X-TREME
POSSIBILITIES

X-TREME POSSIBILITIES

A COMPREHENSIVELY EXPANDED RUMMAGE THROUGH FIVE YEARS OF *THE X-FILES*

Paul Cornell, Martin Day
and Keith Topping

Virgin

This edition published in Great Britain in 1998 by
Virgin Publishing Ltd
Thames Wharf Studios
Rainville Road
London W6 9HT

ISBN 0 7535 0228 3

Typeset by Galleon Typesetting, Ipswich
Printed and bound in Great Britain by
Mackays of Chatham PLC

Introduction

The X-Files has changed everything. Before it, American television, under the influence of series like *Star Trek: The Next Generation*, *Hill Street Blues* and *Twin Peaks*, was just starting to become more innovative, more interested in continuity and texts that could be usefully watched a number of times. *The X-Files* took this idea and ran with it, creating a vast (and difficult) intermittent running story that brought a large supporting cast with it. Having innovated in that direction, it innovated again in the way it used that story arc: the returning characters returned at strange points in the narrative; the central storyline wasn't restricted to episodes in which our heroes discovered something more about it, but informed other episodes as well. It's true that *The X-Files* was a series whose time had come, one of those dead certs that only a TV critic would bet against. With the American psyche turning increasingly against its own government, against all authority, nobody, in the 1990s, can tell an American citizen what to believe. The skies are full of UFOs/black helicopters, containing aliens/UN troops who do experiments on/wilfully destroy herds of cattle. The American public has become thoroughly alienated, shocked that the betrayals of Watergate haven't stopped: Irangate, Whitewater, many other revelations that power is in the hands of people as mortal as those they govern. Their nation, the one that had always believed in freedom and democracy, is being ferociously shown the realities of power and capitalism. That these terrible things have happened cannot be the fault of the public themselves: it's the fault of those in power. Not those fallible presidents and their parties, who are just as much victims of the real world as the public are. The real people in power. Those whose presence among the government makes America such a scary place. The Conspiracy. *The X-Files* is the product of a nation looking for such people to blame.

The second factor in the success of this series is that there is, now, a whole mythos to feed its stories. Thanks to Steven Spielberg (who invented them) and Whitley Strieber (who was abducted by them), the little Grey aliens have become an omnipresent icon, that most miraculous of things, an archetype in a new form. Centuries ago, they'd have been fairies or demons. Now they're from Zeta Reticuli. The innovation is that they bring with them a folk myth of total fear: we are helpless, totally vulnerable, and not safe anywhere. We have to conform to their agenda, we can't bargain with them, they have no human emotions to appeal to. It's a myth, in the end, of bureaucrats from outer space. Their skin colour is no accident. Even the eyes look like spectacles. The Greys are also the dead of Belsen (an image that *The X-Files* takes literally), aborted foetuses, shaved experimental cats: all those things we've done, that we should be guilty about, externalised, mythologised, and back to do to us what we did to them.

The third factor in the series' success is the millennium. It's no surprise that Chris Carter's next show was entirely about the change from twentieth to twenty-first century. It's coming, and lots of things are coming to an end. The human instinct for closure, and the desire for revelation, are once more upon us. *The X-Files* is the expression of that desire. We can look forward, thank goodness, to a party decade in 2001, if previous centuries are anything to go by.

So, with all this in the air, the appearance of a series concerning alien mysteries wasn't really a surprise. The idea would have been floating in many writers' heads. The surprise was that, when it did arrive, this series was actually done so well. Each episode seems to be the product of concentrated creative energy, as if it were a tiny feature film. For once, the design, the direction and the writing are all being urged to be the best they can be. Chris Carter has to be congratulated for his single-mindedness in achieving that, and American television can take a bow for its realisation that a single, driven creator at the helm is the best way to run a TV series. Witness *Star Trek* and *Babylon 5*.

And then there are Mulder and Scully, of course. Intelligent, sexy people, who aren't involved with each other. That's us, these days, that is. That's the Internet Generation writ glamorous. If they shag, the show's over: thank goodness Carter knows that, or we'd have another *Moonlighting* on our hands.

Still, he may surprise us. He may have it happen and do it well. That would almost be the obvious thing to do, in a series that thrives on surprises.

Introduction to the Second Edition

Since the first edition of *X-Treme Possibilities* came out in 1997, the nature of *The X-Files* has changed. From being a cult series, the show has graduated to mainstream success. The movie is a 'blockbuster'; Duchovny and Anderson are major stars (in Britain, when Catatonia's single 'Mulder and Scully' was in the charts they appeared as giant backdrops on *Top of the Pops*); there are Emmy awards and vast audiences. The nature of the storytelling has also changed. Perhaps aware of the impact Darin Morgan's episodes had, perhaps influenced by the commercial success of such shows as *Xena: Warrior Princess* and *Buffy the Vampire Slayer*, *The X-Files* changed from being the most earnest series on television to being one of the most tongue-in-cheek. It's almost as if one can only sustain a level of pre-millennial panic for so long, that sooner rather than later, an intelligent audience (and the series, thankfully, has shown no sign of being 'dumbed down') will start to get restless at being asked to take shivery paranoia so seriously. Perhaps Chris Carter realised that his show was in danger of becoming an anti-establishment cliché in itself, so, very perceptively, he began to emphasise the complicated nature of perception, of how no one version of a story is the objective one. The series started to innovate even further in its storytelling methods, allowing the tone and emphasis of each episode to vary according to its subject matter. The final element in this sea change was that Scully's point of view, that rational inquiry would always prevail over blind faith, came to dominate Mulder's more and more. The one worry we have over this course of action is that the series now finds it hard to do stories that are heartfelt, moving, or simply horrific. Among all the various storytelling methods, 'straightforward' should still be a valid strain, yet it's now underused. Very rarely, in the fifth season, does *The X-Files* produce a sharp, chilling fifty minutes of postmodern horror, and that's a shame. The series' original function has vanished. However, it's thanks to these astute moves that the series remains one that can be proudly discussed in any workplace. Unfortunately, this may have come too late for the UK fan base, which, at the time of writing, is showing the first signs of withering.

One reason for the British lack of interest is doubtless the series' continuing commitment to its Conspiracy story arc. The fact that the 'mythology' stories fail to provide many of the dramatic cues that viewers of series television are used to might be cause for applause (for instance, it's refreshing when we as an audience are given no clue when a character is lying). However, the arc also fails to explain itself as it progresses, often getting cod dramatic set pieces tacked on to its episodes simply to produce an end result that in some way resembles drama. It's an indictment of any series that it requires a book like ours to follow its complexities, even after the story arc is complete. For instance, most *X-Files* fans would not perceive Deep Throat as a lying manipulator who never once acted to help Mulder; however, if we follow the conclusions the story arc presents us with, no other interpretation is possible. The version of the world he describes to Mulder simply isn't the one that the movie reveals to be true. But at no point during the fiction are our heroes or the audience alerted to that. In normal drama, we might expect a line such as 'So Deep Throat was lying all along'. With this series, the fans themselves have to work for that closure, and the general audience are left none the wiser. The Conspiracy has dragged the series from being about the world of nightmare, where anything might happen and men in suits are just symbols of a terrifying bureaucracy, to being about the world of politics, where the same things happen over and over, and we're asked to follow the internal bickerings of those same, now very ordinary, men. Continuity is the enemy of terror.

It doesn't help that the Conspiracy episodes also feature some of the worst scripting in television history. The strange 'poetic' prose which Mulder and Scully spout in voice-over during these episodes is simply bad, and Chris Carter's dialogue in speech for them is sometimes little better. Carter has much, *much*, to be commended for. Nobody betters him for use of budget and materials, talent spotting, dozens of other jobs that producers are hired and fired for. But he should realise that his scripting Emmy was won for the crisp dialogue and dramatic set pieces of 'Duane Barry', not for self-consciously meaningful nonsense. That 'Memento Mori' was submitted for that same award a couple of years later is an index to where the show has gone.

The *X-Files* movie was reported to have 'solved' the Conspiracy arc, and, indeed, it offers clever solutions to some of the problems with the mythology episodes, and provides a degree of closure. What it doesn't do, however, is allow our heroes to do what we've wanted them to do for some time, bring an end to the whole Conspiracy business. It seems that when, with the start of Season Six, *The X-Files* production moves from Vancouver to Los Angeles, the mythology episodes will go with it. At least Mulder and Scully nearly got a snog, which may change the basis of the characters' relationship. Or it may not. Two steps forward, three steps back.

Still, it's good to report that *The X-Files* is alive and well as the millennium approaches, and, through not taking itself seriously, shows every sign of outliving the paranoid phase of American history which produced it.

This Book

There are lots of books about *The X-Files*, and not all of them are good. This one, we can confidently tell you, is different. We've actually delved into the fiction of the episodes, especially in the Conspiracy stories, attempting to make connections, to make sense of what's going on. We theorise about extreme possibilities, and generally pay attention to what the series is trying to say, what it says accidentally, and what it says despite itself. There's a lot of speculation in here, but it's all indicated by words like 'presumably' and 'possibly'. The movie did sort out a lot of the Conspiracy stuff, and we've used that information retroactively, to make clear what was actually going on in the episodes. We've assumed, incidentally, that there always was a masterplan, that Chris Carter with help from, mainly, Frank Spotnitz, meant every detail to fit together. That assumption looks very dodgy on some occasions, especially where the text contradicts itself and during the first two seasons in general, but without it, we couldn't have any fun. Also, we've used Occam's razor with regard to the number of alien races visiting Earth: if we can link a particular happening to the Colonists, we will. There's still a great deal that's open to speculation, as you'll see. Unlike our heroes, we don't have any sources within the establishment – this is a totally unauthorised book – so much of our theorising will doubtless turn out to be wrong. *The X-Files* is a text which rewrites itself: the latest episodes give new meanings to old ones. The text of the first edition has been revised to eliminate sections where we were wrong, and to highlight things which gained in importance later on. A word about 'spoilers': because a lot of *The X-Files* is inter-related, this isn't a good book to read if you want to be surprised by a plot twist in an episode that you haven't seen.

The Headings

At the start of each season, we list the number and length of episodes in that season. Then we run down the production personnel for that season, and the regular cast (by which we mean anybody who appears in more than one story, counting multipart episodes as one story) in order of their first appearance in the series.

For each episode, we give the number of the episode, the title, the US and UK transmission dates, the writer and director credits, and list the cast who don't appear in the regular cast list at the start of the season, together with the roles they play. We summarise the plot, including giving away the ending.

The headings then proceed as follows:

Don't Be in the Teaser: Terrible things happen to people pre-credits in *The X-Files*: this heading documents them. We also include those few times where nothing awful happens, for completeness' sake.

How Did He Do That?: Recording Mulder's extraordinary leaps to the oddest conclusions, plus plot impossibilities and other anomalous material.

Scully Here is a Medical Doctor: As we're continually reminded. Incidents where she snaps on the latex are also reported.

Ooze: Ooze.

Scully's Rational Explanation of the Week: She usually has one, she often has several. Lately, other people have started doing it too. Here they all are.

That's a Mouthful: *The X-Files* has developed its own brand of portentous, quasi-philosophical politicobabble, seemingly informed by the writers having seen a David Mamet film once. Gillian Anderson was quoted in *TV Guide* as saying: 'There's a chance that the cryptic, cultic dialogue we use could prove confusing to people. I hope not. I don't want people walking away from the movie asking, "What was going on with that chick?" ' We ask that.

Phwoar!: This heading charts Mulder and Scully's relationship, and times when they seem especially close. We also mention scenes of unusually obvious horniness. We are grateful for the help of a number of friends of various sexualities in gleefully adding to this section.

Dialogue Triumphs: We quote the bits that sparkle.

Dialogue Disasters: And a few that don't.

The Conspiracy Starts at Closing Time: We try to work out what the Conspiracy's up to, how it works, and who's involved. Big section.

Continuity: This heading keeps track of details concerning Mulder and Scully, their relations, their workmates, their friends, and their foes.

The Truth: This is, as far as we can work it out, exactly what really happened during the episode.

Trivia: We list cultural references, in-jokes, cameo appearances by strange people and stuff that doesn't fit anywhere else. But we still don't think you're interested in things like number plates and how often Scully fires her gun, and we've become too fed up with the series' penchant for numeric in-jokes to pay much attention to that any more.

Scientific Comment: Here comes the science part. Concentrate. Our scientific adviser, Dr Janet Wood of the Astrophysics Group at Keele University, passes comment on things that get her goat concerning the use of science in the episode. (And she supplied our box on missing time.) Rather than being, like the Lone Gunmen, an expert on all things, Dr Wood has consulted many other scientists. Science fiction is about science. When the series goes there, it ought to get its research right.

The Bottom Line: The three of us review the episode separately. Partly to show a series of different critical responses, partly to demonstrate that the Gently Mocking Man, the Well-Mannered Man and Quiet Keithy sometimes disagree rather violently. We divided special responsibility for the episodes between us, a season each for the first three and then largely by subject matter, and the review of the person with that responsibility comes first in every case.

Boxes: Throughout the text, there are a number of boxes which highlight particular issues, or just take the mickey. Marty has updated his essay from the first edition to take account of the series' continuing investigation into the matter of faith.

A note on character names. We've changed to 'The Cigarette-Smoking Man' rather than 'The Smoking Man', and 'The Lone Gunmen' rather than 'the editors of the *Lone Gunman* magazine' for this edition to keep up with standard use, even though these off-screen names aren't established in the show. We have problems with 'The Alien Bounty Hunter' because even when it's really him he's not a bounty hunter as such. You'll see.

The Episodes

First Season

Note: The order of BBC2 transmission runs: 11, 13, 12, 14 . . .

Second Season

Note: The order of BBC2/BBC1 transmission runs: 41, 44, 43, 42, 45 . . .

Third Season

Note: The order of BBC1 transmission runs: 54, 57–59, 62, 71, 60, 64, 65, 69, 66, 61, 67, 68, 70, 72, 63, 55, 56, 73 thus completely messing up the 'tiff' arc and bringing Scully's dog back from the dead. This was allegedly because of the BBC's new guidelines on violence, though this is difficult to believe when some very disturbing episodes were shown in the 9.30 slot ('Grotesque' for instance), while it was '2Shy' and 'The Walk' that were kept back. 'Talitha Cumi' was, according to the *Radio Times*, 'pulled from schedules earlier in the year as it coincided with the Dunblane anniversary' (we could understand it if it was an episode that involved child death, like 'The Walk', for instance . . .) and was finally shown a week before the fourth season premiered on BBC1.

Fourth Season

Note: The order of Sky One transmission runs: 80, 83–88, 81, 82, 89 . . . 'Tunguska' and 'Terma' were held back due to an agreement with Fox over the recent video release of this two-parter. The episodes were eventually shown in movie format in a two-hour time slot. For the first time, the BBC managed to show an entire season of *The X-Files* in the correct transmission order.

Fifth Season

[1] Note the American spelling.

Note: The order of Sky One transmission runs: 102, 105–109, 112–113, 115, 103–104, 114, 116, 110–111, 117. 'Christmas Carol' and 'Emily', and 'Patient X' and 'The Red and the Black', were all held back due to an agreement with Fox over the recent video releases of these two-parters. The first of them was eventually shown in movie format in a two- hour time slot.

The *X-Files* Movie

First Season

24 45-minute episodes

Created by Chris Carter

Line Producer: Joseph Patrick Finn (2–24)
Co-Producers: Larry Barber (11–14),
Paul Barber (11–14),
Paul Rabwin (2–24)
Supervising Producers: Alex Gansa (2–24),
Howard Gordon (2–24),
Daniel Sackheim (1)
Co-Executive Producers: R.W. Goodwin (2–24), Glen
Morgan (2–24),
James Wong (2–24)
Executive Producer: Chris Carter

Regular Cast: David Duchovny (Special Agent Fox
Mulder), Gillian Anderson (Special Agent Dana Scully),
William B. Davis (The Cigarette-Smoking Man, 1,[2] 16,[3] 21,
24), Ken Camroux (Senior Agent, 1[4]), Charles Cioffi
(Section Chief Scott Blevins, 1, 2, 4), Jim Jansen (Dr Heitz
Werber, 1), Jerry Hardin (Deep Throat, 2, 7, 10, 11, 16, 17,
24), Henry Beckman (Detective Frank Biggs, 3, 21), Doug
Hutchison (Eugene Tooms, 3, 21), Scott Bellis (Max Fenig,
10), Don Davis (Captain William Scully, 13), Sheila
Larken (Margaret Scully, 13), Mitchell Kosterman (Detective
Horton, 14), Tom Braidwood (Melvin Frohike, 17), Dean
Haglund (Langly, 17), Bruce Harwood (John Byers, 17),
Mitch Pileggi (Assistant Director Walter Skinner, 21),
Lindsey Ginter (Crewcut Man, 24)

---

[2] Credited here as 'Smoking Man'.
[3] Credited here as 'CIA Agent'. This may or may not be the Cigarette-Smoking Man. See 'Young at Heart' for details.
[4] Credited here as '3rd Man'.

To help you hang on during what is sometimes a very bumpy ride, a few definitions and first appearances to indicate the thinking behind our investigation into how the Conspiracy arc fits together:

The Conspiracy: An international syndicate of powerful people who know the truth behind matters alien, and a good deal more. They first appear together in 'The Blessing Way', but we don't hear their complete plan and motivation until the movie. (And see the box concerning Chris Carter's CD on p. 464.)

The Colonists: A single species or organism that visited Earth in the past and intends to return and conquer. Their actions have consequences from the start of the series, but we first meet a representative in (debatably) 'Ice' or (definitely) 'Piper Maru'.

The Rebel Colonists: Our biggest coup in the first edition was realising that the arc only made sense if there were two sets of warring aliens. The series makes that clear in 'The Red and the Black', but a representative of the Rebels first shows up in 'Fallen Angel'.

The Black Oil, the Greys, the Shapeshifters: All different vessels of the Colonist intelligence, the basic form being the Black Oil. These forms are common to both Colonists and Rebels. ('Ice' or 'Piper Maru'; 'Fallen Angel'; the pilot episode or 'Colony'.)

Human/Colonist Hybrid Clones: Conspiracy-created beings that initially look human, though they have toxic blood, but eventually (perhaps only if exposed to various biohazards) come to resemble the small Grey aliens of lore. Created from abductee ova and Colonist DNA solution ('Colony').

Quasi-Hybrids: US government-created beings, the result of Colonist DNA being injected into existing humans ('The Erlenmeyer Flask').

1: 'The X-Files'/'Pilot'

US Transmission: 10 September 1993
UK Transmission: 26 January 1994 (Sky One)/
19 September 1994 (BBC2)
Writer: Chris Carter
Director: Robert Mandel
Cast: Cliff DeYoung (Dr Jay Nemman),
Sarah Koshoff (Theresa Nemman),
Leon Russom (Detective Miles),
Zachary Ansley (Billy Miles),
Stephen E. Miller (Truitt), Malcolm Stewart (Dr Glass),
Alexandra Berlin (Orderly), Doug Abrahams (Patrolman),
Katya Gardener (Peggy O'Dell),
Ric Reid (Astronomer), Lesley Ewen (Receptionist),
J.B. Bivens (Truck Driver)

Collum National Forest, near Bellefleur, northwest Oregon: four teenagers have been found dead, each with two small marks on their backs. The FBI's Fox Mulder and his new partner Dana Scully order the exhumation of one of the victims and discover an apelike skeleton with a grey metallic implant in the nasal cavity. Later Scully and Mulder 'lose nine minutes' while driving along a stretch of open road, and their motel room is burnt, destroying the evidence so far collected. Mulder comes to the conclusion that Billy Miles, another classmate, is responsible for the deaths, despite being in a persistent vegetative state. Billy claims that during a graduation party in the forest aliens kidnapped the youngsters for experimentation, and that once the experiments were concluded he was used to kill his friends. Scully hands over the only surviving piece of evidence – the 'communication device' – to her bosses.

Don't Be in the Teaser: Karen Swinson dies mysteriously.

How Did He Do That?: It is never explained exactly how Mulder works out that Billy is responsible.

Scully Here is a Medical Doctor: Scully states that she went to medical school, but chose not to practise. She performs an autopsy on Ray Soames.

Scully's Rational Explanation of the Week: The young people might be involved in some sort of cult.

Phwoar!: The bathroom scene in which Gillian Anderson strips to her pants and bra is rather nice. When she shows her mosquito bites to Mulder, it's perhaps the start of that legendary parasexual 'thing' between the two agents.

Dialogue Triumphs: Mulder: 'In my line of work the laws of physics rarely seem to apply.'

Scully: 'Time can't just disappear. It's a universal invariant!' Mulder: 'Not in this zip-code.'

Scully to her superiors: 'Agent Mulder believes we are not alone.'

The Conspiracy Starts at Closing Time: Mulder says that there is classified government information that he has been trying to access but someone at a higher level has been blocking him. He is allowed to continue in his work only because he has made connections in Congress (presumably Senator Richard Matheson who we meet in 'Little Green Men'). The Cigarette-Smoking Man is seen in Blevins' office (Blevins perhaps being the one who's been blocking Mulder's research, as we see in 'Redux II' that he is a Conspiracy agent). The Cigarette-Smoking Man later stores the 'communication chip' (along with five others) in a box marked '100041' in a storeroom deep under (or near to, as we later learn) the Pentagon. Mulder and Scully lose nine minutes of time when their car is enveloped in a bright light. Mulder doesn't seem to regard the fact that, for at least nine minutes, he's been possibly interfered with, as important. Scully, with her knowledge of physics, ought to be jumping up and down in astonishment, but she shrugs it off. Either she simply doesn't believe Mulder, or maybe they've both been got at. (See 'Tempus Fugit' for an examination of the series' treatment of missing time.)

Continuity: Dana Scully has been with the FBI for just over two years. She was recruited out of medical school (her parents at this stage still regard this as an act of rebellion). She taught at the FBI academy at Quantico and did her undergraduate degree in physics. Her senior thesis was 'Einstein's Twin Paradox: A New Interpretation'. (This is a pretty ridiculous subject for a thesis. Einstein's twin paradox is a simple example of how time dilation affects objects travelling near the speed of light: the twin that's been travelling comes home and meets the twin who hasn't been, and finds that twin is now older. Any 'new interpretation' in the field of physics (as opposed to, say, poetry) would have to present a challenge to the laws of relativity! On the basis that Scully actually passed, we might assume that the thesis itself concerns some small topic of relativity research (a new proof is virtually the only possible area), and that, for some reason, Scully gave it a screamingly over-the-top title that referred to little more than an aside in the introduction. Mulder himself is somewhat sarcastic about its contents. In terms of the series, however, the title is poetically apt, darkly alluding to the fate of Samantha, not to mention Mulder's trick with the two watches.) We (possibly) see some of the contents of the thesis in 'Musings of a Cigarette-Smoking Man' and Mulder quotes from it in 'Synchrony'. Scully is aware of Mulder by reputation. She is assigned to assist Mulder and will write field reports on their activities along with her observations on the validity of the work. Fox Mulder is an Oxford-educated psychologist who wrote a monograph on 'serial killers and the occult' that helped to catch Monty Props in 1988. He was considered to be the best analyst in the Violent Crime section. His nickname at the academy was 'Spooky'. He describes himself as 'the FBI's most unwanted'. He has 'developed a consuming devotion to an unassigned project outside the Bureau mainstream'. When he was twelve, his eight-year-old sister disappeared from her bed one night. This tore the family apart. Mulder has undergone deep regression hypnosis with Dr Heitz Werber concerning the events surrounding the abduction. The X-Files are unexplained cases. Mulder says that at first they seemed to be a garbage dump for UFO sightings and abduction reports.

The Truth: The cover-up perpetuated by Billy's father seems to be a localised rather than a governmental activity. Later episodes reveal that Mulder and Scully have actually stumbled upon the work of Japanese and German scientists, working for the Conspiracy, who have been experimenting on the class. The nature of those experiments, is, however, problematic. The kids themselves obviously aren't the Colonist/human hybrids of later episodes (they bleed normal blood). So presumably they're either having their resistance to the Black Oil tested through being given tiny doses of the stuff (which would explain the Greylike state of their corpses (with enlarged cranium and eyes) and the need for blood-monitoring implants, although these nasal ones seem more concerned with control than protection), or they're being injected with the Colonist virus inside an alien bacterium (as with the test subjects of 'The Erlenmeyer Flask'). The latter explanation requires the teenagers to exhibit aggressive behaviour which we don't see onscreen. Both explanations would account for the deposits of an 'organic synthetic protein' found around the puncture marks, and there being no obvious cause of death for the corpses found marked like this. (The Black Oil having presumably left them if the former explanation is correct.) Billy Miles seems under control to an extent unseen again until 'Patient X'. Suspiciously so, in fact. Considering the fact that when we first see him (in a blinding light) his facial features seem blank and shapeless, and that when he's 'returned' at the end of the episode, his injection marks have vanished, is it possible that he's now (become or been replaced by) a fully fledged Shapeshifter, the Black Oil having made his skin malleable? This branch of the Project seem to want to tidy up after themselves, without using the abductees on a long-term basis, or perhaps that's just an artefact of their being discovered. However, there are a number of illogical features to this case which suggest another explanation. We never see the nasal implants again in the series, and it's really strange that the Colonists should decide to take Mulder and Scully out of time for nine minutes just when things are hotting up . . . then do nothing with them. (Although, of course, it's possible that the Colonists, if the DNA explanation is the correct one, know nothing of the Conspiracy's attempts to use their DNA to make humans resistant to the Black Oil, and have arrived to check up on what's going on. That, indeed, may be why from this point onward the Conspiracy never try this again and prevent others doing so.) Add to that the near-miss with the jet that the Colonists would have been able to avoid, the blatant telecommunications interference, and the amount of closure offered by the departure of the apparently benign 'aliens', it's possible that this whole scenario is a set-up designed (by the Cigarette-Smoking Man and Deep Throat?) to send Mulder off on his crusade, with Scully beside him to report to them of his progress. During the course of this story, he comes nowhere near anything of the real nature of the Project (though its standard tools are used to set this up) but is presented instead with the public mythology of aliens, implants and mind control, complete with a set of alien bodies that are swiftly taken from him, so he's left with no hard evidence. This is the mythology that the Conspiracy wish him to go out into the world and propagate, to facilitate their own 'plausible denial', and the teenagers may be being tested with the Black Oil or Colonist DNA mainly in order to stage this.

Trivia: Chris Carter was born in Bellflower, California, and names the locale here in homage. The Pentagon scene is a visual steal from *Raiders of the Lost Ark*, and 'We are not alone' was the poster tagline for *Close Encounters of the Third Kind*. When Mulder knocks on Scully's motel room door and she asks, 'Who is it?' he answers, 'Steven Spielberg!'

The Bottom Line: KT: 'I'm not a part of any agenda. You've got to trust me. I'm here just like you, to solve this.' A fine beginning. The Mulder/Scully dialogue is electric, though the explanations at the story's climax are far too rushed. Little Americana with gothic overtones – chilling and influential. Watching it again, five years on, one still gets the same feeling of freshness.

PC: It's very *Silence of the Lambs* indeed. But it looks different. These dark Canadian forests will soon become as familiar to TV audiences as the dustbowls around LA, but here was where they first made their mark, allowing the series to feel as if it's genuinely moving around the USA, and thus addressing the entire condition of the country. It's as if Canada gives the series an ironic distance.

MD: It's a rattling good yarn, pure and simple. The two key images (the figure standing in a whirlwind of bright light, and the vast storeroom where the communications device is placed) are guaranteed to stick in the memory of the casual viewer. The 'frustration factor' and subversion of expectation – the 'baddies' don't get their comeuppance – certainly marks this out from much American television. I loved this story at the time – it seemed so fresh and vibrant – but it's not surprising that it has visibly aged a bit now, with David Duchovny's performance being a little too mannered. It's very much a pilot script: themes (e.g. familial conflict) that would have been fleshed out in later episodes are briefly sketched here and then pushed to one side.

TITLE SEQUENCES

The pilot episode lacks the familiar title sequence and theme music. It also features a caption that states: 'The following story is inspired by actual documented accounts.' The end credits of 'Space' feature a detailed NASA disclaimer in addition to the usual one regarding the FBI. The usual 'The Truth is Out There' caption at the end of the opening credits is replaced by 'Trust No One' ('The Erlenmeyer Flask'), 'Deny Everything' ('Ascension'), 'Éí 'Aaníígóó 'Ahoot'é' ('Anasazi', which is roughly the same phrase – 'Far away from here, the truth is' – in Navajo), 'Apology is Policy' ('731'), 'Everything Dies' ('Herrenvolk'), 'Deceive Inveigle Obfuscate' ('Teliko'), 'E Pur Si Muove' ('Terma'), 'Believe the Lie' ('Gethsemane'), 'All Lies Lead to the Truth' ('Redux'), 'Resist or Serve' ('The Red and the Black'), and 'The End' ('The End'). Certain stories ('Paper Clip', '731', 'Revelations', 'Apocrypha' and 'Pusher') use a shorter version of the title sequence. From the start of the third season, slight changes are made to the theme music.

2: 'Deep Throat'

US Transmission: 17 September 1993
UK Transmission: 2 February 1994 (Sky One)/
26 September 1994 (BBC2)
Writer: Chris Carter
Director: Daniel Sackheim
Cast: Michael Bryan French (Paul Mossinger),
Seth Green (Emil),
Gabrielle Rose (Anita Budahas),
Monica Parker (Ladonna),
Sheila Moore (Verla McLennen),
Lalainia Lindbjerg (Zoe),
Andrew Johnston (Lt. Col. Robert Budahas),
John Cuthbert (Commanding Officer),
Vince Metcalfe (Col. Kissel),
Michael Puttonen (Motel Manager),
Brian Furlong (Lead Officer),
Doc Harris (Mr McLennen)

Ellens Air Base, southwest Idaho: Mulder and Scully investigate the disappearance (at the hands of the military) of Robert Budahas, an air force pilot. At the base they witness strange lights in the sky, which Mulder believes prove that the air force are using UFO technology. Budahas returns, although his wife says that it's not her husband. Mulder breaks into the base, but is captured and subjected to memory-erasing treatment. Scully overpowers a member of the base personnel and arrives in time to see a dazed Mulder leave the complex, his memory of what he saw gone.

Don't Be in the Teaser: For once, nobody dies. However, Robert Budahas develops a nasty rash and later loses important parts of his memory.

Scully's Rational Explanation of the Week: The pilot's mental instability is caused by stereotypy, a stress disorder that she has studied in zoo animals. The pilots may be the 'washouts' from the government's secret Aurora aircraft project. Budahas's memory loss may be 'selective amnesia'. The UFOs are just lasers reflecting off the clouds.

That's a Mouthful: 'You will pack and leave town immediately, or assume the consequences of intense indiscretion.'

Dialogue Triumphs: Mulder: 'They're here, aren't they?' Deep Throat: 'Mr Mulder, *they* have been here for a long, long time.'

The Conspiracy Starts at Closing Time: 'I think there's a large conspiracy here,' notes Mulder. The USAF are using Colonist technology, and this is the first time that one of their triangular craft is seen, this time in USAF colours. Nothing is revealed about Deep Throat, except that he has taken an interest in Mulder's work, and that he is in a 'privileged' position to pass on classified information. On their second meeting, he informs Mulder that Mulder and Scully's lives may be in danger, and that he is interested in 'the truth'. Mulder says that Ellens was one of six bases to which the UFO wreckage from the 1947 'Roswell Incident' was taken. Mulder has his memory tampered with, but, since he's already been witness to two alien encounters (Samantha's abduction and the car incident in the first episode), this may be part of an ongoing process to, literally, change his mind, making him more paranoid and more liable to speak out about his opinions, thus providing the Conspiracy with the stalking horse they're after to draw the public's attention away from their own activities. It may be that Mulder is 'brain-sucked' (if the same technology is used here as in 'Soft Light') in order to give him the impression that he has seen something meaningful beforehand. It's debatable whether Deep Throat intended to really help Mulder at all, beyond setting up this pawn for his friend the Cigarette-Smoking Man, at least until his (possible) sacrifice at the end of the season. Mind you, this plan might all have been the product of happenstance to begin with: Mulder's exposure to paranoia-inducing gas in 1989 (in 'Unusual Suspects') was totally accidental.

Continuity: Mulder likes guitar rock, is fluent in 'valley speak' ('Later, dude!') and is knowledgeable about American football (discussing the 1968 Superbowl with Budahas). His home phone is tapped in this story.

The Truth: The US Air Force, via the Conspiracy, has developed the capability to erase parts of a person's memory (Budahas and Mulder). As Scully notes in her report, however, there is no positive proof that the technology they are using is alien (though it is certainly far in advance of known scientific achievement). A triangular craft like those flown here is definitely seen to be an alien vehicle in 'Apocrypha' and 'Patient X' (carrying the Black Oil and the Rebel Colonists respectively). What's happening to Budahas physically may be because these things are meant to be piloted by creatures that have the mutable skins (and other alien characteristics) of beings that are hosts to the Black Oil, such as Greys and Shapeshifters.

Trivia: The article on the air base that Scully reads from a microfiche is written by one Chris Carter. 'They're here' was an advertising line for Whitley Strieber's account of alien abduction, *Communion*. When Budahas is first seen after his return he is making a model kit of an F–117A 'stealth fighter'. Mulder refers to one character as 'Uncle Fester' from *The Addams Family*.

The Bottom Line: KT: 'Are you suggesting the military is flying UFOs?' A cracking episode, continuing many of the themes from the pilot (small-town America as a cover for strange doings, etc.). Scully seems more cynical in this story than usual. Some comedy elements don't work (*The X-Files* always seems to have a credibility problem with Generation X), but Duchovny and Anderson are brilliant, developing a sparkling rapport.

PC: Just as well the episode titles aren't shown on screen. This is what I really wanted from this show, a series that would take on all the new American myths presented here. It's bold to take Mulder right into the heart of 'the truth' so quickly, and then pull him away.

MD: 'When does the human cost become too high for the building of a better machine?' This is glorious, and unlike the pilot it's got better with age, now feeling like the entire series in microcosm.

Scully is first seen to wear a small golden cross in 'Deep Throat'. In 'Squeeze' she wears a longer, non-cross necklace, which is stolen by Tooms prior to his attack on her. Maybe this is why she reverts to the cross necklace for 'Conduit' and subsequent stories such as 'Lazarus'. In 'Ascension', we discover that the cross, which Mulder finds, and Mrs Scully asks him to keep, was given to Dana on her fifteenth birthday, or at Christmas if you believe the dream version in 'Christmas Carol' (it might have been an extra Christmas present as an early birthday gift for 23 February). After Scully's abduction, Mulder wears the cross, as seen in '3', and gives it back to her when she returns in 'One Breath'. She wears it in several subsequent stories, including 'Revelations'. She unsuccessfully attempts to pass it on to Emily in the story of that name. Mulder associates it with her, as it forms part of his hallucinations in 'Kill Switch'.

3: 'Squeeze'

US Transmission: 24 September 1993
UK Transmission: 9 February 1994 (Sky One)/
3 October 1994 (BBC2)
Writers: Glen Morgan, James Wong
Director: Harry Longstreet
Cast: Donal Logue (Agent Tom Colton),
Kevin McNulty (Fuller), Terence Kelly (George Usher),
Colleen Winton (Lie Detector Technician),
James Bell (Detective Johnson), Gary Hetherington (Kennedy),
Rob Morton (Kramer), Paul Joyce (Mr Werner)

Baltimore, Maryland: one of Scully's old academy classmates asks for her help in catching a serial killer who takes his victims' livers and leaves no obvious signs of entry. Mulder discovers a fingerprint link to an X-File, and a recurring pattern of five murders every thirty years. A man, Eugene

Tooms, is arrested, but released after he passes a polygraph test. Mulder and Scully are convinced of his guilt. Tooms attacks Scully at her home, using his ability to crawl through very narrow spaces. He is overpowered and imprisoned.

Don't Be in the Teaser: George Usher has his liver ripped out.

Ooze: Yellow bile, used by Tooms in his 'nest'.

Scully's Rational Explanation of the Week: Ignoring the fingerprint evidence, Scully presents the FBI with a very professional (and completely wrong) profile of the killer. Her explanation of the matching of fingerprints to a crime sixty years before is a convoluted genetics theory (see 'Aubrey'!).

Dialogue Triumphs: Colton: 'Does this look like the work of little green men?' Mulder: 'Grey . . . The Reticulan skin tone is actually grey. They're notorious for their extraction of terrestrial human livers due to iron depletion in the Reticulan galaxy.' 'You can't be serious.' 'Do you have any idea what liver and onions go for on Reticula?'

Scully: 'I think it's bile.' Mulder: 'Is there any way I can get it off my fingers quickly without betraying my cool exterior?'

Continuity: Mulder says he thinks Scully will be running the Bureau by 2023. Tom Colton was in Dana's class at the academy. Another classmate, Marty Neal, has just received a Supervisory position. This episode makes it clear that Mulder is not well thought of by many of his FBI colleagues, believed to be incompetent, or an embarrassing crank. Mulder at this point believes that at least some of the aliens visiting Earth (the 'Greys') are from Zeta Reticuli, the star in the Reticula constellation that Barney and Betty Hill, subjects of one of the first alien abduction cases, deduced their assailants came from. However, his speech (note the Reticulan *galaxy*, which turns the whole thing into science fiction) is clearly delivered with the sole intention of winding up Colton.

The Truth: Eugene Victor Tooms lived at apartment 103, 66 Exeter Street in 1903, and continued to use the building during each of his awakenings every thirty years. He is a genetic mutation, the livers providing him with sustenance during his hibernation. His skeletal systems and musculature are abnormal, and his continually declining metabolic rate dips below that found in deep sleep.

Trivia: Further to Mulder's love of seventies television, he mentions *The Waltons*. Tom Colton refers to the World Trade Center bombing.

The Bottom Line: KT: 'He's building another nest.' A magnificent *Silence of the Lambs* variant, with an outstanding twitchy performance by Doug Hutchison. The episode can be faulted for its lack of explanations, but it is dark and nasty with a real sense of evil (though this is almost derailed by Frank Biggs's very obvious speech about death camps and ethnic cleansing).

PC: It's clear that Carter likes the idea that all evil springs from one source, a millennial attitude that says that the horrors of history, in an indirect way, create monsters. That's about the only link between the two sorts of *X-Files* episode: Conspiracy and Monster of the Week. At the time of the first season, I preferred the former, now I'm very much into the latter.

MD: Me too. This is certainly one of the strongest simple monster stories. What we have here is an evil Mr Fantastic whose contortions are grotesquely painful and realistic, although we're never shown Tooms's activities in too much detail, our imaginations doing much of the work. This welcome reticence, and the excellent ending, are particularly dramatic, but it's the little elements that make this story for me – like the outrageously macho way that Mulder shakes Colton's hand.

NUMBERS

Rather than indicate them all as we go, we're going to summarise here the various numbers the production team place in the series as in-jokes, and let you go on to spot them.

11:21: Chris Carter's wife, Dori Pierson, was born on 21 November. (Pity she wasn't born a day or two later . . .) As a way of getting her lots of extra birthday cards, the series makes many references to

NUMBERS

11.21 (note the US inversion of day and month).

10:13: Chris Carter's birthday, and the name of his production company.

9/25: The date of birth, in American format, of Gillian Anderson's daughter, Piper.

208: Particular to the episode 'Leonard Betts', #208 is the number of the ambulance to which Betts is assigned, and Scully wakes up with her nosebleed at 2:08. This may be a reference to the official number of the episode in which she's returned after her abduction, 'One Breath'.

4: 'Conduit'

US Transmission: 1 October 1993
UK Transmission: 16 February 1994 (Sky One)/
10 October 1994 (BBC2)
Writers: Alex Gansa, Howard Gordon
Director: Daniel Sackheim
Cast: Carrie Snodgrass (Darlene Morris),
Michael Cavanaugh (Sioux City Sheriff),
Don Gibb (Kip), Joel Palmer (Kevin Morris),
Shelley Owens (Tessa Sears), Don Thompson (Holtzman),
Akiko Morison (Leza Atsumi), Taunya Dee (Ruby Morris),
Anthony Harrison (4th Man), Glen Roald (M.E. Worker),
Mauricio Mercado (Coroner)

Lake Okobogee, a UFO 'hotspot' near Sioux City, Iowa: the abduction of Ruby Morris bears chilling similarities to the disappearance of Mulder's sister. The girl's young brother seems fascinated with a static-filled television screen, and produces binary drawings that contain fragments from defence satellite transmissions and other coded information. After investigating the murder of Ruby's boyfriend, which is unconnected to the girl's seeming abduction, the agents go back to the lake and find her returned. However, Ruby's mother is unwilling to allow her to talk about where she has been.

Don't Be in the Teaser: Darlene Morris is hit by falling crockery and burns her hand on a doorknob. Her daughter, Ruby, is abducted.

Scully's Rational Explanation of the Week: A 'statistical aberration' explains the nature of Kevin's binary drawings. Even Scully admits this 'isn't much of a theory'. The stunted trees were caused by an electrical storm.

Dialogue Triumphs: Scully: 'Well, what makes this case any more credible than the hundred-year-old mother with the lizard baby?'

Mulder: 'How can an eight-year-old boy who can barely multiply be a threat to National Security? People call me paranoid!'

The Conspiracy Starts at Closing Time: The NSA men may be here as part of the Conspiracy, in order to stop Mulder from receiving transmissions that are either tests by the Colonists, or attempts to communicate by their Rebel faction. It's possible, though, that here they're just involved mundanely, because of the nature of the defence satellite transmissions.

Continuity: Mulder's preoccupation with 'fringe matters' has been 'a major source of friction within the Bureau'. Samantha T. Mulder's case is an X-File opened by her brother. The family address was 2790 Vine St, Chilmarc, Mass. Her date of birth is given as 22 January 1964. (This is flatly contradicted in 'Paper Clip', where her date of birth is given on the medical files as 21 November 1965, and her middle name is Anne. Either Mulder was so upset by her abduction that he got the details wrong when he started the file, or this is a sign that his mind has been manipulated a great deal: there's something ironic and cruel about making Mulder forget his sister's real name . . . Alternatively, this is an indication of the Cigarette-Smoking Man's success-ful attempt to lose Samantha in the bureaucracy of the Project: the change of birthdate might have allowed her to be placed in some different category, the change of initial might have allowed her to be swapped with some other Samantha Mulder.) She disappeared twenty-one years ago (which would be 1974, but we now know the abduction happened in 1973), when she was eight. (It was actually six days after her eighth birthday going by the new date, whereas under the old she would have been nine, going on ten.) Mulder states that he used to have a ritual of closing his eyes before he entered his room in the hope that, when he opened them, his sister would be there. Mulder's hypnotic regression 'number 2B' took place on 16 June (year unknown). A 'voice' during the abduction (revealed by the hypnosis) assured him that Samantha would be OK. (This frequently ignored detail now seems entirely credible. It might even have been that of the CSM!) Mulder appears to read *The National Comet*. He knows a friend of a friend who he says is able to get tickets for Washington Redskins football games. (Considering his conversation with Deep Throat about this matter in 'E.B.E.', it's possible we know who this friend is . . .) Mulder faxes some of Kevin's binaries to Daniel ('Danny') Bernstein at the Cryptology Section at FBI HQ.

The Truth: It certainly seems that Ruby was abducted: when she is recovered her white blood cell count is 'sky high', together with an 'attendant reduction in the lymphocyte population, and a release of glucocorticoids'. (Apart from the high white blood cell count – it should be a low red blood cell count – these *are* all symptoms of prolonged weightlessness.) Ruby was told by 'them' to say nothing. Since no medical experimentation that we know of has been attempted on Ruby, we might have reasonable cause to doubt that this abduction was the work of the Colonists. Presumably, then, this is done by their Rebel faction. Kevin appears to have been in contact with them. Could Kevin be a conduit for information taken from the Voyager probes? A lot of the information he receives seems to be akin to what was sent on disk on these missions, including the 'Brandenburg' Concerto. But none of it is useful. Perhaps the Rebel Colonists are the Greys we see in 'Little Green Men' (who are also perhaps those we don't see in 'Fearful Symmetry') who have found a Voyager probe and are trying to communicate with specific humans using the information on it. It could be that, after the initial defence satellite transmissions, which provoked no response, they decided to send something more obvious to the humans receiving the information, and started to raid this cultural storehouse. Kevin trusts Mulder, telling his sister: 'It's OK, he knows.' That might also indicate that he's now in regular psychic touch with the Rebel Colonists, an aide in their plans to save Earth's wildlife and, perhaps, population.

Trivia: Among the information contained in Kevin's binary drawings are da Vinci's Universal Man, a DNA double helix, an extract from one of Bach's 'Brandenburg' Concertos, passages from the *Qur'an*, and a Shakespeare sonnet. (It is worth noting, however, that even a tiny fragment of a DNA helix in binary would require many millions of characters, and that Kevin would have had to have been writing for decades non-stop to achieve this.)

The Bottom Line: KT: 'I want to believe . . .' In terms of iconography, one of the strongest *X-Files* episodes (the scene in the forest with the wolves, and, particularly, the heart-stopping moment when Scully sees Ruby's face in Kevin's drawings). The plot bears similarities to *Close Encounters of the Third Kind* and *Poltergeist* but is none the worse for this. And it contains one of the series' finest episode endings – the first signs that Mulder is less than the wise-cracking Olympian detective of the first three episodes.

PC: The ending is about the only good thing about an absolutely meaningless runaround that steals nearly all its images (bar the central cool binaries idea) from other people.

MD: There are problems with plot and structure, but unoriginality is rarely the worst crime *The X-Files* can commit (though the quoting of *Poltergeist* is shameless). This is two stories in one: a straightforward, derivative but rather engaging UFO story, and a murder investigation somewhat tacked on via such unexplained leaps as the girl's ability to vanish, Deep Throat-like, from the library, and the pack of almost friendly white wolves. It's interesting to see an early example of how good Mulder is at more traditional FBI activities (such as questioning a suspect), but ultimately it's the back story of Mulder's sister – and that moving ending – that give the story its dramatic root.

5: 'The Jersey Devil'

US Transmission: 8 October 1993
UK Transmission: 23 February 1994 (Sky One)/
17 October 1994 (BBC2)
Writer: Chris Carter
Director: Joe Napolitano
Cast: Claire Stansfield (Jersey Devil),
Wayne Tippit (Detective Thompson),
Gregory Sierra (Dr Diamond),
Michael MacRae (Ranger Peter Boulle), Jill Teed (Glenna),
Tamsin Kelsey (Ellen), Andrew Airlie (Rob),
Bill Dow (Dad), Hrothgar Mathews (Jack),
Jayme Knox (Mom), Scott Swanson (1st Officer),
Sean O'Byrne (2nd Officer), David Lewis (Young Officer),
D. Neil Monk (SWAT Team Officer)

Atlantic City, New Jersey: a homeless man is found dead in the Jersey National Park, apparently the victim of a cannibalistic male. Mulder spends a night on the streets and glimpses a creature but is arrested before he can investigate further. Ranger Peter Boulle finds the body of a naked man in the woods, but this vanishes before the anthropologist Professor Diamond can examine it. Despite local law enforcement opposition, Mulder, Scully, Diamond and Boulle track a creature across the city outskirts. Mulder has a confrontation with the 'beast woman', but she escapes back into the woods. Before the 'creature' can be captured she is killed by police marksmen.

Don't Be in the Teaser: An unnamed man in 1947 is killed by having various appendages bitten off.

How Did He Do That?: How does Mulder work out the creature's gender on such slender evidence?

Scully Here is a Medical Doctor: Almost word for word, the excuse that Mulder gives Detective Thompson to explain their gatecrashing his case.

Phwoar!: Scully looks well-foxy with her hair up on her date. It's nice when Mulder and Scully go to the Smithsonian together at the end (without either of them, of course, regarding *that* as a date).

Dialogue Triumphs: Mulder (looking at a magazine centrefold): 'This woman claims to have been taken on board a spaceship, and held in an anti-gravity chamber without food and water for three days.' Scully: 'Anti-gravity is right!'

Mulder: 'You've been spending too much time in supermarket check-out lines.'

Scully: 'Unlike you, Mulder, I would like to have a life!'

Dialogue Disasters: Scully: 'Mulder, we've put men into space, we've built computers that work faster than the human mind.' Mulder: 'While we overpopulate the world and create new technologies to kill each other with. Maybe we're just beasts with big brains.'

The Conspiracy Starts at Closing Time: The autopsy report from the 1940s disappeared from the police department's files a few years after the original 'Jersey Devil' incident. However, this – and the cover-up faced by Mulder and Scully – is clearly prompted by no more than local concern for the possible impact on Atlantic City's gambling and tourism.

Continuity: Scully has a six-year-old godson (Trent), son of her friend Ellen. She has described Mulder to Ellen as 'cute', and says he is not 'a jerk' but is 'obsessed with his work'. She dates a divorcé, Rob, and later turns down a second liaison with him at Circus au Lait.

The Truth: The woman and her dead mate are descendants of the legendary 1940s Jersey Devil. The male was responsible for the murders; after his death the 'beast woman' was forced to come into town to scavenge for food for her offspring. The woman was twenty-five to thirty years old and she had consumed human flesh. A medical examination of her uterus indicates she has produced children. Both she and her mate are physiologically human. So the menace here is actually . . . poor naked people.

Trivia: This episode sees the first use of the phrase 'extreme possibility'. The policeman mentions Hannibal the Cannibal, so chalk up another *Silence of the Lambs* reference.

The Bottom Line: KT: 'Someone or something out there is hungry.' The first sub-standard *X-Files* episode. Urban myth explanations always have to tread a fine line between cleverness and parody and this episode, full of visual clichés (propeller vents) and bad lighting, falls heavily on the latter. The sub-plot concerning the police cover-up to protect the city's gambling franchises is ham-fisted to say the least. A huge disappointment.

PC: It was at this point that I started wondering if Chris Carter knew what his own series was about. Dull and obvious ecological messages, and a bugbear who is actually just a very poor and uneducated woman who's living wild. (Wouldn't it be the obvious thing for her to have stolen or made clothes?)

MD: Not if she's the descendant of the Jersey Devil! Anyway, this is garbage of the highest order, stuffed full of over-earnest exposition and incredible sub-Freudian sexuality (Mulder describing the 'beast woman' as beautiful). It has all the problems of the pilot episode, only more so, and the ending is just guaranteed to leave you rolling in the aisles.

MULDER AND PORN

In 'The Jersey Devil' Mulder is seen reading *Hanky Panky*, which Scully does not censure him for, and he jokes about a subscription to *Celebrity Skin* in 'Blood'. He finds a porn mag in Oswald's room in 'D.P.O.', and in response to Scully's question says (jokingly?) that he's already read it. In 'Beyond the Sea', Scully comments to Mulder: 'Last time you were that engrossed it turned out you were reading the *Adult Video News*.' At the beginning of 'One Breath', Mulder appears to be watching a porn film (is it an episode of *The Red Shoe Diaries* starring David Duchovny?) and there are references to his porn video collection in 'Excelsis Dei'. Indeed, it seems that Frohike will inherit these videos on Mulder's death ('Paper Clip'), although it's just possible that they're talking about his collection of UFO and bigfoot vids ('Jose Chung's *From Outer Space*', 'Chinga'/'Bunghoney'). The alien autopsy video in 'Nisei' is said by Scully to be 'not your usual brand of entertainment', and Mulder mentions the Playboy Channel in 'Pusher'. His tastes include 'Women of the Ivy League' ('D.P.O.'), so he's into brainy girls. In addition, there's a directory on Mulder's PC called 'spank' ('Little Green Men'), and we see his office girlie calendar in '3'. He seems to have been attending a season of old porn movies in 'All Souls'. In 'The End' Gibson Praise tells him he has a 'dirty mind'. Maybe his job drove him to these dubious delights: at the beginning of 'Little Green Men', he is working on an FBI phone tap, listening to two men talking about a stripper called Tuesday; at the end he's listening to a discussion about table and lap dancing. It somehow fits in with his problems with real relationships. The girl on the answerphone in 'Little Green Men' we might take to be one of a whole series of women whom Mulder has the sheer nerve to approach, but not the social confidence to actually date. And the answerphone message from a telephone sex line in 'Small Potatoes' indicates that he's lately stopped trying, and is maybe more interested in virtual women than real ones. Other than Scully. If Clyde Bruckman's comment concerning autoerotic asphyxiation proves to be about Mulder, rather than about himself, then Mulder's hobby may just be the death of him.

6: 'Shadows'

US Transmission: 22 October 1993
UK Transmission: 2 March 1994 (Sky One)/
24 October 1994 (BBC2)
Writers: Glen Morgan, James Wong
Director: Michael Katleman
Cast: Barry Primus (Robert Dorlund),
Lisa Waltz (Lauren Kyte), Lorena Gale (Ellen Bledsoe),
Veena Sood (Ms Saunders), Deryl Hayes (Webster),

Kelli Fox (Pathologist), Tom Pickett (Cop),
Tom Heaton (Groundskeeper),
Janie Woods-Morris (Ms Lange),
Nora McLellan (Jane Morris), Anna Ferguson (Ms Winn)

Philadelphia, PA: Lauren Kyte, secretary to the industrialist
Howard Graves (a recent suicide victim), is mugged at a
cashpoint, but her attackers die mysteriously. Mulder and
Scully, contending with the attentions of a covert government
agency, question the woman, but are very nearly killed when
their car malfunctions. Surveillance photographs of Lauren
seem to show that Howard Graves is still alive, although this is
soon disproved. Mulder and Scully discover that Graves was
killed by his partner Robert Dorlund, and that the company,
HTG Industrial Technologies, has been selling restricted
military parts to Iranian terrorists. It seems that the 'ghost' of
Graves was seeking revenge and trying to protect Lauren.

Don't Be in the Teaser: Lauren Kyte gets mugged. Her
Iranian terrorist muggers have their throats crushed from the
inside. Just shows that crime doesn't pay!

Scully's Rational Explanation of the Week: 'The mystery
isn't psychokinetic energy, it's her accomplice.' Actually she's
correct, though in ways she can't imagine. Scully is very sceptical of psychokinesis (sarcastically mentioning 'How Carrie got
even at the prom') and poltergeists ('They're here!').

That's a Mouthful: 'If any enquiry about this meeting be
made, we request full denial.'

Dialogue Triumphs: Scully: 'You have seen it before, I could
tell. You lied to them.' Mulder: 'I would never lie – I wilfully
participated in a campaign of misinformation.'
  Scully: 'I think Howard Graves fabricated his own death.'
Mulder: 'Do you know how difficult it is to fake your own
death? Only one man has pulled it off. Elvis!'
  Security Agent: 'I could make her talk.' Mulder: 'My advice
to you: don't get rough with her.'

The Conspiracy Starts at Closing Time: We are never told
exactly who the rival agency who call Mulder and Scully into

the case are. Mulder speculates 'NSA, CIA, some covert organisation that Congress won't cover in the next scandal'. They have been investigating HTG's links to the Iranian terrorist group Isfahan for a year. Their motives in calling in Mulder seem to be genuine, so if they are CIA or NSA, they're not from the parts of those organisations who are involved with the Conspiracy. Unless, of course, the call has gone out to involve Mulder in as much spooky stuff as possible, to boost his paranoia levels.

Continuity: Scully seems to have a fondness for trashy, big-budget horror films.

The Truth: This episode appears to conclude that life after death is a fact – unless Lauren possesses genuine psychokinetic powers and is deluding herself.

Trivia: One of the employees of the company is named Tom Braidwood, after the production person and future Lone Gunman.

The Bottom Line: KT: 'He's watching over you, isn't he?' Apparently an unpopular episode with fans, this is a straight ghost story and, if one manages to suspend disbelief, it works very well. There are many memorable set pieces (the scene in Lauren's bathroom), and the effects are terrific (that flying letter opener). As usual, Scully is conveniently out of the room when something genuinely supernatural happens. But what's all that stuff about Mulder wanting to see the Liberty Bell at the end? Something of an oddity – good in parts, but with little substance.

PC: Some nice effects. It's pretty dull, though, and we've seen every single little bit of it before, done better. Hm? Oh, sorry. Fell asleep.

MD: Wake up, this is great! It's a simple story, but it trots along nicely and is well acted. However, it does feature two ridiculous elements that would go on to be *X-Files* staples, namely the weird character who fills in great chunks of background exposition (in this case the graveyard worker who tells us all about the Graves family), and the photograph that features more information than is visible to the naked eye.

7: 'Ghost in the Machine'

US Transmission: 29 October 1993
UK Transmission: 9 March 1994 (Sky One)/
3 November 1994 (BBC2)
Writers: Alex Gansa, Howard Gordon
Director: Jerrold Freedman
Cast: Wayne Duvall (Agent Jerry Lamana),
Rob LaBelle (Brad Wilczek), Tom Butler (Benjamin Drake),
Blu Mankuma (Claude Peterson),
Gillian Barber (Agent Nancy Spiller), Marc Baur (Man in Suit),
Bill Finck (Sandwich Man), Theodore Thomas (Clyde)

Eurisko Worldwide HQ, Crystal City, Virginia: Benjamin
Drake is electrocuted in his office. Mulder's former partner
Jerry Lamana asks for Mulder and Scully's help with the case.
Suspicion falls on Eurisko's whizz-kid founder Brad Wilczek
and, after Lamana is killed in a Eurisko elevator, Wilczek
confesses. However, Mulder believes that the building's computer, the Central Operations System, has achieved a degree
of sentience and, acting in self-preservation, is responsible for
the deaths. Wilczek creates a virus to destroy the system and,
despite the attempts to stop them by the Defense Department,
Mulder and Scully succeed. Deep Throat tells Mulder that
'the machine is dead'.

Don't Be in the Teaser: Benjamin Drake is electrocuted in
his office washroom.

How Did He Do That?: Mulder displays staggering leaps of
logic in working out that the building itself is killing people.

Scully's Rational Explanation of the Week: Brad Wilczek
did it.

That's a Mouthful: 'That subpoena has been obviated.'

Dialogue Triumphs: Mulder: 'How do you like that, a
politically correct elevator?'
    Mulder, entering Wilczek's home: 'This is what a 220
IQ and a four-hundred-million-dollar severance settlement
brings you!'

The Conspiracy Starts at Closing Time: The Defense Department certainly want to get hold of Wilczek and the COS, and from what we learn of the extent to which the DoD has been infiltrated by the Conspiracy in 'Redux', and Deep Throat's knowledge of this operation, we might gather this is their goal. Perhaps the Conspiracy are interested in any potential military advance in case it gives them an edge on their Colonist 'allies', or perhaps the Colonists aren't keen for any new (and potentially uncontrollable) intelligence to be let loose on Earth.

Continuity: Scully's home telephone number is (202) 555 6431. Her FBI ID number is 2317–616. (See 'F. Emasculata' and 'Paper Hearts' for Mulder's badge number, which has a completely different format.) Mulder knows enough about cars to be able to instantly disable the blaring horn after the attack by the COS. Jerry Lamana was Mulder's partner in Violent Crimes (perhaps Reggie Purdue was AOC to them both). Lamana was something of a high flyer until an incident in Atlanta when he misplaced some evidence which resulted in the disfigurement of a federal judge (which sounds like a pretty involved story in itself!). Since then, his position has been constantly threatened.

The Truth: The technological dream of artificial intelligence has been achieved.

Trivia: Microsoft are mentioned by name (Eurisko were two years ahead of them in terms of 'home control' software).

The Bottom Line: KT: 'I'm gonna figure this thing out if it kills me.' A strange episode, with an unoriginal plot (the 'killer building' has been done in several places before) and a lot of seemingly random elements thrown together. But it is quite involving, and the ending is very enigmatic.

PC: An ordinary episode done with a lot of style (the plunge to video in the camera's-eye-view lift scene is very dramatic).

MD: Now, *this* is derivative rubbish (the death of the COS recalls *2001* in every detail). It's difficult to detest, but it is dull and heartless. About the best thing here is the character of Wilczek, the untidy-minded software programmer into Zen: for him, the worst part about going to prison is having to wear shoes.

8: 'Ice'

US Transmission: 5 November 1993
UK Transmission: 16 March 1994 (Sky One)/
10 November 1994 (BBC2)
Writers: Glen Morgan, James Wong
Director: David Nutter
Cast: Xander Berkeley (Dr Hodge),
Felicity Huffman (Dr Nancy DaSilva),
Steve Hytner (Dr Denny Murphy), Jeff Kober (Bear),
Ken Kirzinger (Richter),
Sonny Surowiec (Campbell)

Icy Cape, Alaska: contact has been lost with the Arctic Ice Core Project, where a team of geophysicists working for the government's advanced research projects agency are drilling into the ice for indications of Earth's past climate. Mulder and Scully, along with three scientists, are sent to the base. Scully finds traces of ammonia in the blood of the corpses, along with a single-cell organism – the larval stage of a worm which causes psychotic behaviour in its human hosts. The expedition's pilot and one of the scientists die, but Scully discovers that larvae from two different worms will kill each other and she is able to prevent further loss of life. After the survivors are evacuated the base is destroyed.

Don't Be in the Teaser: John Richter and Campbell kill themselves rather messily.

Scully Here is a Medical Doctor: She performs an autopsy on the five dead physicists.

Scully's Rational Explanation of the Week: Severe isolation distress explains the physicists' deaths. The tables are turned, however, when her insistence that the single-cell organism could be the larval stage of a larger animal is dismissed by Hodge.

Phwoar!: Everybody takes their clothes off in this one. The sequence in which Mulder and Scully inspect each other's necks is powerful and edgy.

Dialogue Triumphs: Mulder (when told that they'll need to provide stool samples): 'OK, anybody got the morning sport section handy?' Bear: 'I ain't dropping my cargo for no one!'

Mulder (when stripping off): 'Before anyone passes judgement, may I remind you, we are in the Arctic!'

'It's still there, Scully: two hundred thousand years down in the ice.' 'Leave it there.'

The Conspiracy Starts at Closing Time: Somebody torches the base forty-five minutes after Mulder and Scully have been evacuated. Dr Hodge doesn't know who, though he speculates it was probably the military, but we'd bet on the Conspiracy.

Continuity: Mulder again reveals his extensive knowledge of American football when talking to Professor Murphy.

The Truth: This single-celled organism discovered in ancient strata (or possibly in a meteorite, though that's a mistake also made in 'Tunguska') bears striking similarities to the Black Oil (our heroes think it's transmitted via blood or saliva, but that doesn't account for DaSilva's infection), differing only in effect: anger rather than coma or zombiefication. But since the stuff may be sluggish in these low temperatures, perhaps that's a side effect of the environment. We see the Oil in a similar wormlike form in 'Terma'. The creatures seem to feed on the acetylcholine produced by the hypothalamus, triggering increased aggression in the host body, but that might be just a side effect of the Oil's chosen foodstuff here. Maybe Rebel Colonist Black Oil worms kill non-Rebels?

Trivia: Stunt co-ordinator Ken Kirzinger plays Richter.

The Bottom Line: KT: 'We're not who we are.' A shameless 'tribute' to *The Thing from Another World* (and *The Trollenberg Terror*). Claustrophobic, and very nasty – invasion of the killer tapeworms (mark one, see 'The Host'!). A classic 'base-under-siege', with all of the obvious clichés, but very well written and acted for all that.

PC: It's nice to see *Doctor Who*'s old base-under-siege story return to television. Pity it's not very original with its John Carpenter riffs, but it's great fun, anyway, and shows the verisimilitude that was the series' biggest selling point in its first season.

MD: A bit like my old Film Studies teacher's comment on both masturbation and the films of Alan Parker: fun while it lasts, but afterwards you wonder why you bothered. Still, for a few minutes you genuinely think that Mulder must be infected, something that few other programmes could so successfully achieve. It's a shame that the producers have to resort to the old Agatha Christie approach of making the guilty party the most unlikely suspect. (Not only is it never even hinted how DaSilva came to be infected, her character doesn't undergo the expected change of behaviour.) There are other instances of galloping lack of credibility: one moment we're being told that the lack of black spots isn't conclusive, the next Scully uses this as reason enough to believe that Mulder hasn't been infected. Argh!

9: 'Space'

US Transmission: 12 November 1993
UK Transmission: 23 March 1994 (Sky One)/
17 November 1994 (BBC2)
Writer: Chris Carter
Director: William Graham
Cast: Ed Lauter (Lt. Col. Marcus Aurelius Belt),
Susanna Thompson (Michelle Generoo),
Tom McBeath (Scientist),
Terry David Mulligan (Mission Controller),
French Tickner (Preacher), Norma Wick (Reporter),
Alf Humphries (2nd Controller),
David Cameron (Young Scientist),
Tyronne L'Hirondelle (Databank Scientist),
Paul DesRoches (Paramedic)

Houston, Texas: Mulder and Scully are contacted by Michelle Generoo, a NASA worker who believes that the current Space Shuttle programme is being sabotaged. They meet Mulder's boyhood idol, Marcus Belt, a former astronaut who is now project director. He dismisses any suggestion that the programme is being undermined, but the next flight is beset with problems. Belt is haunted by an alien image that he saw in space some twenty years before, an entity seeming to cohabit his body. He states that 'they' have been sabotaging missions for some time because 'they don't want us out there'. The shuttle returns to Earth with Belt's help, but he is hospitalised, and kills himself, much to Mulder's dismay.

Don't Be in the Teaser: Set in 1977, Lt. Col. Belt gets scared witless by the 'face on Mars'.

Scully Here is a Medical Doctor: She aids the medics when Belt suffers his seizure.

Scully's Rational Explanation of the Week: Severe dementia is at the root of Belt's 'possession'.

That's a Mouthful: 'Why would somebody want to sabotage a space shuttle?' asks Scully. Mulder's memorable reply is: 'Well, if you were a terrorist, there probably isn't a more potent symbol of American progress and prosperity. And if you're an opponent of big science, NASA itself represents a vast money trench that exists outside the crucible and debate of the democratic process. Then, of course, there are those futurists who believe that the space shuttle is a rusty old bucket that should be mothballed, a dinosaur spacecraft built in the seventies by scientists setting their sights on space in an ever-declining scale.' 'And we thought we could rest easy with the fall of the Soviet Union,' adds Scully.

Dialogue Triumphs: 'You never wanted to be an astronaut when you were a kid, Scully?' 'Guess I missed that phase.'

And, after the launch: 'I have to admit I've fulfilled one of my boyhood fantasies.' 'Yeah, it ranks right up there with getting a pony and learning to braid my own hair!'

Dialogue Disasters: Mulder: 'You'll get no argument from me, sir, you were true American heroes.'

The Conspiracy Starts at Closing Time: 'The failure of the Hubble telescope and the Mars Observer are directly connected to a conspiracy to deny us evidence,' notes Mulder. 'Evidence of what?' asks Scully. 'Alien civilisation.' 'Oh, of course!' (Every now and then, Mulder's desire to be open to extreme possibilities leads him to go blibber blibber blibber. The Hubble telescope was repaired to enable it to work close to its original specification – and what contribution it might have made to the discovery of alien civilisations is debatable. The loss of the Mars Observer, on the other hand, is rather mysterious, especially considering the possibility raised in 'Tunguska' that the Black Oil, host form of the Colonist consciousness, is also resident on Mars. Is it too much of a stretch to imagine that it might have raised, and consumed, another humanoid host race there?) There is some suggestion that Belt may have covered up sabotage on the Challenger disaster in 1986, or been part of the (actual) attempted hushing up of engineering worries concerning the cause of the disaster. The 'ghost' may be a mental weapon used by the Conspiracy (as in 'Wetwired' or 'Unusual Suspects') to prevent further revelations. It's even possible that the Colonists have a base on Mars and don't want it observed.

Continuity: Lt. Col. Marcus Aurelius Belt was one of Mulder's heroes as a child. Mulder stayed up all night when he was fourteen to watch Belt's spacewalk (this would have been in 1975 or 1976, so presumably Belt was involved in the Apollo/Soyuz link-up).

The Truth: It's possible the gaseous ghostlike thing seen by Belt in space (and by the shuttle astronauts, and by Generoo before the crash, so it's not just Belt's delusions at work) is not Terran in origin. It may originate from Mars: it certainly looks like the 'face' observed there, but this could be Belt's own fears giving it shape. It appears to be malevolent and opposed to mankind's presence in space. But perhaps Belt and the other witnesses are being 'got at' through their water supply or television, and the ghost is purely subjective.

Trivia: When Generoo sees the face, the night is foggy and wet. The weather clears up remarkably as soon as Mulder and Scully arrive. Belt's career included piloting Gemini 8, during which he nearly died, having to make an emergency landing in the Pacific. (The real Gemini 8, piloted by Neil Armstrong and David Scott, made an emergency landing 10 hours and 41 minutes into the flight on 16 March 1966.) Ex-Pixies frontman Frank Black (the source of the *Millennium* character's name) has recorded a song entitled 'Your Face' about the face on Mars.

Scientific Comment: Mention is made of '. . . solar winds that blow across the surface of Mars at 300 m.p.h. ten months a year'. This isn't the solar wind, which is very weak and would do absolutely nothing to sculpt the Martian landscape. It's just the wind, the same as we have winds on Earth. There would be no reason for the solar wind to act for only ten months of the year. And are we talking about Earth years, Martian years or what? A month relates to Earth's moon, so presumably they are talking in Earth terms. Even if they couldn't rotate the shuttle to the proper attitude with respect to the sun it would not 'burn up'. The rotating payload was making a rotating noise when it was released. You wouldn't hear anything, of course. But perhaps one should be charitable and assume that the rotating noise came from the mechanism that spun it, which, since it was attached to the shuttle, the astronauts would hear.

The Bottom Line: KT: 'There's some kind of ghost outside the ship!' For some reason this fine episode proved to be vastly unpopular with fans. Apart from the lack of obvious explanation about what the menace actually is (as though that were an uncommon fault in *The X-Files*!), there's little one can see that's wrong with the episode. It's superbly acted and covers themes of possession and the problematic nature of hero worship. Maybe the fact that the episode disses the American dream by making the villain an archetypal modern folk hero ensured that it was poorly received.

PC: Yeah, I like it too. Another area of the American mythos explored – all the stories of NASA encounters with aliens – and a fun use of stock footage.

MD: It's clever, politically literate and perceptive (it comes as no great surprise that by the episode's end Generoo is lying to the media, too). The suicide of Belt is very moving.

More than any other TV series (with the exception of *Babylon 5*), *The X-Files* is a product of the Internet age. Within weeks of the series beginning, websites, chat rooms and newsgroups had sprung up allowing fans to discuss elements of the series not within days or weeks of broadcast (as *Star Trek* and *Doctor Who* fans had been doing for years through fanzines) but within *minutes*. The production team seem to have noticed this, Chris Carter occasionally going online to answer queries, or give out a few titbits on forth-coming episodes. Actors also are often interviewed online. As a 'thank you' to the more vocal internet fans, many episodes have included character names based on them (see 'D.P.O', for instance). A fan lan-guage of nicknames began to find its way into the series (it was on alt.tv.x-files that calling Krycek 'Rat-boy' and Mulder and Scully 'Moose and Squirrel' became fashionable). While the series' fictional dab-blings with the Internet have ranged from paranoia ('2Shy') to amusing techno-realism ('Kill Switch'), the fact that Mulder, Scully and the Lone Gunmen are all online is surely a sign of the age we live in.

The downside to the instantaneous nature of the Net's influence is that once an episode had been taken apart in the fan community, no amount of revisionist thinking can restore its reputation. Hence 'Space' still regularly comes top of polls of 'Most Hated Episode' despite there being many worse examples of the series than this. IONSHO!

10: 'Fallen Angel'

US Transmission: 19 November 1993
UK Transmission: 30 March 1994 (Sky One)/
24 November 1994 (BBC2)
Writers: Howard Gordon, Alex Gansa
Director: Larry Shaw

Cast: Frederick Coffin (Section Chief Joseph McGrath),
Marshall Bell (Commander Henderson),
Brent Stait (Corporal Taylor), Alvin Sanders (Deputy Wright),
Sheila Paterson (Gina Watkins), Tony Pantages (Lt. Fraser),
Freda Perry (Mrs Wright), Michael Rogers (Lt. Griffin),
William McDonald (Dr Oppenheim),
Jane MacDougall (Laura Dalton),
Kimberly Unger (Karen Koretz)

Townsend, Wisconsin: after the discovery of something in the
woods the town is evacuated on the pretence of a biological
hazard having been found. Deep Throat tells Mulder that it is
really a crashed spaceship and that the air force have sent in a
reclamation group. He has twenty-four hours before the evidence will disappear. Mulder goes in but is apprehended.
Scully arrives to bring him back to Washington for an inquiry
hearing, but Mulder persuades her to stay. He befriends Max
Fenig, a ufologist, and finds evidence of Max's having been
abducted. Max is taken by the aliens, despite the presence of
the military team, and Mulder is forced to return to the inquiry.
However, he is saved from dismissal by Deep Throat.

Don't Be in the Teaser: Deputy Wright, burnt to death by
aliens.

Scully Here is a Medical Doctor: She discusses the finer
points of burn pathology with Dr Oppenheim, and is then
asked for her help in dealing with the badly injured soldiers.

Scully's Rational Explanation of the Week: A downed
Libyan jet with a nuclear warhead is the reason for the
situation. Max is a delusional schizophrenic.

Dialogue Triumphs: Max: 'Let me guess, you're with that new
group, CSICOP, right? Say no more. You're a cautious man,
trust no one, very wise. After what happened to JFK I understand completely!'

Radar Operator: 'Well, sir, the "meteor" seems to be hover-
ing over a small town in east Wisconsin.'

The Conspiracy Starts at Closing Time: Deep Throat's
agenda is the focus of this episode: he sends Mulder into the

area, then he saves his job just when it looks like Mulder's superiors have the perfect rationale for throwing him out of the FBI ('How can I disprove lies that are stamped with an official seal?'). In his encounter with FBI Section Chief McGrath, Deep Throat seems to be playing both sides off against each other ('always keep your friends close but keep your enemies closer'): from the distance of season five, we can now see exactly what he's doing. McGrath, the head of the Office of Professional Responsibility, and a junior representative of the Conspiracy in the FBI (Blevins being the senior one), thinks he's achieved exactly what his employers want, to have Mulder thrown out of the Bureau, but Deep Throat (his CIA contact and someone higher up the Conspiracy hierarchy) pulls rank on him to keep Mulder where he is, and uses a truly feeble excuse (backed up by his usual portentous delivery) to do so. The Cigarette-Smoking Man's agenda may be visible here, as carried out through his friend Deep Throat: to keep Mulder alive, he's told the Conspiracy that he's using him as a stalking horse to keep that particular mixture of public credulity and scepticism that allows the Conspiracy to get away with anything rampant. To justify that policy, he has Deep Throat feed Mulder juicy but ultimately useless snippets. If Mulder were to be thrown out of the Bureau at this point (before he's the household name in UFO circles he later becomes), next time he poked his nose into a Conspiracy operation he'd be dead meat. Deep Throat, as a friend of Mulder's dad, may also have a fondness for the agent, and exceed his orders on occasion, letting Mulder pursue the idealistic crusade Bill Mulder always imagined he would do. But it's hard to read anything fond into him laughing at 'what he (Mulder) thinks he knows', as big an indication as any that Mulder is being presented a cocktail of standard alien abduction myths quite different to what the Conspiracy is really up to. At the end of the episode, Mulder is once more witness to an abduction. He should start checking himself for implants by now, surely? There is another reference to the Roswell incident and its 'cover-up'. The leader of Operation Falcon is Colonel Colin Henderson, the air force's top reclamations officer (during the Cold War his job was to prevent the technology of downed US aircraft from falling into enemy hands). Now his mission is to recover crashed UFOs. (These men may also be the Blue Beret team seen in 'Little Green Men', and supply some of the uniformed gangs of armed men who are at the Conspiracy's command.) At the end of the episode, Henderson says that Max's body was found two hours later in a cargo container, but, since we meet Max again in 'Tempus Fugit', this is a lie to debunk Mulder's story. (Since Mulder shows no surprise at Max's continuing existence in that episode, we may assume that Max resumed his public activities in the UFO community, or perhaps even got in touch with Mulder.)

Continuity: Scully did her residency in forensic medicine. The National Investigative Committee of Aerial Phenomena (or NICAP), of which Max Fenig is a member, has been following Mulder and Scully's exploits with interest ('your travel expenses are a matter of public record'). Mulder has published an article in *Omni* about the Gulf Breeze sightings under the pseudonym M.F. Luder (an anagram of F. Mulder: he didn't think anyone would notice, but is warned that 'Somebody's always paying attention, Mr Mulder'). His photo has appeared in a 'trade publication'. He believes most crop circles are fake.

The Truth: The episode features a crashed alien spaceship and an invisible and lethal alien on the loose, pursued by soldiers who we may take to be representatives of the Conspiracy. So this is our first sighting of a Rebel Colonist, a humanoid being of some sort (not a Shapeshifter, or it'd utilise that ability), cloaked in an invisible field (that also allows it to move through solid objects like camper roofs), moving at normal human running speed (7 mph), presumably containing its own version of Black Oil. It's a reasonable bet to assume this is a cloaked Grey, displaying the same natural radiation weapon as the Oil-infested Krycek used in 'Apocrypha'. Max has already been abducted and subjected to some sort of implantation: he seems to have been called to this area by his implant to gather information to allow a rescue, and to help with that business. (The behind-the-ear implant has a controlling rather than Black Oil monitoring function.) So it seems that the Rebel Colonists are willing and able to conduct abductions too, but only in order to further their faction's plans. The crashed craft looks like it could be a triangular Colonist craft. Invisibility is a trait we associate with the returned zoo animals of 'Fearful Symmetry', and they seem to have been taken by the Rebel Colonists, and we see a Rebel Colonist teleportation device (as used here) in operation in 'The Red and the Black'. So, with a lot of licence, it seems possible that here we see another battle in the ongoing Colonist civil war, with the soldiers representing one side and Max and the invisible alien the other.

Trivia: It's odd that Max assumes that Mulder works for CSICOP (Committee for the Scientific Investigation into Claims of the Paranormal), a group of real-life serious sceptics who wouldn't want Mulder in the same room with them.

The Bottom Line: KT: 'Another intrepid soul in search of a close encounter.' This is a little like biting into a Cadbury's Creme Egg and finding no creamy bit in the middle – a hollow mess with a plot with holes big enough to fly a spaceship through. (What happens to the crashed alien? What is the aliens' purpose in taking Max? Why not take Mulder with him? Is the second spaceship invisible, and, if so, why wasn't the first one?) Despite all of this (and a fairly strong suspicion that Max Fenig is an obvious and pretty insulting parody of SF fans – surely we should be beyond the 'space cadet' stereotypes by now) parts of 'Fallen Angel' are great (particularly Mulder's cool anger at Henderson). Oddly styled, though, with Scully missing for half the episode.

PC: A series of good set pieces put together randomly. The ending is quite meaningless, and a major disappointment.

MD: This left an indelible blank on me when I first watched it, but I quite enjoyed it this time. The complete change of pace was clever, with Mulder thrown straight into a virtual combat zone, and, whatever its flaws, this episode is directed with the brutality of a pop video drenched in testosterone. The little cameos of the harassed doctor who hates fascists and the widow who 'can't afford the truth' are excellent, but one is left with a vague feeling of disappointment after the wordy ending. And, given the deadly nature of the alien, Mulder really shouldn't have survived this episode, either.

11: 'Eve'

US Transmission: 10 December 1993
UK Transmission: 6 April 1994 (Sky One)/
1 December 1994 (BBC2)
Writers: Kenneth Biller, Chris Brancato
Director: Fred Gerber
Cast: Harriet Harris (Dr Sally Kendrick/Eves 6,7,8),
Erika Krievins (Cindy Reardon),
Sabrina Krievins (Teena Simmons),
George Touliatos (Dr Katz), Tasha Simms (Ellen Reardon),
Janet Hodgkinson (Waitress), David Kirby (Ted Watkins),
Tina Gilbertson (Donna Watkins),
Christine Upright-Letain (Ms Wells),
Gordon Tipple (Detective), Garry Davey (Hunter),
Joe Maffei (Guard #1), Maria Herrera (Guard #2),
Robert Lewis (Officer)

Greenwich, Connecticut: a man dies in his back yard from massive blood loss. His daughter (Teena) talks about 'men from the clouds' coming for him. Meanwhile, in Marin County, California, a virtually identical case becomes more of a statistical improbability when it is discovered that the daughter in the California case (Cindy) is the double of Teena. Mulder is told about a forty-year-old eugenics project that created a group of hyper-intelligent psychotic children, one of whom – Sally Kendrick – later worked in the IVF clinic where both Teena's and Cindy's mothers conceived. The girls are kidnapped by Kendrick, but she soon discovers that they are far from innocent eight-year-olds. Mulder and Scully, too, are almost poisoned by the pair, before they are incarcerated with one of their elder 'sisters'.

Don't Be in the Teaser: Joel Simmons suffers 75 per cent blood loss.

How Did He Do That?: So why *did* the girls suddenly decide to drain their fathers of blood?

Scully Here is a Medical Doctor: Mulder tells *Scully* all about the pumping action of the heart. Similarly, *Dr* Scully is told (also for the benefit of the viewer) all about *in vitro* fertilisation at the Luther Stapes Center.

Scully's Rational Explanation of the Week: Real bottom-of-the-barrel scraping here. Two serial killers are working in tandem three thousand miles apart, and the likenesses of the clones are random. As Mulder says, 'I'd like to get the odds on that at Vegas!'

Dialogue Triumphs: 'Mulder, why would alien beings travel light years to Earth in order to play doctor on cattle?'

Mulder: 'One girl was just abducted.' Scully: 'Kidnapped.' Mulder: 'Potato, potahto.'

The Conspiracy Starts at Closing Time: Given Deep Throat's interest in the case, and the fact that the original experiments were sanctioned by the US government, it seems almost certain that the Conspiracy has endorsed Kendrick's renewal of the eugenics experiments. Dr Katz's call for an investigation was ignored, and Eve 6 claims that she is still being experimented on. It is possible that this is a facet of a programme that's attempting to create the perfect soldier (see 'Young at Heart', 'Sleepless'), presumably as a possible defence against the Conspiracy's Colonist 'allies'. Or perhaps Deep Throat's interest is purely that somebody else has been successfully cloning human beings, which is why he uses Mulder to shut that operation down. Deep Throat contacts Mulder via clicks down the phone.

The Truth: According to Deep Throat, the Litchfield experiments were a secret government eugenics project in the early 1950s. A group of children were produced who had 56 chromosomes instead of the normal 46, giving them heightened intelligence (Eve 6 believes her IQ is pushing 265) and strength. However, they were also prone to psychotic behaviour and suicide ('It runs in the family!'). The boys were called Adam, and the eight girls, Eve. Of the Eves, only three are seen during the story. Eve 6 is held in the Whitfield Institute for the Criminally Insane, and Eve 7 has controlled her psychosis with drugs, becoming Dr Sally Kendrick. She has cloned herself in an attempt to root out the 'Litchfield flaws' (which she characterises as psychotic behaviour beginning at seventeen, and homicidal behaviour starting at twenty). Eve 8 appears at the end. Cindy and Teena are the progeny of this 'second-generation' experiment, and they appear to be telepathic, which might be a side effect of their unique genetic make-up (although Eve 7 is surprised by this). Their homicidal behaviour starts much earlier, and Teena and Cindy are renamed Eves 9 and 10 by the story's end.

Trivia: As Mulder and Scully question Ellen Reardon, Cindy watches the cartoon series *Eek the Cat*. The cartoon would later return the favour by featuring an animated Mulder and Scully. Eve 6 quotes from the Beatles' 'I Am the Walrus' ('. . . and we are all together!'). There is a mention of the Jones Town massacre.

The Bottom Line: KT: 'We weren't born, we were created.' A cracking story made more memorable by a series of brilliant set pieces throughout. The pre-titles suggest a simple vampire story – then it gets really weird! Many great directorial touches, a breathtaking multiple performance by Harriet Harris, and a final scene that's crying out for a sequel.

PC: Indeed, here's a story that's written instead of being thrown together. Where do they find these weird-looking child actors? Can you imagine the auditions?

MD: It's not often that we're allowed to be two steps ahead of Mulder, and here it works well, adding to the suspense of the final scenes. The story's only flaw is that the direction sometimes oversteps the mark, making the first abduction, for example, appear to be a supernatural activity when it is in fact nothing of the sort.

12: 'Fire'

US Transmission: 17 December 1993
UK Transmission: 13 April 1994 (Sky One)/
17 December 1994 (BBC2)[5]
Writer: Chris Carter
Director: Larry Shaw

---

[5] Shown as part of BBC2's 'Weird Night'.

Cast: Amanda Pays (Inspector Phoebe Green),
Mark Sheppard (Bob/Cecil L'Ively),
Dan Lett (Sir Malcolm Marsden),
Laurie Paton (Lady Marsden),
Duncan Fraser (Beatty), Phil Hayes (Driver #1),
Keegan Macintosh (Michael), Lynda Boyd (Bar Patron),
Christopher Gray (Jimmie), Alan Robertson (Grey-Haired Man)

Bosham, England: another member of the British establishment burns to death. Mulder's ex-girlfriend, Phoebe Green, now an inspector with Scotland Yard, arrives in America and asks for Mulder's help in protecting Sir Malcolm Marsden and his family. A fire breaks out during an important function, the arsonist seeming to target Marsden's children. Mulder attempts a rescue, despite his pyrophobia. An artist's impression of the arsonist is drawn up, and Scully discovers that he is one Cecil L'Ively, currently working as the Marsdens' odd-job man. L'Ively's attempt to kill the Marsden children is foiled by Mulder and the man self-ignites. Although horribly burnt, L'Ively survives.

Don't Be in the Teaser: A paint-by-numbers member of the British upper classes spontaneously combusts.

Scully's Rational Explanation of the Week: Her profile of the arsonist is spot on in every aspect other than his means of ignition.

Phwoar!: There's some interesting body language from Scully whenever Phoebe is around. Dialogue, too (Mulder: 'I was merely extending her a professional courtesy.' Scully: 'Oh, is that what you were extending?'). Miaow! Mulder wanders round Phoebe's hotel room shirtless, and in a robe, and mention must be made of his tuxedo-wearing skills.

Dialogue Triumphs: Mulder on the mysterious tape: 'Ten to one you can't dance to it.'

Dialogue Disasters: Phoebe: 'Some clever bloke has been giving the aristocracy a scare.'

L'Ively: 'Bloody little cur. I'll skin you alive! See – I'm the caretaker now!'

Mulder: 'Doesn't look like your arsonist is going to make an appearance.' Phoebe: 'That doesn't mean there won't be any fires to put out.'

L'Ively: 'You can't fight fire with fire!'

Phoebe: 'Oh come on, don't tell me you left your sense of humour in Oxford ten years ago?' Mulder: 'No, actually, it's one of the few things you didn't drive a stake through.'

Continuity: Mulder's pyrophobia dates back to his youth: his best friend's house burnt down and Mulder spent the night in the rubble to keep away looters. Following that he suffered years of nightmares about being trapped in burning buildings. He says he has a photographic memory (we don't see any evidence of this – and it's a very rare ability – so he's probably only talking about his acute remembrance of the bad times during his affair with Phoebe). He met Phoebe Green when he was at Oxford and they became lovers. Mulder and Phoebe used to share Sherlock Holmes jokes and Phoebe implies that they once made love atop Arthur Conan Doyle's tomb in Windlesham. (The real tomb is in Minstead in Hampshire. The writer didn't even bother to open a reference book . . .) Phoebe's current lover is Malcolm Marsden. Scully can do a reasonable British accent (better than most of the actors in this episode anyway . . .).

The Truth: Whether L'Ively is a genuine pyrokinetic is debatable. He uses the rocket fuel argotypoline as an accelerant, but his power of ignition seems paranormal. Also, his ability to survive massive burning is said to be 'extraordinary'.

Trivia: Bosham is apparently seventy miles southwest of London, which would place it on the Hampshire coast. The US government, not the British government, used to issue US visas: the FBI should know that!

Scientific Comment: You would get a magnesium residue after an exothermic reaction only if there was magnesium present to begin with. It is stated in this episode that fires burning at 7000 degrees can't be put out with water because it dissociates into hydrogen and oxygen and just adds fuel to the fire, and that rocket fuel burns so hot there are no traces left afterwards. It is true that water would be dissociated at 7000 degrees, but it wouldn't make any difference to the fire: it would not be like adding fuel. However, you'd never get a fire this hot. Anything based on petroleum or hydrocarbons burns at 700–800 degrees, not thousands. You never get fires hotter than 4000 degrees from anything. The only way to get 7000 degrees (which is hotter than the sun's surface) would be to use real rocket fuel, that is: hydrogen and liquid oxygen being brought together in a high-compression engine. Not only that, but concrete is a very good thermal insulator, and apparently can be in a fire for days without really being affected. The only thing that happens is that the outside layer flakes off. It would have to be awfully substandard concrete to be affected much at all.

The Bottom Line: KT: 'God, I just love that accent!' Despite a few (no, qualify that: a *lot* of) dodgy British accents, 'Fire' is another fine episode. The script is full of caricatures (L'Ively especially – we know little more about him at the episode's end than at the beginning), but the effects are amazing and it's got enough genuine scares in it to paper over the logic cracks that pop up every now and then. Mark Sheppard is very good. Amanda Pays chews the scenery.

PC: Put together by people who don't seem to know Britain or the British even slightly (Malcolm Marsden is a knight, a lord, and an MP!), this makes you wonder about how accurately the series treats the other communities it visits. Phoebe would be one of the youngest detective inspectors in Britain, and the most upper-class, and she has a very strange choice of current boyfriend. She wears clothes from the 1980s, as if nobody had seen British fashions since the Royal Wedding. Is Cecil L'Ively really the name of a gardener, and Malcolm Marsden the name of a lord? And there's that standard Americanism, the misuse of 'bloke'. It's annoying that, for a series with the depth of *The X-Files*, the approach to Britain is just as rubbish as that of every other American series. Thank goodness they haven't done one set here, or it'd be cricket, tea, thatched cottages and saving the Queen from aliens at Stonehenge.

KT: Sounds like a good story, actually.

MD: My favourite Americanisms were a 'British Minister of Parliament' and all that guff about Scotland Yard. Oh, and Sheppard's accent is a hoot, changing from Irish to Aussie to

Michael Caine in the blink of an eye (which is a shame because, as Keith points out, he actually puts in a good performance). Still, the episode itself is mostly harmless, and Anderson is great (I love Scully's breezy 'Hello!' to Phoebe).

13: 'Beyond the Sea'

US Transmission: 7 January 1994
UK Transmission: 20 April 1994 (Sky One)/
8 December 1994 (BBC2)
Writers: Glen Morgan, James Wong
Director: David Nutter
Cast: Brad Dourif (Luther Lee Boggs),
Lawrence King (Lucas Jackson Henry),
Fred Henderson (Agent Thomas),
Don MacKay (Warden Joseph Cash),
Lisa Vultaggio (Liz Hawley), Chad Willett (Jim Summers),
Kathrynn Chisholm (Nurse), Randy Lee (Paramedic),
Len Rose (ER Doctor)

Washington, DC: after a visit from her parents, Scully sees a silent vision of her father shortly before receiving the phone call telling her of his death. Raleigh, North Carolina: a couple are kidnapped a year to the day after a similar crime. A death row prisoner, Luther Lee Boggs, claims to have developed psychic powers which will lead the FBI to the kidnapper. He also claims to be able to communicate with Scully's father. Mulder is, for once, sceptical, but Scully, after further visitations, begins to believe in Boggs's abilities. Tracking the kidnapper, Mulder is shot and badly wounded. The kidnapper escapes with one of the two hostages but is identified as Lucas Henry, Boggs's former accomplice. The victim is rescued and the kidnapper falls to his death. As Boggs is executed, Mulder and Scully are still unsure whether his 'gifts' were genuine.

Don't Be in the Teaser: Captain Scully dies (off screen) from a heart attack.

Scully's Rational Explanation of the Week: Having spent nearly an entire episode going Mulder on us, good old Dana ends the story trying to convince herself that Boggs had learnt of her connection to Mulder and researched her, and that her visions of her dead father were grief symptoms (despite the fact that they first occurred before she was aware of his death).

Phwoar!: Mulder touches Scully's face as he says how sorry he is to hear about the death of her father.

Dialogue Triumphs: Mulder (on Boggs): 'When he was thirty, he strangled five family members over Thanksgiving dinner and then sat down to watch the fourth quarter of the Detroit/Green Bay game. Some killers are products of society, some act out past abuses. Boggs kills because he likes it.'

Scully: 'Did Boggs confess?' Mulder: 'No, it was five hours of Boggs's "channelling". After three hours I asked him to summon up the soul of Jimi Hendrix and requested "All Along the Watchtower". You know, the guy's been dead twenty years, but he still hasn't lost his edge.'

Mulder: 'Open yourself up to extreme possibilities only when they're the truth.'

Scully: 'Well, I came here to tell you that if he [Mulder] dies because of what you've done, four days from now nobody will stop me from being the one that throws the switch and gas you out of this life for good, you son of a bitch!'

Continuity: Scully's father was a navy captain, her mother's name is Margaret. Her father always made the family take the Christmas tree down on Boxing Day. She called her father 'Ahab'; his nickname for her was 'Starbuck' (see 'Quagmire'). Scully's house number is 35. Mulder calls Scully 'Dana' for just about the first time, much to her amusement (or discomfort – it's difficult to be sure). Her father's funeral music is 'Beyond the Sea' by Bobby Darin, which was the music played when his ship returned from the Cuban blockade in 1962 – just before he proposed to Margaret. (Since the Cuban missile crisis happened in October 1962, and Melissa Scully was born in that year, are we to assume that she was born out of wedlock?) The song was also played at their wedding. There are five people at Captain Scully's funeral besides Dana and her mother. Presumably these would include her two brothers (see 'Roland'), though her sister (see 'One Breath') doesn't appear to be there.

Mulder's profile helped to capture the serial killer Luther Lee Boggs. Mulder gives Boggs a piece of cloth which Boggs says belongs to Jim Summers. In reality it is from Mulder's New York Knicks T-shirt (see 'Clyde Bruckman's Final Repose'). Mulder is shot in the upper femur, and seriously wounded. An X-File concerning 'visionary encounters with the dead' is code numbered X–167512. (Presumably that's about a specific case, unless Mulder's started to file his library clippings this way, too.)

The Truth: The episode never makes clear whether Boggs is a superb con artist with an accomplice or the genuine possessor of paranormal powers. As Scully points out, it would have been possible (if difficult) for Boggs to have found out a lot about her and her father. And Scully may have indeed been delusional in her grief at her father's death. But, on the other hand, there is nothing to disprove Boggs's claims: after all, more or less everything he predicts (the shooting of Mulder, Henry falling to his death) comes true.

Trivia: The minister who Boggs speaks to quotes from 1 John 3:14–15. Max's NICAP cap (see 'Fallen Angel') hangs in Mulder's office. (Max must get hold of another one before 'Tempus Fugit'.)

The Bottom Line: KT: 'Dana, after all you've seen, after all the evidence, why can't you believe?' 'I'm afraid. I'm afraid to believe.' Magnificent and enigmatic – the zenith of a superb run of episodes with the performance of the season by Brad Dourif. A complex narrative piece, complete with juxtaposed character motivation that could only work if the acting is of the highest quality. A truly great episode.

PC: Still up there with the best episodes of the series. The courage it takes for a series this deep in ratings trouble ('Beyond the Sea' achieved only a 5 rating, the lowest the series has ever sunk, an eminently cancellable position) to do an episode that turns away from the unexplained and denies the audience closure is magnificent. Mind you, there's still that annoying postmodern idea that if you quote from something, then you bring some of the quality of what's being quoted along with you. In this case, the episode takes lots from *Exorcist III*. But it does some original things with the material. Gillian Anderson proves here that she's about ten times better an actor than David Duchovny, by going for restraint and then exploding.

MD: 'Beyond the Sea' is a remarkable episode, *The X-Files* proving that metaphysical reflection is very much its forte. The monochrome nightmare of Boggs going to the chair – and the souls rushing in – is just terrifying. An incredibly brave story, given that many of the viewing public desire the murder of murderers.

14: 'GenderBender'

US Transmission: 21 January 1994
UK Transmission: 27 April 1994 (Sky One)/
22 December 1994 (BBC2)[6]
Writers: Larry Barber, Paul Barber
Director: Rob Bowman
Cast: Brent Hinkley (Brother Andrew),
Michele Goodger (Sister Abigail),
Kate Twa (Marty (Female)), Peter Stebbings (Marty (Male)),
Nicholas Lea (Michael), Paul Batten (Brother Wilton),
Doug Abrahams (Agent #2),
Aundrea MacDonald (Pretty Woman),
John R. Taylor (Husband), Grai Carrington (Tall Man),
Tony Morelli (Cop), Lesley Ewen (Agent #1),
David Thompson (Brother Oakley)

Germantown, Maryland: Mulder and Scully investigate the latest in a series of five deaths linked by the victims dying during or shortly after sexual intercourse with massive levels of pheromones in their bodies. A security camera witnesses the victim arriving home with a female, but a male leaving. Mulder is convinced that they are tracking 'the ultimate sex machine'. Clues point to a link to a reclusive religious cult, the Kindred. He and Scully travel to Steveston, Massachusetts, where they meet the Kindred. Mulder discovers a

---

[6] Originally scheduled for 15 December, but postponed.

secret catacomb area, where a dying man appears to change gender, while Scully finds herself drawn to one of the brothers. The killer is revealed as an escaped member of the sect, 'tainted' by the outside world. After (s)he has killed again, the Kindred arrive to 'take care of their own', and disappear.

Don't Be in the Teaser: An unnamed New York businessman engages in a wild, passionate bout of sex, then chokes to death.

How Did He Do That?: How does Mulder manage to avoid capture in a tunnel system that he's never been in and his pursuers, presumably, know like the back of their hand?

Ooze: There's some frothy stuff that the victims spew up at various points. And Scully vomits (off screen).

Scully's Rational Explanation of the Week: A transvestite, obviously.

Phwoar!: Scully's reaction to Brother Andrew both includes and transcends the sensual.

Dialogue Triumphs: Scully: 'So, what is our profile of the killer? Indeterminate height, weight, sex. Unarmed, but extremely attractive?!'
   Michael: 'The club scene used to be so simple.'

Dialogue Disasters: Cop: 'Cat blew an artery. Must have been some roll in the hay!'

The Truth: The killer, Marty, and his Kindred brothers and sisters are able to vanish at will, and use a regenerative gel in the catacomb that also changes their gender. The pheromones they release contain human DNA, but their final disappearance does suggest a UFO, complete with crop circle landing site. We'd say they were Rebel Colonists, but their method of changing shape is much more complex than that of the Shapeshifters. Perhaps they're Rebel Colonists whose Black Oil content is so low that they can't become true Shapeshifters. Or an escaped community of human/Colonist hybrids, using technology to create individual appearances for themselves, which would explain the DNA. Their attitude of wanting to be cut off from the world seems utterly genuine, but rather strange if they've got transport off-planet arranged. Perhaps they're taken away against their will, or reveal their location to the Conspiracy in order to avoid an investigation.

Trivia: A classic rock fan's dream, Mulder name-checking the Troggs' 'Wild Thing' and Golden Earring's 'Radar Love' and Scully weighing in with a misquote from Lou Reed's 'Walk on the Wild Side' ('She was a he!'). Mulder mentions *The Addams Family* again. The painting that we see Marty standing beside is by H.R. Giger, the designer of *Alien*. Steveston, Massachusetts is named after a real town south of Vancouver, often used by the series for location work.

The Bottom Line: KT: 'Maybe it's the sex that kills.' Difficult to know where to start with this. The episode is a mess, a confusing mixture of about eight different stories all struggling to be understood. Good points first: the juxtaposition of the club scenes with the ordered calm of the Kindred community is well managed, the direction generally being very good. Also, stories about religious cults tend to come over all atheistic and sanctimonious, but this one at least achieves some balance. Yet, for all this, the episode's denouement is a disaster – with seemingly random (and highly implausible) elements thrown in at the last moment to provide a suitably 'enigmatic' climax. The plot has more holes in it than Blackburn, Lancashire. (Who were the Kindred? Aliens? Mutant Hermaphrodites? Bisexuals with a God-complex? How do they 'disappear' from the crime scene?) I'm not in favour of TV spoon-feeding me all the answers, but just one or two would be quite nice. This is also the first episode in which the beauty of the series' initial view of Americana – in which every town has a forest with an alien in it – becomes dissipated. We see the first example of what would soon become the standard *X-Files* visual cliché, a misty inner-city back-alley. For all sorts of reasons, a big disappointment.

PC: Hm? Sorry. Perked up for a bit in the middle of the episode and then dropped off again. Thought that some of the direction and lighting was rather nice, but it didn't keep me awake. Was it any good?

MD: Almost. Some of this actually chugs along quite nicely as a *Witness*-like parable on the corrupting influence of the 'World' (Brother Andrew says that he liked some of what

he saw in the secular magazine, but that much was 'garish'),
but the ending is amateurish in the extreme. What's worse
than the lack of explanation is the lack of a conclusion: the
narrative just peters out completely.

15: 'Lazarus'

US Transmission: 4 February 1994
UK Transmission: 4 May 1994 (Sky One)/
5 January 1995 (BBC2)
Writers: Alex Gansa, Howard Gordon
Director: David Nutter
Cast: Christopher Allport (Agent Jack Willis),
Cec Verrell (Lula Phillips), Jackson Davies (Agent Bruskin),
Jason Schombing (Warren James Dupre),
Callum Keith Rennie (Tommy),
Jay Brazeau (Professor Varnes), Lisa Bunting (Doctor #1),
Peter Kelamis (O'Dell), Brenda Crichlow (Reporter),
Mark Saunders (Doctor #2),
Alexander Boynton (Clean-Cut Man),
Russell Hamilton (Officer Daniels)

Maryland Marine Bank: during an FBI operation to capture
two bank robbers, Warren and Lula Dupre, Scully's former
lover, Special Agent Jack Willis, is critically injured, as is Warren. Willis survives – after thirteen minutes of flatlining in the
emergency room – but Warren Dupre dies. After Willis goes
missing and Warren Dupre's hand is mutilated to remove his
wedding ring, Mulder comes to believe that a psychic transference has taken place. Willis later turns up and appears to be
normal, saying he only wants to capture Lula and close the case.
However, when he and Scully go to arrest the woman, Willis
convinces Lula that he is Warren Dupre and they kidnap Scully.
As Mulder and the FBI close in, Lula double-crosses her lover,
just as she did before. Willis is slipping into a diabetic coma but
he recovers sufficiently to kill Lula just as Mulder arrives.

Don't Be in the Teaser: What a bloodbath! Jack Willis, shot
by Dupre, who is promptly shot by Scully.

How Did He Do That?: The mother of all How Did He Do Thats. Mulder, using only two traces on a heart monitor, comes to the conclusion that a transference of souls has taken place! He even finds a loony scientist to back him up! And, for perhaps the first time in the series, this is all so ridiculous that the audience doesn't believe him either!

Scully Here is a Medical Doctor: Something that she reminds an entire emergency team of when they want to declare Jack Willis dead.

Scully's Rational Explanation of the Week: One of her finest forty-five minutes, and this time we're all rooting for her: 'Post-trauma psychosis' explains Jack Willis's disappearance, 'instrument malfunction' the double EEG print, 'stress' for Willis's changing handwriting, and she dismisses near-death experience as 'some sort of dissociative hallucinatory activity'. Then she says she doesn't discount the near-death experience because it can be explained by stimulation of the temporal lobe. 'I sense a big *but* coming,' notes Mulder, dryly!

Dialogue Triumphs: 'My name is Warren James Dupre, and I was born in Clamett Falls, Oregon, in the year of the rat!'

Willis: 'I feel myself getting into their heads and I'm scared by what I'm feeling. The intoxicating freedom that comes from disconnecting action and consequence – theirs is a world where nothing matters but their own needs, their own impossible appetites. And while the pleasure they derive from acts of violence is clearly sexual, it also speaks to what Warden Jackson called their operatic devotion to each other. It's a love affair I almost envy.'

The Conspiracy Starts at Closing Time: The FBI aren't able to trace Scully through her cellphone, so obviously the Cigarette-Smoking Man (who uses that method to find Mulder in 'Anasazi') has technology they don't.

Continuity: Scully and Jack dated for almost a year when he was her instructor at the academy. (So much for FBI regulations.) They share the same birthday (23 February) and used to celebrate it at 'some dive in Stafford that had a slanty pool table'. Jack was born in 1957 (which makes him seven years older than Scully – see 'Paper Clip'). The couple once spent a snowy weekend after Thanksgiving at Willis's parents' cabin, where Jack taught Scully to fish through the ice.

The Truth: Psychic transference? Difficult to say for sure, but Scully's faith in her ex-lover Willis continues long after he has kidnapped her and, frankly, defies belief (but then, this is Scully we're talking about). The pre-title sequence shows some kind of link between the two bodies, and Scully sees (or seems to see) the face of Dupre when held hostage. However, the suggestion that psychic transference extends to tattoos takes some leap of faith. Thank goodness the killer wasn't circumcised . . .

Trivia: There is some confusion over the dating of this episode. Scully says she bought Willis's watch as a birthday present 'three years ago' (*c.* 1991), but the watch is clearly inscribed 'Happy 35th'. Willis's thirty-fifth birthday would have been in 1992, only two years ago, so Scully must be in error. Callum Keith Rennie – *Due South*'s second Ray – was considered for the role of Krycek after playing Tommy in this story.

Scientific Comment: You can't have two heartbeats from a body with one heart. Two brainwaves would have been more believable. Even if it were true that watches worn by people who have had a near-death experience stop because of a release of electrical energy (and cells are dying all the time, anyway), after their strange experience, the effect would surely cease.

The Bottom Line: KT: 'Baby, you ain't gonna believe where I've been!' An unusual approach to an age-old idea, with a potentially difficult theme (Scully's former love life) well handled. Any episode that includes dialogue references to *JFK* ('You're the FBI, you figure it out!') is OK with this author. Once again, however, the 'enigmatic' ending doesn't work as well as it would have with a bit more opinion about what has actually taken place. One gets the suspicion that the production team at this stage seemed to believe that a lack of explanation was exactly what the audience wanted.

PC: Oh, this is crap crap crap crap! A 'psychotic episode'

that's 'not an X-File'. This doesn't so much suspend my disbelief as stamp it into the floor. How many times have we seen that 'aircraft sound on tape' scene? And there's the annoying 'execution' quote from *Pulp Fiction* (I can imagine the writers who quote stuff shaking their heads in surprise and saying, 'But fanboys love it when we quote stuff!'). This is just silly. And it's nice to know that a nutter can pass the FBI's psychological tests.

MD: Some fair criticisms, but I still rather like this story. Maybe I'm just a sucker for those episodes where we get to see Mulder doing something approaching a 'normal' FBI job. 'It means . . . It means whatever you want it to mean.'

16: 'Young at Heart'

US Transmission: 11 February 1994
UK Transmission: 11 May 1994 (Sky One)/
12 January 1995 (BBC2)
Writers: Scott Kaufer, Chris Carter
Director: Michael Lange
Cast: Dick Anthony Williams (Agent Reggie Purdue),
Alan Boyce (Young John Barnett),
Christine Estabrook (Agent Henderson),
Graham Jarvis (N.I.H. Doctor),
Robin Mossley (Dr Joe Ridley), Merrilyn Gann (Prosecutor),
Gordon Tipple (Joe Crandall),
Courtney Arciaga (Progeria Victim),
David Petersen (Older John Barnett),
Robin Douglas (Computer Specialist)

Washington, DC: a violent bank robbery bears all the hallmarks of Johnny Barnett, a psychopath whom Mulder helped to convict years before. But Barnett apparently died in 1989. Like Barnett, the robber taunts Mulder with threatening notes. After Mulder's friend and former AOC Agent Reggie Purdue is killed, Mulder is convinced that Barnett has returned from the grave. The doctor who signed Barnett's death certificate – Ridley – had previously been disbarred for carrying out human experimentation into premature ageing.

Ridley turns up at Scully's house and tells the agents that his work has continued, with government backing, and that Barnett, his most successful patient, is alive, and, worse, young again. Mulder sets a trap for Barnett at a cello recital with Scully as the bait. Scully is shot, but is uninjured, wearing a bulletproof vest. Barnett takes a hostage but Mulder rights the wrong of his past by shooting him.

Don't Be in the Teaser: Johnny Barnett, seemingly killed in a sinister medical experiment in 1989, actually comes out of the teaser in better shape than the doctor who's working on him.

How Did He Do That?: Not Mulder this time, but Doctor Ridley. How did he know where Scully lived? Indeed, how did he know who Scully was in the first place, and what her connection to Mulder and, via him, Barnett, was?

Ooze: Barnett's 'Salamander' arm is quite disgusting.

Scully's Irrational Explanation of the Week: Barnett is a ghost. No, hang on, she's probably joking and Mulder, and we, have just failed to get it!

Dialogue Triumphs: Mulder tells Scully that Barnett died in prison. 'You're sure?' 'I was paying attention!'

The Conspiracy Starts at Closing Time: The US government has been sponsoring Ridley's latterday research in Mexico and Belize. And, according to Deep Throat, bargaining with John Barnett to buy the research from him once Ridley dies from a rare cerebral-vascular disease. Ridley says that the secret of the US funding goes 'high up the ladder'. A by-product of the original research is a salamander-like ability to regrow injured or severed limbs. 'That guy in the ugly suit is probably CIA,' comments Mulder while watching the attempts to resuscitate Barnett. 'That guy' is played by William B. Davis, the Cigarette-Smoking Man. (Who Mulder and Scully don't get a good look at here, Mulder coming to this conclusion by the CSM's style and presence.) Considering Deep Throat's revelations in 'E.B.E.', it's very probable that the Cigarette-Smoking Man does work for the CIA, as well as for the Conspiracy, and that he's combining both roles here as the Conspiracy continue to use the US military to look into the development of superior soldiers (as in 'Sleepless'), since the ability to regrow limbs would be useful. Mind you, since anti-ageing is the main thrust of the research, perhaps they're looking into ways that they themselves might stay young in order to carry on the human race after the mass arrival of the Colonists.

Continuity: Mulder's first case for the Bureau, fresh from the academy and aged twenty-eight, was Johnny Barnett, who had killed seven people in a string of complex armed robberies. Mulder's AOC (his immediate boss) was Reggie Purdue. Barnett was eventually caught, but agent Steve Wallenburg died because Mulder did not shoot Barnett in the back when he had the chance. (It is against FBI regulations to unnecessarily endanger the life of a hostage: Wallenburg's death explains much of Mulder's subsequent hostility to doing things 'by the book'.) Barnett avoided the death penalty on a technicality and was sentenced to 340 years in prison. He swore revenge on Mulder. Mulder believes (at least in this case) in capital punishment (as did Scully in 'Beyond the Sea'). A friend, and mentor, Purdue always defended Fox against the 'Spooky' nonsense, but was concerned that Mulder's career, which once seemed destined for great things, seemed to be stalled by the cul-de-sac of the X-Files.

The Truth: Thanks to Ridley's work, Barnett has become young again (only his eyes betray his true age). His amputated hand has been 'regenerated' via a technique that derives from research on salamanders.

The Bottom Line: KT: 'Mulder, it's science fiction!' A wildly improbable tale, full of garish set pieces and *non sequiturs* (who, for example, is the buxom blonde in the cycling shorts and cowboy boots in the last scene? – not that it has anything to do with the plot: I'd just like to know). Fundamentally, however, it's a straightforward story of revenge and fear. Includes David Duchovny's best performance of the season and some very good direction. Flawed, but interesting.

PC: Ho hum. Don't you just want Scully to open her door when the incidental music gets operatic to find a male-voice choir out there? I think I get it. This script and the last one were written when it was thought this series was going to be a sort of *Silence of the Lambs* with aliens, and held over into mid-season to get the good stuff up front. You can't see them using ordinary stuff like this in any other season.

MD: It's ordinary only in the sense that 'Aubrey' and 'Irresistible' from the next season are ordinary, i.e. conventional rather than dull. I rather enjoyed it despite its many flaws: the 'salamander arm' seems to be there only for a cheap shock effect, and then there's that ridiculous scene of Scully typing by candlelight. The music is straight from *The Omen*; Barnett's threats make him sound like a minor member of the Corleone clan. The ending, too, is lame, which is unfortunate.

17: 'E.B.E.'

US Transmission: 18 February 1994
UK Transmission: 18 May 1994 (Sky One)/
19 January 1995 (BBC2)
Writers: Glen Morgan, James Wong
Director: William Graham
Cast: Allan Lysell (Chief Rivers),
Peter Lacroix (Ranheim/Frank Druce)

Lexington, Tennessee: a UFO sighting brings Mulder and Scully running, but their interview with a trucker who claims to have shot at an alien creature is curtailed by the local police force. Mulder visits his friends at the magazine *The Lone Gunman*, and then Deep Throat. He discovers that a UFO was recently shot down over Iraq and that the recovered wreckage, and possibly an alien, are being transported across the countryside in a truck. Despite being under surveillance Mulder and Scully meet in Las Vegas, then follow the truck to Washington state where they find a secret government complex. Once inside, Mulder meets Deep Throat, who explains that the alien is already dead.

Don't Be in the Teaser: An Iraqi pilot shoots down a UFO. Good news for him, but terrifically bad for the alien.

Scully's Rational Explanation of the Week: The trucker shot at a mountain lion. The lights he saw were swamp gas. 'Isn't it more plausible that an exhausted truck driver became swept up in the hysteria and fired upon hallucinations?' The Lone Gunmen are 'self-delusional'. The UFO photo is a fake (which it is, actually). 'Why don't you just admit it, Scully? You're determined not to believe,' says Mulder.

That's a Mouthful: Oceans of politicobabble. Deep Throat says he has been 'a participant in some of the most insidious lies, and witness to deeds that no crazed man can imagine. I've spent years watching you [Mulder] from my lofty position to know that you were the one I could trust.'

Mulder: 'Dangerous? You mean in the sense of outrage: like the reaction to the Kennedy assassination? Or MIAs? Or radiation experiments on terminal patients? Watergate, Iran-Contra, Roswell, the Tuskeegee experiments? Where will it end? I guess it won't end as long as men like you decide what is truth.'

Dialogue Triumphs: Byers: 'That's why we like you, Mulder, your ideas are weirder than ours!'

Scully: 'Those were the most paranoid people I have ever met. I don't know how you could think that what they say is even remotely plausible.' Mulder: 'I think it's remotely plausible that someone might think you're "hot"!'

Scully: 'Mulder, the truth is out there. But so are lies.'

Deep Throat: 'And a lie, Mr Mulder, is most convincingly hidden between two truths . . . If the shark stops swimming, it will die. Don't stop swimming.'

The Conspiracy Starts at Closing Time: Mulder contacts Deep Throat by shining a blue light through his apartment window and awaiting a phone call (since Deep Throat seems to hang up immediately, it is uncertain how they arrange where to meet – see 'Eve'). Mulder tells Scully about Deep Throat for the first time. 'All I know is that he's guided us away from harm . . . He's never lied to me . . . I trust him.' Deep Throat promptly lies to Mulder! He tells him that after the Roswell incident in 1947 there was an ultra-secret conference between the USA, the Soviet Union, the People's Republic of China, Britain, both Germanys and France. It was decided that should any Extraterrestrial Biological Entities survive a crash, the country that held them should be responsible for their extermination. (This may not simply be a pack of lies concocted for Mulder's benefit, but a real cover operation staged by the Conspiracy to make sure that any Rebel Colonists would be exterminated rather than interrogated, or, horror of horrors, befriended, while the Colonists themselves enjoyed less difficult landing routes supplied by the Conspiracy.) Deep Throat says that he is one of three men (or perhaps three Americans) to have exterminated such a creature. (Which is possible, since both he and the CSM seem to have such an incident in mind, if 'Musings of . . .' is anything to go by.) He says he was with the CIA in Vietnam when a UFO was shot down over Hanoi by the marines, and that the alien's 'innocent and blank expression' as it was shot has haunted him. (The latter of which is probably a lie designed to offer a fictional explanation of why he's helping Mulder, to 'atone for what he has done'. When we see a fictionalised version of this incident in 'Musings of a Cigarette-Smoking Man', it supports the idea of Deep Throat only partly having a crisis of conscience. However, this is almost certainly a vast rewrite of the (possibly) real events, and it changes the date of the incident by a couple of decades.) From the perspective of future seasons, it seems more and more unlikely that Deep Throat was doing anything other than playing Mulder along. This is the one time Mulder gets close to something he doesn't want him to see, and he thus prevents him from seeing it. Realising that Mulder and Scully have met the truck driver, he gives Mulder a little true information to make him trust him, then the lie which he hopes he'll follow, away from the truck. His mission from the Cigarette-Smoking Man is, after all, to turn Mulder into a very public seeker after the truth, and thus create public paranoia, not give him the corpse of a Rebel Colonist Grey and thus create public panic. His knowledge of Mulder's nature is very subtle: the truck driver has been briefed to appear as an innocent UFO victim, rather than be silent and secret and thus have Mulder follow him. Deep Throat is a CIA man, working for the Conspiracy, the 'dark network' that the Lone Gunmen describe and that is bugging Mulder and Scully. We also, incidentally, meet another alien executioner in this episode, as the truck driver, Ranheim, kills the creature with his gun at the first sight of an alien craft, which is a large, multi-lighted one exactly like Mulder witnesses in 'Paper Clip'. As a Grey seemingly set against the arriving Conspiracy soldiers appeared on that occasion, we may take these to be Rebel Colonist craft, perhaps unique to them. (And maybe this is the sort of large vessel that appears at the end of the movie.) The Rebel Colonists are presumably trying to rescue another of their downed comrades as the Conspiracy try and move it carefully to a holding facility. Ranheim shoots the alien without being masked, but from a considerable distance, and perhaps the containers in his truck hold some refrigerated substance designed to limit any Black Oil released. Ranheim is really a black beret, Frank Druce. Will we ever meet the third alien killer? Presumably the Majestic Project, to which the logs of the Iraqi interception were sent, is an office within the CIA, or within the USAF, who are then reporting to the Conspiracy. Deep Throat says he can get tickets for any American Football game in the country.

Continuity: Scully drinks coffee with cream and no sugar. Mulder has photos of Mars on his walls. Mulder knew that the Gulf Breeze photos were fakes when he saw them (which was probably the subject of his article in *Omni* – see 'Fallen Angel'). He says he has previously investigated multiple UFO sightings at Chesapeake Bay, Okobogee lake (see 'Conduit', although in this story it's 'lakes' plural) and the legendary Area 51, Nevada. None had as much supporting evidence (including anecdotal data, exhaust residue, and radiation levels five times the norm) as this. Mulder describes the three Lone Gunmen as 'an extreme government watchdog', some of their information being 'first-rate: covert actions, classified weapons', though some of their ideas are 'downright spooky!' They are quite prepared to lie to Mulder, and don't trust him enough to switch off their telephone tape recorder when talking to him. Langly refers to Scully as

Mulder's 'sceptical partner', possibly since he knows of previous, non-sceptical partner Diana Fowley (who we meet in 'The End').

The Truth: Aliens exist and governments kill them, ostensibly for their technology, though for the Conspiracy that exists within these governments, this is more a matter of warfare: they must be pleased that they've got officialdom to sanction the execution of their enemies as a matter of policy. What we are seeing here is another battle in the continuing Colonist/Conspiracy vs. Rebel Colonist war. The difference between the two sets of protagonists is made manifest in this story: as soon as a Rebel Colonist craft appears in the sky, the Conspiracy trucker goes to the back of his truck, and executes their comrade. Here Mulder seems to believe that time/space anomalies are caused by every alien encounter, thus his trick with the two watches, which he thinks is conclusive. Initially this makes sense, because he leaves one watch behind while venturing into the area affected by the alien ship we see at the start. (Note that he isn't scared when he loses a few seconds of time in a short walk!) However, the second time is more ambiguous as it appears that he's kept both watches on him. Nevertheless, it is on this basis that he rejects this 'close encounter', thinking that human agencies who could simulate all other effects of alien abduction (via sonic weapons in stealth helicopters) cannot manipulate time. Presumably, the Conspiracy need actual Colonists to do this, and are conducting this operation on their own. Mulder is also surprisingly untroubled by the idea of being unconscious and at the mercy of these abductors: either he's been programmed by them not to worry, or he's merely aware that he can only have been unconscious for moments. There is the possibility that, in this story, both sets of protagonists abduct him! Greys seem to need or like red light: the cell is full of it.

Trivia: At the Washington state complex, Mulder and Scully use fake passes supplied by the Lone Gunmen. Mulder is 'Tom Braidwood' and Scully is 'Val Stefoff'. Since they hacked these identities from computer files it's a little scary to find out that an employee of HTG Industrial Technologies (see 'Shadows') is now working at the facility! Somewhere in this building, maybe there's some research into psychokinesis going on . . . Mulder makes an unflattering reference to Barney the dinosaur.

The Bottom Line: KT: 'I'm wondering which lie to believe.' The best episode of the first season. There are so many good things in this – the first appearance of the Lone Gunmen (the most interesting semi-recurring characters), loads of background on Deep Throat, a marvellous atmosphere of doubt, tension and panic and – best of all – a killer of a script with good lines given to just about everyone. *The* episode to show to non-fans as an example of how good *The X-Files* can be.

PC: I love it, mainly because it needs a lot of work on the part of the audience to figure out what's going on, but, when you get there, there is actually some meat on the bone. One for the video age, then, but it's good to get back to this rough format for what the show is going to be like in the future, which, at this point, they seem to have worked out. It's quite clear that Jerry Hardin has never been given any notes on his motivation: in a certain mood, his fishing for the right note to play his part on is hilarious, but this actually adds to the feeling of imbalance that his character generates.

MD: I think the story works because a lot of the time it's using standard cop- or spy-show motifs (Mulder and Scully losing their shadowy pursuers, tracking the truck across country, breaking into a top-security building). It's only the pre-title sequence – and the nature of the disputed cargo – that makes this a recognisable *X-File*. I love the bit where Scully – in the middle of a rant about how the paranoia of the Lone Gunmen gives them a sense of self-importance – discovers the bug inside her pen.

18: 'Miracle Man'

US Transmission: 18 March 1994
UK Transmission: 25 May 1994 (Sky One)/
26 February 1995 (BBC2)
Writers: Howard Gordon, Chris Carter
Director: Michael Lange

Cast: R.D. Call (Sheriff Maurice Daniels),
Scott Bairstow (Samuel Hartley),
George Gerdes (Reverend Calvin Hartley),
Dennis Lipscomb (Leonard Vance), Walter Marsh (Judge),
Campbell Lane (Margaret's Father),
Chilton Crane (Margaret Hohman),
Howard Storey (Fire Chief),
Iris Quinn Bernard (Lillian Daniels),
Lisa Ann Beley (Beatrice Salinger),
Alex Doduk (Young Samuel), Roger Haskett (Deputy Tyson)

Kenwood, Tennessee, 1983: Samuel Hartley, adopted son of a local preacher, appears to raise a man, Leonard Vance, from the dead. After a string of deaths in the congregation a decade later, the local sheriff, convinced that Hartley and his son are con-men, calls in the FBI. Scully and Mulder attend one of Hartley's services, then help with the arrest of Samuel after a bar brawl. At his arraignment a plague of grasshoppers strikes the court. Hartley tells the agents that he believes his son is innocent, but at the next service a young woman dies moments after Samuel lays hands on her. Convinced of his own duplicity, Samuel is placed in prison, and is beaten to death in his cell. Scully discovers that the girl was poisoned, and she and Mulder realise that Vance was the killer. He has been systematically killing those whom Samuel comes into contact with to discredit him in revenge for bringing him back into a miserable life. Samuel's body disappears from the local morgue and the sheriff is arrested for his part in Samuel's death. Mulder and Scully are left to ponder on the boy's real abilities.

Don't Be in the Teaser: Subversion of the standard opening when Leonard Vance comes back to life. Behold! The miracle of the resurrection.

Scully Here is a Medical Doctor: She is specifically assigned to this case due to her medical background although it is only much later that she is called upon to perform an autopsy on Margaret Hohman. In this episode, Scully actually watches a girl die, then tries to do her bit by feeling her pulse and declaring her dead. A bit of CPR might not have gone amiss.

Scully's Rational Explanation of the Week: Scully states she does not doubt the power of God, just the veracity of Samuel's claims (see also 'The Calusari', 'Revelations', 'All Souls').

Dialogue Triumphs: Mulder: 'The boy's been performing miracles every week for the past ten years. Twice on Sundays!'
And: 'Wait, this is the part where they bring out Elvis!'
Sheriff Daniels: 'Ninety-nine per cent of people in this world are fools, and the rest of us are in great danger of contagion.'

Dialogue Disasters: Mulder: 'Remember, the boy did rise from the dead. That kind of thing only happens once or twice every two thousand years or so.' (Which, flip as it is, might count against Mulder being Jewish.)

Continuity: Scully was raised a Catholic and says *The Exorcist* is one of her favourite films (see 'Shadows'). Mulder says that there are 'dozens' of psychic healers in the X-Files, but none are as well authenticated as Samuel.

The Truth: Few answers are forthcoming here. Samuel may or may not have been a genuine healer (Scully clearly thinks his healings are medical anomalies rather than an indication of God at work). He certainly appears to have some insight into Mulder's sister's disappearance, but seems to know only the information on the subject contained in Mulder's own mind. After all, as we later learn, only a few hundred miles away, a grown-up Samantha is at this point raising a family! Samuel's appearance to Vance may have been as a ghost, or part of a cyanide-induced hallucination.

Trivia: Mulder has seen the movie *Woodstock*, and he and Scully quote from The Who's 'Pinball Wizard' ('How do you think he does it?' 'I don't know.'). Mulder quotes from the King James version of the Bible (Exodus 10:14).

The Bottom Line: KT: 'Miracles don't come cheap.' There are many laudable elements on display. One would have imagined (after 'GenderBender') that *The X-Files*' look at faith healing would be anything but balanced, but this is not the case. Samuel and his father are treated with some sympathy, the villains (Vance and Sheriff Daniels) have plausible reasons for their actions and Scully and Mulder are, for once, pretty much in agreement about cause and effect. A good episode, with only (again) the lack of a few important answers to spoil the effect. Tremendous pre-title sequence (one of the most genuinely scary moments in the entire series).

PC: Why is Samantha in this episode? As glue to try to keep the two different series (Conspiracy and Monster of the Week) locked together? This nothing-special episode is the one I saw with mates in Australia to get them into the series. Of course, it fell victim to Cornell's First Law of TV: 'The forthcoming episode you decide to watch with your friends to persuade them it's a good series is always a crap one.'

MD: At risk of being the first-season apologist, I very much enjoyed this story. For me it's an engaging fable of spiritual pride and redemption, although the 'resurrection' of Samuel is both superfluous and irritating.

19: 'Shapes'

US Transmission: 1 April 1994
UK Transmission: 1 June 1994 (Sky One)/
2 February 1995 (BBC2)
Writer: Marilyn Osborn
Director: David Nutter
Cast: Ty Miller (Lyle Parker),
Michael Horse (Sheriff Charles Tscani),
Donnelly Rhodes (Jim Parker), Jimmy Herman (Ish),
Renae Morriseau (Gwen Goodensnake),
Dwight McFee (David Gates), Paul McLean (Dr Josephs)

Browning, Montana: something 'not human' has been killing cattle. A rancher, Jim Parker, kills what he believes to be an animal, but it turns out to be a Native American, Joseph Goodensnake. Mulder tells Scully the case has links to the first X-File, and they visit the local Indian reservation. The victim's sister, Gwen, is hostile, and the local sheriff denies Scully permission to carry out an autopsy on Joseph. Jim Parker is killed, and Gwen Goodensnake seems to be the prime suspect. However, an old shaman, Ish, tells Mulder the legend of the Manitou, a mythical malevolent spirit with the power to turn men into beasts. Scully is attacked by a beast at the Parker house, but the creature is killed and turns out to be Lyle, Parker's son.

Don't Be in the Teaser: Joseph Goodensnake is shot by Jim Parker after he has badly mauled Lyle Parker. Interestingly, by the end of the story all of these people will be dead, and two of them will die as non-humans.

Scully Here is a Medical Doctor: 'I'm fully qualified,' she tells Sheriff Tscani.

Scully's Rational Explanation of the Week: Goodensnake's enlarged teeth are an abnormal development of calcium phosphate salts. Lycanthropy is 'a kind of insanity'; the beast at the end is a mountain lion.

Dialogue Triumphs: Mulder: 'Charlie, do you believe in shapeshifting?' Tscani: 'This is a funeral!'
Ish: 'I sensed you were different, FBI. You're more open to Native American belief than some Native Americans. You even have an Indian name: "Fox". Should be "Running Fox". Or "Sneaky Fox"!'

Dialogue Disasters: 'It was like nature herself was terrified.'

Continuity: The first ever X-File was initiated by J. Edgar Hoover in 1946 (seemingly in the hope of burying this case: an unsolved series of murders that had occurred during World War II). Presumably, he filed this under 'U' for unsolved, and the secretary of 'Travelers' made it into a true 'X' file later on. Mulder, however, believes the first murders pre-date the X-Files by 150 years. Mulder says he wears a woman's deodorant (he could, of course, be joking). Scully apparently never gets 'the creeps'. She does, however, mention the 'recent' death of her father (see 'Beyond the Sea').

The Truth: The Manitou – an evil spirit of Indian legend whose possession turns people into shapeshifting werewolf-like beasts – is, according to the shaman Ish, behind a string of murders going back hundreds of years. The 'curse' passes from one person to another by a bite, but can also be transmitted to offspring. Thankfully, the episode doesn't bottle it and try to rationalise this: here, a werewolf is a werewolf.

Scientific Comment: If you ingest blood, it doesn't alter your own blood. So it would not show up in a blood test.

The Bottom Line: KT: 'There's something not human out there.' A Native American Werewolf in Montana . . .? Every visual cliché in the book crops up in this episode (full moons, stuffed animals in a thunderstorm, misty woods). There is one terrific transformation scene, although the finished 'werewolf' realisation is less than perfect. But this is one *X-Files* episode without fudged, unclear messages or cop-out endings. For that, if nothing else, the episode deserves much praise.

PC: Ho and Hum. Next! Is the price of acceptance for Native American culture really that they have to have their every myth subsumed into the morass of primetime TV belief?

MD: This shoddy little tale is so simple and derivative that you lose all interest within minutes. Only the American aboriginal setting gives any hint that there might have been a good story here, desperate to emerge from the clichés and the tedium.

20: 'Darkness Falls'

US Transmission: 15 April 1994
UK Transmission: 8 June 1994 (Sky One)/
9 February 1995 (BBC2)
Writer: Chris Carter
Director: Joe Napolitano
Cast: Jason Beghe (Sheriff Larry Moore),
Tom O'Rourke (Steve Humphreys),
Titus Welliver (Doug Spinney),
David Hay (Clean-Suited Man), Barry Greene (Perkins),
Ken Tremblett (Dyer)

Olympic National Forest, northwest Washington state: thirty loggers have vanished and Mulder pulls a few strings to get himself and Scully assigned to the case, which has echoes of a similar one in 1934. Travelling to the site with the sheriff and a representative of the logging company, they find evidence of eco-terrorism, and capture one of the activists, who warns them of the dangers of the coming darkness. They also discover a body cocooned in a shroudlike web in the trees. Mulder finds evidence of insects in the rings of an ancient tree, and speculates that the deadly creatures have been released by tree felling. Although two further attacks follow, the creatures are repelled by light, the cabin generator just holding out until dawn. When Scully, Mulder and Sheriff Moore escape in a jeep they are attacked and cocooned, but are saved from certain death by the arrival of a rescue squad, who remove them to a high-containment facility to recover.

Don't Be in the Teaser: Dyer and Green, two of the loggers, are killed by a swarm of green insects.

How Did He Do That?: Or, rather, why? If the 1934 incident was caused by the same waking of the insects as this one, why is Mulder so worried about the chances of the insects spreading? They don't seem to have in 1934. And how did a swarm of insects lift bodies up into the trees? By all heaving at once?

Ooze: There's the brown oily stuff in the log cabin that Mulder speculates is left by the bugs. And, of course, the cocoons themselves.

Scully's Irrational Explanation of the Week: Bigfoot!

Dialogue Triumphs: Mulder on the loggers: 'Rugged manly men, in the full bloom of their manhood!'

Mulder: 'I think I'm going to suggest we sleep with the lights on.'

Mulder: 'There's actually this lake where they've discovered a kind of amoeba that can literally suck out a man's brain.' Scully: 'Oh, brain-sucking amoebae!'

The Truth: A mutant bioluminescent micro-organism was released from a volcano some six or seven hundred years ago, and has been dormant within the trees of the forest ever since. The insects, when released, kill their victims by cocooning them and drawing the fluids from the bodies. After the attack, the Clean-Suited Man mentions that the chemical Lucipherim was found in Mulder's body, which is normally found in fireflies.

The Bottom Line: KT: 'We're letting ourselves get carried away with this bug story.' A poor, badly plotted episode with a largely artificial atmosphere of tension and two false climaxes before it finally kicks into life in the last five minutes. Good effects and direction are dwarfed by the faults in a plot that staggers through one cul-de-sac after another.

PC: But I really like it! Coming up with a new monster, and then knocking it back and forth through a series of set pieces is something the series does very well. In this case, it's a cottage under siege! Mind you, that isn't a good ending.

MD: The ending is *horrid*, a woeful cop-out that would be used on more than one occasion in the following season (see 'End Game', 'Død Kalm'). This is a shame, as I really enjoyed the previous forty minutes or so: taut, assured, and let down only by the poor special effects for the luminous insects.

THE TRAILER AT THE START OF THE CULT

Just before the end credits of this story's first BBC2 transmission ('neXt week on *The X-Files*'), a lovely minute-and-a-half trailer for the return of Tooms was shown. It was at this point that BBC2 realised that they had a major crossover hit on their hands, and, the series having survived its trough in the States, that there were a few groovy episodes to go. This was the moment, in fact, when the series moved up a gear and the fans went wild. (As further encouragement, another clip of Scully from 'Tooms' was shown after the end credits: 'Wouldn't miss it for the world!') And in those days, we wouldn't.

21: 'Tooms'

US Transmission: 22 April 1994
UK Transmission: 15 June 1994 (Sky One)/
16 February 1995 (BBC2)
Writers: Glen Morgan, James Wong
Director: David Nutter

Cast: Paul Ben Victor (Dr Aaron Monte),
Timothy Webber (Detective Talbot),
Jan D'Arcy (Judge Kann), Jerry Wasserman (Dr Plith),
Frank C. Turner (Dr Collins),
Gillian Carfra (Christine Ranford),
Pat Bermel (Frank Ranford), Mikal Dughi (Dr Karetzky),
Glynis Davies (Nelson), Steve Adams (Myers),
Catherine Lough (Dr Richmond), Andre Daniels (Arlan Green)

Druid Hill Sanatorium, Baltimore: Eugene Tooms gets ready for a hearing on his continued institutionalisation. Meanwhile, Scully has a frosty meeting with the Bureau's assistant director and a man who smokes a lot. Tooms is released after Mulder appears to be a ranting maniac at the hearing. Mulder carries out solo surveillance on Tooms while Scully (with the help of retired Detective Biggs) goes back over the case, and discovers a previously unknown 1930s victim encased in concrete. They conclude that the corpse was disposed of in this way because it could have incriminated Tooms. Mulder prevents Tooms from killing a couple in their home, but is later framed for an attack on Tooms, Scully lying to protect him from disciplinary action. Tooms kills his psychologist and prepares for hibernation, returning to his old nest, now under the escalator shaft of a newly built shopping centre. However, Mulder fights and kills Tooms.

Don't Be in the Teaser: In an episode full of subversions of expectation, Tooms totally fails to kill Doctor Monte, his psychologist, in the teaser despite, clearly, longing to (forty minutes of screen time later, however, the deed is done).

Scully Here is a Medical Doctor: Scully, the queen of the autopsy scene, finds a body encased in concrete, then has somebody else carry out the examination.

Ooze: There's sloppy stuff all over the place in this episode, particularly Tooms's nest, and the blood-and-bile finale.

Phwoar!: The car scene between Mulder and Scully is such a sudden narrowing of the emotional gap between them that you expect the format to change radically at any moment . . .

Dialogue Triumphs: Mulder: 'Excuse me, could you help me find my dog? He's a Norwegian Elkhound. His name is Heinrick. I use him to hunt moose!'

Scully: 'My instinct says that burial in cement is murder!'

Dialogue Disasters: Mr Green: 'I hope you'll be comfortable, Eugene. The room in the back is small, but I'm sure you'll be able to squeeze in.' (Groan.)

The Conspiracy Starts at Closing Time: Walter S. Skinner, an assistant director of the FBI, makes his first appearance in this episode, meeting both Scully and Mulder in his office. The Cigarette-Smoking Man's second appearance (or probably third, see 'Young at Heart') sees him getting his first line of dialogue – 'Of course I do' – when asked by Skinner if he believes Scully and Mulder's story. (Which, since Tooms is too old to be a product of the Conspiracy, merely means that the CSM is aware that there are a lot of weird things out there, that his friend's son Mulder wouldn't lie about them, and that the genetic pool of humanity has been muddied from the very start.) There is no hint here of whom he represents, but Skinner seems to defer to him. (As McGrath deferred to Deep Throat.) This is, of course, not the standard relationship between the FBI and the CIA. Skinner tells Mulder towards the end that he was 'close' (presumably meaning, close to having the X-Files shut down on him), and that 'any closer and a thousand friends in the Capitol won't be able to help you'. (As the Cigarette-Smoking Man is present in meetings between Skinner and both Mulder and Scully, we can only presume that, since neither knows his name later, he isn't introduced to them. This, perhaps, stretches credibility somewhat, although it is later confirmed (see 'Talitha Cumi') that Skinner doesn't know his name either.) Since the CSM had known Mulder as a child, he must be wondering if he's going to be recognised (unless he knows that that was one of the memories Mulder had erased in 'Deep Throat'), and is doubtless ready to deny any recognition.

Continuity: Scully calls Mulder 'Fox' for just about the first time. He tells her that he even made his parents call him 'Mulder' (but they never do in any of the encounters we see!).

Skinner says Mulder is 'one of the finest, most unique agents' in FBI history. Most of the FBI, including Skinner and the (unseen) director, feel his talents are wasted on the X-Files. Mulder watches *The Fly* (1958) on TV in his apartment. He sleeps on the couch. Mulder and Scully have a 75 per cent 'conviction or conclusion' rate, well above Bureau standard (this is, says Skinner, their only saving grace). Considering the inconclusive nature of the cases we've seen, they must do a lot of hard work off screen! Mulder worked for three years at the FBI Behavioural Science Unit, profiling serial killers.

The Truth: Dr Pamela Karetzky has been unable to find any organic or physiological dysfunction in Tooms, although his attorney has blocked further study. At the time of the arrest abnormalities were found in Tooms's striated muscles and axial bones.

The Bottom Line: KT: 'Maybe your mind has become too open.' The first thing to say about 'Tooms' is that it's a great *X-Files* episode. The second thing to say is that it's the worst 'great' episode possible. It has flaws that are manifest from the first scene, and it seems to be the beginning of a worrying (and pretentious) stagger into the realms of continuous narrative that the series could well do without (it forms, with 'The Erlenmeyer Flask' and 'Little Green Men', the series' first multipart storyline). There are many fine elements present, however (that entire five-minute sequence of Tooms's entry into a couple's house through the toilet is full of little touches that make the viewer laugh and squirm in equal measure). Again, the performances are top-notch, and for the most part the story carries its message with a thuggish charm that is difficult to criticise. But 'Tooms' is also a sign of difficulties to come, and at its nihilist core, is a mass of 'might have beens'.

PC: Toilets in American TV! One of the ways that the series has been influential is in bringing the little details of real life, left behind long ago at the point of *I Love Lucy*, back to the small screen. This is apt for a show about US mythos, and helps to suspend disbelief. Together with the depictions of different parts of America, it also adds a degree of universality. In what other show, ask yourself, would we be aware, as we are in 'Eve', of one of our leads going to the lavatory? Oh, and 'Tooms' is as good as it has to be, letting us see Mulder as others see him (aren't you just willing him to lie at the judicial review?) and getting the format moving again with the idea that this is one continuous universe and characters can recur.

MD: This contrived and stuttering mess isn't a patch on the original, despite some excellent interplay between the leads (the scene with a tired Mulder in the car is priceless). 'Tooms' seems incapable of making up its mind what sort of story it wants to be, and (er) ends up falling between numerous stools (sorry). I've never seen a lock on a toilet seat before, but perhaps I've led a very sheltered existence.

HAVE THEY ALREADY DONE IT?

Mulder and Scully's relationship is generally acknowledged to be full of sexual tension, but certain signs in the early seasons indicate a different reading. Work partners, no matter how close, don't touch each other in the intimate way that Mulder and Scully do. It's generally frowned upon for FBI agents to get too close to agents with whom they work, but that's a rule that Scully and Mulder have both already broken. Aware that their colleagues, never mind the Conspiracy, are looking out for any disciplinary problem, it looked possible for a while that Mulder and Scully had already started an affair, only they'd been very discreet, and it had never been shown on screen. The car scene in 'Tooms' appears to show two people finally acknowledging that they're attracted to each other, an attraction we saw developing through the early episodes of the first season. Perhaps, after that, they dated until Scully's abduction, but went no further. Mulder's reaction to her vanishing is that of somebody who's lost a lover, not a dear friend. Upon her return, the relationship could be said to become deeper. By 'Red Museum', he's wiping her face clean in the way that only people who've been to bed together do. From then on, there are many of these moments, until Mulder's

HAVE THEY ALREADY DONE IT?

beliefs at the end of '731' add new tension to the relationship, tension which only eases after the cathartic affirmation of their bond in 'Grotesque'. Unfortunately, 'Small Potatoes' makes it clear that they haven't been intimate, although Scully's willingness to give it up in that episode, plus her incredibly unsubtle flirting in 'Detour', and the ease of the dance in 'Post-Modern Prometheus' hint that she might see possibilities in their relationship (when Mulder isn't driving her up the wall as in 'Bad Blood') that Mulder hasn't even considered. Her jealousy over Diana Fowley seems to confirm that, perhaps forcing Scully to consider how she feels. The derailed kiss in the movie indicates that, at least in a moment of vulnerability, something is finally happening between them.

22: 'Born Again'

US Transmission: 29 April 1994
UK Transmission: 22 June 1994 (Sky One)/
23 March 1995 (BBC2)
Writers: Howard Gordon, Alex Gansa
Director: Jerrold Freedman
Cast: Brian Markinson (Tony Fiore),
Mimi Lieber (Anita Fiore),
Maggie Wheeler (Detective Sharon Lazard),
Dey Young (Judy Bishop), Andrea Libman (Michelle Bishop),
P. Lynn Johnson (Dr Sheila Braun), Leslie Carlson (Dr Spitz),
Richard Sali (Felder), Dwight Koss (Detective Barbala),
Peter Lapres (Harry Linhart)

Buffalo, New York state: Detective Barbala apparently throws himself through the window of a police interview room moments after being left alone with Michelle Bishop, an eight-year-old girl. Michelle states there was another man in the room. Despite her mother's claims that the girl is disturbed, Mulder believes her, although a photofit representation of the mysterious man does seem uncannily like Charlie Morris, a respected police officer killed, apparently by Chinese Triads, some nine years ago. Mulder and Scully visit Morris's ex-partner, Fiore, who is unhelpful and nervous. An ex-policeman, Felder, is killed in a freak accident; again, Michelle is nearby. Discovering that Morris, Felder, Barbala and Fiore were all involved in a drug deal before Charlie Morris's murder, Mulder speculates that the girl may be his reincarnation, seeking revenge, especially against Fiore, who has married Charlie's wife. Michelle goes to Fiore's house but is prevented from killing Fiore by Mulder and by the man's confession to his crimes. Although her mother will not allow the girl to undergo further deep-hypnosis therapy, she appears to be 'cured'.

Don't Be in the Teaser: Detective Rudolph Barbala goes into a room to interview an eight-year-old girl, and ends up getting flung out of the fifth-storey window. Wimp.

How Did He Do That?: All right, so he's seen at one point looking closely at the aquarium diver model, and the autopsy does show that Morris was drowned in a small amount of salt water, but Mulder recognising the distorted image on the video is still a bit of a leap.

Scully Here is a Medical Doctor: She does the autopsy on Barbala – 'That's your department,' notes Mulder – and discovers what Mulder had suspected: signs of electrocution.

Scully's Rational Explanation of the Week: Scully (more or less correctly) states that the marks on Barbala's body were caused by 'an intense concentration of electrothermal energy'. However, she believes that Michelle is simply disturbed, and that the photofit of Charlie Morris is down to the girl seeing a photograph of the dead man in the police station. As a thoroughly pissed-off Mulder notes, 'Short of her growing a moustache, how much more apparent does it have to become for you to accept it?'

That's a Mouthful: 'Metempsychosis, transmigration, re-embodiment, call it what you will.'

Dialogue Triumphs: Sharon Lazard on Barbala: 'The only time he ever looked at himself was in the mirror. And he always liked what he saw.'

Continuity: Mulder writes his notes on this case (and presumably others) longhand, in a leather-bound field journal (a neat juxtaposition with Scully's use of laptops). It's a pity we so rarely see it: 'The Walk' is one of the few other examples. Lazard's brother is a Baltimore cop who worked on the Tooms case, and recommended Mulder and Scully to her.

The Truth: The story is based around the concepts of re-incarnation (with the possibility of the personality from one incarnation being carried into the next) and of continued existence beyond death. Michelle Bishop – conceived at about the time that Morris was killed – *was* Charlie Morris, reborn. She also possesses telekinetic powers, which may or may not be linked to this.

Trivia: Possibly the most staggering coincidence in TV history: in this episode one of the villains is a cop named Tony Fiore, and in the *Forever Knight* episode 'Dead Issue' (first broadcast on 6 October 1992), the main villain is a cop named Tony Fiori. Maggie Wheeler, the actor who plays Sharon Lazard, appeared with David Duchovny in the movie *New Year's Day*.

The Bottom Line: KT: 'Status: unexplained.' A chilling, well-directed episode, with a lot of memorable set pieces. The climactic scenes are a special effects *tour de force*, and the acting is universally good. There are only occasional problems with sustaining the pace of the episode with such slight subject matter (there is only one plot, it doesn't need a genius to work it out, and the fact that it takes Scully and, especially, Mulder so long reduces our faith in them). Great performance by the little girl.

PC: The nadir of the monster/concept-of-the-week stories. It's just dull, darlings! And obvious, and not scary, and bland . . . I could go on.

MD: Please don't – it's lovely, like *Hamlet* with a psychic girl with an origami fixation in the lead role. The image of the underwater diver is memorably bizarre, as is the completed paper menagerie. The only flaw for me is Felder: yet another minor character looking towards *The Godfather* for inspiration.

23: 'Roland'

US Transmission: 6 May 1994
UK Transmission: 29 June 1994 (Sky One)/
2 March 1995 (BBC2)
Writer: Chris Ruppenthal
Director: David Nutter
Cast: Zeljko Ivanek (Roland Fuller/Dr Arthur Grable),
Micole Mercurio (Mrs Stodie),
Kerry Sandomirsky (Tracey), Garry Davey (Dr Keats),
James Sloyan (Dr Frank Nollette),
Matthew Walker (Dr Ronald Surnow),
David Hurtubise (Barrington), Sue Mathew (Lisa Dole)

Mahan Propulsion Lab, Washington state: a scientist working on a secret project to create a jet engine capable of Mach 15 is killed in his own wind tunnel. The only witness to the death is Roland Fuller, an autistic man employed as a janitor. This is the second death associated with the project, after a car crash in which a brilliant scientist, Arthur Grable, was killed. Soon after Mulder and Scully arrive another scientist on the project is killed with liquid nitrogen. Suspicious of Roland, the agents discover that Grable was Roland's identical twin brother, and that the dead scientist's head has been cryogenically frozen. Mulder speculates that he may have a psychic link with his twin from beyond the grave and that he is 'directing' Roland to kill the others and to complete his work on the project. After Grable's colleague, the sinister Nollette, has sabotaged Grable's cryogenic unit, Roland attempts to kill Nollette, but is prevented from doing so by Mulder and Scully, and by Roland's own personality forcing its way through Grable's faltering hold on him. Despite Mulder and Scully's recommendations, Roland is taken away for psychiatric treatment.

Don't Be in the Teaser: Dr Ronald Surnow, chopped into lots of little bits by a jet engine in a wind tunnel.

How Did He Do That?: How did Mulder guess the password on the basis of some of Roland's doodles?

Mulder's Rational Explanation of the Week: Arthur Grable faked his own death. (Second time this season for that theory!)

Dialogue Triumphs: Scully (holding a copy of a photo of the car crash in which Grable died): 'By the look of this, he's hamburger!'

Scully (on learning that only the head of Arthur Grable has been cryogenically preserved): 'Wouldn't your client find it somewhat inconvenient to be thawed out in the future only to discover he had no functional mobility?'

Continuity: Scully has two brothers, one older, one younger (presumably the two men seen at Captain Scully's funeral in 'Beyond the Sea').

The Truth: There is a psychic link between the identical twins, one that survived death and cryogenic freezing.

Scientific Comment: The liquid nitrogen is referred to by Scully as being at −320 degrees. All the cryogenic chambers are set at −320 degrees. Whether this is plausible depends on what sort of degrees are intended. Liquid nitrogen only cools to about −180 degrees centigrade. And −273 degrees C is absolute zero: you can't get cooler than that. So this number must be in Fahrenheit, though no scientists (e.g. cryogenicists) would use that system. Minus 320 degrees F is −196 degrees C, which is only a little cooler than one would expect for liquid nitrogen.

The Bottom Line: KT: 'Tell me about your dreams, Roland.' A rather sad, confusing, and heartless episode, that contains illogical elements, and in which sympathetic characters are treated like scum, and the genuine twenty-four-carat bastard, Frank Nollette, doesn't get his comeuppance at the end. Maybe that's the effect that the production team were going for (hey, life isn't fair), but it's a bit of a choker to find poor old Roland getting carted off to the funny farm at the end. Despite a good climax, and the touching final scenes, 'Roland' is an unsatisfactory mixture of too many ideas, and too little humanity.

PC: Yeah, but there's lots of good jokes, a real atmosphere, and an interesting, albeit instantly obvious, central idea . . .

MD: 'People die. They go away, and they're not supposed to come back.' How radical this is for US TV! Forget toilets, such a moving and distressing episode stands out from the bland soup of much so-called entertainment. While I'm not in favour of stories that pursue miserabilism to the exclusion of all other emotions, this episode does smack of real life to me. Nollette's survival and Roland's institutionalisation are balanced by the joyful finishing of the equation and the tender expression of love at the conclusion: small victories made all the more glorious for being in the face of corporate evil and immoral prejudice. Nods towards *Rain Man* (Roland counting items in the blink of an eye), and a wicked sense of humour (I love the headless scene-of-the-crime corpse outline!), only add to the satisfaction derived from this simple story.

24: 'The Erlenmeyer Flask'

US Transmission: 13 May 1994
UK Transmission: 6 July 1994 (Sky One)/
9 March 1995 (BBC2)
Writer: Chris Carter
Director: R.W. Goodwin
Cast: Anne DeSalvo (Dr Anne Carpenter),
Simon Webb (Dr William Secare),
Jim Leard (Captain Roy Lacerio),
Ken Kramer (Dr Terence Allen Berube),
Phillip MacKenzie (Medic), Jaylene Hamilton (Reporter),
Mike Mitchell (Cop), John Payne (Guard)

Deep Throat rings Mulder and tells him to watch Channel 8, currently carrying a news report about a fugitive evading police capture after a lengthy chase. Mulder and Scully investigate what seems to be a routine case, but discover some puzzling anomalies concerning the car at the scene. They trace the car to a Dr Berube at the Emgen Corporation, Gaithersburg, Maryland. However, there doesn't seem to be anything worth investigating, and Mulder is ready to give up until Deep Throat tells him he has 'never been closer'. After Berube's apparent suicide Scully checks the contents of a flask found in his lab, while Mulder follows a lead to a storage facility and finds several live bodies stored in liquid. He takes Scully to the site but the evidence has been removed. Mulder finds the fugitive – Dr Secare, a human-alien hybrid – but is overcome by toxic fumes given off by Secare when shot. All traces of the investigation begin to disappear, and the doctor whom Scully worked with on the flask dies in a car crash. Deep Throat arranges for Scully to gain access to a secret facility and steal an alien embryo for use in a trade to get Mulder back. This succeeds, but Deep Throat is killed during the exchange. Later, Mulder tells Scully that the X-Files have been closed down.

Don't Be in the Teaser: Dr William Secare, chased by the police, shot and apparently drowned.

How Did She Do That?: Of thousands of possible passwords (and on the basis only of a labelled flask), Scully plumps for the correct one in the containment facility.

Scully Here is a Medical Doctor: Scully's medical background enables Deep Throat to get her into the Fort Marlene High Containment Facility. This kind of thing happens a lot in *The X-Files*, and often it's pretty baffling: if they can forge her credentials for the containment facility they could just as easily forge her original qualifications.

Ooze: Green toxic blood. Lots of it.

Dialogue Triumphs: Mulder and Scully discuss Deep Throat's cryptic nature: 'Do you think he does it because he gets off on it?' 'No, I think he does it because you do.'

Scully after Mulder has asked her to find out what the contents of the 'Purity Control' flask are: 'If this is monkey pee, you're on your own.'

Crewcut Man: 'Your cellular phone's been ringing off the hook.' Mulder: 'I'm a popular guy!'

The Conspiracy Starts at Closing Time: 'Inside the intelligence community,' notes Deep Throat, 'there are so-called black organisations, groups within groups, conducting covert activities unknown at the highest levels of power.' (An absolute definition of how the Conspiracy functions, and one that definitively separates them from 'the government' as a whole.) He confirms that 'they have had alien DNA since 1947' and tells Mulder that the Roswell incident was 'just a smokescreen' and that 'they've had half a dozen better salvage operations than that.' (The use of 'better' indicates that there was a real crash of some kind at Roswell, but that the ensuing media circus (most of it, in real life, being a long time after the fact) was a Conspiracy misinformation project.) The other salvage operations would have been of Rebel Colonist ships and what the Conspiracy could get away with in the area of examining the equipment of their 'allies'. (We may see one such better salvage operation turned into a base at the end of the movie.) For once, Deep Throat may well be telling Mulder something approaching the truth. The Conspiracy seems to have been in operation since around 1947 (fifty years or so before 1998), the 'alien DNA' in question being that of the virus that is the essence of what the Colonists are (as the movie reveals), contained within alien bacteria, that being the solution that is found within the 'Purity Control' flask. (The bacteria also contain plant cells, possibly to allow the virus to be passed into crops and thus into bees through this means, the movie demonstrating this to be the chosen method of spreading the virus among humanity.) The Conspiracy's main mission is to mix this solution with carefully selected human ova from female abductees to produce Colonist/human hybrid clones. However, the above is clearly not what is going on in this episode: Dr Berube is not creating Colonist/human clones, he's injecting volunteer humans with Colonist DNA, creating powerful humans with both normal red and toxic green blood who don't sizzle into nothingness when killed. In fact, considering how set against him and his work Crewcut Man is, Dr Berube doesn't seem to be working for the Conspiracy at all. Which explains why Deep Throat feels so able to talk about this project, and why we need a box like:

The mainstream US military have somehow got hold of the foetus of a Colonist/human hybrid (we know it can't be that of an actual Grey, because, as we see in the movie, those gestate full size inside a host). They know this has been taken from a shady quasi-government project that calls itself 'Purity Control', so that's the name under which they keep it on ice. (Alternatively, the US military wing of the Conspiracy always called itself 'Purity Control', this being the project name under which Bill Mulder worked. Now that the Conspiracy have gone international, and are run by a group of unaccountable Conspirators, the rump of US military control that remains are holding on to the foetus doggedly, using the DNA contained therein in all sorts of tests, no longer aware of the greater purpose of the Conspiracy. See the box on Chris Carter's explanation at the end of the movie entry for the source of the confusion over 'Purity Control'.) Obviously, the Conspiracy don't want DNA from this foetus continuing to be used in projects like Dr Berube's. The resulting quasi-hybrids are stronger than normal humans, and, unlike the Conspiracy's own clones, prone to human loyalties and disobedience. (They may also know of some sort of instability on the part of these quasi-hybrids, which explains why they never follow up this line of enquiry themselves.) When one of Berube's experimental subjects panics at the sight of a police car, he blows Berube's cover, and brings this latest use of Colonist DNA to the notice of the Conspiracy. The Cigarette-Smoking Man devises a plan to hinder the Conspiracy's foes and get the foetus back from Fort Marlene. Deep Throat sends Mulder after Dr Secare, while the Crewcut Man misdirects all other law enforcement agencies. Then the Crewcut Man kills Berube (missing, we must assume, a hidden phial of Colonist DNA, or perhaps he was disturbed and makes good his mission to tidy up by killing Scully's medical contact) and follows Mulder as he tracks down both the warehouse of quasi-hybrids and (later) Secare himself. These are all eliminated and the evidence of the quasi-hybrids is whisked away (by X, if this was still his job as it was in 'Unusual Suspects'). Mulder is presented with tracking down illegal government use of alien DNA as his mission in life by Deep Throat, as if that were the nature of the Conspiracy itself. Scully is made aware of all of this. Then Mulder is kidnapped. (This is the biggest clue to the true nature of this plot: Deep Throat and the Cigarette-Smoking Man are utterly in command of the Conspiracy's troops at this point. If they wanted to have Mulder released (and the CSM certainly would want no harm to come to him) they could just have made it so.) Scully is told that she can swap the foetus for Mulder. She thinks she's giving back the Conspiracy something they already own. But in actual fact, she's been used as the fall girl in an elegantly deniable operation to steal something they want. Meanwhile, the CSM has told his masters in New York of his operation. True to form, they are appalled by the risks he's taken in showing Mulder the truth of the existence of alien DNA. Equally true to form, he blames it all on someone else: it was all Deep Throat's idea. At the last moment, Deep Throat gets the feeling that something's not quite right with the set-up rendezvous. Maybe he sees Crewcut Man in the car, and wonders why they've sent an assassin to do this little bit of set-up drama. Instead of letting Scully take the foetus to the other car, he goes himself, maybe to ask about Mulder's condition, or worrying that they're going to kill Scully (and there's absolutely no reason for him to expose himself like this if Scully's version of the truth is correct and the foetus belongs to the Conspiracy). The Conspiracy hoods in the other car are hardly going to be surprised at his presence: they planned this together with him. He's surprised when he's shot by Crewcut Man, however: that he's the fall guy for the CSM's rash behaviour, and another cue for paranoia on Mulder's part. This also explains his dying words: 'Trust no one', because he thought he had this set-up all worked out, and is amazed that his comrades would kill him to complete the charade. If we take it that as well as in fiction, the Cigarette-Smoking Man in reality has a lighter with those words engraved on it (as in 'Musings of . . .') then Deep Throat implicates the CSM in his killing as he dies. (Alternatively, this may be all part of the set-up, meaning that, funeral apart, Deep Throat lives!) The CSM successfully argues for Mulder's life, on the condition that the X-Files be closed down: Mulder is never going to be allowed that close again. The final clue to the nature of this plot is that the foetus is not returned to Fort Marlene, but placed in the Conspiracy's sub-Pentagon vaults, held not in pristine storage, but in a cardboard box with others like it.

Deep Throat states that Mulder is 'too high-profile' to kill, but this is a lie, a cover for the Cigarette-Smoking Man's plan to keep Mulder alive by turning him into an instigator of public paranoia and the smasher of government misuse of Colonist DNA. At the end of the episode Mulder says that Skinner rang him to tell him of the closure of the X-Files, and that the decision had come from 'the highest level of government'. (It is hinted that Skinner, and even the unseen Director, did not agree with this decision, but could do little about it. Presumably, the Conspiracy has clout above the FBI's level of command, and are thus allowed to intrude down into the FBI command structure. The Conspiracy – which we know is international in nature (see 'E.B.E.', 'Anasazi', etc.) – seems to have become part of a number of security agencies and governmental bodies.) Scully and Mulder are reassigned to other duties. The next time we see Colonist DNA being misused by the government rather than the Conspiracy, it's in 'Red Museum'. (Note the aggression of Dr Berube's injected monkeys.)

Continuity: Again we see that Mulder sleeps in his front room with the television on (see 'Tooms'). (This is almost certainly a reaction to his sister's abduction. If electromagnetic disturbance is a sign of alien incursion, then it's a great early warning. Duane Barry shares the TV habit. But perhaps it's a reaction to the end of his marriage, too. Indeed, if he'd been repressing the whole abduction memory thing until the paranoia gas incident of 'Unusual Suspects', then sleeping alone with the TV on is something he must associate hugely with his solo crusade.) This time *Journey to the Centre of the Earth* (1959, starring James Mason) is the film that has sent him to sleep (probably Pat Boone's performance). Mulder speaks to 'Danny' again (see 'Conduit'). This episode is the first indication that the blood of certain aliens (and alien/human hybrids) is toxic (with horrific results for Mulder). This is the first episode in which Deep Throat is referred to by that name (sarcastically, by Scully). Rather wonderfully, Mulder tells Deep Throat that he's 'been the dutiful son', not realising that, in terms of fulfilling Bill Mulder's mixed hopes for his destiny, he's being terribly ironic.

The Truth: Trust no one.

Trivia: Mulder makes an oblique reference to *Star Wars*, further establishing his 'classic SF fanboy' credentials. The police captain makes a scathing reference to *The Silence of the Lambs*.

The ending of this episode mirrors the ending of 'The X-Files': Mulder calls Scully at 11.21 (she takes the call at 11.22), and the Cigarette-Smoking Man puts the alien embryo in the Pentagon storage facility (in a box marked '6604' along with other embryo jars). Zeus Storage is at 1616 Pandora Street (quite applicable considering what's 'in the box', as it were). The flask of the title is the one labelled 'Purity Control', and not the one containing the foetus.

The Bottom Line: KT: 'Trust no one!' A fine, tense episode, from its *Bullitt*-style car chase in the pre-title sequence to the shocking execution of Deep Throat. But ... we still know nothing at the end of it. Again, there are more questions than answers (chiefly, who are the 'they' that Deep Throat has been banging on about all season?). And the final scene, for all its terrific impact, seems to have been tacked on as an afterthought. Memorable for all the right reasons, but a few of the wrong ones, too – the pacing of the episode is hopeless, beginning like a runaway train and getting slower and slower. Mulder's investigation of the Zeus warehouse is one of the best scenes ever, awesomely lit and chillingly realistic. But it's a shame that this and other undeniably great moments aren't followed through to a logical conclusion. Good effort but, ultimately, no cigar.

PC: Like a lot of the Conspiracy episodes next season, it does leave you unsatisfied. Signifying nothing.

MD: Any episode that has Scully saying, 'There's just one thing I don't understand ...' and features a hitman who looks like a satanic hybrid of Peter Schmeichel and Stephen Berkoff, can't be all bad. Although the first two-thirds of 'The Erlenmeyer Flask' are splendid, the implausible stealing of the embryo and the horribly contrived exchange to free Mulder threaten to derail proceedings entirely.

ROADS NOT TAKEN

Big theories of ours that turned out to be totally wrong between the first edition and this one:

That the Shapeshifters are into racial purity, and killing off those who want to breed with humans.

That Scully's neck chip is a monitoring device.

That X was responsible for the killing of Deep Throat.

That the Greys abducted Samantha before the Conspiracy could.

That the *rebel* alien faction are the ones represented by Samantha in 'Colony'.

That the Conspiracy needed the Grey Chimeras to pilot the triangular aircraft.

ROADS NOT TAKEN

That Deep Throat was really interested in helping Mulder.

That Mulder and Scully are secretly lovers.

That the Greys and Shapeshifters are different, and possibly at odds, with the Greys helping Mulder.

That Scully, as per Clyde Bruckman's comment, was somehow immortal after her abduction.

Second Season

25 45-minute episodes

Created by Chris Carter

Line Producer: Joseph Patrick Finn (25–27)
Co-Producer: Paul Rabwin
Producers: Rob Bowman (38–49), Paul Brown (25–33),
Joseph Patrick Finn (28–49), Kim Manners (43–49),
David Nutter (27–37)
Supervising Producer: Howard Gordon
Co-Executive Producers: R.W. Goodwin,
Glen Morgan (25–38), James Wong (25–38)
Executive Producer: Chris Carter

Regular Cast: David Duchovny (Special Agent Fox Mulder), Gillian Anderson (Special Agent Dana Scully, 25–30, 32–49), William B. Davis (The Cigarette-Smoking Man, 25, 28, 30, 32, 46, 49), Ken Camroux (Senior Agent, 49), Don Davis (Captain William Scully, 32), Sheila Larken (Margaret Scully, 30, 32), Mitchell[7] Kosterman (Detective Morton, 28), Tom Braidwood (Melvin Frohike, 27, 32, 42, 49), Dean Haglund (Langly, 27, 32, 49), Bruce Harwood (John Byers, 27, 32, 42, 49), Mitch Pileggi (Assistant Director Walter Skinner, 25, 26, 28, 30, 32, 40, 41, 46, 49), Lindsey Ginter (Crewcut Man, 34), Raymond J. Barry (Senator Richard Matheson, 25), Vanessa Morley (Young Samantha Mulder, 25), Steven Williams (X, 26,[8] 28, 30, 32, 39, 41, 47), Nicholas Lea (Alex Krycek, 28–30, 49), Michael David Simms (Senior Agent, 30,[9] 49[10]), Melinda McGraw (Melissa Scully, 32), Tegan Moss (Young Dana Scully, 32), Christine Willes (Agent Karen E. Kosseff, 37), Peter Donat (Bill Mulder, 40, 41, 49), Megan Leitch (Samantha Mulder, 40, 41), Brian Thompson (Rebel Leader,[11] 40, 41), Rebecca Toolan (Teena Mulder, 40), Paul McLean (Special Agent Kautz, 49)

[7] Known here as Mitch Kosterman.
[8] Uncredited.
[9] Credited here as 'FBI Agent'.
[10] Credited here as '2nd Senior Agent'.
[11] Credited here as 'The Pilot'.

25: 'Little Green Men'

US Transmission: 16 September 1994
UK Transmission: 21 February 1995 (Sky One)/
28 August 1995 (BBC2)
Writers: Glen Morgan, James Wong
Director: David Nutter
Cast: Mike Gomez (Jorge Concepcion),
Les Carlson (Dr Troisky), Marcus Turner (Young Mulder),
Fulvio Cecere (Aide), Deryl Hayes (Agent Morris),
Dwight McFee (Commander), Lisa Anne Beley (Student),
Gary Hetherington (Lewin), Bob Wilde (Rand)

The X-Files have been closed down, Mulder and Scully reassigned and prohibited from meeting. While working on electronic surveillance as part of a fraud investigation, Mulder is informed by a friendly senator that the Arecibo ionospheric observatory in Puerto Rico – although officially closed – has been picking up possible extraterrestrial signals. Mulder travels there and finds evidence that aliens are transmitting information found on one of the Voyager spacecraft back to Earth. Mulder confronts an extraterrestrial, but Scully's arrival is soon followed by a truckload of Blue Berets. Although Mulder and Scully escape with their lives, the one piece of evidence they have – a reel of tape – proves to be completely blank.

Don't Be in the Teaser: It features only Mulder's voice and the machines in the observatory kicking into life.

Scully Here is a Medical Doctor: Scully is seen teaching students how to perform an autopsy. Mulder gets to do his own (non-invasive) post-mortem later.

Scully's Rational Explanation of the Week: An electrical storm wiped the tape – she's probably right.

That's a Mouthful: Mulder's opening narration, an early specimen of Mouthful: 'We wanted to believe, we wanted to call out . . . We wanted to listen . . . I wanted to believe, but the tools have been taken away, the X-Files have been shut down. They closed our eyes. Our voices have been silenced, our ears now deaf to the realms of extreme possibilities.'

Phwoar!: Mulder and Scully hold hands as he tells her, 'I still have you.'

Dialogue Triumphs: Mulder's greeting to Scully in an underground car park: 'Four dollars for the first hour of parking is criminal. What you've got better be worth at least forty-five minutes.'

The Conspiracy Starts at Closing Time: By implication, the lack of follow-up to Voyager and the abrupt ending of NASA's high-resolution microwave survey of the universe might be down to the Conspiracy (who wouldn't want their own signals to the Colonists, or those of the Rebel Colonists, to be heard). Mulder may or may not go through a period of missing time in this story. Previously, the whiteout effect has been used to indicate this. He doesn't seem unduly concerned. The Blue Berets are an elite crash retrieval unit (similar to or the same as the one seen in 'Fallen Angel') who are authorised to kill civilians (and act this way, astonishingly, outside US territory in convoys in broad daylight, presumably sanctioned by the local government apparatus too). The Greys who appear to Mulder do so with an associated whiteout effect that we don't see linked to the Colonists until 'The Red and the Black', but from that distance it seems clear that these are Rebel Colonists. They are, for some reason known only to them, broadcasting material from the Voyager space probe back to Earth (as we have already seen in 'Conduit'?). Is this their rather complicated way of saying hello? Showing up at the Arecibo project is also a very odd thing to do, unless they wanted to erase the data that was sent there (if it's an ionosphere research lab, the data could have bounced there accidentally off the ionosphere, so what we're witnessing isn't an attempt at contact, but at hushing up the material we saw being passed along in 'Conduit'). Mulder's memories of his sister's abduction are different in this episode from when he recalled them in 'Conduit'. In that version, they were both asleep when she was taken, and the whole experience sounded more gentle. Either this is the result of the fuzzy nature of hypnotic regression, or Mulder's memories are being tampered with to make him more aggressive about aliens. Certainly, firing his gun at them would previously

have seemed most out of character . . . but suits the aims of
the mainstream Colonists and the Conspiracy.

Continuity: When Mulder's sister was abducted, on 27
November 1973, their parents were out and he and Samantha
were playing Stratego – a very apt game, considering the way
Mulder's life went. (Stratego involves finding out what the
nature of the pieces on the other side is, which ones are
dangerous, and where the most vital piece of information is
being hidden.) Aptly, an item concerning Watergate was on
the news. (Mulder was in fact waiting for *The Magician* at 9
o'clock – a further example of Mulder's love of tack TV, as is
a later reference to the quiz show *Jeopardy* – see 'Deep
Throat', 'Squeeze' and 'Jose Chung's *From Outer Space*'.)
He saw his sister floating away, and then a 'stickman' at the
door. (This might be one of the Conspiracy's Grey Chimera
hybrids (perhaps what becomes of Colonist/human hybrids
towards the end of their lives) seemingly being used to give
credence to abduction scenarios. Alternatively, it could be a
genuine Grey Colonist. The similar stickman who appears at
Arecibo is a Rebel Grey Colonist, since the Conspiracy most
certainly don't want Mulder to encounter it.) There is a
message on Mulder's answerphone from a nameless (and
husky-voiced) female who complains that, after his constant
attempts to get her to have lunch with him, he has stood her
up. In the absence of Deep Throat, Mulder is fed information
by Senator Richard Matheson, who seems only to have the
aims of an interested and empowered amateur. Mulder can
recognise one of Bach's 'Brandenburg' Concertos (though he
gets the precise passage wrong), yet he seems not to know
that this was the first selection of music on the Voyager
spacecraft. He speaks very little Spanish. Deep Throat was
buried at Arlington Cemetery (which implies a military or
CIA career). Mulder watched this from a safe distance. The
Cigarette-Smoking Man smokes Marlboro cigarettes here (he
changes to Morleys later on). Skinner seems annoyed by the
Cigarette-Smoking Man's use of an illegal phone tap. He
doesn't smoke.

The Truth: Unless Mulder imagined all the events in the
observatory (and he is emotionally unstable in this story),

there is a definite encounter with aliens: an experience which seems similar to the abduction of his sister. Once more, a line is drawn between the Rebel Colonists and the Conspiracy: the Blue Berets arrive, presumably on Conspiracy orders, to stop Mulder from contacting them.

Trivia: Mulder is travelling as (*X-Files* novel author) Charles Grant. He actually boards the plane under the name of George E. Hale, who was mentioned earlier in the episode as having been chasing Elvis all his life.

Scientific Comment: Voyager 1 did not pass the 'orbital plane' of Neptune, but the 'orbit' of Neptune. The episode implies that the only thing that Arecibo Observatory ever did was search for extraterrestrial signals. They have done some of that, but their main job is proper radio astronomy. The place would not be closed up if the SETI project was no longer funded, so having Mulder find a deserted control room is totally wrong. It would not be isolated in the middle of the jungle, either. There really was a high-resolution microwave survey started on 12 October 1992, and terminated after only a year.

The Bottom Line: MD: From the extraordinary Voyager sequence to the downbeat ending, this is a cracking opener, albeit not quite what most fans were probably expecting. It's even darker than average – and I don't just mean the lighting – with a sense of pessimism permeating much of the dialogue. Chinks appear in Mulder's self-belief, and the whole thing – with its limited number of characters and dingy observatory location – becomes an exercise in separation. Mulder – on his own, but 'narrating' for Scully – is forced to ponder the nature of reality and the proof that has eluded him ('Even if I could see them, would they really be there?'). Despite everything we might have expected, but very much in keeping with our humanity, when Mulder is finally confronted by the alien creature of his childhood, he is terrified and tries to shoot it.

KT: 'What if they come?' I found this episode a staggering disappointment on first broadcast, but it has aged quite well. The underground car-park scene is a shameless parody of *All*

The President's Men, but after this the episode picks up, with the balletic Shakespearean Matheson/Mulder sequence and Scully's brilliant losing of her 'shadows' at the airport. And there's the mother of all cross-country car chases at the climax. Skinner's protection of Mulder is the first sign of depth in his character, too. Not the classic it could have been, but worthy of a second chance.

PC: Not from me. This is the episode that convinced me at the time that Fox had decided to shove the series back into the shape of a generic TV show. The unexplained plot lapses, the idiocies (why is part of the vast Arecibo telescope complex out in the jungle, and why is it abandoned, and just what the hell are the aliens up to?), and the cartoon nature of the opposition (look out, it's the Blue Beret UFO team, headed by that crusty soldier type who's always going to be growling, 'I'll get you, Fox Mulder!') make this firmly the Saturday-morning version of the show. I still can't watch it without a little shudder, and wonder how they managed to recover from it.

26: 'The Host'

US Transmission: 23 September 1994
UK Transmission: 28 February 1995 (Sky One)/
4 September 1995 (BBC2)
Writer: Chris Carter
Director: Daniel Sackheim
Cast: Darin Morgan (Flukeman),
Matthew Bennett (First Workman),
Freddy Andreiuci (Detective Norman),
Don Mackay (Charlie), Marc Bauer (Agent Brisentine),
Gabrielle Rose (Dr Zenola), Ron Sauve (Foreman),
Dmitri Boudrine (Russian Engineer), Raoul Ganee (Dmitri),
William MacDonald (Federal Marshall),
Hrothgar Mathews (Man On Phone)

Mulder is assigned to another case that he thinks is meaningless and insulting: a corpse found in the sewers of New Jersey. However, when Scully comes to perform the autopsy she finds a fluke worm within the body. A worker is later attacked in the sewerage system, the bite mark on his back – although much too large – seeming to have come from a fluke worm. A human/worm creature becomes trapped in the sewage processing plant, but tries to head back to sea. Scully discovers that the original corpse came from a Russian ship that had been used in the Chernobyl clean-up operation.

Don't Be in the Teaser: The poor young Russian has to clear a blockage from the ship's tanks, and you just know he's not gonna make it . . .

How Did He Do That?: Mulder spends the entire episode making brilliant (and completely irrational) guesses about where the flukeman is heading for or can currently be found, the most staggering being his convenient spotting of a passing sewage tanker in Betty Park when all leads have failed.

Scully Here is a Medical Doctor: She gets to do an autopsy on the dead sailor, complete with wriggling fluke worm.

Ooze: Some serious goo after the workman cleans his teeth.

Scully's Rational Explanation of the Week: Scully pins the blame for the fluke/human creature on Chernobyl, and she would appear to be correct. For once everyone agrees with her assessment.

That's a Mouthful: 'Reinstatement of the X-Files must be undeniable!'

Dialogue Triumphs: Scully: 'Is this seat taken?' Mulder: 'No – but I should warn you I'm experiencing violent impulses.'

Mulder, after Scully has said that some 40 million people are infected with flatworm worldwide: 'This isn't where you tell me some terrible story about sushi, is it?'

The Conspiracy Starts at Closing Time: Mulder is told (during an anonymous phone call) that he has a friend in the FBI who considers it imperative that the X-Files be reopened. Subsequent episodes point to that friend being Skinner, despite his claims just to be following orders. He accepts that this case should have been an X-File and that Mulder and Scully's full involvement might have saved the workman's life. Scully is passed a copy of *National Comet* (see 'Conduit' – there's a headline concerning 'Nirvana stars' and a teddy bear!) containing a story about a monster on a Russian ship. This and Mulder's two phone calls are subsequently shown to have been the work of X (see 'Sleepless'). Here his main aim is probably to begin contact with Mulder in a way that doesn't relate directly to the Conspiracy.

Continuity: Mulder has recently considered leaving the Bureau.

The Truth: A genetic mutation triggered by abnormal radiation levels – a fluke worm with humanoid physical characteristics.

Scientific Comment: Scully says that an animal with no sex organs is a hermaphrodite. But a hermaphrodite has both sets of sex organs.

The Bottom Line: MD: 'You know, they say three species disappear off the planet every day. You wonder how many new ones are being created.' Terrifying (if predictable) scenes on the ship and in the sewers add up to B-movie homage that just pulls back from being the ultimate 'monster-in-the-bog' fable. The story briefly grapples with the difficulty one has prosecuting such a creature through normal channels of law and justice, but suffers from too many endings. The exchanges between Mulder and Scully continue to make up for any shortcomings, and the scene where he bursts into Skinner's office is delightfully underplayed.

KT: 'It looks like I'll have to tell Skinner that his murder suspect is a giant blood-sucking worm after all!' Gross! In fact mega-gross, with terminal potential! Do not, under any circumstances, watch this immediately after eating. There's more good work on Skinner on display, while Duchovny (denied Anderson's presence for most of the episode) gets to display quite a decent range. The ending is very messy.

PC: A decent monster story in a series still shaken up by the change of format (I was very scared that this situation was going to last a long time). Mulder on his own is really a bit too morose to be enjoyable. The partial escape of the flukeman means that there's another monster out there in S&M's own version of Arkham Asylum (Tooms is about the only one they've finished off). And the monster suit is pretty terrible, so terrible that I was worried at the time that the monsters were being standardised and rationalised too. It's good to know that it's my hero, Darin Morgan, in there, though.

THE REPERTORY COMPANY

Several actors make numerous appearances in *The X-Files* in many different supporting roles. You may remember them from such episodes as:

Hrothgar Mathews: Five appearances, including the movie. His greatest moment is being healed and gaining a new insight on life from Jeremiah Smith as Galen Muntz in 'Talitha Cumi'.

Doug Abrahams: Five appearances, mostly tiny, but puts in a splendid turn as Paul Vitaris in 'Die Hand die Verletzt'.

William MacDonald: Five appearances, specialising in policemen, with a near-starring role as the troubled Buddy Riggs in 'Chinga'/'Bunghoney'.

Malcolm Stewart: Five appearances, highlighted by his 'comatose in a suit from *Outbreak*' turn as Dr Sacks in 'Tunguska' and 'Terma'. He even got to be on the video cover!

Bonnie Hay: Five appearances, specialising in medics, and making an attempt to get into our Regular Cast lists by playing (we assume, two different, sorry!) night nurses in 'D.P.O.' and 'Talitha Cumi'.

Chilton Crane: Four appearances, but you know her as Sharon Graffia in 'Tempus Fugit' and 'Max'.

Garry Davey: Four appearances, graduated from roles like 'Hunter' in 'Eve' to Bob Spitz in 'Syzygy'.

Michael Dobson: Four appearances, gets to shine as Sgt. Hynek in 'Jose Chung's *From Outer Space*'.

Lesley Ewen: Four appearances, really kicks arse as the bereaved serviceman's wife, Renee Davenport, in 'Unrequited'.

Dwight McFee: Four appearances, most memorable as credulous Detective Havez in 'Clyde Bruckman's Final Repose'.

Larry Musser: Four appearances. Tends to get meaty and memorable roles, like that of bleeping Detective Manners in 'Jose Chung's *From Outer Space*'.

Gordon Tipple: Four appearances, notably as Hepcat Helm in 'Humbug'. (Do we take it that Darin Morgan likes having familiar faces in his episodes?) He was also the Master before he got exterminated in a minuscule role at the start of the *Doctor Who* TV movie.

Michael Puttonen: Four appearances for this character actor with rather too much presence to go unnoticed. He's instantly recognisable as the scared railway conductor in '731'.

Of course, such well-liked faces often go on to better things, Chris Owens's guest roles leading him to not one but two appearances in our Regular Cast listings.

27: 'Blood'

US Transmission: 30 September 1994
UK Transmission: 7 March 1995 (Sky One)/
11 September 1995 (BBC2)
Writers: Glen Morgan, James Wong,
from a story by Darin Morgan
Director: David Nutter
Cast: William Sanderson (Edward Funsch),
John Cygan (Sheriff Spencer),
Kimberly Ashlyn Gere (Bonnie McRoberts),
George Touliatos (County Supervisor Larry Winter),

Gerry Rosseau (Mechanic),
Andre Daniels (Harry McNally), Diana Stevan (Mrs Adams),
David Fredericks (Security Guard),
Kathleen Duborg (Mother), John Harris (Taber),
B.J. Harrison (Clerk), William McKenzie (Bus Driver)

Mulder investigates an outbreak of 'spree killings' in the town of Franklin, Pennsylvania. The murderers were perfectly normal individuals with no previous history of violence or antisocial behaviour, although Scully's post-mortems reveal abnormally heightened levels of adrenalin (each person seeming to have suffered from a phobia) and traces of an artificial substance, LSDM. LSDM is an experimental synthetic insecticide that releases pheromones to scare away flies, and Mulder believes that it is having a similar effect on certain people. He is sprayed by a helicopter working under cover of darkness, but seems to be unharmed. He and Scully track down the remaining phobic individual suffering from exposure to LSDM and prevent a massacre.

Don't Be in the Teaser: A soon-to-be-unemployed postal worker, Edward Funsch, not only survives the teaser but the whole episode (completely against the viewers' expectations, considering that the perceived mental health of American mail workers is the origin of the expression 'going postal').

How Did He Do That?: Mulder's sudden deduction that the town is the subject of some weird subliminal-message experiment, which remains unproved until his phone 'message' at the end.

Scully Here is a Medical Doctor: She performs an autopsy on Mrs McRoberts.

Scully's Rational Explanation of the Week: The LSDM seems to be at the root of the problem, although Scully lacks the evidence she needs to be 100 per cent certain of even this.

Dialogue Triumphs: Frohike: 'So, Mulder, where's your little partner?' 'She wouldn't come. She's afraid of her love for you.' And: 'You know, Frohike, it's men like you that give perversion a bad name.'

Mulder on the local cop: 'He's probably one of those people that thinks Elvis is dead.'

The Conspiracy Starts at Closing Time: We see an early attempt by the Conspiracy to release paranoia-inducing gas in 'Unusual Suspects'. Here, they're presumably the ones experimenting in the same manner, with a different substance. The messages would be a refinement of the original experiment, similar to the mind control of 'Wetwired'. (Perhaps such attacks on the public psyche will vastly increase as the date for Colonisation draws near, or is the aim simply to up the level of public craziness, and thus make those who discover facets of the Project seem crazy themselves when they report their findings?) Mulder is certainly exposed to the same substance (which somehow allows you to perceive messages which other people don't see), and those who controlled this experiment wanted him to know that. (Which keeps him playing his part in the Conspiracy's paranoia plans.) Alternatively, since the effect of the paranoia-inducing gas is to make the victims believe their greatest fear is coming true, perhaps the message Mulder sees is just a reflection of *his* biggest fear, that the Conspiracy are going to get away with it. It would be nice to see the return of the subliminals some day, if only because that would make such a neat pre-titles cliffhanger.

Continuity: Mulder played right field at baseball. The April edition of *The Lone Gunman* featured details of the CIA's fibre-optic micro-video camera, which is small enough to be carried by a fly(!); the August edition described LSDM. Frohike is very keen on Scully (see 'E.B.E.'). Scully makes a sarcastic comment about Reticulus (see 'Squeeze').

The Truth: Fear-inducing insecticide, possibly in conjunction with (probably subliminal and visible only to those affected by the chemical) messages via electronic devices.

Trivia: A few seconds of a Basil Rathbone Sherlock Holmes movie are glimpsed just before the 'Do It!' advert. The nurse buzzing on the door is buzzing the word 'kill' in Morse code.

The Bottom Line: MD: Strangely gripping. The script extends far beyond its initial interest in (and disgust at) the use of DDT in the 1950s, featuring subtle nods towards Middle American decline and a critique of US gun culture. The direction, too, is top-notch: look out for a Charles Manson/Waco montage on television and a memorable tracking shot over the photos of the victims. Only Mulder's barmy theory about subliminal messages jars, but this is easily forgotten when it's so swiftly followed by Fox seeing 'Do it!' on a TV screen – which turns out to be an advert for a fitness club.

KT: 'A forty-two-year-old real estate agent murders four people with his bare hands. That's not supposed to happen anywhere.' OK, I'm the one who usually engages in hyperbole, but this is magnificent. A horrifying central concept (suburbia goes psycho) chillingly played. The 'subliminal messages' are by turns terrifying and hilarious, particularly the sequence in the garage involving Mrs McRoberts ('He'll rape you. He'll kill you. Kill him first!'). One great set piece after another, full of elegant touches and iconography. The clock tower finale with its visual links to Hitchcock's *Vertigo*, and echoes of the real-life 1966 Charles Whitman murders, is dazzling. And this is one occasion when an underplayed, enigmatic ending actually works.

PC: At the time, I thought the ending was a real cop-out (I get nostalgic about this period of the show, when everybody I knew had given up on it as having bottled out, because it came through it all so wonderfully), but, in retrospect, this is a very well-realised episode, dealing with some really sticky stuff about guns, university towers and grudges that America is still nervy about coming to terms with. A jolly good source of screensavers too.

MULDER'S EXPOSURES

Fox Mulder isn't the most sane of individuals, for several very good reasons. During the course of the show he:

Is infused with paranoia-inducing drugs ('Unusual Suspects').

Is taken out of time for nine minutes by the Rebel Colonists ('The X-Files').

Has his memories tampered with by the Conspiracy ('Deep Throat').

Loses a few more seconds of time ('E.B.E.').

Might lose more time with the Rebel Colonists ('Little Green Men').

Is infused with paranoia-inducing drugs ('Blood').

Might lose more time with the Rebel Colonists ('Fearful Symmetry').

Is infused with paranoia-inducing drugs ('Anasazi').

Encounters the dead while travelling on the astral plane ('The Blessing Way').

Is regressed to a past life ('The Field Where I Died').

Loses another nine minutes with the Rebel Colonists ('Max').

Is infused with memory-stimulating drugs that can bring on suicidal psychosis and has holes drilled in his head ('Demons').

Thus gets to the point of suicide ('Redux').

Has his memories plundered by an artificial intelligence ('Kill Switch').

Is drugged to the point of professional irresponsibility ('Bad Blood').

And is shot in the head (the movie).

Weird how we still trust his judgement, eh?

28: 'Sleepless'

US Transmission: 7 October 1994
UK Transmission: 14 March 1995 (Sky One)/
18 September 1995 (BBC2)
Writer: Howard Gordon

Director: Rob Bowman
Cast: Jonathan Gries (Salvatore Matola),
Tony Todd (Augustus Cole), Don Thompson (Henry Willig),
David Adams (Dr Francis Girardi),
Michael Puttonen (Dr Pilsson), Anna Hagan (Dr Charyn), Paul
Bittante (Team Leader),
Claude de Martino (Dr Saul Grissom)

Mulder receives a newspaper report on the demise of a prominent doctor specialising in sleep disorders and an audio cassette of the man's final 911 call before his death. Although the man claimed that his apartment was on fire, no evidence for this was found by the fire crew, although Dr Grissom had discharged his fire extinguisher. Mulder and his new partner Alex Krycek investigate, Scully performing an autopsy on the corpse, which shows secondary physiological responses to having been in a fire ('as if his body believed that it was burning'). In a similar case, a man is 'shot', but no bullets are found. The common link seems to be that both men were involved in (or subjects of) experiments on an elite group of soldiers during the war in Vietnam. One of only two survivors of that group – Augustus Cole, 'the Preacher' – seems to have developed an ability to physically influence other people, even to the point of 'suggesting' that they are dying. Mulder tracks the man down, but just as he is becoming rational, Krycek shoots him, thinking the Bible he was holding was a gun.

Don't Be in the Teaser: Dr Grissom fights a fire (that doesn't exist) in his apartment, and dies as a result.

How Did He Do That?: Mulder jumps from the Vietnam sleep experiments to Cole's ability to project his unconscious with little real explanation (beyond a vast amount of sub-Jungian guff about building a bridge between the conscious and unconscious worlds). Also, as Salvatore Matola seems to still be alive at the episode's conclusion, why doesn't Mulder simply use him as proof of the experiments?

Scully Here is a Medical Doctor: Another two autopsies (one interrupted!).

Phwoar!: The phone calls between Mulder and Scully in this episode have a certain charge to them.

Dialogue Triumphs: Krycek: 'You don't know the first thing about me.' Mulder: 'Exactly!'

The Conspiracy Starts at Closing Time: The newspaper report, 911 tape and (later) a file concerning the sleep experiments come from X, a man who is aware of Mulder's dealings with Deep Throat. He says he has no intention of making the same 'sacrifice' as Deep Throat: 'The truth is still out there – but it's never been more dangerous.' He seems to be a follower of Deep Throat with the same connections, thus probably CIA. (In 'Wetwired' we see that he's a close lieutenant of the Cigarette-Smoking Man, and in 'Unusual Suspects' we see that in 1989 he was in charge of the Conspiracy's 'sanitation' team.) Krycek – who claims to be open to 'extreme possibilities' – is actually working for the Cigarette-Smoking Man, stealing Mulder and Scully's copies of the Vietnam files. The Conspiracy seems to be interested in creating superhuman soldiers, possibly one of the lines of research pursued in its search for options against the unbeatable might of the Colonists, and/or in its search for weapons for the aliens to use against Earth. Since the CSM claims to have saved Scully's life in 'Zero Sum', we might assume that he realises that an eager young Conspiracy lieutenant like Krycek will remark on Scully's 'problematic' nature in his report to the CSM's masters, and thus arranges for her to be abducted, rather than killed. He even manages to use the trick he pulled with Samantha (albeit too late, in Scully's case, to preserve her fertility) in having her returned quickly. All this to spare Mulder's feelings!

Continuity: Mulder uses the pseudonym George Hale when contacting Scully at Quantico, as he did before in 'Little Green Men'. Krycek claims that many at the academy admire Mulder and follow his career (however, this may be, along with much else that Krycek spouts, a load of bollocks).

The Truth: Cole and the others were part of an elite group (J7) of Vietnam soldiers who volunteered for sleep 'eradication' experiments on Paris Island. Absence of sleep – made possible by an operation and use of antidepressant drugs – was supposed to make the soldiers more aggressive. However, they stopped obeying orders and went on a killing spree, murdering hundreds of civilians. Cole – who like the other vets hasn't slept for twenty-four years – discovered a way of psychically affecting other people's sense of reality. There is the problem of whether the gun/Bible Cole is holding is real or not to Krycek. Perhaps Cole was making Krycek see a gun because he wished to die (as he, sort of, indicates to Mulder). On the other hand, what we see may be Mulder's subjective view and Krycek, with his own agenda, may have killed Cole without any help from the veteran himself.

Trivia: Dr Grissom may be named after the astronaut Gus Grissom, who also died in a fire, on board Apollo I in 1967.

The Bottom Line: MD: *The X-Files* does *First Blood*, only better! Gripping stuff, with wonderful splashes of surrealism, most notably the dead Vietnamese people 'haunting' the ex-soldier. 'Sleepless' is a rare example of a story that mixes strange goings-on and the Conspiracy-based back story without either element suffering.

KT: 'Scully's . . . a much larger problem than you indicated.' 'Every problem has its solution.' A story with a load of references to the American psyche, and the guilt complex surrounding Vietnam (My Lai is mentioned). The template for this seems to have been Adrian Lyne's *Jacob's Ladder* (with a couple of nods at *Apocalypse Now*). Another fine, dark, complex, multi-layered episode.

PC: Erm, a bit dull, but Krycek is initially very convincing as a cool little follower for Mulder (and, with what the fans knew was going to happen concerning Scully, the expectations set up by television are used cleverly to make us, initially, trust him).

It's clear from the conclusion to 'Wetwired' that X is not following the Cigarette-Smoking Man's original policy, via Deep Throat, of giving Mulder titbits of largely false information to make him a paranoid public spokesman. That policy ceased with the death of Deep Throat. The information X leaks to Mulder is information that the Conspiracy don't want to come out: so it's considerably more reliable. If he was involved in the clean-up operation seen in 'The Erlenmeyer Flask', then X would presumably have been aware of the nature of Deep Throat's sting operation in that episode, and was possibly appalled to find that the sting was completed with the betrayal and killing of Deep Throat himself. Therefore, he decided to betray the Conspiracy in order to gain revenge for the death of his mentor: only he's determined not to die that way himself. (He wants, for instance, a Colonist-killing weapon for himself.) He knows of one other person within the Conspiracy who is willing to betray it: Marita Covarrubias, as he reveals on his death. Alternatively, if Deep Throat is still alive, but wants to maintain deep cover, then he's getting his pupil to pursue *his* revenge agenda, in which case no wonder X seems so continually pissed off.

29: 'Duane Barry'

US Transmission: 14 October 1994
UK Transmission: 21 March 1994 (Sky One)/
25 September 1995 (BBC2)
Writer: Chris Carter
Director: Chris Carter
Cast: Steve Railsback (Duane Barry),
C.C.H. Pounder (Agent Lucy Kazdin),
Stephen E. Miller (Tactical Commander),
Frank C. Turner (Dr Del Hakkie),
Fred Henderson (Agent Rich), Barbara Pollard (Gwen),

Sarah Strange (Kimberly), Robert Lewis (Officer),
Michael Dobson (Marksman #2), Tosca Baggoo (Clerk),
Tim Dixon (Bob), Prince Maryland (Agent Janus),
John Sampson (Marksman #1)

Mulder is flown to Richmond, Virginia, to take part in
a hostage negotiation. Duane Barry, who believes he is
regularly abducted by aliens, has escaped from a psychiatric
institute. Mulder talks to Barry, and recognises the man's use
of FBI terminology. Duane Barry left the FBI in 1982. When
one of the hostages is shot Mulder goes in, disguised as a
paramedic, and continues to gain the man's trust, talking
about his abducted sister. He gradually encourages Barry to
release his hostages, but Scully discovers that Barry was shot
in the head in 1982 and might well be a delusional
pathological liar. Barry is shot, bringing the situation to a
satisfactory close, but X-rays reveal metal fragments in the
man's gums, sinus cavity and abdomen, and holes in his
molars, which would seem to back up what he said about
being abducted. Scully discovers that one of the metal
fragments has a barcode-like marking on it, but Barry escapes
from hospital and attacks and kidnaps her.

Don't Be in the Teaser: The eponymous Duane Barry has a
very bad time in his home having an 'encounter'. Allegedly.

Scully's Rational Explanation of the Week: The metal
items in Barry are shrapnel from Vietnam.

Phwoar!: The scene that is, for many people, the most
pivotal moment in *The X-Files*. Mulder swims in Speedo
trunks (actor's own). And it must have been quite a warm
swimming pool . . .

The Conspiracy Starts at Closing Time: From the Cigarette-
Smoking Man's words at the end of the previous episode, we
gather that Barry is, at the end, directed to Scully's home via
his implants, and sent to a prearranged site where she can be
collected by the Conspiracy's scientists. (We see a similar
summoning, on a larger scale, in 'The Red and the Black'.)

The Truth: 'The government knows about it, you know. They're in on it sometimes, right there in the room when they come. They work together,' says Duane. And, as we see from later episodes, he's absolutely right. Duane's been abducted on to an advanced USAF craft, meets either USAF staff disguised as Greys, or Grey hybrids, or Grey Colonists (though the latter isn't very likely: a real Grey, as seen in the movie, is very big and very aggressive), and, having had his memory wiped, is experimented on by Conspiracy scientists. The nature of these experiments is problematic: it seems to be research into the physical structure of humans. Perhaps it's a search for candidates with suitable genetic lineage to provide Colonist/human hybrid material in the next generation, or perhaps the Colonists want to know every detail of which individual humans they themselves will be inhabiting after humanity is dosed with the Black Oil. However, it's difficult to know how much of what Duane says is real (or what reality is for him – his speech about aliens experimenting on children seems to be entirely for Mulder's benefit), so perhaps the more tortuous passages of the tests are fictional. Although the scientists do genuinely seem interested in his teeth. (The movie suggests that Greys need a lot of calcium in their host bodies to grow their fearsome incisors . . .)

Scientific Comment: The barcode is only ten microns across. It is doubtful that supermarket barcode readers could detect this.

The Bottom Line: MD: 'Duane Barry is not what Mulder thinks he is.' A gripping hostage scenario – almost free of generic trappings – is intercut with Barry's memories of the aliens and a 'dentist-from-hell' scene. Pared to the bone, and all the better for it. Marvellous.

KT: 'There's a situation going down.' Yes, this one's got pretty much everything too. Startling pre-title sequence (and an even more impressive cliffhanger), and a lot of classic one-room, dialogue-heavy drama. Somebody's clearly been given a strobe machine for Christmas.

PC: Yes, it's brilliant, mainly because it succeeds in turning all this murky back-story stuff into pointed, dramatic encounters, something the Conspiracy stories very rarely manage. This is indeed good drama. This particular siege scenario is actually going to happen one of these days.

30: 'Ascension'

US Transmission: 21 October 1994
UK Transmission: 28 March 1995 (Sky One)/
2 October 1995 (BBC2)
Writer: Paul Brown
Director: Michael Lange
Cast: Steve Railsback (Duane Barry),
Meredith Bain Woodward (Dr Ruth Slaughter),
Peter LaCroix (Dwight), Steve Makaj (Patrolman),
Robyn Douglass (Video Technician),
Bobby L. Stewart (Deputy)

Mulder replays his answerphone message from Scully, and is shocked to hear the sounds of an attack. He rushes over to her house to find the police already there. Scully is missing, and Skinner orders Mulder not to get involved with the FBI's attempts to track her down. However, Mulder realises that Barry is taking Scully to Skyland Mountain in Virginia, hoping that the aliens will take her rather than him. He persuades Krycek to accompany him, in contravention of Skinner's orders, and races to the summit in a cable car, only for Krycek to turn off the machinery. When Mulder does reach the summit, Scully is nowhere to be seen, Duane Barry claiming that the aliens have taken her. Barry dies, and Mulder is blamed. However, Krycek vanishes just as Mulder is about to make a claim against him, having finally realised that the young agent is part of the Conspiracy. Skinner can't do anything, but says he will order the reopening of the X-Files. 'That's what they fear the most.'

Don't Be in the Teaser: It's just a recap, via Mulder listening to his answerphone message, intercut with images of Scully's abduction by Barry.

How Did He Do That?: Mulder seems to have psychic 'flashes' at the scene of the crime. (Probably just a dramatic way of showing how his thought processes zap their way over clues: we see the way he does it, but we still don't quite follow how . . .) Shades of *Millennium*.

Dialogue Triumphs: Krycek: 'You know Chernobyl, Valdez, Three Mile Island, they were all linked to sleep deprivation. The US Department of Transportation estimates that over a hundred and ninety thousand fatal car crashes every year are caused by sleeplessness.' Mulder: 'Do they estimate how many people are put to sleep listening to their statistics?' (It's cool that Krycek, who's obviously quite similar to Mulder, has that cute way with hard data too . . .)

The Conspiracy Starts at Closing Time: The Cigarette-Smoking Man is in on the discussion about Scully's absence. He still isn't introduced by name to Mulder despite this being their second – possibly third – meeting (with Mulder as an adult), and he continues to direct Krycek's actions. Barry either tracked Scully down via the implant or was informed of her address by the Conspiracy (the latter seems reasonably plausible, given the speed with which the authorities arrive on the scene of the abduction – indeed, the look that Krycek gives the Cigarette-Smoking Man when Mulder asks how Barry knew where Dana was speaks volumes). Mulder goes to see Senator Richard Matheson, but is intercepted by X, who tells him that the Conspiracy have something with which they could incriminate the senator. Mulder believes that Krycek killed Duane Barry, and that the military pathologist's autopsy was incomplete, with no toxicological analysis.

Continuity: Margaret Scully had a dream that her daughter would be 'taken away'. (Did a faceless man come to her and talk in iambics? See 'The Blessing Way'.) She describes Dana as a sceptic. At the end of the episode, angered by Scully's abduction, Skinner takes his first overt action to disobey the Conspiracy, and reopens the X-Files, allowing Mulder to continue his work more easily.

The Truth: Scully is abducted by the Conspiracy. We see a glimpse of her on an operating table having her stomach enlarged. (Possibly, that's the ova extraction process at work.) At the time, various official materials made it clear that this was Mulder's imagined view of what was happening to her (the weirdo!), but in '731' Scully remembers the scene herself, so it happened. The second 'UFO' that so frightens Barry is a helicopter. (Mulder seems to believe that the first one was also a helicopter, and, judging by later episodes, he may well be right. A helicopter fitted with a sonic weapon was certainly enough to fake just the same kind of event in 'E.B.E.'.) It's interesting that Skinner already knows of an existence of a 'they'. He's been an unwilling but knowledgeable accomplice to the Conspiracy, and we might assume that, once it became clear that they were on the same side, Mulder grilled him off screen for all the (limited) information he had.

Trivia: Duane Barry's reported reference to a 'Stairway to Heaven' is more likely to be about the 1946 Michael Powell and Emeric Pressburger film (UK title: *A Matter of Life and Death*) than that song by Led Zeppelin. The song on the radio in his car is 'Red Right Hand' by Nick Cave and the Bad Seeds.

The Bottom Line: MD: 'They only have one policy: deny everything.' Despite being just about the only mainstream US TV show to feature the music of Nick Cave this is a tremendous disappointment, largely because it has twenty minutes of plot stretched over twice that time. It's exciting up to a point, but then peters out completely, having about ten possible endings leading into each other.

KT: The lack of plot is the most annoying thing here. The episode is full of great moments (the final shot is staggering), but it's too bitty to be fully effective. A disappointing end to a fine run of episodes.

PC: I thought it was OK, and it was brave to have Scully taken away, but it's just an excuse to have a scene on top of a cable car, isn't it? Actually, thinking about it, it is a pretty good cable-car-top scene, and we need more of those, so what the hell?

31: '3'

US Transmission: 4 November 1994
UK Transmission: 4 April 1995 (Sky One)/
9 October 1995 (BBC2)
Writers: Chris Ruppenthal, Glen Morgan, James Wong
Director: David Nutter
Cast: Justina Vail (The Unholy Spirit),
Perrey Reeves (Kristen Kilar), Frank Military (The Son/John),
Tom McBeath (Detective Munson),
Malcolm Stewart (Commander Carver),
Frank Ferrucci (Detective Nettles),
Ken Kramer (Dr Browning), Roger Allford (Garrett Lorre),
Richard Yee (David Yung), Brad Loree (Fireman),
Gustavo Moreno (The Father), John Tierney (Dr Jacobs),
David Livingstone (Guard), Guyle Frazier (Officer)

Mulder reopens the X-Files, and is almost immediately called to Los Angeles. The LAPD are investigating a murder in which the body was drained of blood, which Mulder links to murders committed in other states by the self-styled 'unholy trinity'. He apprehends John ('The Son') in a blood bank, and thinks that the man is suffering from a mental illness. However, when exposed to sunlight John immediately suffers fourth-degree burns and dies. A stamp on the man's hand leads Mulder to Club Tepes, where vampire fetishists and young people into 'blood sports' gather. He meets Kristen, who is involved with 'The Father', John, and 'The Unholy Spirit'. John returns to life, but Kristen destroys the trinity of vampires.

Don't Be in the Teaser: Garrett Lorre becomes food and drink for the vampires.

How Did He Do That?: Mulder arrives at the crowded Club Tepes and (incredibly) goes straight up to Kristen. If (as John claims) the vampires believe they cannot be seen in mirrors, then how do they shave?

Phwoar!: It's odd to see Mulder getting off with a woman. It's as if, without Scully, he's throwing himself into things head first (in 'Grotesque' we see that, before he met her, this is how much of a bulldozer he was). When he's distant from her, or hurt, as we see in the 'tiffing' story arc of season three, he also tends to throw himself at women (and 'throw' is about all Mulder can do in the field of the chat-up), as if daring fate to hurt him. In this case, what with the shaving and the blood sports, he's got to his most cliff-teeteringly self-destructive. And, with the former, his most toe-curlingly sexy. He spends quite a bit of time with his shirt hanging half off as well. And all this while still wearing Scully's cross.

Dialogue Triumphs: Does Mulder want to live for ever? 'Not if drawstring pants come back into style.'

Dr Browning after Mulder has admitted he is beginning to believe in vampires: 'You're really upsetting me ... on several levels.'

Continuity: Mulder says he hasn't slept since Scully's disappearance. He uses the alias 'Marty Mulder' when investigating the Hollywood Blood Bank (and to telephone sex lines! See 'Small Potatoes'). Scully's personal X-File is numbered 73317.

The Truth: Mulder has been tracking the 'Trinity Killers' for a year. They have previously killed six times in two states (Tennessee and Oregon). This presumably means that Mulder and Scully worked on the case as an X-File during the period covered by the first season. In each instance the corpse is drained of blood and every mirror on the scene is smashed. The perpetrators are, to all intents and purposes, vampires. They can be seen in mirrors (although John thinks he can't) and don't react to crucifixes, but suffer burns when exposed to sunlight and need to ingest large amounts of blood. (So these are very different from the large clan of vampires depicted in 'Bad Blood'.) John 'dies' of his burns, but comes back to life: beyond that, their claimed longevity is not proved, and Kristen's sacrifice seems to kill the 'unholy trinity'.

Trivia: The writing on the wall in the victim's blood is 'John 52:54', which Mulder claims is the biblical passage 'He who eats of my flesh and drinks of my blood shall have eternal life, and I will raise him up on the last day'. However, this should be John 6:54 (there are only 21 chapters in John's gospel).

The Bottom Line: MD: 'I'll do things with you no one's ever done.' *The X-Files* rips off, well, just about every modern vampire variant, and adds little to the genre, although there is a clever allusion to the shaving scene in the original *Dracula*. Instead of making vampirism an AIDS allegory, '3' has the two running in parallel (Mulder enquires if Kristen is afraid of catching AIDS through her interest in 'bloodsports'). As an *X-Files* episode it's not unacceptable, however, especially for the poignant scene where Mulder puts a folder concerning Scully's disappearance into the filing cabinet. The chemistry between Duchovny and his then girlfriend Perrey Reeves is remarkable, and the atmosphere and iconography – the forest fires, the loaf filled with blood – are vivid. Also memorable is the scene where John describes a terrifyingly humanist universe where death is the end and only grotesque vampires can achieve immortality. The conclusion, though, is too muddled for words.

KT: 'Are you going to ask what a normal person like me is doing in a place like this?' With a list of roots as long as a very long arm (*Forever Knight*; *Count Yorga, Vampire*; *Scream and Scream Again*; *Near Dark*; the works of Anne Rice; the *Kolchak* episode 'The Vampire'; the *Blacula* films, etc.) this veers haphazardly from schlock to brilliance (often with little stopover in between). There's some good stuff here, but the Sadean abuse subplot seems disturbingly out of place in this fantasy setting, and the finale is a right mess. One gets the impression that the entire episode was written purely as a device to keep Scully's crucifix on display and therefore provide a link between the previous episode and the next.

PC: Tough assignment, this one, and it doesn't quite make it, despite some awesome photography and design. It's truly weird to see Mulder in a sexual encounter (again, at the time – and I know I do go on – I saw this as another bit dropping off the format). The vampires are just so . . . ordinary, that it's hard to believe there isn't some kind of technological twist on the legend coming up. Though the idea of having a delve through the goth club thing is interesting, it isn't pursued, leaving this a very unbalanced and weird episode.

32: 'One Breath'

US Transmission: 11 November 1994
UK Transmission: 11 April 1995 (Sky One)/
16 October 1995 (BBC2)
Writers: Glen Morgan, James Wong
Director: R.W. Goodwin
Cast: Jay Brazeau (Dr Daly),
Nicola Cavendish (Nurse G. Owens),
Lorena Gale (Nurse Wilkins), Ryan Michael (Overcoat Man)

Northeast Georgetown Medical Center, Washington, DC: Scully has been found in unknown circumstances. She is unconscious and is being kept alive artificially. Mulder notices that a phial of her blood has been stolen from the hospital, and chases the thief. X rescues Mulder and shoots the thief, but refuses to tell Mulder what happened to Scully. Her medical records show that her immune system has been decimated by very advanced genetic experimentation. Mulder receives details of the location of the Cigarette-Smoking Man via a message in a packet of Marlboro cigarettes, and tries to interrogate him. X arranges for Mulder to kill some individuals who are involved in Scully's disappearance, but, instead, Mulder chooses to stay by Scully's bedside. Scully eventually recovers.

Don't Be in the Teaser: Young Dana Scully murders a poor little snake.

Scully Here is a Medical Doctor: On Scully's living will: 'Dana is a doctor. Her criteria for terminating life support is quite specific.'

That's a Mouthful: X: 'At eight seventeen tonight, they will search your apartment. They will be armed, you will be waiting . . . to defend yourself with terminal intensity.' 'This high-capacity compact . . . high calibre weapon is pointed at your head to stress my insistence that your search for whoever put your partner on that respirator desist immediately.'

Phwoar!: Scully's unfeasibly large bosoms. Mulder smiles in such a wonderful way when she wakes up, and weeps as he gives her back her cross.

Dialogue Triumphs: The Cigarette-Smoking Man: 'Don't try to threaten me, Mulder. I've watched presidents die.' (Note only *watched*, and see our critique of 'Musings . . .')

Frohike explains how he stole Scully's medical records: 'Stuck 'em in my pants.' Mulder: 'There's plenty of room down there.'

Langly: 'We're all hopping on the Internet to nitpick the scientific inaccuracies of *Earth 2*.'

The Conspiracy Starts at Closing Time: X says that he used to be like Mulder. (Presumably, his own investigations took him to the heart of the Conspiracy.) He knows (but cannot explain) why Scully was taken, indicating that, like Deep Throat before him, he is actually privy to the nature of the Conspiracy, but doesn't want to reveal all of it (possibly because the information could only have come from him: Krycek's use of secrets in later episodes may change that position). Later, we see that he still does real work for the Conspiracy (or the CIA) on occasions ('Soft Light'), which is obviously something he has to do to stay out of suspicion. He is, however, prepared to allow Mulder to kill off some of the agents who participated in Scully's abduction. (That's got to be a pretty unique situation: the agents in question must be freelancers like Cardinal from 'Apocrypha': they can't be members of any intelligence organisation or there'd be too many questions. And X must have come across the knowledge of their impending break-in in such a way that the Conspiracy doesn't know he knows. And he must be confident that these agents don't know enough about anything to give the game away if Mulder just injures them. All in all, it seems that he's either trying to keep Mulder sane, by giving him some revenge in anticipation of Scully's death, or maybe just settling some scores of his own, pursuing his revenge for the killing of Deep Throat.) X himself can (just about) kill a junior agent of the Conspiracy and get away with it. (One wonders if the Conspiracy think that Mulder killed the blood thief.) Scully has obviously been returned earlier than the Conspiracy would like (probably due to the intervention of the Cigarette-Smoking Man), and they thus need to take a final blood sample after she's been given back, perhaps to check that the neck implant is controlling the Colonist DNA in her system. (The presence of which is almost certainly a result of her having had her eggs impregnated with the Colonist virus in an alien bacteria (like the 'Purity Control' flask contents) while still inside her body. The union between human eggs and Colonist DNA must happen internally, and the multiple ova extracted after fertilisation, otherwise how are the abductees exposed to alien DNA at all?) Skinner slips Mulder the note about the Cigarette-Smoking Man. Odd that he knows his home address, though. The Cigarette-Smoking Man is willing to die, not for the cause, but seemingly out of a sense of ennui. This, as we later discover, is a rather brave act to conceal all the things he's trying to save from the point in the future where, he thinks, most of humanity will die out.

Continuity: Dana was a 'tomboy' as a child. One of her brothers is called Bill Jnr (we meet him in 'Gethsemane'), which indicates that, like Mulder's, her father is named William. She was (and presumably still is) afraid of snakes. Her middle name is Katherine, and this episode confirms she was born in 1964. Scully's gravestone bears the inscription 'The Spirit is the truth', attributed to 1 John 5:07 (with an unusual use of a zero in the verse number). It should be 1 John 5:6 ('. . . the Spirit is truth'), with no definite article. Perhaps the mason got it wrong? Mulder signed Dana's will as her witness. He buys the recovered Scully a Superbowl video as a present (presumably as a joke). Skinner volunteered for service in the marines in Vietnam when he was eighteen (he had an out-of-body/near-death experience and says he is afraid to explore further extreme possibilities – see 'Avatar'). The Cigarette-Smoking Man (called 'Cancer Man' by Mulder) says he has no wife or family, but as we later learn, he's protecting at least two children here. He drinks bottles of Budweiser. Mulder attempts to contact X by taping an 'X' in his window (so is someone always watching his apartment?). Frohike appears at the hospital with a bunch of flowers for Scully. Melissa, Dana's older sister, is a bit of a hippie. The Cigarette-Smoking Man's address is 900 West Georgia Street. (It's reasonable to assume that he moves after this episode! See 'Talitha Cumi'. But Skinner still knows where to find him in 'Zero Sum'.)

The Truth: Scully is returned having been used as a breeder of Colonist/human hybrids (we meet one in 'Emily', and her blood is tainted with Colonist DNA, as revealed in 'Redux') with a microchip in her neck to control the cancer otherwise caused by exposure to Colonist DNA. The nature of the mysterious Nurse Owens – who helped Scully through her coma but doesn't in fact work at the hospital – is never explained.

Trivia: Skinner makes an oblique reference to *The Godfather* ('Then what? He sleeps with the fishes?'). The Thinker is modelled after an Internet fan, Yung Jun Kim.

The Bottom Line: MD: Hospital drama, conspiracies and suspense, plus splashes of dreaming surrealism: an atypical X-File, but a strangely beguiling one.

KT: Beguiling, certainly. There are many tremendously vivid scenes, particularly Mulder's confrontation with 'Cancer Man' and his attempted resignation with Skinner. And the symbolic Dana-on-the-river sequences are worthy of considerable praise. But all the stuff about branch DNA seems to be a complete red herring. And why does every *X-Files* episode of this era seem to end up in a dark underground car park?

PC: This is a weird combination of dullness and 'too much, too soon'. Now that Mulder knows the Cigarette-Smoking Man's address, why isn't he round there every night? It's genuinely touching to see Mulder and Scully back together, though.

33: 'Firewalker'

US Transmission: 18 November 1994
UK Transmission: 18 April 1995 (Sky One)/
23 October 1995 (BBC2)
Writer: Howard Gordon
Director: David Nutter
Cast: Bradley Whitford (Dr Daniel Trepkos),
Leland Orser (Jason Ludwig),
Shawnee Smith (Jesse O'Neil),

Tuck Milligan (Dr Adam Pierce),
Hiro Kanagawa (Peter Tanaka),
David Kaye (Eric Parker), David Lewis (Vosberg),
Torben Rolfsen (Technician)

Mulder and Scully investigate recent events at a volcanic research post at Mount Avalon in the Cascade mountains. They find the brilliant but erratic leader has gone AWOL and appears to be killing the remaining members of the research team, and that the Firewalker robot seems to have videoed the shadow of a lifeform that can exist at impossibly high temperatures. It transpires that all the members of the expedition – except the leader, Trepkos – have been infected by a fungus brought back by Firewalker, and that Trepkos is striving to ensure that the infection does not spread further. With the infected team members dead, Scully and Mulder are rescued, and spend a month in quarantine.

Don't Be in the Teaser: The folk at the California Institute of Technology manage to activate Firewalker remotely, revealing the body of a team member, Pil Erikkson, and the shadow of . . . something.

Scully Here is a Medical Doctor: She just can't wait to whip out her test tubes and analyse those spores. Mulder even feels the need to inform Tanaka of her 'medical doctor' credentials when his cough gets worse.

Scully's Rational Explanation of the Week: Post-traumatic stress.

Phwoar!: Mulder risks being shot to go and warn Scully. He touches her neck when he gets to her.

Dialogue Triumphs: Mulder: 'I'm going to find Trepkos.' Scully: 'What if he's already dead?' Mulder: 'Then he'll have a lot of trouble answering my questions.'

Continuity: There are references to recent events, including Scully saying, 'I'm back, and I'm not going anywhere.'

The Truth: The parasitic fungus seems to be a silicon-based lifeform that is resistant to high temperature. Sand (silicon dioxide) found in the lungs of one of the victims would seem to indicate respiration.

Scientific Comment: The temperature in the caverns is stated as being 130 degrees, but people go into them during the episode. They must therefore mean 130 Fahrenheit, a system which scientists don't use. What's the point of charting all the crevices and fissures so Firewalker doesn't trip? The robot is meant to go where people can't go.

The Bottom Line: MD: 'Mulder, that is science fiction!' This season's hot equivalent of 'Ice' proves to be another undemanding adventure. It's not the richest nor most engrossing of episodes, although an interesting contrast is established between Mulder and Trepkos, a man obsessed with 'truth' almost to the point of insanity. The gross body effects and the gripping conclusion – as Scully strives to evade being covered with spores – are quite capable of diverting one's attention, however.

KT: 'The truth is an elephant described by three blind men . . .' A quite rubbishy remake of 'Ice' without an original idea anywhere on display. No poetry. No soul. Just line after line of great dialogue ('You still believe you can petition heaven to get some penetrating answer . . . If you found that answer, what would you do with it?') that doesn't mean a damn thing. Depressingly lacking in even the most basic emotion. And the way in which Scully's recent adventures are dismissed casually in two minor scenes and about five lines of dialogue stinks of tokenism.

PC: At the time (OK, that's the last time I'm going to say that) I thought that this was the point when the series got back on form. A solid, tight series of set pieces in the base-under-siege format are one of the things the show should never forget it's good at (though, in the Conspiracy stories, it often has). I'm quite happy for it to lack depth once or twice in return for moments of original horror. That is one of the things this show was designed to do, after all . . .

34: 'Red Museum'

US Transmission: 9 December 1994
UK Transmission: 25 March 1995 (Sky One)/
30 October 1995 (BBC2)
Writer: Chris Carter
Director: Win Phelps
Cast: Paul Sand (Gerd Thomas),
Steve Eastin (Sheriff Mazeroski),
Mark Rolston (Richard Oden), Gillian Barber (Beth Kane),
Bob Frazer (Gary Kane), Robert Clothier (Old Man),
Elisabeth Rosen (Katie),
Crystal Verge (Woman Reading the Text),
Cameron Labine (Rick), Tony Sampson (Brad),
Gerry Nairn (1st Man), Brian McGugan (1st Officer)

Mulder and Scully investigate a number of cases in Wisconsin involving hysterical teenagers who the local sheriff believes have been possessed. Suspicion initially points towards the Church of the Red Museum, a New Age vegetarian sect in the heart of 'cattle country'. After a further attack the leader is arrested, but an old farmer takes Mulder and Scully out to see livestock being injected with genetically engineered growth hormone. It is this that he blames for the escalating violence and unease in the town. Later a plane containing Gerry Larsen, the local doctor, crashes. The man was carrying details of various families and what proves to be a phial of alien material similar to that in the Erlenmeyer flask. He has been conducting illicit experiments on the children of the town, and the 'abductions' were the attempt of a local man (a paedophile who was watching and videoing the members of a particular family) to draw attention to them. The assassin who shot Deep Throat appears on the scene, trying to tidy away the loose ends, but is himself shot before Mulder can question him.

Don't Be in the Teaser: Gary Kane survives, despite being found in his underwear in the woods with 'He is one' written on his back in marker pen.

Phwoar!: Mulder wipes barbecue sauce off Scully's face in a very fond way.

Dialogue Triumphs: Mulder: 'You know, for a holy man, you've got quite a knack for pissing people off.'

Scully: 'Kind of hard to tell the villains without a scorecard.'

The Conspiracy Starts at Closing Time: It seems that Larsen, the local doctor, has been paid by the government (not by the Conspiracy) to inject certain children with regular doses of the Colonist virus contained within an alien bacteria (that is to say, the substance contained within the 'Purity Control' flask). This has resulted in highly aggressive children (immune to disease) who haven't yet shown much sign of Colonist power and speed (we're talking about much smaller doses, obviously, than those of 'The Erlenmeyer Flask'). They display only human blood when shot, but then, Dr Secare did also have red blood in 'The Erlenmeyer Flask'. We learn in 'Redux' that this solution can be grown in bovine serum: perhaps that's just what's happening here: with living cattle. Which explains why the townsfolk who eat the cattle are also very aggressive. (This aggression is just what the Conspiracy don't want in the human race, which is why they're hostile to these experiments, and why their own, cloned, hybrids are created to be passive. However, in going by the cloned route, they seem to have been unable to keep the immunity and power of these quasi-hybrids. Real human/Colonist cloned hybrids are relatively weak.) The death of Kane Snr some years previously – after he expressed worries about his son's growth – would seem perhaps to be more than a simple 'accident'. The Crewcut Man is in town to arrange the death of the medic carrying out this government misuse of Colonist DNA, kill those injecting the 'growth hormone' into cattle and destroy the meat plant, thus erasing all evidence.

Continuity: Once again, Mulder talks to Danny at the FBI (see 'Conduit', 'The Erlenmeyer Flask').

The Truth: The disappearing teenagers are down to Gerd Thomas, the voyeur/paedophile who has been spying on the Kane household for some years. It's not clear how he came by the drug used to sedate the young people, which is also responsible for their nightmarish visions, but there is no suggestion that Gary and the others were psychically attacked as initially suggested. Thomas wanted to expose Dr Larsen's experiments – thus the cryptic messages on the teenagers' backs. The Church of the Red Museum believe in soul transference (or 'walk-ins' as Mulder describes it), but are ultimately innocent of any wrongdoing. Indeed, it's only the nature of Larsen's injections – alien DNA in an experiment with the Red Museum people as a control group – that makes these events an X-File at all. The aggression of the locals is, apparently, genuinely down to what's being pumped into their meat. (It's worth noting in passing, however, that Larsen's experiments stretch back to when these children were born, but according to Mulder, Oden and the others have been in the area for only three years. Presumably, changes in the children were only anticipated recently.) An episode of red herrings!

The Bottom Line: MD: The excellent and diverse introduction – switching from the meat factory to a peeping Tom to the young man being found by policemen – gives something of the flavour of this story. The galloping changes of emphasis – it's really like watching four or five stories rolled into one – at least keeps the viewer's interest, although they do lead to a lack of explanation and a desperately contrived plane crash which is there purely to get our heroes one step closer to the solution. Still, there's a marvellous confrontation between Mulder and the local jocks – it almost looks like he's spoiling for a fight – and the return of Deep Throat's assassin leads to a marvellously tense conclusion.

KT: 'I'm a sick man.' Gorgeous to look at (the colours are so vivid – the entire episode is streaked with images of red, from the car Mulder and Scully drive, to the turbans worn by the Museum), if a bit paint-by-numbers. And, as noted above, there is so much going on it's difficult at times to remember which one of the subplots you're supposed to be concentrating on at any given moment. There are a few staggering coincidences, too (not only the plane crash, or the fact that Mulder and Scully are in town on an unrelated case, but that 'they' seem to have chosen this exact moment to pay Dr Larsen for his work).

PC: It's cool that this script suddenly becomes a Conspiracy story out of nowhere, and that the two plots blend very well, but this is one of those *X-Files* stories that aren't really 'about' something, that can't be summed up in twenty-five words or less, like a *Friends* episode title: 'The one with the Werewolf'. When the show loses focus like that, it's often in trouble, but that's not very evident here.

35: 'Excelsis Dei'

US Transmission: 16 December 1994
UK Transmission: 2 May 1995 (Sky One)/
6 November 1995 (BBC2)
Writer: Paul Brown
Director: Stephen Surjik
Cast: Teryl Rothery (Nurse Charters),
Sheila Moore (Mrs Dawson),
Jerry Wasserman (Dr Grago),
Tasha Simms (Laura Kelly), Jon Cuthbert (Tiernan),
Paul Jarrett (Upshaw), Ernie Prentice (Leo),
Frances Bay (Dorothy),
Eric Christmas (Stan Phillips),
David Fresco (Hal Arden),
Sab Shimono (Gung Bittouen)

A nurse working with the elderly claims she was the victim of a violent rape – and that her attacker was invisible. Scully and Mulder's arrival at the Excelsis Dei nursing home in Worcester, Massachusetts, is swiftly followed by the deaths of a patient and of an orderly, seemingly pushed to his death from an upper window. One of the female patients claims to see 'spirits' patrolling the building. The autopsy on the old man shows traces of poison in his bloodstream, and Mulder concludes that the patients are taking other medication in addition to that supplied by Grago, the nursing home's doctor. The culprit is a Malaysian staff member, who has been growing mushrooms in the cellars. Although the drug made from the fungus appears to combat Alzheimer's disease, it is also to blame for the manifestations of the 'angry spirits' and is, ultimately, a poison. Mulder is saved from death by drowning, and the old people – now deprived of the mushroom-derived tablets – succumb to Alzheimer's once more.

Don't Be in the Teaser: Michelle Charters, patronised by male colleagues, has her butt pinched by a septuagenarian, and then gets raped by an invisible entity.

Scully Here is a Medical Doctor: She tries to resuscitate Hal, and checks the (lack of) pulse on the orderly.

Scully's Rational Explanation of the Week: The woman was either raped by an elderly patient in a semi-schizophrenic state brought on by Dr Grago's Alzheimer's treatment, or (more accurately, as it turns out) there must be some fungal or other environmental factor causing delusional and violent behaviour.

Dialogue Triumphs: Mulder, finding Scully watching a video in his office: 'Whatever tape you've found in that VCR, it isn't mine.' Scully: 'Good, because I put it back in that drawer with all those other videos that aren't yours.'

Mulder: 'Are you saying that the building's haunted? Because if you are you've been working with me for too long, Scully.'

Scully: 'Mushrooms aren't medication. They taste good on hamburgers, but they don't raise the dead.'

Continuity: Mulder says he has several X-Files concerning alleged 'entity rape'. This is one phenomenon he seems pretty sceptical about.

The Truth: Difficult to say for sure, but it seems that Gung's mushrooms have in some way 'reactivated' the angry spirits of those who died in the nursing home. The connection between the old folk's recognition of the 'ghosts' and their ability to cause damage isn't really explained, unless either the patients are exhibiting psychic abilities, or everyone's perceptions are at fault.

Trivia: This episode is sometimes erroneously known as 'Excelsius Dei'.

Scientific Comment: Nobody would ignore a cure for Alzheimer's just because it used an illegal mushroom.

The Bottom Line: MD: This strange mixture of *Ghost*, *Cocoon* and *One Flew Over the Cuckoo's Nest* proves, ultimately, to be a simple *X-Files* story about ghosts. Or something. Although hampered by a complete lack of explanation (why do the 'spirits' depart at the end?), it's atmospheric stuff, and an interesting examination of filial responsibility and of different cultural attitudes towards ageing. The 'ghosts' are really quite spooky, and there's a nice shot of the building at the end, moving from darkness to light with an echo of the malevolent spirits. Only the scenes with Mulder about to drown prove to be unexciting and poorly executed.

KT: 'They've taken revenge for their mistreatment.' Influenced largely by the films *Awakenings* and *The Entity*, this rumbles along without much point for a long time before bursting into life with the scene of Mulder and Michelle trapped in a bathroom that is filling with water (let's not, for the moment, consider how long it would take a room of that size to fill from a couple of burst pipes . . .). The concepts look good on paper (growing old is horrible and the young don't help), but the realisation is disappointing. And can anybody explain the motivation behind murderous attacks on Mulder and Scully (who haven't done anything to anybody at the home) while both Dr Grago and Mrs Dawson (a memorably dodgy pair of hypocritical gangsters) seem to go through the entire episode untroubled?

PC: No for the water scene, yes for the theme and the atmosphere. It's interesting to note that, originally, the rape victim was going to be a lesbian, but, in the final cut, she's just surly. OK, so let's give them some credit, maybe they didn't like that juxtaposition either. Mind you, I'm uncomfortable about a fantasy show, even one as committed as *The X-Files*, dealing with rape. At least the victim doesn't get happy by the end of fifty minutes, but we are left with the vague impression (because this episode only does vague impressions) that (a) the event was somehow unreal, and (b) she 'deserved' it for being nasty to the patients. Ick.

36: 'Aubrey'

US Transmission: 6 January 1995
UK Transmission: 9 May 1995 (Sky One)/
13 November 1995 (BBC2)
Writer: Sara B. Charno
Director: Rob Bowman
Cast: Terry O'Quinn (Lieutenant Brian Tillman),
Deborah Strang (Detective B.J. Morrow),
Morgan Woodward (Harry Cokely),
Joy Coghill (Mrs Thibedeaux),
Robyn Driscoll (Detective Joe Darnell),
Peter Fleming (Officer #1), Sarah Jane Redmond (Young Mom),
Emanuel Hajek (Young Cokely)

Aubrey, Missouri: the remains of an FBI agent are discovered – some fifty years after his murder – by B.J. Morrow, a woman police officer whose visions appear to be giving her glimpses of events in 1942. The agent seems to have been a victim of the very killer he was investigating, the word 'brother' having been carved into his chest. A similar attack took place in Nebraska, Harry Cokely having raped a woman and cut the word 'sister' on to her chest with a razor. He was never accused of the similar murders in Missouri. Now the 'sister' attacks seem to be happening again. Cokely, although released, is an old man, but Morrow accuses him of attacking her. Scully and Mulder interview Mrs Thibedeaux, the woman who survived Cokely's attack in the forties, and she reveals that she was pregnant as a result of the rape. The boy – who turns out to be B.J.'s policeman father – was given up for adoption. Morrow seems to have inherited her grandfather's violent impulses, and is responsible for the modern-day murders.

Don't Be in the Teaser: Technically, it's just B.J. Morrow discovering a body, but we also witness, in flashbacks, the murder of Special Agent Sam Chaney, whose body it is that she finds.

How Did He Do That?: Scully and Mulder discuss the latter's amazing leaps of logic in a joking manner: 'I seem to recall you having some pretty extreme hunches.' 'I never have.'

Scully Here is a Medical Doctor: She confirms that the two X-rays of the teeth match, examines the unearthed bones, and pronounces Cokely dead towards the end.

Ooze: Plenty of blood. B.J. is sick at one point.

Scully's Rational Explanation of the Week: B.J.'s 'psychic flashes' are events she heard her father discussing emerging through her unconscious. (And not a product of the coming together of ideas that inspired *Millennium*?)

Dialogue Triumphs: Mulder: 'I'd like to know why this policewoman would suddenly drive her car into a field the size of Rhode Island and, for no rhyme or reason, dig up the bones of a man who's been missing for fifty years . . . unless there was a neon sign saying "dig here"!' (Compare the events at the start of 'Paper Hearts'!)

Scully: 'The man we're talking about is seventy-seven years old.' Mulder: 'George Foreman was forty-five when he won the heavyweight crown. Some people are late bloomers.'

Continuity: Mulder says he has always been intrigued by women named B.J. In the 1930s, Special Agents Sam Chaney and Tim Leadbetter used their spare time to work on so-called 'stranger killings' (what would these days be referred to as the work of serial killers). They were pioneers of behavioural science. There are hints that they were regarded as pariahs in the FBI of their era in the same way that Mulder is today. They disappeared in 1942 working on the 'slasher' murders.

The Truth: Mulder proposes that Morrow has inherited her grandfather's psychotic gene, which skipped a generation but has now been triggered by her pregnancy.

Trivia: Mulder's fascination with women named 'B.J.' might be down to his then-girlfriend, Perrey Reeves, playing a character named B.J. on *Doogie Howser M.D.* at the time. Cokely seems to be watching *His Girl Friday* (1940) on TV during the final scenes. Exactly twenty-six minutes into the episode, in the scene where B.J. is in the cellar discovering

Leadbetter's skeleton, keep your eyes on the staircase behind her. While descending, Gillian Anderson trips and almost falls, steadying herself, with some help from David Duchovny.

The Bottom Line: MD: A little cracker, this. A twisting plot, some fine suspense, and peerless performances. The script and direction are inspired, and one can almost imagine this story working as a 'weird' episode in a 'straight' cop show.

KT: 'Someone's gotta take the blame, little sister, and it's not gonna be me!' It's a pity this is so close in the season to 'Red Museum', as both episodes concern strange messages left on people's bodies. This is a nasty piece that works largely because every sympathetic character has a dark secret (Tillman's insistence on B.J. aborting their baby, Mrs Thibedeaux's hatred of her own son conceived out of rape). The scene of B.J. attacking Mrs Thibedeaux is one of the best of the season.

PC: Ordinary, good, and solid, and sets the standard for these 'filler' episodes – that is, the ones that could marginally sneak into other series and are generally written by outside writers. It is, thematically, a bit of a mess, though.

SUNFLOWER SEEDS

In 'Deep Throat' Mulder is seen eating seeds of some sort while driving the car. He offers Scully some in 'Squeeze' ('Seeds?' he asks: she declines). In 'Eve', 'E.B.E.' and 'Miracle Man' he's seen eating them again; in the third story they're obviously sunflower seeds. He also eats them in 'Little Green Men' when doing the 'bugging' job, and in 'Hell Money' and 'Wetwired', among others. In 'Aubrey' we get a kind of explanation: he used to have nightmares as a child that he was the only person left alive, and when he awoke his father would always be in the study eating sunflower seeds. (Extreme paranoia department: since Mulder's dad knew so much, did he know something about the protective biological effects of sunflower seeds, and has Mulder been inadvertently protecting himself all these years?) In 'The Blessing Way', the Navajo

give Mulder a pouch of seeds; in 'Teso dos Bichos'
Dr Lewton's small intestine reveals that he had been
eating sunflower seeds ('A man of taste,' comments
Mulder). Sunflower seeds do protect Mulder directly
in one instance: in 'Bad Blood', the vampire has to
stop and pick them all up before he can attack. The
implication is that this is another reason why he
often carries them with him: they're his version of
Scully's cross.

37: 'Irresistible'

US Transmission: 13 January 1995
UK Transmission: 16 May 1995 (Sky One)/
20 November 1995 (BBC2)
Writer: Chris Carter
Director: David Nutter
Cast: Bruce Weitz (Agent Moe Bocks),
Nick Chinlund (Donald Pfaster), Deanna Milligan (Satin),
Robert Thurston (Jackson Toews), Glynis Davies (Ellen),
Tim Progosh (Mr Fiebling), Dwight McFee (Suspect),
Denalda Williams (Marilyn), Maggie O'Hara (Young Woman),
Kathleen Duborg (Prostitute), Mark Saunders (Agent Busch),
Ciara Hunter (Coed)

An FBI agent in Minnesota investigates a desecrated grave
and, thinking it the work of extraterrestrials, he calls in
Mulder and Scully. Mulder believes that the cutting away of
nails and hair points instead to a human fetishist, and he is
concerned that the man will escalate towards killing in order
to satisfy his cravings. A prostitute is murdered, and Scully
takes the corpse to Washington for further analysis. A fingerprint of the murderer – Donnie Pfaster – is found on the body,
but when Scully returns to Minneapolis she is forced off the
road by the man and captured. However, Mulder and Agent
Bocks find Pfaster's location in the nick of time.

Don't Be in the Teaser: The story begins with a funeral . . .

Scully Here is a Medical Doctor: Yet another autopsy. She says that in medical school she developed a clinical detachment from death.

Phwoar!: Having found Scully, Mulder holds her as she cries, and kisses her hair.

Dialogue Triumphs: Agent Mo Bocks: 'You're saying some human's been doing this?' Mulder: 'If you want to call them that.'

Mulder: 'Some people collect salt and pepper shakers. Fetishists collect dead things – fingernails and hair. No one quite knows why, though I've never understood salt and pepper shakers myself.'

Mulder: 'You know, people videotape police beatings in darkened streets, they manage to see Elvis in three cities across America every day, but no one saw a pretty woman being forced off the road . . .'

Continuity: Mulder has really come to Minneapolis to watch the Vikings play the Washington Redskins, for which he has a pair of tickets. He seems quite annoyed that he and Scully will have to miss the game. Scully says she trusts Mulder with her life. She has never seen a case of grave desecration before, though she has read about them.

The Truth: Pfaster is just a psychotic death fetishist. Or is he? Scully (without any explanation) sees him morph into other human 'shapes' and into some sort of alien creature. However, given that no mention is made of this in the dialogue, and that Scully also sees the alien thing in a nightmare, it is difficult to state categorically that Pfaster isn't human (and Scully is pretty disturbed during this particular episode).

Trivia: The music being played at the funeral is 'Trios Gymnopedies' (first movement) by Erik Satie. In the football game, the (real life) player making the touchdown is called Cris Carter.

The Bottom Line: MD: 'It is somehow easier to believe . . . in aliens and UFOs than in the kind of cold-hearted inhuman monster who could prey on the living to scavenge from the dead.' The theme of this episode in a nutshell (although

somewhat ruined by attempts to make the human killer some
sort of 'creature' from Scully's point of view). Unfortunately,
coming hard on the heels of another fairly 'straight' episode,
it doesn't provide the ideal juxtaposition (it would be lovely
to have this episode following after, say, 'The Host'), though
it still gives an idea of what *The X-Files* might have been like,
had it not so firmly placed itself in a fantasy milieu. As I've
said before, it's nice to see Mulder acting as a 'normal' agent
(we've been told that he was very successful before getting
involved in the X-Files, and here we see why), and Pfaster –
Norman Bates's spookier cousin – is far creepier than any
number of weird aliens or half-human hybrids. Mind you, it's
difficult to understand how a man so strange he almost makes
Eugene Tooms look normal is so easily given a delivery job
and accepted by the unsuspecting middle-class family on his
rounds – still less why his strange behaviour (and insistence
on returning to his apartment) doesn't start any alarm bells
ringing in the prostitute's mind. As well as featuring a
tiny homage to *Taxi Driver* ('You talking to me?') and an
ending photo montage somewhat reminiscent of *Peeping
Tom*, 'Irresistible' is one of the very best Scully stories. But
do people in Minnesota really leave their doors open?

KT: 'The conquest of fear lies in the moment of its
acceptance.' This story of 'the devil in a button-down shirt'
by the middle of the following season would become somewhat commonplace in *The X-Files*, which is a pity as, taken in
isolation, they work really well. 'Irresistible' is great, though,
with vague necrophiliac undertones (that's got to be a first for
US TV!) and some good performances, chief among them
being Gillian Anderson who, again, proves she's the best
actor on this show by miles. Scully's nightmares are brilliantly staged, and her scene with the FBI psychologist is one
of the highlights of the season (although it's rather sad that,
after a brilliant set-up, there's no concrete reason given for
why this case should upset her any more than any other –
after all, she's seen some weird shit over the last couple of
years). There's also a fine performance from Bruce Weitz
(late of *Hill Street Blues*), who makes an oblique reference to
the real-life serial killer Jeffrey Dahmer at one point.

PC: So what does this killer want, exactly? Too bowdlerised

by a long way. It's a bit disturbing, as well, that having Scully tied up and helpless is now a recurring motif. And why do that crap morphing business just to let us know we're watching *The X-Files*? All these factors insult the audience in a big way, and it's nice to know that they're all addressed and turned around during season three, when the scripts allow us to deal with the realities of violent abuse ('Oubliette'), Scully as a professional (notably '2Shy' but generally all round), and stories without supernatural elements ('Grotesque').

38: 'Die Hand die Verletzt'

US Transmission: 27 January 1995
UK Transmission: 23 May 1995 (Sky One)/
27 November 1995 (BBC2)
Writers: Glen Morgan, James Wong
Director: Kim Manners
Cast: Dan Butler (Jim Ausbury),
Susan Blommaert (Phyllis H. Paddock),
Heather McComb (Shannon Ausbury),
Shaun Johnston (Pete Calcagni),
P. Lynn Johnson (Deborah Brown),
Travis MacDonald (Dave Duran),
Michelle Goodger (Barbara Ausbury),
Larry E. Musser (Sheriff John Oakes),
Franky Czinege (Jerry Thomas),
Laura Harris (Andrea), Doug Abrahams (Paul Vitaris)

A teenager is killed in Milford Haven, New Hampshire, an area associated with witchcraft, and nervous police officers call in Mulder and Scully. Despite Scully's scepticism, toads fall from the sky, water runs down basins anticlockwise, and Shannon Ausbury, a friend of the dead boy, makes claims of ritualised abuse when she was young. The girl appears to commit suicide, but the focus of the investigation moves from her father to the mysterious woman teacher whom no one can remember appointing. Jim Ausbury is consumed by what appears to be an enormous snake; Mulder and Scully are captured by the remaining adherents of the dark religion practised by some of the schoolteachers, but are saved from ritual sacrifice by the psychic intervention of Mrs Paddock, the mysterious temporary teacher. Paddock vanishes from the scene, leaving a taunting message.

Don't Be in the Teaser: No deaths, but a remarkable sequence as we realise that the 'Nice School of Christian Bigots' is actually the 'Spooky School of Nutter Diabolists'. (More of a 'pre-title sequence' actually takes place immediately after the credits, with the death of Jerry Stevens after the summoning of dark forces.)

Scully's Rational Explanation of the Week: The falling toads are due to tornadoes in north Massachusetts. She does at least concede that the man with the gun looked as if someone else was controlling him. Why can nobody remember hiring Mrs Paddock? 'A bureaucratic oversight.'

Dialogue Triumphs: Mulder to Scully after the local cop has been dribbling on about 'Heavy Metal bands that influence kids': 'Better hide your Megadeath albums.'

Continuity: Scully's expertise on snake digestion leads Mulder to suspect that she watches the Learning Channel.

The Truth: Paddock – presumably a human acolyte with incredible evil powers, although this is never made clear – can influence others, especially if she has an item that belongs to the person, and controls a (supernatural?) snake of vast proportions. It's quite possible that she's the cause of the power cut (the lights come back on after she has left) and other phenomena seen during the course of the episode (including the toads?). She has presumably come to the area to punish the followers of the 'forces of darkness' who have lost their faith, and is somehow summoned by the teenagers' invocation, attacking a teacher with 'flesh-eating bacteria' so that she can take over his position for a while.

Trivia: The title is German for 'The Hand, The Pain' – presumably a reference to Mrs Paddock's burning of her hand on a candle to control the actions of others, translated by the cultists as 'His is the hand that wounds'. Paddock is an old

English word for toad. The Ausbury family is named after a fan, Jill Ausbury, and Jerry for another fan, Jerry Jones. Pete Calcagni is the husband of another fan.

Scientific Comment: It is true that Coriolis forces in the northern hemisphere would make the water go down clockwise, but this can be disturbed by other forces. For instance, if you get out of a bath in such a way as to create vorticity, that could overcome the Coriolis forces. If the water fountain was asymmetric, it could go the other way. It's not necessarily evidence of Satanism!

The Bottom Line: MD: 'Did you really think you can call up the Devil and ask him to behave?' The themes raised – loss of faith (in 'evil' rather than 'good' forces), ritual abuse, repressed memories – are a tad more interesting than the somewhat lumpen execution. The (rather nice) lack of closure and (more annoying) lack of anything resembling an explanation (just what was the nasty old woman with the pet snake?) means that it's exciting and frustrating in equal parts. Still, there are great set pieces aplenty, and the plot executes just enough twists to prevent it being a complete retread of old *Omen*-type ground.

KT: 'So . . . lunch?' 'Mulder, toads just fell from the sky!' Another good mixture of small-town American myths, and pseudo-something-or-other horror. Love Mulder's description of Paper Lace's 'The Night Chicago Died' as 'devil music'. The naming of High School Crowley is a good in-joke, as is a genuine line of Aleister Crowley lore ('Do what thou wilt'). Great music, too (hugely influenced by *The Omen*, but, given the subject matter, that's pretty inevitable!).

PC: Again, it's a pity that the show is allowing itself time off from closure. The nature of the evil teacher is a vast unanswered question, and one that's very troubling in a show that's concerned with seeking the truth. In the second season, all the rules about how far from the rational the show is going to go seem to have been suspended, leading to a number of episodes where, to put it bluntly, bizarre things happen for no reason. Groovy set pieces, though.

39: 'Fresh Bones'

US Transmission: 3 February 1995
UK Transmission: 30 May 1995 (Sky One)/
4 December 1995 (BBC2)
Writer: Howard Gordon
Director: Rob Bowman
Cast: Bruce Young (Pierre Bauvais),
Daniel Benzali (Colonel Wharton),
Jamil Walker Smith (Chester Bonaparte),
Matt Hill (Private Harry Dunham),
Callum Keith Rennie (Groundskeeper),
Kevin Conway (Private Jack McAlpin),
Katya Gardner (Robin McAlpin), Roger Cross (Private Kittel),
Peter Kelamis (Lieutenant Foyle),
Adrien Malebranche (Skinny Man)

The FBI are called in after the second suicide in under a
month at an immigration processing centre in North Carolina.
Although there is no evidence of foul play, the widow of
Private McAlpin is convinced that he would not take his own
life. A voodoo symbol was found on the tree which McAlpin
crashed into, and suspicion focuses on Bauvais, the leader of
the Haitians who make up most of the immigrants. As Mulder
and Scully investigate, McAlpin's body vanishes from the
morgue, the man later being found – alive – beyond the camp
perimeter. Although McAlpin appears to murder his friend
Harry Dunham, the real instigator of all the violence is the
brutal camp commander, Colonel Wharton. He lost men
during the US invasion of Haiti, and is systematically beating the immigrants as revenge, using voodoo to stop the
two soldiers testifying against him. Bauvais – killed by the
colonel – is 'resurrected', and ensures that Wharton receives
a suitably grotesque punishment for his crimes.

Don't Be in the Teaser: Jack McAlpin steps into a scene
straight from *Poltergeist*, then crashes his car into a tree.

Scully Here is a Medical Doctor: She is about to perform an
autopsy on McAlpin, but the corpse has been replaced by that
of a dog.

Ooze: Some nasty stuff flows from Scully's palm. McAlpin vomits off screen, and there's a cereal bowl full of maggots.

Scully's Rational Explanation of the Week: Voodoo works purely on suggestion and fear. Bauvais has switched McAlpin's body for the dog despite his being in a cell. This is the first episode in which the phrase 'old wives' tale' is used!

The Conspiracy Starts at Closing Time: X turns up (contacting Mulder via a playing card – the ten of diamonds) and sketches in the political dimension to the events at the processing centre, basically saying that everything will soon be swept under the carpet. Mulder says he is surprised to see the man again (after disobeying his orders in 'One Breath'). Maybe this encounter is simply to re-establish contact with Mulder, or maybe, for X, this case is personal (has he got a Haitian background, or is he an illegal immigrant, like that other agent of the Conspiracy, Luiz Cardinal of 'Apocrypha'?). It doesn't seem likely that the Conspiracy would have an interest in this matter, although they might be interested in a chemical which turns people into zombies . . . There is a suggestion that the military are sanctioning Wharton's actions in retaliation for the death of three soldiers in Haiti. That might be enough for the vengeful, anti-establishment X to take an interest.

The Truth: Wharton 'went native' in Haiti to such an extent that he returned to the US conversant with voodoo. A poison (possibly extracted from frogs) can induce a zombie-like state in small quantities. The nature of Chester Bonaparte – who died during the riot ten weeks previously but seems like a normal kid (albeit one who can change into a cat!) to Mulder and Scully – is unclear, but his 'new life' is presumably also linked to voodoo.

Trivia: Doesn't Private Dunham seem a little short for a marine? He's not much taller than Scully. The card that X leaves Mulder appears to be a coded reference to where they should meet (County Road 10).

The Bottom Line: MD: Darker than Dracula's underpants. The whole thing romps along, blessed with some lovely direction (there's a nice zoom into the cracked face of the statue in the pre-title sequence, later mirrored by the rotten face glimpsed in the car mirror). A grotesque scene with Scully's hand ripping open leads into a lovely double-twist ending.

KT: 'They will only warn you once. After that, no magic can save you.' As Kenny Lynch said in *Doctor Terror's House of Horror* (1964), 'You don't want to mess with that voodoo!' Partly objectionable because it takes every Caribbean folk myth and mixes them up without much intelligence (as if just mentioning the words 'voodoo' and 'zombie' will make the audience happy), there are good things on offer (Daniel Benzali is excellent), and the candle-filled graveyard finale is effective. There are a few nods at Edgar Allan Poe, too (notably *The Premature Burial* in the final shot).

PC: Eek! Scary! The last bit is really scary! It's all done so terribly well that you don't realise until a few days after that it's basically a load of set pieces glued together with expectation. Which could be one of the secrets of this show's success: do the lighting and design well, and the rest will follow (as *Doctor Who*'s finest script editor, Andrew Cartmel, once noted).

40: 'Colony'

US Transmission: 10 February 1995
UK Transmission: 6 June 1995 (Sky One)/
11 December 1995 (BBC2)
Writers: Chris Carter, from a story by David Duchovny,
Chris Carter
Director: Nick Marck
Cast: Dana Gladstone (Dr Landon Prince/Gregors),
Tom Butler (CIA Agent Ambrose Chapel),
Tim Henry (Federal Marshall),
Andrew Johnston (Agent Barry Weiss),
Ken Roberts (Proprietor), Michael Rogers (1st Crewman),
Oliver Becker (2nd Doctor), James Leard (Sgt. Al Dixon),
Linden Banks (The Reverend Sistrunk),
Bonnie Hay (Field Doctor), Kim Restell (Newspaper Clerk),

Richard Sargent (Captain), David L. Gordon (FBI Agent),
Michael McDonald (Military Policeman),
Capper McIntyre (First Jailer)

Arson attacks on abortion clinics have claimed the lives of
three doctors who were unrelated but apparently identical.
Mulder and Scully try to track down the other clones, but
during the course of their investigation an FBI agent is killed,
as is the doctor they were trying to protect – although, as with
the others, no corpse remains to be analysed. Despite being
'grounded' by Skinner, Mulder and Scully are contacted by a
CIA agent who claims that the cloned men are the result of
Soviet cold-war experiments, and that they are being systematically destroyed by a Russian assassin at the behest of
the US authorities. Suddenly Mulder is forced to return home
on important family business: his sister has reappeared after
all these years. Scully continues the investigation and eventually finds the remaining clones. However, the protection she
organises for them proves inadequate. Samantha Mulder, now
the adopted daughter of one of the doctors, explains to Fox
that the assassin is in fact a shapeshifting alien. Mulder tries
to contact Scully, but it is too late: she has just let another
Mulder into her room.

Don't Be in the Teaser: Mulder's heart stops in the Arctic.

Scully Here is a Medical Doctor: She reads the autopsy of
the dead agent: his blood seems to have coagulated.

Ooze: Lots of it as the clones and the assassin are stabbed or
shot. Scully steps in some ooze at one point and it ruins her
shoe. And there's whatever is in that blood bag she's holding
in the warehouse (looks suspiciously like a hybrid foetus
that's been stamped on!).

Scully's Rational Explanation of the Week: The arsons are
the work of militant pro-lifers. Nevertheless, in a great subversion, she's less than willing to believe the moronic state-
sanctioned-murder nonsense that 'Chapel' spouts.

That's a Mouthful: Mulder: 'I have lived with a fragile faith
built on the ether of vague memories from an experience I

could neither prove nor explain . . . What happened to me out on the ice has justified every belief. If I should die now it would be with the certainty that my faith has been righteous, and if through death larger mysteries are revealed I will have already learnt the answer to the question that has driven me here: that there is intelligent life in the universe, other than our own, that they are here among us, and that they have begun to colonise.'

Dialogue Triumphs: Mulder: 'You've got to wonder about a country where even the President has to worry about drive-by shootings.'

Scully: 'Whatever happened to "trust no one"?' Mulder: 'I changed it to "trust everyone". Didn't I tell you?'

Continuity: Mulder's parents are separated. Samantha mentions Stratego (see 'Little Green Men'). Both Mulder and Scully are on the Internet, and receive anonymous e-mail tip-offs. Mulder's father now lives in West Tisbury, Massachusetts.

The 'Truth': According to 'Agent Chapel', the cloned doctors are the result of the Gregor programme in the former USSR, and they entered the States in the 1970s on German passports, infiltrating medical establishments in case of war. However, 'Chapel' is a shapeshifting alien killer, with green toxic blood, so this simply isn't true: see the next episode.

Trivia: Ambrose Chapel is named after a church in the Hitchcock movie *The Man Who Knew Too Much*. In that film, the name is wrongly believed to be that of a person. Exactly Mulder and Scully's mistake!

The Bottom Line: MD: Uneven but good, despite the contrived events (a broken pencil, Scully taking a shower) that work towards that breathtaking cliffhanger.

KT: Impossible to like because it cheats for just about the first time in the series' history (the lie about Samantha returning being unresolved until the next episode). The episode features several great set pieces (the UFO crashing into the sea); the CIA stuff is well played, even if it is a complete red herring; and the *Terminator* influence that marbles the opening scenes becomes less obvious as the episode progresses. But it's still chock-full of dark back-alley chases that smack of a lack of ideas. A series is usually in trouble when it allows the actors to start thinking that they're writers!

PC: A mate of mine who'd given up on the series because of its nebulous and unresolved nature asked another friend what was happening these days. 'Oh, an alien bounty hunter has arrived to kill the clones of Mulder's sister' was the reply. And that's just the trouble. After all these shadows and grey areas, a dirty great, large-as-life, shapeshifting, alien bounty hunter takes some swallowing. It's a tightrope walk the series loves to do: have they gone too far? And in season three, they manage to totter their way along quite well. But here they fall right off and plummet to the floor screaming, 'But it's true!'

41: 'End Game'

US Transmission: 17 February 1995
UK Transmission: 13 June 1995 (Sky One)/
18 December 1995 (BBC2)
Writer: Frank Spotnitz
Director: Rob Bowman
Cast: Colin Cunningham (Lieutenant Terry Wilmer),
Garry Davey (Captain), Andrew Johnston (Agent Weiss),
Allan Lysell (Able Gardener),
J.B. Bivens (Sharpshooter), Oliver Becker (2nd Doctor),
Beatrice Zeilinger (Paramedic),
Bonnie Hay (Field Doctor),
Dana Gladstone (Dr Prince/Gregor)

Scully is captured by the alien, 'disguised' as Mulder, who wants to exchange her for Samantha. Skinner arranges for a sniper to shoot the alien during the hostage swap, but the plan fails and both Samantha and the assassin tumble over a bridge. Fox tells his father about Samantha's death, and he gives his son a note from her, encouraging him to travel to an abortion clinic in Rockville. Although Scully is on the scene when Samantha's body is recovered from the river, Mulder meets other 'Samanthas' in the clinic. They are alien clones, just like the other Samantha, and are being hunted down by the assassin. Mulder cannot save them, but pursues the killer to the Arctic sea, where his ship originally came down. Left for dead by the bounty hunter, Mulder is saved by a rescue team. He has been contaminated by the alien's blood, but Scully oversees his recovery.

Don't Be in the Teaser: A recap, and then the USS Allegiance's abortive attempt to destroy the bounty hunter's craft.

Scully Here is a Medical Doctor: Scully's conclusions regarding the retrovirus that killed Agent Weiss save Mulder's life. She does the electrocardio treatment on Mulder.

Scully's Rational Explanation of the Week: 'Several aspects of this case remain unexplained,' she concludes with characteristic understatement. At the end, she finally addresses all the extreme things she's seen on her travels with Mulder, and concludes that science is still a useful tool and a crutch for her, even when dealing with the paranormal.

Dialogue Triumphs: Mulder: 'How was the opera?' X: 'Wonderful, I've never slept better.'

X: 'Is the answer to your question worth dying for?'

The Conspiracy Starts at Closing Time: X says that a fleet has been dispatched from Anchorage to make sure the alien assassin doesn't leave. That's because, as becomes clear from 'Patient X', this alien (popularly known as the Alien Bounty Hunter) isn't the same one who's working for the Conspiracy in such episodes as 'Herrenvolk'. This Shapeshifter is the important member of the Rebel Colonist faction who modifies his face to attack the plans of the Conspiracy in 'Patient X'. (The Shapeshifters seem to have only a certain number of template human shapes, the use of which perhaps depends on function, rather in the way that all the same-looking hybrids are given the same task.) The Rebel Leader is touring the country, destroying the work of Conspiracy scientists who are creating batches of human/Colonist hybrid clones of the kind we see in 'Memento Mori'. (This is the first time we've seen the Conspiracy's own hybrids.) The Samantha clones shamelessly use Mulder for protection, employing him once again as a Conspiracy stooge, in a plan that the CSM may also somehow see as 'comforting' for Mulder. Bill Mulder doesn't tell his son that by going after the Rebel Leader, he's actually helping the Conspiracy. (The Cigarette-Smoking Man must have gained great kudos from his Conspiracy masters for this one.) The Samantha clones must have been created from Samantha's ova, so she may have been very lucky to be able to have a family of her own ('Redux II'), and may still wear a cancer-control chip in her neck. X frustratedly tells Mulder that the government/Conspiracy aren't on the side of the Rebel Leader by mentioning the pursuing fleet, but Mulder still doesn't take the hint. X presumably won't tell Scully where Mulder is because he doesn't want the whole might of the FBI pursuing his enemies' enemy also, or perhaps he just doesn't want the Conspiracy to realise that the knowledge of the passage of the Rebel Leader has gone beyond their own forces (he also didn't encourage Mulder to pursue the Rebel Leader on that basis). Skinner appears to be aware of X's connection to Mulder, or perhaps he just realises that whoever he meets in the building is going to be the contact. The detail of the Rebel Leader's cover story while he's Ambrose Chapel indicates the depth to which the Rebel Colonists have done their homework. (He's either gained enough knowledge to pilot a nuclear sub, or he finds the technology simple; or he has some method of stealing knowledge from those whose appearances he duplicates.) His knowledge of Mulder includes the information that he's been shot before, which indicates a day-to-day knowledge of Mulder's life. Shapeshifters can survive leaps from great heights, and can recognise each other no matter what face they're wearing. The phrase 'bounty hunter' is part of the cover story the cloned Samantha gives Mulder (this batch of clones obviously have no protective attachment to their mother, unlike those in 'Memento Mori'), because it doesn't describe the mission or credo of their assailant at all. The Rebel Colonist ship is 800 metres across (so it's not one of the triangular ones), and emits radio noise all across the spectrum (indicating perhaps, as does 'Apocrypha', that Colonist ships can communicate with their owners). It can hover, and zap human hearing and communication systems with what is, apparently, a sonic weapon (of the type referred to in 'E.B.E.'? – maybe that's one of the things that the Colonists have given the Conspiracy, assuming the technology is common to both factions). We might see this very ship again arriving at the start of 'Patient X', since it belongs to the same individual and looks exactly the same in-flight. Mulder doesn't usually have to get authorisation or do (much of?) the normal paperwork on X-Files cases. But the death of a fellow agent is enough to put Skinner's place as his protector in jeopardy from quite ordinary sources. Would Skinner normally call Mulder into his office for a 'family emergency', or does he know how weighted this particular event is? But Bill Mulder knows better than to trust telephones . . . (This story reveals that he's also a 'cigarette-smoking man'. Must be the company he keeps.)

Continuity: The Rebel Leader says that (the real) Samantha is still alive. (And since he has no reason to make a wild guess, then we might suppose that the Rebels know every detail of the Conspiracy's operation on Earth.) It's strange that he doesn't seem to consider confiding in Mulder (although his questioning about what Mulder feels is worth dying for may be an attempt to discover his loyalties), but then, Mulder has given no sign of not being the utter Conspiracy stooge that both sides of the conflict may regard him as. The Samantha clones also say they know where Samantha is, but since the CSM has taken care to get her away from the Project, that information is probably confined to 'on Earth and out of our organisation'.

The Truth: As above, Mulder is tricked into saving Conspiracy facilities and personnel. It's a lovely detail of the lie that the Samanthas tell him they believe their people will one day 'inherit' the Earth, which may be exactly the point of the view of their Rebel enemies (considering their actions in 'Fearful Symmetry'). Shapeshifters can be killed only if the base of the neck is pierced. Their blood is fatal to humans as it contains a retrovirus that triggers an immunological response to produce excess amounts of red blood cells (given that the biology of human response to Black Oil-based Colonists is constant throughout the series, it is probable that exposure to small amounts over a long period is carcinogenic, as we see with Scully and the other 'abductees'). Shapeshifters could be either specialised Colonist/human hybrids who utilise the Black Oil component of their blood to liquidise their features (which explains the back-of-neck control-chip weakness common to both) or human bodies made animated and mutable via the Black Oil inside them. (Which explains why the Conspiracy seem to employ, rather than create, them.) It's possible that they come in both types. The Colonist virus, and all aspects of Colonist biology, become dormant at low temperatures.

Trivia: In this episode we see that the number of Mulder's apartment is 42 – either a brilliantly conceived Douglas Adams in-joke, or a complete coincidence.

The Bottom Line: MD: Poor Scully – another day, another lunatic (what's that, her third psycho/alien weirdo this season?). On the surface, this is the closest the show gets to 'straight' SF thriller (alien bounty hunter tries to kill another group of extraterrestrials who are colonising Earth), and if anything it's a notch up from the previous episode. I love the scrap between Skinner and X, and the incredible descending sub tower!

KT: 'It's a good story. I've heard a lot of good stories lately.' There are actually about six stories here (some of them very good, some less so), and the episode ends up with so much going on that it's often difficult to keep track of what, exactly, we're supposed to be concentrating on. The bridge sequence is great, and Skinner's got a couple of brilliant little cameos, but the whole thing is so complicated that this was the point I began to wonder how much of a corner the production team had painted themselves into with this whole Conspiracy malarkey. And, can somebody please tell them to turn the lights on once in a while?

PC: I concur about the Conspiracy, if not the lighting. It was at this point that you started to need not only to have seen the previous Conspiracy episodes, but to have studied and discussed them at length, in order to enjoy the latest ones.

Fortunately, between, I suspect, this season and the next, Frank Spotnitz (who has the most apt name) sat down with Chris Carter and got all the Conspiracy stuff sorted, leading to the run of coherent (if still somewhat audience-shredding) Conspiracy episodes in the next season. These episodes, however, are a mess. They seem to go on forever, because there are many slow-paced threads all continuing at once. Worse, the Conspiracy distracts us from the human drama. Bill Mulder's bizarrely casual reaction on hearing that his daughter has vanished again alienates us from the whole thing, because it's just not how a human being would behave. Later information backs up his apparent insensitivity (it's doubtful that he ever believed that this was the real Samantha, since he could have phoned up the Conspiracy and asked). But the moment is sacrificed for a back story that we don't yet know about, resulting in what's almost an anti-drama.

FOREIGN TITLES

Countries where *The X-Files* is shown, and what the show is called there (translations for titles other than the original):

Albania: *Fajllat X* ('The X Case').

Argentina: *Los Expedientes Secretos X* ('The Secret Cases of X').

Austria, Germany and Switzerland: *Akte X – Die unheimlichen faelle des FBI* ('X Files – Uncovered FBI cases').

Belgium: *De X-dossieren* ('The X Dossiers').

Brazil and Portugal: *Arquivo X* ('The X Archive').

China: *X-Dang An*.

Croatia: *Dosije X* ('X Dossier').

Czech Republic: *Akta X*.

Denmark: *Strengt Fortroligt* ('Strictly Confidential').

Finland: *Salaiset Kansiot* ('The Secret Folders').

FOREIGN TITLES

42: 'Fearful Symmetry'

US Transmission: 24 February 1995
UK Transmission: 20 June 1995 (Sky One)/
23 January 1996 (BBC1)
Writer: Steve de Jarnatt
Director: James Whitmore, Jr
Cast: Jayne Atkinson (Willa Ambrose),
Lance Guest (Kyle Lang), Jack Rader (Ed Meecham),
Jody St Michael (Sophie), Charles Andre (Ray Floyd),
Garvin Cross (Red Head Kid), Tom Glass (Trucker)

The death of a construction worker and the mysterious escape of an elephant from a nearby zoo bring Mulder and Scully to Idaho. Although much damage was caused in the town of Fairfield, no one saw the creature, and there is no sign that the cage was tampered with. However, Scully remains convinced that the WAO, a radical anti-zoo group stationed in the area, are to blame, and she follows a man as he breaks into the zoo. He is killed, seemingly by a tiger, but video footage of his death reveals no attacking animal. Mulder discovers that no pregnancy at the zoo has ever successfully come full term, and an autopsy on the elephant shows that it was pregnant. Mulder postulates that extraterrestrials are harvesting the animals for embryos and returning the creatures to the wrong location. He shares a 'whiteout' encounter with Sophie the gorilla, who has learnt to communicate in sign language. After their encounter, she delivers an ecological warning to humanity.

Don't Be in the Teaser: A construction worker is killed by an invisible elephant.

Scully Here is a Medical Doctor: She performs an autopsy on the elephant (which involves stepping into the corpse!), despite it being beyond her 'job description'. She also examines Kyle Lang's body and finds evidence of manslaughter.

Scully's Rational Explanation of the Week: The lights used by the workers affected their night vision, and the video cameras were of such poor quality that they couldn't pick out a grey elephant in the dark. About as plausible as Mulder's invisible elephant.

Dialogue Triumphs: Mulder: 'I'd be willing to admit the possibility of a tornado, but it's not really tornado season. I'd even be willing to entertain the notion of a black hole passing over the area . . . but it's not really black hole season, either.'

The Conspiracy Starts at Closing Time: Mulder is once more present during a 'whiteout' effect, and may thus have lost time again. (It's becoming a way of life for him.) If the aliens featured here are Rebel Colonists (and, as established in 'The Red and the Black', Colonists are definitely capable of organising both 'whiteouts' and missing time) then this faction want to save Earth's animals. There would be many easier ways for the Conspiracy and their own Colonist friends to nick animal DNA if they wanted it. Presumably, the Rebel Colonists may want to save some of Earth's biosphere from the imminent attack by their foes, and their motives here may be highly ethical.

Continuity: Mulder once saw a David Copperfield show (possibly on TV – see 'Little Green Men') in which the magician made the Statue of Liberty disappear. Frohike was arrested at a 'Free James Brown' rally. Langly has a 'philosophical problem' with having his image bounced off a satellite.

The Truth: Animal embryos are being harvested by extra-terrestrials. It's not explained, however, what causes the 'invisible creatures', or the animals' return to the wrong place (Mulder blathers on about disruption in the spacetime continuum), or – given the aliens' poor map-reading – how they manage to locate Sophie, the ape having been moved.

Trivia: Blake Towers seems to have been named after the author of the poem ('The Tyger') from which the title comes, William Blake.

Scientific Comment: When Mulder says that the aliens are suffering from 'an astrological variation, a trouble with the spacetime continuum', at the very least he should have said astronomical, not astrological!

The Bottom Line: MD: 'Man save man.' Marvellous, a great example of how rich a brew *The X-Files* can be, with a quite different example of alien interaction with our planet from that seen in the previous story. Presumably this is why the BBC showed this one out of sequence, as they didn't want to start their BBC1 run with something so atypical. But what makes a classic *X-Files* anyway? OK, so this is a 'message episode', but who cares? It's a great message, and the opening sequences are wonderfully bizarre.

KT: 'Unless it's trick photography, that kid was killed by some kind of phantom attacker.' A hell of a pre-title sequence. Apart (again) from the lack of a clear motivation for the animal abductions (three or four theories are put forward, but most seem like Mulder grabbing at straws), this is a really good episode. There's an anger in the writing that is unusual in *The X-Files* (which is normally much more cynical – even when it's getting on its soapbox).

PC: Oh come on! Let me get this straight: these aliens, who have been scaring the hell out of our heroes with their abduction stuff (or at least, the Conspiracy's panto version of their abduction stuff), have now started abducting gorillas to save our planet's wildlife from humanity? The reason the BBC showed this one out of order was, I suspect, that it's bloody ridiculous. I mean, what next, the gorilla abduction support group? Otters with implants? Can we be sure of the safety of Mulder's poor goldfish? This whole Grey alien/snatched-from-your-bed business started out as a hard, scared response to all that hippie space brothers nonsense. Shoehorning abduction mythology back into green crystal dolphin politics is just a ridiculous, rabbitlike response to the new mythos, both in fact and in fiction like this. *The X-Files* should be more cynical than this, but with the hippie Indians on the horizon, it got worse before it got better. This was just an excuse for an elephant autopsy, wasn't it?

43: 'Død Kalm'

US Transmission: 10 March 1995
UK Transmission: 27 June 1995 (Sky One)/
16 January 1996 (BBC1)
Writers: Howard Gordon, Alex Gansa,
from a story by Howard Gordon
Director: Rob Bowman
Cast: John Savage (Henry Trondheim),
David Cubitt (Captain Barclay), Vladimir Kulich (Olafsson),
Stephen Dimopoulos (Ionesco), Claire Riley (Dr Laskos),
Robert Metcalfe (Nurse),
Dmitry Chepovetsky (Lieutenant Richard Harper),
Mar Anderson (Halverson), John McConnach (Sailor)

The only survivor of the USS *Arden*, which went missing in the Norwegian sea, appears to have aged prematurely, and Mulder and Scully decide to investigate. They charter a ship to the area – which has seen an unusually high incidence of disappearing vessels over the years – and find the rusted remains of the *Arden*. Stranded on board the prematurely aged ship, they find one survivor, who soon dies, and a pirate whaler, who has not aged. The FBI agents discover that the water supply has become infected, and that only the recycled sewage water is safe to drink. This supply is dwindling, and Mulder and Scully begin to age. However, they are rescued and, thanks to Scully's detailed notes, even Mulder recovers fully.

Don't Be in the Teaser: The men of the USS *Arden* mutiny in a desperate attempt to escape the ageing, but by the time of their rescue it's already too late for them.

Scully Here is a Medical Doctor: Mulder is able to get her a clearance code to see Lt. Richard Harper, the only survivor of the *Arden*. Later, her notes help to save Mulder's life.

Scully's Rational Explanation of the Week: Free radicals – highly reactive chemicals containing extra electrons that can attack DNA and cause body tissue and cell membranes to oxidise, thought to be at the root of natural ageing – are being released as the ship is drifting towards a large metallic source (e.g. a meteorite), with the ocean acting as a battery.

Phwoar!: Neither of them will drink the last water. Aww . . .

Dialogue Triumphs: Mulder: 'I always thought when I got old I'd take a cruise . . .'

The Conspiracy Starts at Closing Time: According to Mulder, scientists involved in the Philadelphia Experiment, which attempted to make battleships invisible to radar, were not, as is commonly believed, moved to the Manhattan Project. They continued their work at Roswell, New Mexico, utilising alien technology, and less than nine months later caused the USS *Eldridge* to disappear from the Philadelphia Naval Yard and reappear minutes later in Norfolk, Virginia. That sounds like Conspiracy scientists getting hold of the spacetime warping equipment of the Colonists, but they don't seem to have done much with it since.

Continuity: Mulder gets seasick; Scully doesn't. Scully refers back to the events of 'One Breath', and says that she no longer fears death. (Then consider this a rehearsal . . .)

The Truth: Your guess is as good as ours. Mulder knows of nine unexplained cases of ships vanishing as they passed through the 65th parallel, dating back to 1949, which suggests a long-standing phenomenon. No explanation is made for the problems with instrumentation (particularly radar) in the area, and suggested causes of the ageing moves from wormholes and the Philadelphia Experiment to free radicals released because the ship is drifting towards a large metallic meteorite, to a water supply infected with what Scully calls 'heavy salt'. This seems to be at the root of the human ageing at least, as her theories are proved correct when Mulder is treated in the naval hospital, but it's difficult to see how infected water would cause the entire ship to degenerate. No explanation is given for how or why the water was infected or for the disappearing vessels in the past or for the true role played by the crashed meteorite (if indeed that's what the recent light in the sky was). And why, exactly, was Olafsson unaffected?

Trivia: Leeds isn't on the coast, so how can a Royal Naval ship disappear between there and Cape Perry? There is a port of Leeds, but it's a canal port, so a warship wouldn't be sailing from there. (Given the destination, Hull or Newcastle upon Tyne would seem the likely port of origin.)

Scientific Comment: The battery theory wouldn't work. The positively charged meteor, the sea and the battleship wouldn't form a circuit.

The Bottom Line: MD: 'Time got lost.' A triumph of style over substance and the shaggiest of shaggy-dog stories, 'Død Kalm' is a bit of a mess. It's atmospheric and well-directed, and the enclosed survival play that it becomes is well acted by the regulars, but the complete lack of explanation, the gross contradictions and the cop-out ending (echoing that of 'End Game', only two episodes previously) relegates this to an also-ran among 'X-Files without monsters'. No amount of Norse mythology and fog can disguise the fact that the story simply hasn't been thought through properly.

KT: 'I think I hear the wolf at the door.' I'd forgotten just how bad this one was. Boring isn't a word normally used in connection with *The X-Files*, but this is a bland, mindless episode full of culs-de-sac and blind alleys. It grabs on to any passing horror movie clichés (rats, the 'bleeding' ship) and waves them in the air saying 'Be afraid'. No thanks, I was too busy laughing. Even the much-admired make-up isn't really very good (that's when you can see it – turn the lights on, please).

PC: My God, are we anywhere near the end of the season yet? The best *X-Files* episodes trip their way lightly through all the possibilities, and then settle on one, even if they don't tell us which it is. This story is based on the 'throw enough phenomena at the wall, and some of them will stick' theory. As usual, everything looks great, but having our heroes just escape from things, instead of settle them, is always unsatisfactory, and wasn't regarded as fair play before the second season. This story, by the way, seems heavily influenced by *Miss Smilla's Feeling for Snow* by Peter Høeg which, incidentally, has a suspended ending too, only that's a literary masterpiece, and this isn't.

44: 'Humbug'

US Transmission: 31 March 1995
UK Transmission: 4 July 1995 (Sky One)/
9 January 1996 (BBC1)
Writer: Darin Morgan
Director: Kim Manners
Cast: Jim Rose (Dr Blockhead/Jeffrey Swaim),
Wayne Grace (Sheriff Hamilton),
Michael Anderson (Mr Nutt), The Enigma (The Conundrum),
Vincent Schiavelli (Lanny), Alex Diakun (Curator),
John Payne (Jerald Glazebrook),
Gordon Tipple (Hepcat Helm), Alvin Law (Reverend),
Debis Simpson (Waiter), Blair Slater (Old Glazebrook),
Devin Walker (Young Glazebrook)

The murder of an 'Alligator Man' (the forty-eighth attack by a similar assailant in twenty-eight years across America) brings Mulder and Scully to Gibsontown, Florida, a town populated largely by former circus 'freaks' and sideshow artists. After another savage killing the FBI agents become suspicious of Sheriff Hamilton – who used to be Jim-Jim the Dog-Faced

Boy – and Dr Blockhead, whose blood matches that found at the scene of the second murder. However, the real culprit seems to be an atrophied Siamese twin, who can detach from his brother and is searching out a more suitable carrier. He finds this in the form of the jigsaw-tattooed man who can eat anything – including, it seems, the murderous twin.

Don't Be in the Teaser: Jerald Glazebrook, the alligator man, killed in his swimming pool.

How Did He Do That?: Why suddenly start a hunt for the Fiji Mermaid on the basis of a drawing on a restaurant menu?

Scully Here is a Medical Doctor: She does the autopsy on Lanny, the 'normal' twin.

Phwoar!: That remarkably clever scene with Scully's semi-exposed breast and Lanny's deformed stomach/brother.

Dialogue Triumphs: Dr Blockhead (after removing a bloody nail from his nose): 'For instance, did you know that through the protective Chinese practice of Tubu Shon, you can train your testicles to drop into your abdomen?' Mulder: 'I'm doing that as we speak.'

Mr Nutt: 'Not all women are attracted to overly tall, lanky men such as yourself. You'd be surprised how many women find my size intriguingly alluring.' Mulder: 'You'd be surprised how many men do as well.'

Dr Blockhead (with numerous hooks in his chest): 'If people knew the true price of spirituality, there'd be more atheists.'

Continuity: Scully's uncle was an amateur magician who taught her sleight of hand. Seemingly Mulder also had an uncle with similar abilities.

The Truth: Just as Scully says: it's Lanny's brother (not the Fiji Mermaid!).

Trivia: This episode was aired in the USA on the day before April Fool's Day. The trailer park is named Gulf Breeze, after the place where those sightings that Mulder doesn't believe in occurred.

The Bottom Line: MD: 'We're exhuming . . . your potato.' *The X-Files* does *Basket Case*! Having been wobbling on for ages about the diversity of the format, I must begin by saying that I'm not sure such an obviously surreal and *Twin Peaks*-y episode really does *The X-Files* any favours. When everything is strange, it's difficult to take anything seriously (but then I expect that is the point). Even Scully is wildly out of character: far from being the rationalist foil to Mulder, here she's swapping bizarre one-liners, pulling off sleights of hand and coming up with a theory so weird that no one believes her ('Now you know how I feel,' remarks Mulder). And the plot is almost non-existent. Still, with a script this clever, I'm not complaining too much. The sequences in the wonderfully named Hepcat Helm's 'Tabernacle of Terror' are especially memorable.

KT: 'You recall what Barnum said about suckers?' Now this is funny! Quite why, at this stage in its history, a series as po-faced as *The X-Files* should attempt a comedy episode (even one as surreal as this) is interesting. The reducing of one of the series' most important sacred cows (Mulder) to a straight man is inspired. There are loads of brilliant characters, set pieces and plot devices (Michael Anderson excels as a dwarf made angry by society's stereotyping). There's also a great little rant against genetic engineering towards the end that is out of place, but strangely compelling.

PC: Never mind the comedy aspect, this is simply the best-written show of season two. Morgan, as always, has some weight behind his parody, and the many syntheses between the normal and the not, not to mention the simple and solid ending (an ending! *The X-Files* this week had a proper ending!) make this very satisfying indeed.

45: 'The Calusari'

US Transmission: 14 April 1995
UK Transmission: 11 July 1995 (Sky One)/
30 January 1996 (BBC1)
Writer: Sara B. Charno
Director: Michael Vejar

Cast: Helene Clarkson (Maggie Holvey),
Joel Palmer (Charlie/Michael Holvey),
Lilyan Chauvin (Golda),
Kay E. Kuter (Head Calusari),
Ric Reid (Steve Holvey),
Christine Willes (Agent Karen E. Kosseff),
Bill Dow (Dr Charles Burk),
Jacqueline Dandeneau (Nurse Castor),
Bill Croft (Calusari #2),
Campbell Lane (Calusari #3),
George Josef (Calusari #4),
Oliver and Jeremy Isaac Wildsmith (Teddy Holvey)

A photograph taken just before the mysterious death of
two-year-old Teddy Holvey at the Lincoln amusement park,
Virginia, apparently shows the boy following a balloon
moving against the prevailing wind. When the image is
enhanced there seems to be a childlike figure holding the
balloon. Scully is sceptical, and is particularly suspicious of
Mrs Holvey's superstitious Romanian mother, Golda, who
began living with the family soon after Teddy's birth. She
seems both protective and afraid of Teddy's older brother,
Charlie. Mr Holvey is killed in a freak accident, and Golda
dies when trying to perform a protective ritual, her eyes
apparently pecked out by birds. Charlie blames events
on Michael, his stillborn brother. The poltergeist/spirit of
Michael takes on physical form to masquerade as Charlie and
is taken home by Maggie Holvey, although when she tries to
perform a Romanian rite over the 'boy' he attacks her and
Scully psychically. They are both saved by the Calusari,
Romanian religious elders who sever the link between
Charlie and 'Michael'.

Don't Be in the Teaser: Teddy Holvey, killed by a fairground
train while following a balloon.

Scully's Rational Explanation of the Week: The moving
balloon is blamed on the wind (despite it blowing in the
wrong direction), and Teddy's escape from his harness is
down to two-year-olds being 'slippery'. (Mulder says that it

would be impossible for the boy to free himself, unless he were the reincarnation of Houdini – 'and that would be an X-File in itself'.) Scully blames everything else on the old woman, accusing her of Munchausen's-by-proxy and of wielding a vicious garage-door remote-control unit. This is one of those episodes in which the viewer gets perverse satisfaction from watching Scully thrown about like a rag doll towards the end. Explain that away, then!

The Truth: 'Michael' – the 'spirit' of Charlie's stillborn brother – is the root cause of the mayhem. Exactly how Golda and the Calusari open the garage door, however, is never explained (or maybe it was Charlie who opened it). Mulder is told that it 'knows' him, but we might take that to mean that Mulder has just got on the being's nerves during the course of the episode.

The Bottom Line: MD: 'This programme contains scenes that some viewers may find upsetting,' said the BBC announcer before the initial terrestrial transmission of this episode, and certainly the opening sequences are horrifying for any parent or, indeed, any normal human being. Hugely derivative (chiefly *Damien – The Omen II* and *The Exorcist*), but there's just enough pace to keep your interest, and the audience's changing attitude to the grandmother (who moves from bogeywoman to tragic heroine) is well handled.

KT: 'There were three strange men. They were performing some kind of ritual.' I like this episode a lot, chiefly because it plays with audience expectations and then throws the expected climax back in the viewer's face with a gigantic 'Stuff you!' Mind you, if Scully seeing Mrs Holvey dangling ten feet in the air isn't final concrete proof of the existence of some form of supernatural phenomenon, then . . . Ah, what's the point? Almost certainly the first *X-Files* story to use the word 'diarrhoea'.

PC: But not the last! The opening scenes are so deeply scary that reducing it all to mumbo-jumbo seems a bit of an anticlimax. Again, for the umpteenth time this season, Mulder and Scully just stand around watching the climax.

46: 'F. Emasculata'

US Transmission: 28 April 1995
UK Transmission: 18 July 1995 (Sky One)/
6 February 1996 (BBC1)
Writers: Chris Carter, Howard Gordon
Director: Rob Bowman
Cast: Charles Martin Smith (Dr Osbourne),
Dean Norris (US Marshall Tapia), John Pyper-Ferguson (Paul),
Angelo Vacco (Angelo Garza),
Morris Panych (Dr Simon Auerbach), Lynda Boyd (Elizabeth),
John Tench (Steve), Alvin Sanders (Bus Driver),
Kim Kondrashoff (Bobby Lawrence),
Chilton Crane (Mother at Bus Station),
Bill Rowat (Dr Torrence), Jude Zachary (Winston)

Mulder and Scully are somewhat confused by their latest assignment from Skinner: to liaise with the police searching for two escaped convicts. They notice that the prison from which they absconded is quarantined, and when one of the inmates is found dead his corpse is taken away by men in protective suits. Scully learns that the epidemic at the prison is highly contagious, and that it was a botched experiment by a large American pharmaceutical company. The government, as Mulder discovers when he confronts Skinner and the Cigarette-Smoking Man, are now actively suppressing information and destroying all the evidence, hoping to prevent the spread of infection without causing a panic. Mulder and the police track the remaining prisoner to a bus depot, but the infected man is shot before Mulder can question him in detail.

Don't Be in the Teaser: Dr Robert Torrence comes to a sticky end in the jungle. Literally.

Scully Here is a Medical Doctor: She uses this as justification to muscle in on the contagion investigation.

Ooze: Oh, just gallons of it.

Dialogue Triumphs: US Marshall: 'FBI run out of crooked politicians to sting?'

The Conspiracy Starts at Closing Time: Yes, the Cigarette-Smoking Man could very well be using his information-management skills on behalf of his nominal government employers, to prevent an ordinary scandal. But does this sound likely? This is either another sign that the Conspiracy are trying to develop a hardier strain of human in order to be able to develop a soldier capable of resisting the Black Oil and thus their nominal 'allies', or the first sign that they're choosing such a biological weapon to test their Black Oil delivery system (and end up discarding this one in favour of Smallpox as seen in 'Zero Sum'). They're working, in this case, through Pink Pharmaceuticals (who manage things to the extent of finding a prisoner with the same name as Torrence so that the entire episode can be passed off as a postal error). The Cigarette-Smoking Man states that there was an outbreak of haemorrhagic fever in Sacramento, California in 1988, which was covered up. The occupant of the railway car in 'Apocrypha' is reputed to be infected with haemorrhagic fever, so it's a good bet that the case he refers to was that of a previous escapee. The Conspiracy ensure that Mulder and Scully's evidence is discredited. Skinner is still trying, at this point, to have an easier life by keeping Mulder and the Conspiracy's agendas both going at once.

Continuity: Mulder's badge number is JTT047101111.

The Truth: F. Emasculata is a beetle that carries a parasite that attacks the human immune system, usually causing death in thirty-six hours. The disease is transmitted via exploding pustules that contain the beetle larvae.

The Bottom Line: MD: 'There'll be a time for the truth, Mulder, but this isn't it.' An X-File only because it smacks of Conspiracy (the disease has nothing to do with aliens or the supernatural). 'F. Emasculata' is a great take on the apocalyptic speculation that swept the world after the outbreak of the Ebola virus in Africa. It's chilling but somehow lifeless, and it was probably a mistake to split Mulder and Scully up so early. The moment Scully tells Mulder that there is no evidence left at the prison, and that he must take a statement from the remaining prisoner, you just know that the episode is going to end with a whole lot of fresh air as 'proof'. The special effects are gross, and I swear I'll never complain about zits again.

KT: 'You can't protect the country by lying to it.' 'It's done every day.' Echoes of *The Satan Bug*, *The Andromeda Strain* and even the *Survivors* episode, 'The Last Laugh'. Good fun this, although at heart it's a hoary old B-movie full of ciphers and clichés. Somewhere in the middle of a procession of obvious set pieces is a smashing little story about disinformation struggling to get out. There's a great scene with Skinner towards the end ('Where do you stand?' 'Right on the line that you [Mulder] keep crossing!').

PC: For once, we don't get all the set pieces we expect. There are loads more good disease moments to be had, but, instead of pushing them to the maximum, the script falls back on the Conspiracy to provide drama in what seems to be frantic desperation. Sorry to be so negative, but I really think that this season has problems.

47: 'Soft Light'

US Transmission: 5 May 1995
UK Transmission: 25 July 1995 (Sky One)/
13 February 1996 (BBC1)
Writer: Vince Gilligan
Director: James Contner
Cast: Tony Shalhoub (Dr Chester Ray Banton),
Kate Twa (Detective Kelly Ryan),
Kevin McNulty (Dr Christopher Davey),
Nathaniel Deveaux (Detective Barron),
Robert Rozen (Doctor), Donna Yamamoto (Night Nurse),
Forbes Angus (Government Scientist),
Guyle Frazier (Barney), Steve Bacic (Second Officer),
Craig Brunanski (Security Guard)

Detective Kelly Ryan, an ex-student of Scully's, asks for the FBI agent's help on her first case: a man has vanished from within a locked room, in a Virginia hotel, leaving behind only a black shadowlike stain. Clues gained from two similar disappearances, and the deaths of two policemen at the railway station, eventually point to Polarity Magnetics, a research lab. Dr Chris Davey explains that his partner, Dr Chester Banton, was subject to a massive quantum bombardment some weeks previously in a freak accident. He's been missing since then, but Mulder and Scully apprehend the man at the station. He claims that since the bombardment his shadow has become dark matter – a deadly black hole – and that the government are after him. The people died when his shadow accidentally touched them. Moved off the case by the local police force, Mulder contacts X, who attempts to rescue Banton. Another death in the Polarity Magnetics lab seems to indicate that Banton killed himself, but Mulder instead suspects that Dr Davey – who was secretly working for the government – has been disposed of. X and his associates embark on a programme to investigate Banton.

Don't Be in the Teaser: Patrick Neuwith, a tobacco company executive, is reduced to a pile of carbon.

How Did He Do That?: How did Mulder so swiftly notice the 'killer' on the video tape?

Scully's Rational Explanation of the Week: Despite all that she's seen recently, Scully is still sceptical. Mulder says that he suspects that it's all down to spontaneous human combustion; Scully says that there's no scientific proof for this. By the time she comes round to this theory, Mulder has moved on to a new idea.

Dialogue Triumphs: Scully: 'Nonsensical repetitive behaviour is a common trait of mental illness.' Mulder: 'You trying to tell me something?'

Mulder: 'As a favour, we just handed over an A-bomb to the boy scouts.'

The Conspiracy Starts at Closing Time: Davey was working for the government; Banton fears a 'brain suck' that will reveal all his secrets. With good reason: X, too, is interested in the man. (Why, though, does he let him go after the initial botched attempt? Do they recognise each other, and has X already decided to kill Davey?) X is still annoyed that his identity has been revealed to Mulder's associates (presumably meaning Scully and Skinner – see 'End Game'), although Mulder says that he can trust them. X claims not to have killed Banton (which is true: though it seems he kills Davey), but his sinister agenda means that Mulder won't contact him again. 'You're choosing a dangerous time to go it alone, Agent Mulder,' says X, who also talks about his 'loyalty' to his predecessor. Mulder suspects that X is merely using him as his 'stalking horse', that is, relying on his ability to find the mysterious and supernatural so that X can steal it for his masters. (But that's simply untrue, and presumably X is all too eager for Mulder to resume their relationship so that he can continue to betray the Conspiracy.) Kidnapping Banton so that the Conspiracy can steal his knowledge of this useful new weapon (which they presumably want to use either for or against the Colonists) is presumably the sort of everyday work X does for the Conspiracy. (Having Mulder appear in the middle of his 'day job' must make him feel very insecure.) The 'brain suck', while it resembles the Conspiracy's ability to record people's memories or erase them, isn't something we've seen them use before. Those who work around the fringes of the Conspiracy's world (such as Banton) seem to fear the tales they've heard of such things.

Continuity: There's a lovely moment in homage to Eugene Tooms when Scully looks at the ventilation grille in the dead man's room. ('You don't think anybody could squeeze in there?' 'You never know!') Scully implies that she has been on the receiving end of sexual discrimination within the Bureau.

The Truth: Thanks to Banton's 'two-billion-megawatt X-ray', his shadow – thrown by harsh light – is deadly dark matter that kills humans on contact (but oddly it has no effect on inorganic matter).

Trivia: The cigarette company executive worked for Morley's, the brand that the Cigarette-Smoking Man finally favoured. Scully says she intends to buy Mulder a 'utility belt' for his birthday, indicating a knowledge of *Batman* (either the comics or, more likely, the TV series).

Scientific Comment: Probably the worst episode scientifically because they were trying to be scientific. It's stated that quantum particles, neutrinos, gluons, mesons and quarks are dark matter and that no one knows if these really exist. Problems with this: A: Everything obeys quantum mechanics so everything is a quantum particle. It's a meaningless description. B: Neutrinos and mesons can be detected, so definitely do exist. The presence of three quarks in a particle has been seen through diffraction, so there's very strong evidence that they exist. C: The nature of dark matter has not been determined. It's known to exist because the behaviour of galaxies and galaxy clusters does not fit with the gravitational forces you'd expect for the amount of mass that you can see. The dark matter (that is, simply, the matter that's not alight like a star is) must be there to provide the mass, but must be dark so we can't see it. Suggestions for what it is range from massive black holes, brown dwarfs, white dwarfs, mini black holes and massive neutrinos, to as yet undiscovered elementary particles, e.g. Weakly Interacting Massive Particles (WIMPs). It's the elementary-particle explanation that *The X-Files* seems to be going for. Also, there are problems with burning the man's shadow into the wall: (i): If the elementary particle hasn't been discovered yet it must be difficult to detect. That means its interaction with matter would be very weak and it would go straight through objects (including people) without affecting them (like a neutrino); (ii): Even if the particles would produce an effect like this, why didn't the chairs, desks and so forth get their shadows burnt in as well? Also, it's stated that the shadow is like a black hole, splitting molecules into atoms, unzipping electrons from their orbits and changing matter to energy. Problems with this: (a): A black hole doesn't do any of that. A heat source would split the molecules and ionise the atoms. (b): If the shadow is like a black hole it should have a strong gravitational attraction and pull things towards it. You wouldn't have to be touching it. (c): Why don't non-organic things fall in?

The Bottom Line: MD: A great central idea – a reverse on *Peter Pan* with a deadly rather than an absent shadow – is somewhat marred by its bland execution, although there is still much to enjoy here. The scene where Ryan and her 'boss' stop Mulder and Scully questioning Dr Banton is great: while Scully makes a valid point about Ryan's struggle for survival in 'the boy's club', you just want to punch Detective Ryan's lights out ('We'll call you if there's any more you can do,' she says patronisingly, after Mulder and Scully have just solved her case for her). And then, of course, she dies in tragic circumstances, and you feel really bad . . . The ending is superb.

KT: 'My shadow isn't me . . .' The 'forgotten' X-File (I didn't remember this at all when rewatching it for this review). There are a few oddities here (Scully's line 'You don't have a clue, do you?' suggests she believes that Mulder often makes up his investigations as he goes along, which may be true (see How Did He Do That?) but it is not the impression she normally gives). There are some powerful scenes, but the episode does have something of a feeling of going through the motions. For Vince Gilligan, life would never be the same again!

PC: Very bland, but with a nice and odd twist on X to stop us from trusting him too much. I really hate it when the series gets scientific things like 'dark matter' so wrong, though, especially when they could have so easily made up something fictional.

48: 'Our Town'

US Transmission: 12 May 1995
UK Transmission: 1 August 1995 (Sky One)/
20 February 1996 (BBC1)
Writer: Frank Spotnitz
Director: Rob Bowman
Cast: Caroline Kava (Doris Kearns),
John Milford (Walter Chaco),
Gary Grubbs (Sheriff Tom Arens),
Timothy Webber (Jess Harold),
John MacLaren (George Kearns),
Robin Mossley (Dr Vance Randolph),
Gabrielle Miller (Paula Gray),

Hrothgar Mathews (Creighton Jones),
Robert Moloney (Worker), Carrie Cain Sparks (Maid)

Mulder and Scully's latest case is the disappearance of an inspector at Chaco Chicken's poultry processing plant. Despite a strange fire witnessed on the night of the man's disappearance, the case seems nothing out of the ordinary, and the local sheriff believes that he was leaving his wife for another woman. However, the man was about to recommend the closure of the plant on health and safety grounds, and a young woman working there suffers a psychotic episode and is shot. An autopsy reveals that she was suffering from Creutzfeldt-Jakob Disease, while her records show that she should be forty-seven years old. Mulder orders the dredging of the local river, which reveals numerous skeletons stretching back many years. Scully is almost the next victim of the area's cannibalistic cult, but she is saved by Mulder.

Don't Be in the Teaser: George Kearns is in for more than a bit of rumpy-pumpy in the foggy woods.

How Did He Do That?: If it weren't for the truck driver having a fit just as Mulder is driving along it is doubtful that he would ever have thought of getting the river dredged.

Scully Here is a Medical Doctor: Her autopsy on Paula Gray shows conclusive evidence of CJD, which is, er, as rare as hen's teeth. Do you think the people who abducted her were actually British farmers?

Scully's Rational Explanation of the Week: Bonfires explain the scorch marks in the field (the sheriff suggests an 'illegal trash burn').

Phwoar!: Mulder strokes Scully's hair after he rescues her from the headlock.

Dialogue Triumphs: Scully: 'She claims that she saw some kind of a fox-fire spirit. I'm surprised she didn't call Oprah as soon as she got off the phone with the police.'

Mr Chaco: 'Not many people I know are as useful as these chickens!'

Continuity: Mulder says that a documentary on an asylum he saw in college gave him nightmares (Scully: 'I didn't think anything gave you nightmares.' Mulder: 'I was young . . .').

The Truth: All the guff about fire spirits is a complete red herring. Walter Chaco has been educating the townsfolk in the delights and benefits of cannibalism, chief of which among the latter seems to be the absence of ageing. He lived with a cannibalistic tribe in New Guinea in 1944. Presumably the presence of the CJD prion in Kearns's spinal tissue spread it to the other townsfolk. Chaco Chicken (slogan 'Good People, Good Food!') seems not to be implicated, despite the fact that the creatures are being fed on the ground remains of the unusable bits from dead hens.

Scientific Comment: CJD doesn't develop in ten weeks; it's certainly not time for an epidemic to develop. During the autopsy, Mulder looks at a slice of Paula's brain, but her head is still intact. Wasn't aware you could do that!

The Bottom Line: MD: An explicit take on the BSE crisis. It starts brilliantly, but peters out just a tad towards the end: what works well via innuendo and suggestion (cannibalism, small-town niceness) just looks plain daft when presented unblinkingly. The spectacle of townsfolk queuing up for their spoonful of human stew from the big pot seems silly, and the ending reeks of *Scooby Doo*. You're just dying for Mulder to say 'Sheriff Arens!??!' after ripping his mask off. Plus, we've got Scully in jeopardy again. Oh, and for a series that prides itself on its gruesome special effects, the head Paula sees on a spike is rubbish beyond description.

KT: 'Who knows, Scully? This could turn out to be even more interesting than fox-fires.' I don't think this has anything to do with BSE (despite Scully's throwaway line about cows being burnt to stop the spread of 'mad-cow disease'). I'm not convinced that this worry had reached the American consciousness yet and the winter 1995 CJD panic was still months away when this episode was first broadcast. On the contrary, it's actually an age-old variant on the 'small town with hidden secrets' strain of writing (is a town of cannibals any more ridiculous than a town full of Satanists?

Discuss . . .). Taken as a piece of modern gothic Americana, it works on most levels (I love the bit where Scully looks at the skeletons, thinks about what Mulder has been suggesting regarding what's in the food supply, and elects not to eat her family bucket of Chaco Chicken!).

PC: I agree with Marty: cannibalism's one thing, but all the ritualistic trappings are another. It'd be scarier if they ate people blandly and coolly, as real cannibals (not that anybody's ever proved there ever were any such people on an organised basis) probably did.

49: 'Anasazi'

US Transmission: 19 May 1995
UK Transmission: 9 August 1995 (Sky One)/
27 February 1996 (BBC1)
Writers: Chris Carter,
from a story by David Duchovny, Chris Carter
Director: R.W. Goodwin
Cast: Floyd 'Red Crow' Westerman (Albert Hosteen),
Renae Morriseau (Josephine Doane),
Dakota House (Eric Hosteen),
Bernie Coulson (Kenneth Soona), Aurelio Dinunzio (Antonio),
Byron Chief Moon (Father), Mitch Davies (Stealth Man)

A hacker nicknamed the Thinker has gained access to a classified Defense Department file which details the international Conspiracy that has kept the existence of extraterrestrials a secret since the 1940s. The file has been encoded into Navajo. Mulder, who complains of not having been able to sleep, attacks Skinner and risks being thrown out of the FBI. Meanwhile, the Cigarette-Smoking Man discusses developments with Mulder's father, who is implicated in the cover-up. Bill Mulder asks Fox to come to see him, but before he can tell his son of his involvement he is shot by an assassin. Scully, hoping to clear her partner's name, takes Mulder's gun away for ballistics analysis, but this leaves him vulnerable to attack by the assassin – Krycek. Scully is forced to shoot Mulder to prevent him from killing Krycek, and reveals that LSD or amphetamines have been pumped into Mulder's water supply in an attempt to induce psychotic behaviour. Scully takes a recovering Mulder to New Mexico, where Albert Hosteen, a Navajo, translates the Top Secret files. Mulder is shown an old boxcar, revealed by a recent earthquake, which is full of seemingly alien corpses. However, troops under the command of the Cigarette-Smoking Man unknowingly torch the enclosed metal carriage with Mulder inside . . .

Don't Be in the Teaser: The box car is uncovered. Amazingly, no one dies.

That's a Mouthful: The Cigarette-Smoking Man: 'As always, maintain plausible denial. The files are only as real as their possible authentication.' And: 'I strongly encourage you in that event . . . to deny everything.'

Phwoar!: Scully starts taking Mulder's clothes off and tells him to lie down on her bed . . . because he's ill. Plus, an interesting shot of Mulder in his boxers.

Dialogue Triumphs: Mulder (after the Lone Gunmen tell him about the 'trained killers' who are following them): 'You boys been defacing library books again?'

The Thinker: 'I don't want you to know my real name – I just don't think it's that important that you know.' Mulder: 'Sounds like a line I used in a bar once.'

Mulder on the fourth commandment and alien life: 'The part where God made heaven and Earth but didn't tell anyone about his side projects . . .'

The Conspiracy Starts at Closing Time: The Conspiracy involves representatives from Italy, Japan and Germany. It probably includes many more, perhaps those listed in 'E.B.E.'. Bill Mulder's involvement stretches back to the 1940s. He has kept this secret from his son ('Forgive me,' he says, as he dies in his son's arms), he and the Cigarette-Smoking Man having agreed never to meet again (so Bill at least attempted to retire, presumably thinking he could inform Fox of the terrible things that were going to happen when they were imminent, or that his son would uncover everything in time). The Cigarette-

Smoking Man claims to have protected Fox Mulder until now. (He's telling the truth.) When Mulder calls for X he does not turn up (see 'Soft Light'). Scully's name is in the Top Secret file, along with Duane Barry's. It has something to do with 'a test' (see 'Nisei' and '731'), so the experiments on human beings are concerned with more than stealing ova. (Perhaps they're intended to fully discern the weaknesses of human biology? Perhaps the Colonists have gone so far as to prepare humanity to be consumed by the Black Oil by programming human genes to produce specific individuals intended to play host to specific Colonists? Maybe that's how it's become obvious to everyone that the date of the Colonisation is close at hand: that those individuals have started to be born.) The Cigarette-Smoking Man says that Fox's father was the originator of the Project, but this is not substantiated, except in fictional form in dialogue put into Deep Throat's mouth in 'Musings of . . .'. (Perhaps Bill Mulder was the first person to realise that resistance to the Colonists was impossible, and put forward the idea that if a group of humans cooperated, covertly preparing the ground for the Colonisation, rather than having the Colonists do it, then there would be time to find some way to resist.) The Cigarette-Smoking Man also tells Mulder that he did not authorise Bill Mulder's murder. (In the light of the attempted elimination of Krycek as a loose cannon later on, that may very well be true. Perhaps somebody else in the Conspiracy wanted Bill Mulder dead, and was getting tired of the Cigarette-Smoking Man protecting his friends. So the assassination attempt on Krycek was either the Conspiracy covering the fact that they and the Cigarette-Smoking Man sometimes have different ends, or the Cigarette-Smoking Man taking revenge.) After the War, Axis scientists, granted amnesty, experimented on 'merchandise', i.e. the beings Mulder finds the remains of in the boxcar. There are two possible alternatives concerning the nature of these beings: a): they were once human, hence the smallpox vaccination scar on one of them, and have been transformed via the injection of the Colonist virus solution over a period of time (like the corpses seen in the pilot episode, only prior to their deaths). Which means that the Conspiracy once carried out such experiments and have since abandoned them and discouraged them in others. Or b): these are what becomes of true Colonist/human hybrids, killed off when their Colonist nature became too obvious for them to pass for human. The smallpox vaccination scars in that case are evidence that they too are recorded in Bill Mulder's bank of genetic information concerning humanity, presumably with a note to the effect that such creatures aren't to be infested with the Black Oil upon Colonisation (the 'Chimera' found in 'Gethsemane' doesn't have a scar, but then, that would have invalidated the purpose for which that hybrid was chosen). These are not real Greys, Rebel Colonist hosts to the Black Oil, because the Conspiracy knows of the corpses' existence, yet still regard the killing of Greys as a rare event ('E.B.E.') and also because there would be no possible reason to vaccinate them. Therefore, it seems the secret railroad and human experimentation camps of '731' have been running for decades, and that the end result for the unfortunate subjects remains a mass death. The aliens who took the Anasazi six hundred years ago, and 'come here still', seem to have a similar preservation instinct to that of the ones who took the animals in 'Fearful Symmetry', and we might suppose that these are the Rebel Colonists.

Continuity: Scully's father told her about the use of Navajo in World War II codes. The Thinker was briefly mentioned in 'Colony'. The Cigarette-Smoking Man speaks fluent German. (Was he, perhaps, the liaison officer in the 1950s responsible for the Nazi scientists smuggled to the States at the end of the war? If he was Werner Von Braun's case officer, then he might, indirectly, be behind the entire American space programme (bet that would blow Mulder's mind!) and still have good enough contacts to effect the cutbacks mentioned in 'Space'.)

The Truth: See The Conspiracy Starts at Closing Time above.

Trivia: The Thinker is seen reading a book called *50 Greatest Conspiracies of All Time*. Chris Carter appears as one of the FBI agents interrogating Scully. R.W. Goodwin appears as a gardener.

The Bottom Line: MD: Plotted more tightly than a gnat's naughties, this is just marvellous, and the pinnacle of *The X-Files*' unique line in 'aliens-as-absence' stories. The twists and turns (how cleverly the woman who shoots her husband further down the corridor turns from being a piece of dramatic fluff into an intrinsic component of the plot) keep one on tenterhooks, and the sudden presentation of Mulder as a nutter is compelling.

KT: 'What is this?' 'The Holy Grail!' Like 'Little Green Men', I loathed this when it was first transmitted (how odd that the bookends of a slightly disappointing season should have been those that set my teeth on edge, rather than rubbish like 'Død Kalm'). Now, rewatching it, I can't believe how wrong I was. The episode is a bit cluttered (Krycek seems only to be there for Mulder to beat up – Nick Lea hardly gets to utter a word) with far too many plot strands being laid down for a conclusion that could never hope to deliver all of the answers. But, for all that, the ideas are impressive: turning Daddy Mulder into a dark figure; Fox going to pieces; the first example of 'Skinner Baiting' as a sport (see 'Piper Maru', 'Pusher' and others), and the amazingly well-handled climax. From here in, the series was about to deliver.

PC: Yes, this sets things up nicely for the next season. You can almost hear the clunk of the series moving up a gear as decisions start to be made regarding the nature of the aliens and the Conspiracy. In many ways, that gear is reverse, because things we've assumed concerning Scully's abduction and the aliens are overturned in order to give the series a more distant sell-by date. The mysteries are taken further away, and we're told that what we've seen so far is horrid, but actually quite ordinary. I like that a lot, and I like the final coherence of this trilogy. If it had gone wrong, though, it could have smelt worse than those poor things in the boxcar.

Third Season

24 45-minute episodes

Created by Chris Carter

Co-Producer: Paul Rabwin
Producers: Rob Bowman, Joseph Patrick Finn,
Kim Manners
Supervising Producer: Charles Grant Craig
Co-Executive Producers: R.W. Goodwin, Howard Gordon
Executive Producer: Chris Carter

Regular Cast: David Duchovny (Special Agent Fox Mulder), Gillian Anderson (Special Agent Dana Scully), William B. Davis (The Cigarette-Smoking Man, 50, 51, 59, 65, 70, 72, 73), Jerry Hardin (Deep Throat, 50, 73[12]), Sheila Larken (Margaret Scully, 50, 51, 72), Tom Braidwood (Melvin Frohike, 50, 51, 58, 65, 72), Dean Haglund (Langly, 51, 58, 65, 72), Bruce Harwood (John Byers, 51, 58, 65, 72), Mitch Pileggi (Assistant Director Walter Skinner, 50, 51, 58, 63–66, 70, 72, 73), Raymond J. Barry (Senator Richard Matheson, 58), Steven Williams (X, 58, 59, 72, 73), Nicholas Lea (Alex Krycek, 50, 51, 64, 65), Michael David Simms (Senior Agent, 50, 70[13]), Melinda McGraw (Melissa Scully, 50, 51), Tegan Moss (Young Dana Scully, 64), Peter Donat (Bill Mulder, 50, 51, 73[14]), Rebecca Toolan (Teena Mulder, 50, 51, 73), Lenno Britos (Luiz Cardinal, 50, 51, 64, 65), Ernie Foort (FBI Gate Guard, 50, 66), John Moore (2nd Elder, 50,[15] 51[16]), John Neville (Well-Manicured Man, 50, 51, 65), Stanley Walsh (Other Elder,[17] 50, 64, 65), Don S. Williams (Elder, 50, 51, 59, 65[18]), Jaap Broeker (The Stupendous Yappi, 53, 69), Gillian Barber (Penny Northern, 58), Brendan Beiser (Agent Pendrell,

[12] Here playing an image of, and not the actual, Deep Throat.
[13] Credited as 'Senior FBI Agent' in this episode.
[14] Here playing an image of, and not the actual, Bill Mulder.
[15] Credited as '3rd Elder' in this episode.
[16] Credited as '3rd Elder' in this episode.
[17] Credited (confusingly) as '2nd Elder' in all his appearances.
[18] Credited as 'Elder 1' in this episode.

58, 59, 65, 70), Tyler Labine (Stoner, 61, 71), Nicole Parker (Chick, 61, 71), Morris Panych (Grey-Haired Man, 64, 70), Julia Arkos (Holly, 66), Robert Wisden (Robert Modell, 66), Brian Thompson (The Shapeshifter Assassin, 73[19])

50: 'The Blessing Way'

US Transmission: 22 September 1995
UK Transmission: 5 March 1996 (Sky One)/
12 September 1996 (BBC1)
Writer: Chris Carter
Director: R.W. Goodwin
Cast: Floyd 'Red Crow' Westerman (Albert Hosteen),
Alf Humphreys (Dr Pomerantz), Dakota House (Eric Hosteen),
Forbes Angus (MD), Benita Ha (Tour Guide),
Ian Victor (Minister), Tim Michael (Albert's Son),
Mitch Davies (Camouflage Man)

Mulder has apparently died in the boxcar fire. Scully is ambushed and forced to hand over her copy of the MJ files, and is suspended on her return to Washington. Her back-up tape is missing. The Cigarette-Smoking Man informs the Conspirators that Mulder is dead and that the files are recovered. Frohike tells Scully that the Thinker has been killed. Albert Hosteen and his Navajo comrades find Mulder in a hole in the desert, and set up a healing ceremony for him, during which he has visions of Deep Throat and of his father. Scully discovers an implant in the back of her neck, but gets only partway through a hypnotherapy session intended to establish how it got there. She visits Bill Mulder's funeral, where the Well-Manicured Man warns her that her life is in danger: she'll be killed either by somebody she trusts or a pair of assassins. She tries to stop her sister from coming to her apartment, but is intercepted by Skinner. Melissa is shot by Krycek's partner, who mistakes her for Dana. Meanwhile, Scully – distrustful of Skinner – tricks him into being held at gunpoint. He pulls out his gun too.

[19] Credited as 'The Pilot' in this episode, and universally known as the Alien Bounty Hunter, though this term is incorrect.

Don't Be in the Teaser: Albert and his relatives are roughed up. Mulder seems to be dead.

How Did He Do That?: Mulder gets out of the burning boxcar and into the rocks surrounding it! (To be fair, we know that two of the little mutants managed this in the past, so presumably there's a hole in the wall of the boxcar, with a narrow rock tunnel.)

Scully Here is a Medical Doctor: And like all good doctors, she doesn't try to treat herself.

That's a Mouthful: Even after he's dead, you can't shut Deep Throat up. 'Moving backward into the perpetual night. It consumes purpose and deed, all passion and will. I come to you, old friend, with the dull clarity of the dead . . .' Dull, yes, clear, no. Isn't it interesting that all of the 'dead' people in this episode talk in a mannered, poetic fashion (Deep Throat, Bill Mulder, even Fox himself in Scully's dream: 'I have returned from the dead to continue with you')? Maybe this is a device the dead use to convince the living that when they are speaking to them in dreams, it's illusion rather than reality! Or maybe it's just that somebody wants, desperately, to win an Emmy.

Phwoar!: Scully's purple pyjamas are . . . sort of sexy in that they're designed to be incredibly unsexy, and that's her all over. This episode sees an awful lot of Mulder undressed, being bathed and generally looking gorgeous.

Dialogue Triumphs: Mulder, on being told he must not change clothes or bathe for four days: 'That's really going to cut into my social life.'

The Well-Manicured Man: 'We predict the future. The best way to predict the future is to invent it.' (Or to put it more accurately, perhaps: 'We can't help what's going to happen, so we're going along with it for now.')

The Conspiracy Starts at Closing Time: The Conspirators are a kind of consortium, representing global interests (so Scully's continuing reduction of them to 'the government' is very naive). They meet in what seems to be a club, and have been working together for at least forty years. They include the Elder and the Well-Manicured Man, with at least six others. They have always handled the FBI 'internally' (through the Cigarette-Smoking Man, who is scared enough of the Conspiracy to lie and make excuses to them, and through Blevins). They can sway (but not, seemingly, control) federal judges. They have two standard ways of having somebody killed: a): one or two men do the killing, with an unregistered weapon, which they leave at the scene; they have false documents and immediately leave the country; b): somebody the victim trusts kills them. (These are an exact description of the working methods of human and Shapeshifter agents, the person of trust almost certainly being a Shapeshifter.) The Well-Manicured Man seems to think such killings unnecessary or, at least, that they have been poorly handled recently (by the Cigarette-Smoking Man). In 1972 (or 1973, according to the next episode), William Mulder was pictured with several members of the Conspiracy (including Deep Throat, the Cigarette-Smoking Man, the Well-Manicured Man and Klemper). They often used to visit the Mulder household. Bill was with the State Department (but that covers a multitude of sins). Vultures won't eat the corpses of the little Grey hybrids, presumably because their biology just doesn't smell like flesh to them. It's interesting that they're buried in a boxcar, which is still the chosen method of transportation for them these days ('731'), and near Los Alamos, where radiation releases would be harder to detect. (If we believe Mulder's research in 'Død Kalm', the Conspiracy have a facility there.) The Grey hybrids were killed by hydrogen cyanide.

Continuity: Scully has an implant in her neck (a computer chip), put there during her abduction, of which she has no recollection. Under hypnosis she says that she was afraid that she'd die, but she was cared for by a man. Was this one of the Conspiracy scientists ('Nisei'/'731')? Or maybe she's talking about Mulder looking after her in hospital ('One Breath'), or even the Cigarette-Smoking Man, who seems to be the one responsible for her swift release ('Zero Sum'). Her memory of the sounds is 'all screwed up' (a reaction to the drugs used to wipe her memory, or is this the effect of a 'sonic weapon', which in 'E.B.E.' Mulder suggests are used to fake an abduction experience?) During Scully's abduction an alarm sounded (a test, something routine, or was the place she was taken under attack from some enemy? Perhaps this was the ruse the CSM used to have her returned?). Scully says that she's not wearing her necklace today (see 'Deep Throat', 'Tooms', etc.). William Mulder is buried in Parkway Cemetery, Boston, Massachusetts. Scully is brought before the Office of Professional Conduct Articles of Review. She's given a leave of mandatory absence, with no pay or benefits, for direct disobedience, and has to hand in her weapon and badge. We see her key to Mulder's apartment (it's labelled 'Mulder'). Frohike describes Mulder as a good friend, 'a redwood among mere sprouts'.

The Truth: 'There is truth,' Deep Throat says about the afterlife, but then adds that there is 'no justice', without which the truth is meaningless. Then he paraphrases Nietzsche. So, are Mulder's experiences a genuine near-death glimpse into the afterlife, or a load of hallucinations? Mulder hears from his father, who tells him that he, Fox, will find the truth that will destroy him (Bill, that is, and he's presumably talking about having his sense of worth, or, since this is in Mulder's mind, his son's sense of his father's worth, destroyed, since he's already dead). This indicates (since, as far as Mulder is concerned, it turns out to be untrue: Bill Mulder wasn't completely responsible for the horrors caused by the Conspiracy) that all these visions really are from his imagination. Certainly, they all talk with the heightened language Mulder uses for his reports. Deep Throat is pontificating as always, and, as we have seen, represents the place as having truth, but not justice or judgement. (In other words, Mulder feels that, even though they're dead, this bunch of, literally, faceless men, to which his father and Deep Throat belong, have not been brought to justice.) His sister isn't there (this is death, and Mulder has faith that she's alive). It's interesting to speculate, however, that, beyond its archetypal and psychological reality, this place Mulder finds himself in may also be a physically real place. It's described as being a bridge between two worlds, having no time, and being a point of origin. We know that the Colonists can take people out of time quite literally (the missing nine minutes being one of the few concrete instances). The Holy People of the Navajo are summoned along this path, and the Anasazi are hinted to have been taken by aliens, after all. And the dead, in this series, do have somewhere they communicate from (Melissa, for instance, in 'Christmas Carol'). Certainly, this space is real enough for Mulder to communicate with Scully from it. (But that's the trouble with being reductionist about mystical experiences. The whole thing is subjective.) All of this isn't helped by Albert's non-committal answer to Mulder's question: 'It wasn't a dream?' 'Yes,' he says. Does he mean 'yes it was' or 'yes it wasn't'?

The Bottom Line: PC: The least satisfactory part of the trilogy, because not a lot happens, and what does looks alarmingly like the writer has lost control of the plot – a sort of giddy veer away from a through line. The crap second-hand poetry in the near-death experience doesn't help. Krycek's angst at killing the wrong person is a nice touch: he still believes in what he's doing at this point. And it's interesting how Scully's chat with Mulder's mum is a reflection of Mulder's chat with her mum in the previous season. There's also a great dissolve from spacey death to the Stars and Stripes. Oh, and the new version of the title music (and the shortened opening credits used for the next episode) is fab, a pulling in of the hems and cutting away of flab that reflects the new discipline this season was to impose upon the series.

MD: Another slow and reflective season opener, albeit one blessed with a wonderfully silly ending. The dream dialogue and Navajo narrative – you can tell this is a Chris Carter script, can't you? – do indeed wobble close to being purple prose of the worst kind, but for me this is an enjoyable and engrossing attempt to turn American TV into something more lyrical.

KT: 'These sons of bitches, they're rigging the game.' This is OK – another one where it seemed disappointing on first broadcast because we had all had six months to get worked up and expect a masterpiece. Terrific cliffhanger, and a good double bluff in making the audience briefly think that Skinner is Scully's would-be assassin. And we have John Neville, another great actor, given a part without any motivation and trying, desperately, to find a character in there. And succeeding.

51: 'Paper Clip'

US Transmission: 29 September 1995
UK Transmission: 12 March 1996 (Sky One)/
19 September 1996 (BBC1)
Writer: Chris Carter
Director: Rob Bowman
Cast: Walter Gotell (Klemper),
Floyd 'Red Crow' Westerman (Albert Hosteen),
Robert Lewis (ER Doctor), Peta Brookstone (ICU Nurse),
Martin Evans (Factotum), Stanley Walsh (2nd Elder)

Mulder arrives and halts the stand-off between Scully and Skinner. Skinner says he has Scully's copy of the tape. Scully's mother finds Melissa in hospital. Mulder takes the photograph of his father and the conspirators to the Lone Gunmen, who identify one of the men as the war criminal Victor Klemper. Mulder and Scully visit Klemper, who directs them to a disused mine, but then informs the Well-Manicured Man that Mulder is still alive. Klemper meets his death in suspicious circumstances shortly after. Albert Hosteen comes to the aid of Melissa, but when Skinner visits the ward he is attacked and the tape he is carrying is stolen. The Cigarette-Smoking Man, realising that the Conspirators are becoming aware of his bungling, violent methods, tries to kill Krycek with a car bomb, but it fails to destroy him or the tape. At the mine, Mulder and Scully find thousands of records of American citizens, complete with tissue samples. Mulder finds that a file on his sister was planned to be his. Scully encounters some small grey humanoids, while Mulder sees a vast spaceship overhead. Gunmen rush in, but the agents escape. Skinner tells them that he's come to an arrangement with the Cigarette-Smoking Man: he gets the only copy of the tape back, and Mulder and

Scully are in the clear. Although the Cigarette-Smoking Man knows that Skinner no longer has the tape, Skinner says that Hosteen and twenty other Navajo have memorised the contents of the tape. Melissa Scully dies.

Don't Be in the Teaser: Native Americans, bears, buffalo, all unscathed. It turns out that there's trouble in store for the buffalo's immediate family, though.

How Did He Do That?: How does Albert memorise the contents of the tape when Skinner loses it moments after meeting the guy for the first time? This is obviously part of an elaborate bluff on Skinner's part, as the Cigarette-Smoking Man guesses, but can't take the risk of trying to prove it so.

Scully's Rational Explanation of the Week: It's the Nazis. There were no experiments on or by aliens, just on and by humans.

That's a Mouthful: Skinner hangs out with the Cigarette-Smoking Man far too much in this episode: 'I just thought you should know of certain potentialities' and 'I'm quite aware of your policies in those regards.'

Phwoar!: It's lovely that Mulder can embrace Scully at the end and comfort her.

Dialogue Triumphs: Scully: 'I've heard the truth, Mulder. Now what I want are the answers.'

Skinner (relishing his escape from the power of the Cigarette-Smoking Man): 'This is where you pucker up and kiss my ass!'

Dialogue Disasters: Klemper's Dr Von Scott moment: 'Progress demands sacrifice!'

The Conspiracy Starts at Closing Time: The Conspiracy meet in a room, perhaps in a club, in New York City. One of them, the English Well-Manicured Man, seems to dislike the Cigarette-Smoking Man's violent methods of getting things done, because he sees them as inefficient and gaudy. The Cigarette-Smoking Man is a servant of this group, willing to lie to them to avoid exposing his failures. He's been handling 'security' for them, not very well. Skinner calls the Cigarette-Smoking Man 'sir', contemptuously, in this instance, but thinks that it would be hard for the Conspiracy to have him killed. They can, apparently, arrange deaths by botulism, heart attack or plane crash. (We've probably seen evidence of the latter in 'Red Museum'. They almost certainly bump off Klemper for saying too much.) The Well-Manicured Man tells Mulder and Scully that in 1947 a body was recovered from the Roswell UFO crash, and that Klemper used the knowledge gained there to try to create human/alien hybrids. This is either an attempt to keep Mulder at the same level of truth as Deep Throat maintained him on, that the nature of the Conspiracy concerns government infection of civilians with alien DNA, or the simple truth, that the Conspiracy initially tried to use the DNA in this fashion before their Colonist masters told them not to (or found out they were doing so). They're also told that William Mulder collected information on American citizens for use in disaster management after a nuclear war (the medical database covers almost every US citizen born since 1950), which is a lie, as is the detail that he objected to the use of the data in selecting citizens to be abducted and mutated, Bill Mulder having been up to his neck in the Conspiracy from the start. It's also a lie that Samantha, his daughter, was abducted to keep him silent. Rather, he wanted her abducted (or the CSM did) so that his genetic line would continue, even through hybrid clones. (See the movie entry for more information on this conclusion.) That may be why somebody (the CSM or Bill Mulder) changed the prospective abductee from Fox to Samantha, since it was discovered that this generation of hybrids were probably to be the last before Colonisation, so the collection of eggs, rather than information about what the future genetic line of the Mulders would be like, became the important thing. When the Elder, having despaired of the Cigarette-Smoking Man's latest excuse, calls up some 'friends' to help, he summons the armed men in CIA fleet sedans (who would, presumably, be usually under the Cigarette-Smoking Man's control). It seems unlikely that he summons the dirty great spaceship that hovers over the old mine, because here we have the series' first proof of the existence of Greys other than the Conspiracy's Grey hybrids (the second being in 'Tempus Fugit'). The presence of a single, tentatively exploring Grey (the one Scully sees in silhouette, the distinction from the Grey hybrids who run past her being underlined) is hardly the strong action that the Elder would expect a summoned ship to take, and the Conspiracy are just trying to move Mulder and Scully on at this point, not trying to make them believe in anything (and presumably, even if so, the Grey hybrids would have been enough to show to Scully). The large spaceship is also fairly similar to the one at the start of 'E.B.E.'. The Rebel Colonists seem to have learnt about this place, and sent one of their Greys in to have a look, just at the moment that the Conspiracy order it closed down. (Maybe the Rebel Colonists are interested in rescuing the Grey hybrids?) It boggles belief that the Grey hybrids are actually still living down there, but maybe we're dealing with a colony of escaped lab subjects.

Continuity: Scully has a recent tissue sample in her file (presumably taken during her abduction experience). There is no file on Fox Mulder. Samantha Ann Mulder is here stated to have been born on 21 November 1965, and her ID number on the file is 378671. The birth date flatly contradicts the one that Fox wrote down for her when he opened her X-File (see 'Conduit'). Since Bill Mulder created this database, it's probably his lie on display here. (It's pretty naff, actually, to turn over established continuity for the sake of a numerical in-joke.) Fox William Mulder was born on 13 October 1961, his (unused) ID number being 292544 (the numbering system would seem, then, to be based on date of birth, or date of abduction). Here, we're led to believe that the hatred Mrs Mulder feels towards her husband extends directly from his choosing Samantha rather than Fox to be 'abducted' (when she herself was unable to choose between the two of them). However, later events prove that the Cigarette-Smoking Man forced the Mulders' hand in choosing Samantha, his own daughter, either because he knew that he could protect her (and might want to have taken the opportunity to be a real father to her), or because he (and Bill Mulder, if he thought she was his) wanted his line to continue. The subsequent break-up of the marriage seems to be a vast case of guilt projection on Mrs Mulder's part. Scully knows Napier's constant off the top of her head: the Lisa Simpson of the FBI.

The Truth: Operation Paper Clip, the US plan to offer Nazi scientists sanctuary in return for their skills, was the project that brought Werner Von Braun to the USA and started the space programme. (All this is real-world true, astonishingly. In 1945, the British wanted Von Braun, the inventor of the Vl and V2 rockets, to be arrested for war crimes, but he was spirited out of Germany by the Americans.) But it continued after the 1950s. Victor Klemper, who had conducted medical experiments on Jewish subjects (it is implied that he was working either with or under Josef Mengele), arrived as part of the project, and either started to abduct humans and experiment on them, or aided in the Conspiracy's hybrid cloning programme. Perhaps the cloning only came later, when the aggressive nature of the quasi-hybrids became obvious. Bill Mulder is said to have been against these experiments, but, as we see later, as a close friend of Deep Throat and the Cigarette-Smoking Man, he is very much implicated in this, despite Mulder's cosy conclusion that he was acting under duress. In 'Musings of a Cigarette-Smoking Man', the whole scheme is even referred to as 'Bill Mulder's Project'.

Trivia: (Well, extreme seriousness, really ...) A white buffalo is born on the farm of a northern tribe of Native Americans, indicating great changes coming. The mother buffalo dies, seemingly sacrificing herself for her child in (yes!) a clunking great metaphor.

Scientific Comment: Napier's constant (e, as in log to the base e) is used as the door code. However, the writer screwed up. First of all, Scully is asked if she knows the formula for Napier's constant. It's a number, not a formula. Then Mulder asks Scully if 27828 is right and she says it is. But $e = 2.71828$, not 2.7828. The writer missed out the 1 (or at least David Duchovny did). But why have a coded door at all since there's an unlocked one at the other side of the hill?

The Bottom Line: PC: The closing coup by Albert is very satisfying, but, as with many of the Conspiracy episodes, that closure is partly a sigh of relief that next week they might get back to some monsters. *Sophie's Choice* is an original choice as this week's cultural quote. When I originally saw these three episodes, I was incredibly pissed off by them, thinking that Carter and Co. were deliberately sacrificing narrative coherency for a vague sense of paranoia, that they were never going to be able to tie all these threads together in a satisfactory way. In other words, that they'd decided the show was *Babylon 5*, but had improvised a master plan after the fact. In retrospect, seeing the Conspiracy episodes again for this guide, I've found them to be linked much better than I'd thought, the kind of intelligent, video-age television that I'd always argued for, where you have to look back over the page to understand. But that doesn't stop them from being very alienating for the casual viewer who's trying to follow the plot. Their success with the casual viewer suggests that, worryingly, it's possible to get by in series TV by just presenting a lot of atmosphere and gravitas in place of drama. In terms of fiction, it's nice to see Mulder so driven, and Scully acting on a leap of faith. The problems of the Conspiracy stories, and many other weaknesses in the format, were about to be dealt with in great style, in the best season of the series so far.

MD: A satisfyingly hectic conclusion to the trilogy.

KT: 'I don't work deals.' This is great. It's full of unanswered questions, though, which is a pity: why do Mrs Scully, and later Skinner, place such trust in this Navajo Indian they have only just met (especially as Skinner surely knows that nothing should be taken at face value)? There's a fine example of the 'Skinner-baiting' trend that would become farcical by the end of the season, with Krycek and mates kicking seven grades out of poor old Walter, but, again, why doesn't Krycek just kill Skinner? He must realise that he'll be identified by his former boss. And Klemper has all of the menace of American television's previous Nazi creation, Colonel Klink of *Hogan's Heroes*. There's a huge 'but' coming here though! The scene of Mulder seeing the spaceship is one of *the* moments on *The X-Files*. Final proof that everything he has always believed in is for real, and Scully's not with him! Of course, she's busy having her own close encounter.

52: 'D.P.O.'

US Transmission: 6 October 1995
UK Transmission: 19 March 1996 (Sky One)/
26 September 1996 (BBC1)
Writer: Howard Gordon
Director: Kim Manners
Cast: Giovanni Ribisi (Darren Peter Oswald),
Jack Black (Zero), Ernie Lively (Sheriff Teller),
Karen Witter (Sharon Kiveat), Steve Makaj (Frank Kiveat),
Peter Anderson (Stan Buxton), Kate Robbins (Mrs Oswald),
Mar Andersons (Jack Hammond),
Brent Chapman (Traffic Cop),
Jason Anthony Griffith (First Paramedic)

A series of probable electrocutions bring Mulder and Scully to the countryside around a lightning research centre. They find a local car mechanic who survived a strike, and was near one of the fatal ones. Darren Peter Oswald proves to be a frustrated kid with a crush on his former remedial teacher and an ability to conduct lightning and manipulate electrical objects. He restarts his boss's heart after causing him to have a cardiac arrest, and Mulder and Scully have Oswald arrested, although he is released by the sceptical local sheriff. Oswald kidnaps his teacher, having killed his best friend in a fit of pique. Cornered, he summons the lightning again, but this time it hits him. Oswald survives, and is locked up, his electrical powers apparently returning.

Don't Be in the Teaser: Jack Hammond, who makes the crucial *X-Files* error of 'Shoving the Weird Kid Around', gets zapped in his car.

How Did He Do That?: Mulder takes some tiny anomalies and makes a case out of them. When he begins to guess that Oswald can conduct or control lightning he does at least admit that 'It's a leap'.

Scully Here is a Medical Doctor: 'Based on my opinion as a medical doctor . . .' She does an autopsy on the charred body of one victim.

Ooze: Mulder's melting cellphone appears to exude treacle!

Scully's Rational Explanation of the Week: Erm, no: the first sign that this season they're trying to get away from the comedic inevitability of her doubts. She highlights the statistical improbabilities of lightning striking so many times, and challenges the police chief's rational explanation.

Phwoar!: Scully has used that vast FBI fashion budget to get herself some vampy sunglasses.

Dialogue Triumphs: Mulder (admiring Scully's plaster cast of a boot print): 'That's great. Now can you make me a little cherub that squirts water?'

The Truth: Darren Oswald, having survived being struck by lightning, gains an electrolyte imbalance and a conductive body (unless these qualities were latent in him already), can affect all manner of electrical systems, and attract lightning.

Trivia: Mulder is familiar with T.S. Eliot ('April is the cruellest month'). For a story that depicts a Stephen King community, there's appropriately a lot of pop music involved, including james's 'Ring the Bells' on the jukebox, Filter's 'Hey Man, Nice Shot', the under-car view set-up from Bruce Springsteen's 'I'm On Fire' video, and T-shirts celebrating the Vandals (whose memorable song is 'Live Fast, Diarrhoea'). The Rosemarys play 'Mary Beth Clark I Love You' on TV, which is actually an excuse to name her, J. Hartling and Deb Brown, all Internet fans. The Astadourian Lightning Observatory is named after Chris Carter's PA, Mary Astadourian.

Scientific Comment: It's stated that lightning emits radio waves at a particular frequency: 8 cycles/sec. It does emit radio waves, but not just at one particular frequency.

The Bottom Line: PC: Mulder and Scully's version of Arkham Asylum continues to fill up with weird kids. The atmosphere of small-town yuck is very nicely drawn, and it's good to get back to weird kids and monsters, though the ending is (necessarily this time, I think) arbitrary. Chris Carter's credit is shown inside the drama itself at the end, on a television set that Oswald is watching, which says all sorts of things about how the series has become a defining and limiting factor in exactly the sort of mythology that Mulder investigates (an idea which it would later take Darin Morgan to mine effectively). One of these characters really should say: 'This is like an episode of *The X-Files*!' But Carter probably just thought it looked cute.

MD: I thought this was lame and bland in the extreme, with many ridiculous elements (the cop who knows all about lightning because there's a research station nearby, which we never see and has no bearing on the story) and a plot that's so slight it threatens to vanish without trace at any moment. Instead, events limp along via such contrived notions as the sheriff releasing the kid from jail. The fact that from the outset the audience knows what's going on ensures that 'D.P.O.' has about as much tension as an average episode of *George and Mildred*.

KT: 'Bummer!' As far back as 'Deep Throat' (episode two!) I discovered the series had a real problem with presenting Generation X as anything other than a joke. Here it is turned into full-blown paranoia of the worst middle-aged, middle-class bollocks imaginable. And yet, for all that, the episode is quite tasty in places. Even the groan-inducing 'He is lightning, we have to get to him before he strikes again' line (think about it!) doesn't blow it. It's Son of *Firestarter* of course, but with a mad, stressed-out quality that grows on you.

53: 'Clyde Bruckman's Final Repose'

US Transmission: 13 October 1995
UK Transmission: 26 March 1996 (Sky One)/
3 October 1996 (BBC1)
Writer: Darin Morgan
Director: David Nutter
Cast: Peter Boyle (Clyde Bruckman), Stu Charno (Puppet),
Frank Cassini (Detective Cline),
Dwight McFee (Detective Havez),
Alex Diakun (Tarot Dealer), Karin Konoval (Madame Zelma),
Ken Roberts (Clerk), David MacKay (Mr Gordon),
Greg Anderson (Photographer)

Fortune-tellers are being murdered by a serial killer. A mystic, the Stupendous Yappi, is called in to psychically trace the killer, but Mulder is sceptical of the man's abilities. Another body is found by an insurance salesman, Clyde Bruckman, who seems to be cursed with the ability to know how people are going to die. Bruckman foresees Mulder's murder by the killer, and predicts that Scully will hold his own hand in bed. The killer comes after Bruckman, as he had expected, but Mulder chases and, thanks to Bruckman's warning and Scully's intervention, emerges unscathed. Bruckman, however, has taken an overdose, Scully holding his hand as he dies.

Don't Be in the Teaser: Madame Zelma fails to foresee being murdered.

How Did He Do That?: Mulder leaps to the conclusion that Bruckman is precognitive, rather than the more obvious one that he's the killer. He's 'got a feeling' about it.

Scully Here is a Medical Doctor: She performs an autopsy off-screen.

Ooze: Blood, entrails, eyeballs, mud, putridity and liquescence.

Scully's Rational Explanation of the Week: She and Mulder think that Yappi is just playing the odds. People see what they want to see, and Clyde is just lucky. 'I'm not one who readily believes that kind of thing.'

Phwoar!: Scully deals with Bruckman's pass with sublime calm: 'There are hits, and there are misses, and then there are misses.'

Dialogue Triumphs: Scully to Mulder, after the latter has been expelled from the room by Yappi because of his scepticism: 'I can't take you anywhere.'

Mulder: 'Mr Yappi, read this thought: –'

Bruckman reading Mulder's badge: 'I'm supposed to believe that's a real name?'

Mulder's wonderful reaction to Bruckman's apparently precognitive verdict of auto-erotic asphyxiation: 'Why are you telling *me* that?'

Bruckman to the killer: 'You do the things you do because . . . you're a homicidal maniac.'

Continuity: Scully refers to Ahab, who died, like Macbeth, because he misinterpreted a prophecy. (In 'Quagmire', we're hammered over the head with a Mulder-as-Ahab metaphor, but here he successfully interprets the prophecy, so is Mulder someday going to fall into this trap again? We may have already seen this thread play out, as he nearly falls victim to the words of a Cassandra (in 'Demons') and just as wrongly fails to believe another (in 'Patient X').) Scully, asking how she's going to die, is told, 'You don't.' Does this mean that Scully is going to get lost in 'missing time' for ever? Or does Bruckman simply mean that when Scully thinks she's going to die (of cancer), she will in the end be saved? (Bruckman's words must occur to her during that ordeal.) Or is Bruckman just being very nice to the object of his desire? Mulder isn't convinced by the reading of tea leaves, and claims not to be a Freudian (despite his Oxford degree in psychology), but he does believe in psychic ability (if not Yappi's!). He's had prophetic dreams (we see an example in 'Paper Hearts'). Bruckman misidentifies a bit of cloth as having come from Mulder's New York Knicks T-shirt, in a neat reversal reference to 'Beyond the Sea'. Satanists usually take the eyeballs and leave the body, according to Mulder, which indicates that he has investigated Satanic cults before. Scully gets to keep Mrs Lowe's dog at the end of the episode (see 'War of the Coprophages', 'Quagmire').

The Truth: Ever since he reflected on the circumstances of the Big Bopper's death in 1959, Clyde Bruckman can calculate how anybody is going to die. The universe thus seems preordained. But then a chaotic element suggests that that may not be completely true. If Bruckman was talking about himself, and not Mulder, when he referred to auto-erotic asphyxiation being an undignified way to die, he commits suicide in a more dignified way as soon as he realises that there actually is such a thing as free will.

Trivia: Bruckman's non-winning lottery numbers (if anybody fancies trying this) are 9, 13, 37, 39, 41 and 45. (The winners are all one digit lower.) *Midnight Inquisitor* is a tacky national tabloid. References are made to J.D. Salinger, Madonna and Kato Kalin, and to Buddy Holly returning from the dead to do the Lollapalooza tour with the Crickets. Mulder (inevitably!) quotes from 'Chantilly Lace' ('You *know* what I like'). Jaap (pronounced 'yapp') Broeker is actually David Duchovny's stand-in. When playing cards with Scully, Bruckman holds 'dead man's hand' (aces and eights), the poker hand that Sheriff 'Wild Bill' Hickok was holding when he was shot in the back. Interestingly, it is said that carrying a (real) dead man's hand will ensure a restful night's sleep. Several of the character names in this episode are drawn from the silent comedy film era, including Clyde Bruckman himself, who directed films by Laurel and Hardy and W.C. Fields among others. (One of his films plays in the *Space: Above and Beyond* episode 'R&R', in which David Duchovny appeared, which was written by Darin Morgan's brother Glen.) The hotel the killer works at is El Damfino, a nod to Buster Keaton's boat Damfino in *The Boat*. Detective Cline is named after the silent movie director Eddie Cline. Detective Havez is named after Jean C. Havez, a collaborator with the original Clyde Bruckman. The dead man under the car is Claude Dukenfield, which was the real name of W.C. Fields (another Bruckman associate). Scully watches the Laurel and Hardy movie, *The Bullfighters* (1941), their final movie for Fox during their twilight years. (It's interesting that old comedy, with all the alienation of time passing that it implies, and its contrast with the glossy production on display here, is used as a metaphor for mystery and the occult in this . . . . . 'Syzygy').)

The Bottom Line: PC: What an extraordinary piece of work. The story concerns the nature of freedom of choice, following two men who see reality as predetermined. One becomes a psychotic killer (because he can?) while the other becomes resigned and sells insurance. There are all sorts of sidelong commentaries on the nature of free will, from the dog's ghoulish actions, for which he can't really be blamed, to Bruckman's oddly beautiful view of his own destruction. But a custard pie shows that the future is actually up for grabs. The usual ghoulish and comedic, as well as deeply insightful, joys of a Darin Morgan episode are all evident, and this story shows off something he's particularly good at: an ordinary person is the centre of the story, even favoured by the direction, and Mulder and Scully are seen from his distant, slightly alienated, point of view. Altogether gorgeous.

MD: Duller than a dull thing with dull knobs on. I mean, yes, it's all very clever and well acted, but it's extremely tedious, like watching metaphysical paint dry. What actually happens here, dramatically or literally? There's a constant undercutting of tension (Bruckman being more concerned by the nature of the pie than Mulder's fate) and even the *A Zed and Two Noughts*-style surrealism seems thrown in to make up for the complete absence of plot.

KT: '. . . And so was your old man!' I'm with Paul all the way on this one. A little gem that benefits from the funniest opening in *The X-Files* (the scene immediately after the introductory credits is astonishing) and loads of great little asides (Bruckman trying to sell Mulder insurance, 'Say "Hi" to the FBI', etc.). However, 'if coincidences are just coincidences why do they feel so contrived?' The episode runs entirely on coincidences, from Bruckman and the killer almost meeting in the pre-titles, to the 'highly improbable' safehousing of Bruckman in the very hotel where the killer works. I suspect Darin Morgan might be having another joke on his audience with this, but it reduces the impact of a brilliant episode.

PRIMETIME EMMY AWARDS

At the 1994 Emmy Awards ceremony *The X-Files* won a single award, that for Individual Achievement in Graphic Design and Title Sequences, won by James Castle, Bruce Bryant and Carol Johnsen. The next year was barren, despite seven nominations, but 1996 brought something of a bounty. This was the season that the series won five Emmys . . . Outstanding Writing in a Drama Series: Darin Morgan, for 'Clyde Bruckman's Final Repose'. Outstanding Guest Actor in a Drama Series: Peter Boyle, for 'Clyde Bruckman's Final Repose'. Outstanding Sound Editing for a Series: Thierry J. Couturier, for 'Nisei'. Outstanding Sound Mixing

PRIMETIME EMMY AWARDS

for a Drama Series: Michael Williamson, David West and Nello Torri, for 'Nisei'. Outstanding Individual Achievement in Cinematography for a Series: for 'Grotesque'. 1997's ceremony added three more awards to the total: Outstanding Individual Achievement in Art Direction for a Series: Graeme Murray. Outstanding Sound Editing for a Series: Thierry J. Couturier, for 'Tempus Fugit', and, best of all, a long-deserved win for Gillian Anderson as Outstanding Lead Actress.

54: 'The List'

US Transmission: 20 October 1995
UK Transmission: 2 April 1996 (Sky One)/
10 October 1996 (BBC1)
Writer: Chris Carter
Director: Chris Carter
Cast: Bokeem Woodbine (Sammon Roque),
Badja Djola (Napoleon 'Neech' Manley),
John Toles-Bey (John Speranza),
Ken Foree (Vincent Parmelly),
April Grace (Danielle Manley),
J.T. Walsh (Warden Leo Brodeur),
Greg Rogers (Danny Charez), Mitchell Kosterman (Fornier),
Paul Raskin (Ullrich), Denny Arnold (Key Guard),
Craig Brunanski (Guard), Joseph Patrick Finn (Chaplain),
Bruce Pinard (Perry Simon)

Taken to the electric chair, Napoleon 'Neech' Manley vows revenge. Days later, a prison guard is found murdered. Mulder and Scully discover that Neech had a list of five persecutors he was going to kill. Danielle, his widow, now has a new lover, having promised Neech that she would never love another. As more bodies are found, and all other explanations exhausted, Mulder and Scully fail to prevent the deaths of Danielle's lover and the brutal prison governor, Neech's revenge precisely concluded.

Don't Be in the Teaser: Neech Manley is executed, and we are spared none of the horrors of the electric chair. Mr Simon appears for only about thirty seconds, but he's dead meat, too.

Scully Here is a Medical Doctor: She questions the prison doctor about his autopsy, as though only her autopsies count.

Ooze: Maggots and peeling skin.

Scully's Rational Explanation of the Week: It's a conspiracy among prisoners and guards, with an uncaught accomplice.

Dialogue Triumphs: Scully, asked who would be on her hit list: 'I only get five?' (Which isn't like her at all, really.) Mulder responds, 'I remembered your birthday this year, didn't I, Scully?'

Scully, on Neech's wife's new partner: 'A woman gets lonely. Sometimes she can't wait around for a man to be reincarnated.'

Continuity: Scully mentions being taught by catechism, the first strong indication (beyond her cross necklace) that she was raised a Catholic.

The Truth: Neech has, somehow, returned to life, possibly in the form of various animals ('transmigration of the soul' as he calls it). The governor and the guards are involved in systematic abuse.

Trivia: The chaplain in the teaser is played by the series producer Joseph Patrick Finn.

The Bottom Line: PC: The series isn't good at doing heat: Vancouver doubles for Florida mostly using interiors. Carter raids the media cupboard again: *The Silence of the Lambs* (again), *Candyman*, *Shocker*, and *Pulp Fiction*. The pace is slower than a sloth watching county cricket, and the twist is that the supernatural shtick is ... exactly who and how we thought it was, right back to the teaser. The sheer professionalism of the series by now stops it being as dull as a dull first-season episode, but it's still pretty damn dull. At least Carter's social conscience is on display: capital punishment is shown as barbaric, the governor is keen to beat up his prisoners (killing them if necessary), and death row is the place where the US puts its black male prisoners.

MD: What Paul says about the good stuff is true, but what's saddest about this episode isn't so much its sampling of other texts, but its cannibalism of its own, being little more than a retread of 'Fresh Bones' (with a hint of 'Beyond the Sea' thrown in for good measure). As with the previous story, there's a crushing lack of drama, and a feeble ending that beggars belief. I'm really not sure that this is in any form an improvement over the less exciting first-season stories. Mind you, any actor with a name like Bokeem Woodbine deserves an Oscar or something in my book.

KT: 'I will return!' This is rubbish. Like all of the worst bits of every bad horror film you've ever seen stitched together into a long, disorganised, nasty mess. Good social themes and con-science, bad drama. Dreadfully incoherent ending too. Why are Mulder and Scully in this episode? They solve nothing, they achieve nothing. All that happens is that a lot of men die (some deservedly, though that's not really the point) and, at the end of the episode, Mulder and Scully leave town none the wiser – not only is there no closure, there's no point either.

55: '2Shy'

US Transmission: 3 November 1995
UK Transmission: 9 April 1996 (Sky One)/
27 February 1997 (BBC1)
Writer: Jeffrey Vlaming
Director: David Nutter
Cast: Timothy Carhart (Virgil Incanto),
Catherine Paolone (Ellen Kaminsky),
James Handy (Detective Alan Cross),
Kerry Sandomirsky (Joanne Steffen),
Aloka McLean (Jesse), Suzy Joachim (Jennifer),
Glynis Davies (Monica), Randi Lynne (Lauren Mackalvey),
William MacDonald (Agent Kazanjian)

A man on a blind date kills his companion in a car, covering her in a dissolving ooze. Scully discovers the nature of the ooze, and meets a sexist cop, while Mulder traces a suspect from similar previous killings, theorising that the man needs fatty tissue. The man kills again, and Mulder and Scully reason his identity from the poetry he quotes to lure victims to dates. They find his computer files, and alert every woman named in them. While Mulder is sidetracked, Scully protects the latest target and captures the killer.

Don't Be in the Teaser: Don't finish a date in a car overlooking Cleveland. You'll get cocooned like Lauren Mackalvey.

How Did He Do That?: For once, Mulder takes longer to reach the silly conclusion than the audience does.

Scully Here is a Medical Doctor: 'You're a medical doctor?' 'You sound surprised.' For once there isn't an autopsy, much to Scully's relief.

Ooze: Viscous hydrochloric acid plus traces of pepsin. It sucks the fat out of you, apparently.

Phwoar!: Mulder puts his arm around Scully in the police station, for no reason other than he likes it.

Dialogue Triumphs: Mulder: 'It's not the finely detailed insanity that you've come to expect from me . . .'

Dialogue Disasters: Reaction of a man with a prostitute on discovering a corpse: 'Uh-uh! Forget this!'

Continuity: Wendy Sparks, the Cleveland police department FBI liaison, knew of Mulder's expertise in serial killings (and weird stuff?).

The Truth: Virgil Incanto is a 'genetically different' human who needs fatty tissue to survive, and has been getting it in the most horrid way.

The Bottom Line: PC: Despite several dodgy moments (the world's most gorgeous hooker, a villain called Virgil Incanto, the idea that being a 'freelance translator of Italian literature' is a good living and that sixteenth-century Italian poetry would turn anybody on), this is a highly effective, and rather gooey, examination of the darker areas of the patriarchy. If the sexist cop is very clichéd, the further examination of a female nightmare is very subtle. Incanto's message that his victims don't have to do what's expected of them is extremely seductive, but it's a feminist message used to a sexist end. This monster preys, literally, on those with body-image problems (although, typically, Lauren is hardly some-body with 'a weight problem'). Scully is ambushed in a bathroom (again), but this time wins the bout, part of the third season's empowering of the character, and also apt for the story. The actor playing the killer is fab, he's given a great theme by Mark Snow, and the script is realistic about the frailty of human desire. At the end, Mulder and Scully's personal Arkham Asylum gets another inmate. Odd moment: Duchovny's weird and bad reaction shot on 'There is not going to be an autopsy'.

MD: Looks fine to me. Anyway, I like the feminism that runs through this story, as Paul indicates (most notably Scully and the 'victim' defeating the masculine manipulator), but it is a shame to watch *The X-Files* treading water so. This reminds one of an unused Tooms script, and it's not even that good.

KT: 'I don't know too many scorpions who surf the Inter-net.' It's a nice idea, using an Internet background to the murders, though only a technophobe would seriously suggest (as this episode seems to) that the medium is populated by ugly fat girls and psycho-killer men. And there's that cock-and-bull back story about that annoying woman who wants the killer to read her poems (her death doesn't come a minute too soon for this writer), and her blind daughter. Your point being, Jeffrey? OK, now, here's the Major Inconsistency: Incanto requires fat to replace a chemical imbalance in his body. An imbalance he has, presumably, had since birth (he tells Jesse as much). So, how did he survive until he dis-covered that he could suck fat from others? How old was he when he started killing? At least with Tooms there is a plausible explanation for why he's never been caught (he hibernates for thirty years between murder sprees). Incanto is an academic, which suggests a long period spent in education of one sort or another. How on Earth hasn't he made a mistake before now? (As a friend of mine pointed out shortly after this episode was broadcast, his school life must have been a laugh and a half: 'Now I'd like the person who sucked all of the fat out of Jennifer Smith in form 2B to own up . . .')

56: 'The Walk'

US Transmission: 10 November 1995
UK Transmission: 16 April 1996 (Sky One)/
6 March 1997 (BBC1)
Writer: John Shiban
Director: Rob Bowman
Cast: Thomas Kopache (General Thomas Callahan),
Willie Garson (Quinton 'Roach' Freely),
Don Thompson (Lt. Colonel Victor Stans),
Nancy Sorel (Captain Janet Draper),
Ian Tracey (Leonard 'Rappo' Trimble),
Paula Shaw (Ward Nurse), Deryl Hayes (Army Doctor),
Rob Lee (Amputee), Andrea Barclay (Frances Callahan),
Beatrice Zeilinger (Burly Nurse),
Brennan Kotowich (Trevor Callahan)

Mulder and Scully investigate a number of apparent suicide attempts at an army veterans' hospital, and find their way blocked by General Callahan. The ghost of a soldier seems to be haunting the place. After more deaths, Quinton Freely, a meek nurse, is arrested, since he delivered mail to all the victims' homes. But it turns out that he's working for Sergeant Leonard Trimble, an amputee who has killed all the victims remotely through some kind of telekinesis. Quinton is suffocated, and, his wife and child having been attacked, the general goes to execute Trimble, stopping when he realises that that's just what Trimble wants. One of Trimble's former victims, badly burnt, suffocates Trimble.

Don't Be in the Teaser: Lt. Col. Victor Stans fails to die by boiling himself; his third failed suicide in as many weeks ('He won't let us die').

How Did He Do That?: Mulder accuses a quadruple amputee of murder. Talk about going for it!

Ooze: Stans's face.

Scully's Rational Explanation of the Week: Shell-shock, post-traumatic stress syndrome, and (she's getting a bit more open-minded) she won't rule out Gulf War Syndrome. The general is protecting his men from prosecution for the murder of their families.

Dialogue Triumphs: Mulder: 'Sometimes the only sane response to an insane world is insanity.'

Trimble (to Scully): 'If I could leave my body right now, I could think of something else I'd rather be doing!'

Continuity: Scully is familiar with how to get her way in a military bureaucracy, doubtless a family life skill. Mulder is still writing his reports longhand into his journal.

The Truth: Trimble can use astral projection to affect objects at a distance, send backward phone messages, and appear as a remote image. He receives some help from Roach, stealing mail to provide Trimble with a 'psychic connection'.

Trivia: Trimble mentions Fred Astaire, while watching a Fred and Ginger movie.

Scientific Comment: If a dental X-ray plate was exposed to radiation it would be fogged all over, not show stripes; although, if it was covered by something like a comb, you'd get a picture of the comb.

The Bottom Line: PC: It's good to see Scully taking Mulder's side so much by now, as the third season's subtle character arcs get under way. There's a nice *Cat People* quote in the pool scene, which works because it surprises with a menace from another direction: inside the pool. It is also a surprise that dental X-rays can pick up astral projection, but a pleasant one that the series' only use of 'back-masking' is for a cool sound effect. This is, however, one of those stories in which the cause of the problem is obvious straight away, with an ending full of mock weight, and ends up being oddly dull.

MD: A definite improvement on previous stories, with a newish *modus operandi* and an age-old hatred of war on display.

KT: 'He kills our wives and children, but he won't let us die.' Hmmm . . . The swimming-pool scene, and little Trevor's death in his sandpit, are terrifying. But I can't help thinking this is just a series of nice set pieces strung together for effect. Mind you, a touch of Gulf War Guilt Syndrome (like Vietnam Guilt Syndrome but less defeat-orientated!) gives the episode a nice edge. And I love that line about people sitting at home watching the war on cable as if it was a video game. Which is exactly what I and, I suspect, most of the rest of the audience did, too. Part of an ongoing hidden agenda by the producers to get the viewer to confront his/her own demons (see also the next episode).

57: 'Oubliette'

US Transmission: 17 November 1995
UK Transmission: 23 April 1996 (Sky One)/
17 October 1996 (BBC1)
Writer: Charles Grant Craig
Director: Kim Manners
Cast: Tracey Ellis (Lucy Householder),
Michael Chieffo (Carl Wade), Jewel Staite (Amy Jacobs),
Ken Ryan (Special Agent Walt Eubanks),
Dean Wray (Tow Truck Driver), Jacques LaLonde (Henry),
David Fredericks (Mr Larken), Sidonie Boll (Myra Jacobs),
Robert Underwood (Paramedic),
Dolly Scarr (Fast Food Supervisor), Bonnie Hay (Woman),
David Lewis (Young Agent)

Amy Jacobs is kidnapped, and Lucy Householder, who was held for five years in similar circumstances, seems to know too much about the case. The blood from her nosebleed is of Amy's rather than her own blood group, and she becomes a suspect, despite Mulder's sympathy for her and his conviction that she's experiencing Amy's plight directly. Mulder and Scully track down the real kidnapper, Carl Wade. Lucy goes to the oubliette under Wade's house, where she was imprisoned long ago. Wade has already fled with Amy, but, from Lucy's reaction, Mulder realises where they are. Mulder shoots Wade in a nearby river. Amy stays underwater too long, but Lucy 'drowns' in her place, thus saving her and ending the trauma.

Don't Be in the Teaser: Amy Jacobs gets snatched from her bed, and, at the same time, Lucy falls into a mumbling trance.

How Did He Do That?: Mulder doesn't leap to the obvious weird conclusion in front of the others if it means that Lucy's a suspect. But the idea that, having been in front of dozens of witnesses when Amy was taken, she is a suspect at all strains credibility.

Scully Here is a Medical Doctor: She investigates the blood types of Amy and Lucy.

Scully's Rational Explanation of the Week: Mulder's identification of Lucy with his sister stops him acting rationally. Lucy is Wade's accomplice in a reverse abused/abuser scenario.

Phwoar!: Mulder is very huggable and vulnerable when he introduces a slight stutter into the line about his sister. The geek beneath the cool exterior is revealed.

Dialogue Triumphs: Mulder (in response to Scully's assertion about Samantha): 'Not everything I do and say and think and feel goes back to my sister . . .'

Continuity: Mulder seems to have a good working knowledge of resuscitation technique (standard FBI training?). Neither Mulder nor Scully seems to smoke. (Although we later learn that Scully has in the past and is apt to again upon mystical provocation ('Syzygy') and Mulder also gave up sometime in the nineties ('Travelers').)

The Truth: Lucy gains an instant empathy with Amy when she is kidnapped by the same man, to the extent of seeing what she sees, bleeding for her, and transporting water from her lungs into hers, breaking all sorts of physical laws. Mulder's explanation, 'empathic transference', is logically impossible, but seems to fit.

The Bottom Line: PC: This looks great, and manages to create another female nightmare without a hint of exploitation. The wet leafy countryside becomes a character, as it does in all the best episodes. Just a hint of the paranormal, and it doesn't detract from Amy's terrible situation in the slightest.

MD: Indeed, one of the better 'almost normal' episodes, though the pace is somewhat pedestrian. It's fascinating to observe that initially Scully is shown as pursuing a theory based on 'coincidence' (the second blood type found on Lucy's clothes) and Mulder is more interested in compassionately protecting a former victim.

KT: 'I've got my own set of problems now, thank you.' Kidnapping is a federal crime, so it's surprising that it has taken Mulder and Scully two years to get invited on to a case. Then again, this is a strange kidnapping. There's another *JFK* reference (the 'photo-cutting' scene). It's difficult to know exactly what the writer was trying to say here, except that no one is innocent. In a nutshell, this disturbing episode forces the viewer to focus on their own dark corners. Scully's normal persona of disbelief can be very irritating (e.g. 'The Calusari'), but in 'Oubliette' it would be downright insulting if the persecuted Lucy were a slightly more sympathetic character. But here is the problem: this poor woman has every reason to be pissed off given what she had been through. However, viewer expectation requires that she accept her fate without complaint. Which makes her sacrifice all the more upsetting. Not one to watch after a few beers if you're looking to get cheered up. Amy seems to be wearing her socks in bed. Hasn't anybody told her that they get covered in fluff when you do that?

58: 'Nisei'

US Transmission: 24 November 1995
UK Transmission: 30 April 1996 (Sky One)/
24 October 1996 (BBC1)
Writers: Chris Carter, Howard Gordon, Frank Spotnitz
Director: David Nutter
Cast: Stephen McHattie (Red-Haired Man),
Robert Ito (Dr Takeo Ishimaru),
Corrine Koslo (Lottie Holloway), Lori Triolo (Diane),
Paul McLean (Coast Guard Officer),
Yasuo Sakurai (Kazuo Sakurai)

A group of Japanese scientists examine an apparent alien in a railway car, and are killed. Mulder buys a video of the autopsy, and investigates the supplier, only to find that he's been murdered. At the scene, a Japanese agent is captured, but is freed when it is discovered that he is a high-ranking diplomat. His briefcase contains satellite photos of a ship and a list of local members of a UFO group, MUFON. Scully meets a group of former abductees, who recognise her as one of their number, and Mulder searches the shipyard, seeing a strange craft at the docks, apparently brought in on the ship. He is visited by Skinner, who says that the Japanese man has been murdered and that his briefcase is being sought. Mulder turns to Senator Matheson, who tells him to give the photos from the case back, for his own safety. Scully gets her implant examined, and remembers some details of her abduction, enough to recognise that one of the men who took her was a Japanese war criminal, who was in the railway car. Mulder finds a train carrying another apparent alien, and, despite Scully and X's pleas not to do so, boards it.

Don't Be in the Teaser: A group of Japanese scientists are shot down by armed men.

How Did He Do That?: How did Steven Zinzer get hold of a video copy of the autopsy and the murder of the scientists? That story about pulling it off the satellite at 2 a.m. sounds false, but can only be true, considering his fate. He must have just happened to intercept the Japanese scientists transmitting the images home (and, considering the contents of the diplomat's briefcase, he may have hacked one of their spy satellites too!).

Dialogue Triumphs: Scully, on the video: 'This is even hokier than the one they aired on the Fox network.'

On the green substance: 'Olive oil, snake oil . . . I suppose you think it's alien blood.'

The Conspiracy Starts at Closing Time: X knows exactly what Mulder is up to, indicating that he is under surveillance most of the time. He wants to get Mulder away from the boxcar, because he knows the Conspiracy have sent the Red-Haired Man to destroy it. Skinner is still acting suspiciously in wanting to recover the Japanese agent's briefcase, but, having broken ties with the Cigarette-Smoking Man, he probably just wants to avoid a diplomatic incident (and to protect Mulder and Scully – though when he realises the extent of the hot water they've got themselves into he backs off like a scalded cat). Scully remembers a bright, white place, a drill bit, and her stomach being distended. She bears a mark on the back of her neck from where the implant was extracted. Many of the abductees suffer from cancers, and are proved correct, eventually, in their belief that they will all be fatal, because the fools have all had their microchips removed! The doctors doing the autopsy on the dead Grey hybrid, and the soldiers who kill them, are protecting themselves, presumably from the green blood of the alien, an early indication that Grey hybrids are a later stage in the life of a human/Colonist hybrid. (Presumably, since the Grey hybrid Mulder finds in 'Gethsemane' hasn't got a chip in its neck, after a certain point control of the Black Oil inside the hybrid can't be maintained, and it's then that the transformation into a Grey hybrid occurs.) Betsy has been being abducted since her teens, so the hybrid cloning programme has been going on for at least two decades.

Continuity: Senator Richard Matheson is on the Intelligence Committee, and can't tell Mulder everything he knows (a significant step up on his earlier position, where he seemed to be in the dark and trying to discover the answers: see 'Little Green Men') – although there are, in turn, things that he is not aware of. Scully has told Mulder of her experiences in the deserted mine, and a reference is made to her attempted regression hypnosis in 'Paper Clip'. Mulder carries a second gun in an ankle holster (the implication being that this is a recent development – 'I get tired of losing my gun'). Scully seems to have moved since 'The Blessing Way'. She now lives in an apartment (number 5).

The Truth: The commander of Japanese Medical Corps unit 731, who experimented on captives during the war, was Dr Ishimaru. He was brought to the USA as part of Paper Clip, and was one of the humans who presided over Scully's abduction. He was part of the Conspiracy, but decided to reveal all to Japanese intelligence, who seem to have started monitoring Conspiracy activities. (Perhaps they were tipped off by the incorrectness of the Conspiracy's first cover story

about the raising of the alien craft, that the ship was
recovering a Japanese submarine.) This implies that the
Conspiracy hasn't penetrated the Japanese government. When
the Japanese video broadcast of an autopsy on one of
Ishimaru's Greys was intercepted, the Japanese sent an agent
to recover the data and hunt down his contacts. The Japanese
motivation in all this is seemingly to be able to recreate the
biology of a hybrid and apply it to their own soldiers, to
create an army immune to radiation (which everything
involving Black Oil biology seems to thrive on).

Trivia: The series' first mention of Vancouver. Agent
Pendrell is named after Pendrell Street in Vancouver.

The Bottom Line: PC: The revelation that Scully was
abducted by human beings is very shocking, and pulls the
tablecloth from under one's expectations so much that one is
tempted to forgive these Conspiracy episodes all their other
flaws. A step back from the mystery was needed, and, while
leaving the audience going 'but . . . but . . .', this is a brilliant
coup. The investment in this episode is huge: trains and boats,
all there before our eyes, and there's a wonderful camera pan
in the teaser. That said, this episode emphasises that the icons
and design of the Conspiracy episodes are all the same: cases
in car boots; helicopters; running gunmen; McGuffin pieces
of evidence; boxcars; war criminals; lengthy speeches in the
series' patent form of Diet David Mamet. There are also the
trademark Stupid Moments, those images that work only
because of the utter commitment of all concerned. Why, for
example, does Skinner come all the way to Pennsylvania for
three lines? How do the Lone Gunmen make out the name of
a ship with their magnifying glass? And isn't the scene of all
the abductees sitting in the lounge wonderfully silly? ('Why
are you all at her house?') Oh, and Paul McLean, who
plays the Coast Guard Officer, turns in a truly horrible
performance.

MD: This starts well but tails off a little, although the many
set pieces try to make up for this.

KT: 'Monsters begetting Monsters!' A very confusing
episode, albeit one that seems to have an idea where it's
going. Some great touches (the first scene with a man waving

at passing children from the Boxcar of Death! Or that great
bit where all of the abductees get out plastic bottles containing their implants and rattle them at Scully!). The Japanese
diplomat Mulder tackles is the worst Kung Fu ninja in the
history of US television (Mulder beats him, for goodness'
sake!). Visually stunning, however.

59: '731'

US Transmission: 1 December 1995
UK Transmission: 7 May 1996 (Sky One)/
31 October 1996 (BBC1)
Writer: Frank Spotnitz
Director: Rob Bowman
Cast: Stephen McHattie (Red-Haired Man),
Michael Puttonen (Conductor),
Robert Ito (Dr Takeo Ishimaru),
Colin Cunningham (Escalante)

Mulder hunts for Ishimaru on the train. Scully, investigating
her implant, finds that a shipment of them were sent to a Dr
Zama, at an institute in West Virginia. The place is a camp for
victims of Hansen's Disease, a cover for a group of deformed
beings who were experimented on by Zama. Recently, these
victims were all killed, their bodies thrown into pits. Mulder
sees a similar creature on the train, in a separate boxcar. He's
attacked by the Red-Haired Man who has already killed Zama
(who is in reality Ishimaru). The man's mission was to stop
Ishimaru getting the creature out of the country. He tells
Mulder that there's a bomb on the train. Scully, meanwhile,
meets the Elder from the Conspiracy, who tells her that the
Hansen's Disease victims were, along with various other
minority groups, exposed to diseases and radiation. Scully
manages to deduce the exit codes for the boxcar, but the
Red-Haired Man attacks Mulder again. He leaves, but is shot
dead by X, who saves Mulder from the ensuing explosion.
Mulder has Ishimaru's journals, but he discovers that they're
useless, having been rewritten. The Cigarette-Smoking Man
has the real ones.

Don't Be in the Teaser: Hundreds of Grey hybrid beings are herded into vans, taken out and shot by the US military.

Scully Here is a Medical Doctor: She knows that Hansen's Disease is the proper name for leprosy.

Scully's Rational Explanation of the Week: 'There is no such thing as alien abduction.' She's right about the activities of the Conspiracy, at least, but not (as we see in 'Max' and elsewhere) about the activities of the Rebel Colonists. She swallows the Conspiracy's latest cover story, that the inmates of the camp were human to begin with, and that the crashed alien craft was a Russian submarine. Her righteous anger is used to turn her into a stooge, and thus Mulder takes the first step on the road that will lead him to lose belief and contemplate suicide. Nice going, Scully!

Phwoar!: Agent Pendrell has a boyish crush on Scully.

Dialogue Triumphs: Mulder: 'Scully, let me tell you, you haven't seen America until you've seen it from a train!'

The Conspiracy Starts at Closing Time: The Red-Headed Man (whose ID is probably a sign that the Conspiracy have penetrated the NSA) says that the creature in the boxcar is suffering from haemorrhagic fever. (However, given that this is the very disease that the Cigarette-Smoking Man mentioned he'd been involved in preventing the spread of ('F. Emasculata'), it's possible that either this is one of the diseases that the Grey has been exposed to as a non-suffering carrier, and the earlier incident involved a similar experimental escapee, or that this is the standard cover story for such escapes.) By the end of the episode, however, it seems pretty clear that the man is a Grey hybrid soldier 'prototype', immune to radiation poisoning and the effects of biological warfare. Whether or not the hybrid was human to begin with (in which case the Elder tells Scully some of the truth) or was a human/Colonist clone hybrid (that is, created as such from before birth) is hard to say. It's possible that the Japanese wouldn't have an interest if the former wasn't true: they wouldn't be able to create their super-army otherwise. It's also possible that Ishimaru may have been part of the US government's perversion of the Conspiracy's aims, the use of alien DNA through injection continuing this strand of research even though the Conspiracy forbade him. (Or perhaps he was simply put in charge of the mutated individuals created when the Conspiracy themselves followed this path and grew more and more certain that it could lead to useful results.) It's possible (the impression the episode gives emotionally, but confusingly not supported anywhere in the back story) that the Grey hybrids don't look like Greys until they've been exposed to various biohazards and radiation (one naturally feels that the cause one's sympathy has been caught by, in an involving drama of suffering, really ought to be 'true' within that drama! But that's not always the case in this series). The Elder tells Scully that he doesn't know if she's been exposed to radiation or disease or not (but since that would be a silly thing to do to the women breeding the hybrids, that's another sign that he's just trying to conceal the whole idea of humans birthing cloned hybrids here). The Grey hybrids may have toxic blood: they're shot from a safe distance at the start of the episode. Altogether, the jury is still out on the origins of these creatures. Either they're the last gasp of the ex-Conspiracy/various governments' attempts to use Colonist DNA to create supersoldiers through injection, or Scully is just being told to believe that (so she and Mulder will continue to help the Conspiracy hunt such things down) while these creatures are actually what becomes of cloned Colonist/human hybrids. Either way, they're tested by being exposed to diseases and radiation, possibly in order to perfect the process so that the US government can use them in future wars (if the Elder is telling the truth and the Conspiracy disapprove of this project) or the Conspiracy can use them against the Colonists (if he isn't and they were running this place). Scully's computer chip is a neural network that records and backs up her memories (but obviously doesn't broadcast them or she would have been located by the Conspiracy on many awkward occasions, and X would have been a dead man much sooner). We know the chip can also cause the recipient to go into a trance and move to a desired location ('Patient X'), and has a most important use in blood toxicity control, but this memory recording is more rarely mentioned.

Is this where the Shapeshifters gain their knowledge of human institutions and procedures (as shown by the Rebel Leader in 'End Game'), the information being read every time a subject is abducted? Or is the plan for some sort of mass uploading of human memories when the Project is complete and the bodies of humans have become so much Grey-fuel? Is this what Clyde Bruckman meant when he said that Scully doesn't die? The chip is made by a Japanese company (presumably using Conspiracy knowledge). Possibly it's something as simple as keeping continual tabs on Scully's memory as a way of monitoring any ailments or medical conditions she reports, and thus keep the state of her blood checked. X knows about the shooting of Scully's sister, but says he doesn't know everything. He seems fascinated by the Grey hybrid: perhaps he hasn't seen one this close before. It's almost certain that he hands Ishimaru's journals over to the Cigarette-Smoking Man, arriving at the boxcar on orders to help the Red-Haired Man but killing him because he might have prevented the saving of Mulder (and, following his revenge motive, because he knew he could get away with it).

Continuity: Scully was brought to a Conspiracy boxcar during her abduction, and was attended by Dr Ishimaru. Mulder studied French (and not Japanese!) at high school. Mulder's home telephone number is 550199. In 'Kill Switch' we see Mulder's home phone number on his computer file – it's (202) 555 9335. Either he's moved and kept every detail of his apartment the same (which sounds like him), or in the world of the series, the local codes changed.

The Truth: Ishimaru, who had presided over both microchip implantations of abductees in the Conspiracy's boxcars (including Scully), and the mutation of (either Colonist/human hybrids or humans) into Grey hybrids that could withstand biological weapons and radiation exposure, decided to tell the Japanese government all, presumably reasoning that his government could create their own army of immune soldiers. Thus, he and his comrades left their base camp, taking a living and a dead Grey hybrid with them. The attempt to beam the results of the dead Grey hybrid autopsy to Japan failed, and his comrades were killed, so he tried to take the living example with him out of the country. The Conspiracy sent the Red-Haired Man to kill him and destroy the Grey hybrid, having wiped out every other result of his experiments (presumably in a panic move, thinking the information could at any moment be made public: it would have been just as easy to transport them away. Perhaps the Conspiracy wouldn't know what to do with a batch of Grey hybrids with varying degrees of infection and disease-carrying).

The Bottom Line: PC: I thought at the time that this was a triumphal rabbit-out-of-a-hat trick. Not only did we now have a solid plot under the Conspiracy stuff, but it was one with an incredible moral potency. (What other series would dare suggest that the American government is actually following a Nazi eugenics policy? Can you imagine the British equivalent? Tony Clark of *Between the Lines* stumbles across MI5 systematically exterminating Pakistanis.) However, time has not treated this story well, the Conspiracy arc telling us that Scully was wrong, when I wanted her to be right, for this series to be about something more than aliens. The image of US soldiers casually killing scores of creatures because they're ordered to (and because they look weird) is still shocking and true, though, and it's pleasing that the show went for the army fatigues option rather than Conspiracy black.

MD: '731' works less well than some of the other Conspiracy stories, although there are nice touches (notably the Scully–Pendrell interchange).

KT: 'What was he exposing those people to?' 'Terrible things.' A huge, allegorical fascist nightmare (anybody who doesn't think 'Belsen' when Scully looks into the open grave clearly isn't following where this storyline is going). A complex narrative that, in its final moments, suddenly, and quite without warning, changes the focus of the series. The *Between the Lines* simile suggested by Paul is interesting in that it is possibly the only other series recently to get into the grey areas of government and disinformation that *The X-Files* is playing with here. A work of terrible beauty.

The X-Files was shown in Japan in a primetime slot on Wednesday evenings (whereas *Star Trek: The Next Generation*, for example, was shown after midnight) in a bilingual format (most televisions and VCRs in Japan having a bilingual button so you can watch imported shows in English or Japanese, or both simultaneously). Each episode was followed by a five-minute feature entitled *X-Files Fan* (similar to BBC2's *X-Philes*), presented by a terribly enthusiastic Japanese woman called Rie Eto, about the programme's production, stars, merchandising and followers. The Japanese language hardly has any plural forms. It also lacks articles, so although the show is named *The X-Files* on screen, Japanese people therefore always simply refer to it as 'X-File'. The end credits for each season had a different song over the titles, and that of the third season became a popular hit. Gillian Anderson's BBC TV documentary series, *Future Fantastic*, started its Japanese broadcast in January 1998, and *Millennium* videos were eagerly rented far in advance of that series being screened. Despite its early evening TV timeslot, and despite the Japanese predilection for fantastical horror and violence, many Japanese people say that *The X-Files* is simply too terrifying to watch. Perhaps that was a factor in the sudden withdrawal of the series (following the episode 'Home') from the schedules, to be replaced by *Chicago Hope*. But presumably such a popular hit won't remain buried for long.

60: 'Revelations'

US Transmission: 15 December 1995
UK Transmission: 14 May 1996 (Sky One)/
27 November 1996 (BBC1)
Writer: Kim Newton
Director: David Nutter

Cast: Kevin Zegers (Kevin Kryder),
Sam Bottoms (Michael Kryder), Kenneth Welsh (Simon Gates),
Michael Berryman (Owen Lee Jarvis),
Hayley Tyson (Susan Kryder),
R. Lee Ermey (Reverend Finley),
Lesley Ewen (Carina Maywald), Fulvio Cecere (Priest),
Nicole Robert (Mrs Tynes)

Mulder seeks the killer of eleven fake stigmatics. Kevin, a boy who is a real stigmatic and has a religious maniac for a father, looks like being the next victim when he's kidnapped by a man called Jarvis. Mulder and Scully find Kevin, but Jarvis escapes, and is murdered by the real killer, Gates, a man with hands that can burn. Mulder and Scully try to protect Kevin, but the killer abducts him again, and takes him to a recycling plant where he intends to kill him. Scully, based on the merest hint from Kevin's father, intuits that she needs to go there, and she saves the boy.

Don't Be in the Teaser: A (false) stigmatic priest is killed by a member of his congregation.

How Did He Do That?: This time, he doesn't. Mulder is rational in the face of Scully's leaps of faith, going so far as to allege, with a straight face, that the killer used an acetylene torch to melt the bars, and that the man is being driven by the 'Jerusalem Syndrome' (a real-life psychotic illness). One gets the feeling that he's enjoying showing Scully how it feels to be on the receiving end of unbreakable rationalism.

Scully Here is a Medical Doctor: She does an autopsy on Jarvis, and comes to the unmedical conclusion that the body isn't decaying and smells of roses. (Mulder appears not to agree, at least on the latter point.)

Scully's Leap of Faith: 'I believe He can create miracles.'

Mulder's Rational Explanation of the Week: Kevin, disturbed by his father's institutionalisation, wounded himself. Religious stories are 'hagiographic fabrications, not historical truths', and, 'parables, metaphors for the truth'.

Phwoar!: Scully getting all maternal is strangely arousing. Mulder complains that she never runs a bath for him after she does this for Kevin.

Dialogue Triumphs: Mulder: 'Looks like Kevin was abducted by Homer Simpson's evil twin.'

Scully (during the autopsy): 'Mulder, would you do me a favour? Would you smell Mr Jarvis?'

Mulder on the 'fanatics': 'They give bona fide paranoiacs like myself a bad name.'

Continuity: There's another mention made of catechism (see 'The List'). Scully believes in Armageddon, was raised a Catholic (see 'Miracle Man'), but it's been six years since her last confession. She says she's not sure why she drifted away from the Church. Mulder thinks that the Bible is metaphorical, not the truth itself, and he doesn't get out of bed on Sundays (which, if Duchovny is right and Mulder is Jewish, isn't entirely a matter of being without faith). There are more hints in 'Kaddish'.

The Truth: Simon Gates, a rich executive, returns from Jerusalem with the ability to heat things with his hands. His quarry, Kevin, can (intermittently) appear in two places at once, and can disappear from sight (as, it seems, can Jarvis!). He seems to suffer from genuine stigmata (although, as with much real-world stigmatism, one is somewhat puzzled by the positioning of the 'nail wounds': in the palms, as per tradition but at variance with biological possibility, rather than in the wrists, as attested archaeologically). From their behaviour, one might assume that Kevin is a deity of some kind, and Simon an agent of a dark force, but this is never made explicit. Gates may be trying to bring on Armageddon (an odd aim for an agent of Satan, considering that the Bible has the Devil losing that final battle), or avoid it and usher in a 'New Age' (in which case he's not working to the Christian agenda, and you wonder why he's concerned with it!).

Scientific Comment: The sun turning to darkness and the moon to blood are references to solar and lunar eclipses.

The Bottom Line: PC: The tension in Mulder and Scully's relationship becomes greater, the wisecracking muted, along the same issue as last week: are Mulder's obsessions really what intelligent people should concern themselves with? Or are there even more things in heaven and earth? This episode very neatly reverses their roles, managing to make Scully's scepticism understandable, open her up and increase her role. The episode also succeeds in mining the vast divide between religious belief and paranormal belief, exploring why the two can't sit together comfortably. One such titbit thrown up is the delicious question of whether antipsychotic drugs can prevent religious experiences. Amid such depth and subtlety, it's sad that, because of fears about offending the audience, we're not actually allowed to discover what the nature of the battle represented here is. If the villain is working for the 'New Age', then that's the whole of the New Age community (and what percentage of the viewers would that be?) branded as Satanists. If it's the other way round, and Gates is trying to bring on Armageddon, then we've actually had the Antichrist and the Messiah in this week's exciting episode, struggling in a recycling plant. Hmm, I begin to see the problem. Whatever, it's still an extraordinary episode.

MD: I wouldn't worry too much about the New-Agers-as-Satanists thing: one nutter does not a blanket generalisation make (and if I had a pound for every time that Christians are presented as bigots, busybodies, puritans or simply insane by the media . . . I'd be quite rich by now, actually). Still, as you say, this is the episode's major flaw: you're not left with any option but to see Gates as a loony and Kevin as a lad who, by the episode's end, is beginning to believe his mad father's 'hype'. Despite the unusual abilities on display, the episode is purposefully shorn of any biblical power or symbolism, making the whole thing somewhat lifeless (compare 'All Souls'). It works reasonably well as an X-File, but Scully's character changes beyond all recognition, and you've got to be worried by any writer who thinks St Ignatius is a character in the Bible.

KT: 'You must come full circle to find the truth.' If *I* had a pound for every time *The X-Files* has shagged up its religious position, I'd have almost enough to buy a copy of this book. This is halfway towards being a great episode (*The X-Files* doing the second coming is a delicious idea – even if the Son of God is known as Kevin this time around). But then they ruin it, and they ruin it through a very unlikely source. Mulder. Having Mulder 'go Scully' on us (and her) in 'Beyond the Sea' was inspired because it had conceptual depth. Here it's just an angry rant from a writer who seems to have gained all of their understanding of religion and the religious from an afternoon in Sunday school. That apart, visually influenced by *The Dead Zone*, and conceptually by *The Omen II* (well, sort of!), and with a good ending, 'Revelations' works on most levels. And, even for a series that seems to delight in hiring weird-looking actors, this episode takes the biscuit.

61: 'War of the Coprophages'

US Transmission: 5 January 1996
UK Transmission: 21 May 1996 (Sky One)/
9 January 1997 (BBC1)
Writer: Darin Morgan
Director: Kim Manners
Cast: Bobbie Phillips (Dr Bambi Berenbaum),
Raye Birk (Dr Jeff Eckerle), Dion Anderson (Sheriff Frass),
Bill Dow (Dr Newton), Alex Bruhanski (Dr Bugger),
Ken Kramer (Dr Ivanov), Alan Buckley (Dude),
Maria Herrera (Customer #1), Sean Allan (Customer #2),
Norma Wick (Reporter), Wren Robertz (Orderly),
Tom Heaton (Resident #1), Bobby L. Stewart (Resident #2),
Dawn Stofer (Customer #4), Fiona Roeske (Customer #5)

Mulder stumbles across a series of killings apparently caused by cockroaches with very hard exoskeletons. He visits a Department of Agriculture building that turns out to be a replica of an ordinary house, given over to studying cockroaches. There he meets Bambi, an entomologist. He goes to see an inventor of robot insects, who speculates that the metal bugs might be alien probes. Scully arrives amid panic in the town. The director of the local methane plant, where Mulder thinks the bugs might be refuelling on dung, goes crazy because of the infestation, and fires his gun, blowing the place up. Bambi and the inventor walk off into the twilight, the bugs having flown away.

Don't Be in the Teaser: To full-on horror-movie music, Dr Bugger (!) the exterminator is killed by cockroaches! If you have lunches, prepare to lose them now.

Ooze: Oh no! Ick! Grooooo! Apart from the bugs themselves, there's a continuing meditation on the theme of dung. Scully even eats Choco Droppings.

Scully's Phone-In Rational Explanation of the Week: The whole idea of alien life is, apparently, anti-Darwinian (what?) and astronomically improbable. The victims have (in order) an allergy to cockroaches (anaphylactic shock), died as the result of a psychotic drug-induced fantasy (Ekbom Syndrome, a real-life delusion of parasitosis), and have, erm, been straining too hard on the toilet.

That's a Mouthful: Scully: 'I'm not going to ask you if you just said what I think you just said because I know it's what you just said!'

Phwoar!: Mulder is fascinated by Bambi, who thinks UFOs are nocturnal insect swarms. They manage about a quarter of a kiss, nodding their heads towards each other invitingly. 'Does my scientific detachment disturb you?' He's obviously into weird sceptics, but that doesn't stop Scully getting a bit snappy. As she tells Bambi, loading her gun in a very professional manner, 'This is no place for an entomologist.'

Dialogue Triumphs: 'Dr Bugger', on freezing roaches: 'Where's the fun in that?'

Mulder to Bambi: 'What's a woman like you doing in a place like this?'

Mulder hangs up on Scully while he's with Bambi: 'Not now.'

Scully: 'Her name is Bambi?' Mulder: 'Both of her parents were naturalists.'

Mulder on his close encounter with the praying mantis: '. . . as a result I screamed – not a girlie scream . . .' (See 'Jose Chung's *From Outer Space*'!)

Bambi (on the cockroach under the microscope): 'He's hung like a club-tailed dragonfly.'

The Conspiracy Starts at Closing Time: Notice how Sheriff Frass's conspiracy theory involving killer bees is spot on in almost every respect?

Continuity: Scully's exciting weekend at home involves eating a plate of greens and a tub of ice cream, with a glass of water, reading *Breakfast at Tiffany's*, and defleaing her dog (see 'Clyde Bruckman's Final Repose', 'Quagmire'). She always assumes it's Mulder on the phone (so much for that life she claimed to want a couple of seasons back). Mulder hates insects, having had a 'praying mantis epiphany' in a tree, although he's quite happy to handle them. (The head of a mantis does look very like the head of a Grey . . .) Mulder spends his spare time chasing lights in the sky.

The Truth: There may have been some robot insects feeding on dung, and they may have been alien probes. But the deaths might well have been incidental, exacerbated by hysteria.

Trivia: Five seconds of *The Seven Year Itch* is glimpsed as one of the characters in the hotel is changing TV channels. (We suspect a joke, but, aside from the 'itch' bit, we don't get it.) The movie *Planet of the Apes* is quoted from. Twice! (A cool sidelong glance at another species inheriting Earth.) On the subject of invasion, there are lots of visual references to *The War of the Worlds* (and the town's name, Miller's Grove, is derived from Grover's Mill, the location of the first Martian landing in Orson Welles's radio version). *Breakfast at Tiffany's* was the answer (or, to be exact, the question) that cost David Duchovny the game when he appeared on *Jeopardy*. The TV news reporter, Skye Leikin, is a reference to fan Leikin Skye, who won a trivia contest to be named on screen. The name A. Ivanov is a nod to Isaac Asimov, who devised the Three Laws of Robotics. Dr Bambi Berenbaum is named after Dr May R. Berenbaum, Head of Entomology at the University of Illinois, and an authority on insects. Darin Morgan's subsequent *Millennium* script 'Somehow Satan Got Behind Me' includes several behind-the-scenes jokes about the production of this episode, and of 'Jose Chung's *From Outer Space*', most notably the Network Standards officer stating, 'You can say "crap" if you mean "crap" but not if you mean "excrement"!'

Scientific Comment: It is impossible to agree with Scully when she dismisses the possibility of extraterrestrial life on grounds of anti-Darwinianism. Given the size of the universe, it's almost inconceivable that there would be no other life out there. Once you have life, Darwinian evolution implies that it will become intelligent through survival of the fittest. And keeping beer in liquid nitrogen would freeze it solid.

The Bottom Line: PC: Wa-hey! Not only an honest-to-goodness monster story that has viewers crawling up the walls (the 'bug across the lens' gag is fab), but a hilariously ironic commentary on Mulder and Scully's relationship (they're trying to get back to their friendship, but they're physically separated, and Mulder wants to demonstrate to Scully that he's a single man), and an inquiry into the nature of mystery to boot. You get the feeling that Morgan would have liked to have his insect protagonists vanish into mist completely, and that only the concrete nature of the typical *X-Files* plot stopped him. Still: there's only one Darin Morgan. In any other series, his literate, passionate, scatological and ironic ventures into sheer style would stick out like a sore backside. Here, to the series' credit, he seems to be at home.

MD: The best Darin Morgan script so far: the balance is flawless, and the running gag about Scully not coming to Massachusetts is gorgeous. I love the scene of Scully in the supermarket, encountering the woman who's not seen roaches, 'but they're everywhere', and the man fearful of the Ebola virus ('We're all going to be bleeding from our nipples!'). The ensuing chaos when she tries to reassure everyone says a lot about most people's attitude to authority when it comes to matters of health and safety. The direction is flawless, although – and despite the horrible toes of the man who dies in the motel! – for once I'm not sure it's nasty enough. And as I typed those words a shield bug landed on my monitor. Spooky.

KT: I think this might be one we all agree on! Flawlessly researched (every character seems to be an expert on something – except Scully who's an expert on everything), and with a neat line in 'bugs' jokes (that roach-crawling-across-the-screen sequence made me fall out of my chair the first time I saw it). And we've got two of the grossest moments in TV history (the dude with cockroaches in his arm, and, even worse, the guy on the toilet). It seems churlish to criticise any aspect of this, though they've done Generation X up the Khyber again. *Star Trek: The Next Generation* hire Steven Hawking. *The X-Files* takes the piss. A necessary difference, I think! Can I skip the next few episodes and go straight to reviewing 'Jose Chung'?

62: 'Syzygy'

US Transmission: 26 January 1996
UK Transmission: 28 May 1996 (Sky One)/
13 November 1996 (BBC1)
Writer: Chris Carter
Director: Rob Bowman
Cast: Dana Wheeler-Nicholson (Detective Angela White),
Wendy Benson (Margi Kleinjan),
Lisa Robin Kelly (Terri Roberts), Garry Davey (Bob Spitz),
Denalda Williams (Zirinka),
Gabrielle Miller (Brenda Summerfield),
Ryan Reynolds (Jay DeBoom),
Tim Dixon (Dr Richard W. Godfrey), Ryk Brown (Minister),
Jeremy Radick (Eric Bauer), Russell Porter (Scott Simmons)

Three high-school boys are killed, the townsfolk blaming Satanic cultists. Two girls, Terri Roberts and Margi Kleinjan, who were with the last victim, have confirmed the involvement of dark rituals. The boy's coffin combusts at the funeral, and, against Scully's protests, Mulder and his new friend, Detective Angela White, visit a local astrologer. The two girls psychically trap a boy who offends them behind the seating in the gym, killing him. The local people dig up a field and find some bones, but they turn out to be those of a dog. Terri and Margi terrorise and murder another girl. While Mulder and Scully are distracted by Mulder's out-of-character tryst with White, the girls fall out over a boy, who gets killed in the crossfire, and accuse each other of the murder. They confront each other in the police station as the mob arrives, causing havoc, but, as midnight passes, their powers pass with it.

Don't Be in the Teaser: Jay DeBoom falls into the clutches of the Psychic Spices and gets well hung.

Scully Here is a Medical Doctor: She investigates the coffin.

Scully's Rational Explanation of the Week: Embalming fluid combusts, and the people are subject to 'rumour panic'.

Phwoar!: 'I was hoping you could help me solve the mystery of the horny beast . . .' Mulder, in the middle of a vast lovers' tiff with Scully (continuing their alienation following the death camp incident), goes after Detective White, allowing her to leap on top of him. Of course, it's because everybody's acting out of character, Mulder drinking rough vodka and orange while Scully smokes (and paces like an alley cat) in the next room. When she bursts in on him, it's as if the ghosts of Hattie Jacques and Kenneth Williams have entered the building. She's certainly upset that he's still trying to display his sexuality: 'the big macho man . . .' Mulder sniffs Scully at one point.

Dialogue Triumphs: According to Mulder, Scully is 'rigid in a wonderful way'.

Mulder to Scully on the plastic gloves: 'I know how much you like snapping on the latex.'

Mulder on why he usually drives: 'I was just never sure your little feet could reach the pedals.'

'That's a bad thing?' 'Bad like an Irwin Allen movie!'

The continuing mantra of disaffection between the two agents: 'Sure. Fine. Whatever.'

Continuity: Mulder says he doesn't normally drink (compare 'Deep Throat'). His credit card is good for three hundred dollars, which isn't very much!

The Truth: An alignment of Mercury, Mars and Uranus on the day that the girls were born in 1979 focuses the energy of the cosmos through them on their birthday, and causes everybody else to act out of character too. Especially when they're in the house of Aquarius. Or something.

Trivia: The Keystone Kops on television, with Aram Khachaturian's 'Sabre Dance' on the soundtrack, seem to be a symbol of the occult at work (and is used in a similar way in the *X-Files* computer game). (See 'Clyde Bruckman's Final Repose' for more silent-movie chaos motifs.) The high school is named Grover Cleveland Alexander after another of David Duchovny's incorrect *Jeopardy* answers. (Can't they leave him alone? One day he'll just snap.) The name of the town, Comity, means courtesy, and we see signs on the way in and way out of town that indicate that Mulder and Scully are now leaving and then now entering that state of mind.

Scientific Comment: Oh no, astrology. One can suspend one's disbelief for liver-eating mutants, UFOs, invisible elephants . . . but not astrology. However, leaving that aside: the girls' strange behaviour was supposedly caused by a conjunction of Mercury, Mars and Uranus. At the end of the episode a full moon with three planets next to it is shown. Presumably, this was meant to be the conjunction. However: A: Since Mercury is very close to the sun, the only way you can get those planets aligned is to look from Earth to Mercury then Mars and Uranus with your line of sight going very close to the Sun. So you'd only be able to see it, if at all, at dawn or dusk. To see a full moon, the moon must be on the far side of Earth from the Sun, so you have to look directly away from the Sun to see one. Therefore, you can't possibly see that conjunction next to a full, or even quarter, moon. B: There have been murders for three months. A conjunction with Mercury involved wouldn't last long, since it's got a short orbit. Even Earth has moved a lot in three months. The effect switched off miraculously at 12.00 on the girls' birthday, which is not consistent with the three-month lead-up. The mention of a geological vortex or high-intensity meridian is total junk. A meridian is a line of longitude, like the Greenwich meridian, a line on a map. So how can you have a 'high-intensity' one?

The Bottom Line: PC: The subtle character arc of Mulder and Scully's falling out continues, played, unlike everything else in this season, at a level where the casual viewer wouldn't be disturbed by it. True, the script suffers from Carter Syndrome: the menace is . . . exactly what we're told it is in the teaser. But there's lots of fun to be had in this cut-price *Carrie*. The character play more than makes up for the silly astrology plot, and who cares if a gun going off in your holster would leave you maimed for life? There are moments of Darin Morgan charm around the discovery of the dog. Things are spoilt a bit, though, by what is, even for Mulder, a very silly summing up.

MD: Silly is the word. From the ridiculous idea of an 'upright' school with a demonic goat for a logo to the excruciating dancing-tables ending, this is a stinker. What was doubtless intended as being a witty parody of the True Love Waits campaign and Satanic-abuse stories spiralling out of control comes unstuck because the dialogue lacks any of the sparkle that Morgan would have brought to it. And I'll swallow some pretty incredible concepts in the cause of watching *The X-Files*, but, as with our scientific friend, the reality of astrology is not one of them!

KT: 'Did you hear who the cult is supposed to be going after next? A blonde virgin.' *Heathers*! Or not. Interesting mention of the (real-life) McMartin pre-school trial. This is good fun in small doses (I love the 'Mr Tippy' sequence), with a healthy slice of self-aware dialogue. But, as for Mulder's bollocks speech at the end . . . Hated it.

63: 'Grotesque'

US Transmission: 2 February 1996
UK Transmission: 4 June 1996 (Sky One)/
13 February 1997 (BBC1)
Writer: Howard Gordon
Director: Kim Manners
Cast: Levani [Outchaneichvili] (John Mostow),
Kurtwood Smith (Agent Bill Patterson),
Greg Thirloway (Agent Greg Nemhauser),
Susan Bain (Agent Sheherlis),
Kasper Michaels (Young Agent), Zoran Vukelic (Peter)

A serial killer claims that he was possessed by a spirit, then another killing occurs after he's been arrested. Mulder's old teacher, Bill Patterson, resents Mulder's involvement in the case and his support for the man's claims that the spirit has inhabited a new killer. Mulder finds a roomful of the killer's victims, made into gargoyles. It turns out that, baffled, Patterson actually requested Mulder's involvement. Mulder becomes very involved, decorating his apartment with the killer's art and sleeping in the man's room, during which time he's disturbed by an attacker. Scully finds the killer's blade, with Mulder's fingerprints on it, stolen from evidence, and becomes afraid for her partner's sanity. Patterson's lieutenant is killed. It turns out that Patterson is the killer, driven mad by the case, and crying out for Mulder to catch him.

Don't Be in the Teaser: A life model is attacked and facially mutilated, and an artist is brutally arrested.

How Did He Do That?: Mulder's leap to Patterson's being the killer is very intuitive: but that's the whole point. However, in the scene where Mulder moves his thumbs across the gargoyle's eyes, don't you think that the gargoyle looks very like Patterson? Maybe he left a big clue under Mulder's nose.

Ooze: Clay!

Scully's Rational Explanation of the Week: Mostow, the killer, has an accomplice.

Phwoar!: Scully's having a go at Patterson for pushing Mulder too far is incredibly sexy: she really cares for Mulder. And here we see what he was like before he had her to save him all the time: driven, consumed, going right to the edge and then just teetering back when he can see over it. He turns his mobile phone off: in this series, that's like becoming a hermit. You could say that, hurt by the distance that's now between him and Scully, Mulder deliberately throws himself into this self-destruction, crying out for Scully to save him in exactly the way that Patterson cries out to him. The difference between the two, ultimately, is that Mulder will always have Scully there for him.

Continuity: Bill Patterson runs the Investigative Support Unit at Quantico, a behavioural science guru. Although he was a good student, Mulder 'couldn't worship' Patterson, and so quit the ISU eight years ago.

The Truth: If we assume that Patterson had a gargoyle

mask, then there's no supernatural element whatsoever, just a psychologically acute picture of what battling monsters and staring into the abyss do to you. There's an extraordinarily realistic look at the human psyche going on here. Patterson taught Mulder about how to become a monster in order to catch them, but these days he's in complete denial of that side of himself, saying that the killer says this stuff 'because he's insane', refusing to look into the pit any more. He tells stories about Mulder when he's drunk: on one level, he's deeply in love with his former student, because he's transcended his teachings. The two things came together in his need to call Mulder in to solve this case: to punish Mulder for leaving him, to baffle this bright boy, to turn him into something like what Patterson has become, and, as the just bit of him wants, to capture and stop him.

Trivia: The gargoyle art is reminiscent of Clive Barker's drawings. And at least one gargoyle is very like Davros in *Doctor Who*. Agent Nemhauser is named after the post-production supervisor, Lori Jo Nemhauser. (All this naming of characters after production staff ought to seem too cute for words, but the effect is actually to give the series a great variety of ethnic and everyday-strange character names, making it actually seem the most realistic TV series in this regard.)

The Bottom Line: PC: Utterly magnificent: a script that could have been a movie or a novel, represented just as well in series television. There are echoes of *Manhunter*, certainly, but nothing that the format itself doesn't demand. Otherwise, bar the old cat-leaps-out gag, this is completely original, with psychological depths that, these days, only *The X-Files* explores. It also looks gorgeous, designed and lit in many shades of grey. Mind you, Skinner is in it only to remind us that he still exists.

MD: An American Gothic *Cracker*, indeed. The themes explored here remind me very much of a factual book I read on criminal psychiatry and psychological profiling, which had the effect of making the 'real world' seem a very frightening and potentially insane place. 'Grotesque' makes the cartoon killings of 'Syzygy' fade yet more into insignificance.

KT: 'Why didn't it kill me like it killed the others?'
A mature, thoroughly bewildering step into the heart of
darkness. A miniature Thomas Harris novel with echoes of
Dostoevsky and *From Hell* into the bargain.

64: 'Piper Maru'

US Transmission: 9 February 1996
UK Transmission: 11 June 1996 (Sky One)/
4 December 1996 (BBC1)
Writers: Frank Spotnitz, Chris Carter
Director: Rob Bowman
Cast: Robert Clothier (Commander Johansen),
Jo Bates (Jeraldine Kallenchuk),
Stephen E. Miller (Wayne Morgan),
Ari Solomon (Bernard Gauthier), Paul Batten (Dr Seizer),
Russell Ferrier (Medic), Kimberly Unger (Joan Gauthier),
Rochelle Greenwood (Waitress),
Joel Silverstone (First Engineer),
David Neale (Navy Base Guard),
Tom Scholte (Young Johansen),
Robert F. Maier (World War II Pilot)

A French diver, investigating a crashed aircraft on the ocean
floor, is surprised to see a human form inside. He becomes
possessed, and transfers that possession to his wife. The rest
of his crew suffer from radiation burns. Scully sees an old
navy friend of her father, who was sent on a submarine
mission to retrieve a downed atom-bomb-carrying B-52 many
years ago. Mulder, still on the trail of the 'craft' he saw in
the dockyard after his previous investigation into the alien
autopsy video, follows Krycek to Hong Kong, where he,
together with his salvage company partner, Jerry, has been
selling secrets from the MJ Files on the DAT (digital audio
tape). The diver's possessed wife follows Mulder to Hong
Kong, and attacks a squad of French agents with a burst of
radiation. Skinner is shot in what seems to be a coffee-shop
argument. The possessed woman passes her alien infestation
on to Krycek.

Don't Be in the Teaser: Gauthier, a French diver, gets ambushed by the Black Oil.

Scully Here is a Medical Doctor: 'I'm a medical doctor,' she tells the doctor examining the crew of the Piper Maru.

Ooze: Inside victims' eyes.

Phwoar!: This sees the end of the Scully/Mulder tiff arc, marked by a rather self-conscious affirmation of their respect for each other at the start. She was, after all, there for him in the last episode, and he doesn't seem to need to test the bounds of their relationship again. She seems to have forgiven him for his obsession with aliens at the cost of what she thinks is true, and this two-parter unites their points of view again. Mulder's reaction to Scully's instant aircraft knowledge: 'I just got very turned on.'

Dialogue Triumphs: Scully to Mulder: 'They could drop you in the middle of the desert and tell you the truth is out there, and you'd ask them for a shovel.'

The Conspiracy Starts at Closing Time: The Conspiracy men who threaten Skinner are from 'the intelligence community'. We might speculate the CIA or NSA as their cover organisation. Krycek says he didn't kill Mulder's father, but, since there would be little point in sending a Shapeshifter to do it in a disguise that Bill Mulder wouldn't recognise, we can only assume he's lying.

Continuity: Commander Johanson used to be a friend of Scully's father. The Scullys lived three doors away from the Johanson house at Miramar naval air base. Scully went to school with his son, Richard (who was recently killed in the Gulf). Scully watched her dad and brothers building model aircraft, and has a vast knowledge of aircraft.

Not The Truth: Allegedly, a B-52 crashed at coordinates 42 North, 171 East, during World War II. It was carrying the third nuclear bomb (to follow the Hiroshima and Nagasaki weapons) to be dropped on Japan. The submarine *Zeus Faber* was sent on a mission to recover the bomb, but the crew of the sub suffered from what appeared to be radiation burns. This is the third cover story the Conspiracy have told about this affair (see 'Apocrypha'). What is true is that Submarine Captain Sanford was possibly the first known victim of the Black Oil for several thousand years.

Trivia: Piper Maru is the name of Gillian Anderson's daughter. Gauthier is named after the effects supervisor, Dave Gauthier.

Scientific Comment: How did the oil get into an airtight suit, and out of an airtight submarine? How could the crew be irradiated without their ship being irradiated?

The Bottom Line: PC: Another wild lurch along the tightrope. This episode is a mess, using all the regular Conspiracy episode props one after the other, seemingly in desperation. One gets the feeling of this cookie jar being raided once too often, but then, next episode, miraculously . . . It's really strange that anybody should suspect the French of wanting to nick a forty-year-old nuclear weapon when they have modern ones of their own. Gauthier and his wife had their photo taken in front of a crap backdrop of the Eiffel Tower, and the model shot of the submarine is truly awful, sub (sic) *Blake's 7*. Somebody on the production team is still reading *Miss Smilla* . . .

MD: Preferable in many ways to 'Nisei', this is really a rather jolly exercise in compulsive storytelling, although the switch to Hong Kong seems little more than a desperate attempt to paint parts of the episode with international colours.

KT: 'We bury the dead alive, don't we?' On first broadcast, this was the first Conspiracy episode since 'The Erlenmeyer Flask' that I had (a) fully understood, and (b) enjoyed. With hindsight, I was as wrong about this as I was about 'Paper Clip', '731' et al. This is an episode that sees the series treading water. Literally. Some good set pieces, though (Scully's visit to Johanson, Skinner's shooting). Although rather obvious attempts are made to soften Dana's 'navy brat' past with soft lighting and mood music, the effect isn't badly handled. The fact that Skinner's secretary calls Scully when he is shot says much about how far Scully and Mulder have climbed in the FBI hierarchy.

65: 'Apocrypha'

US Transmission: 16 February 1996
UK Transmission: 18 June 1996 (Sky One)/
11 December 1996 (BBC1)
Writers: Frank Spotnitz, Chris Carter
Director: Kim Manners
Cast: Kevin McNulty (Agent Fuller),
Barry Levy (Navy Doctor),
Dmitry Chepovetsky (First Government Man),
Sue Mathew (Agent Caleca), Frances Flanagan (Nurse),
Peter Scoular (Sick Crewman), Jeff Chivers (Armed Man),
Martin Evans (Major Domo)

Skinner is taken to hospital, while Mulder rides with Krycek, hoping to retrieve the DAT from its hiding place. Their car is ambushed, but Krycek attacks the assailants with a radiation burst. The Cigarette-Smoking Man orders these victims destroyed. Scully finds out that the man who shot Skinner also shot Melissa, and petitions the FBI to pursue Krycek. Mulder believes that the alien is inhabiting oil, and gets the Lone Gunmen to open the safe-deposit box where the tape is meant to be, only to find it has gone. Krycek has it. The Conspiracy, meanwhile, want the Cigarette-Smoking Man to get the man who shot Skinner out of the country before he's caught. Mulder arranges a meeting with the Well-Manicured Man, and swaps the knowledge that Krycek has been selling secrets from the tape for a warning that Skinner is still in danger. Scully protects Skinner, and apprehends his assailant, but the man offers Krycek's destination in return for his life. Krycek is heading for a North Dakota missile site, to which the recovered UFO has been moved. Mulder, Scully, the Cigarette-Smoking Man and a squad of his troops arrive there. The Cigarette-Smoking Man stops Mulder and Scully entering, and the Black Oil leaves Krycek, returning to the craft. Skinner's assailant dies in his cell. Krycek is left trapped in the silo.

Don't Be in the Teaser: On 19 August 1953, a survivor of the submarine crew tells his story to Bill Mulder, the Cigarette-Smoking Man and, possibly, Deep Throat, who are very much a unit at this point. They seem to be investigating in exactly the way that Mulder does now. Only we can be fairly sure they know all about the truth behind what they're hearing.

Scully Here is a Medical Doctor: She checks on Skinner's condition.

Ooze: Fifty-weight diesel oil, a medium for an alien creature that inhabits bodies.

Phwoar!: Scully's passionate confrontation with Luiz Cardinal. And Agent Pendrell still has a crush on her. Her assertiveness with two junior agents at the hospital is way cool. It's good that Mulder puts his arm around Scully beside Melissa's grave.

Dialogue Triumphs: Langly: 'We show a talent for these G-men activities.'

The Conspiracy Starts at Closing Time: The Conspiracy don't seem to feel that they've missed anything in their retrieval of the craft, despite not initially finding any Black Oil or the body of any host creature for it. It may be that, at this point, they're quite ignorant of the true nature of their 'allies', as seen in the movie. (Mulder's speculation in '731' about the source of the creature in the boxcar being undermined in that episode itself). Perhaps they assume that, over the years, sea creatures have disposed of any body. The Black Oil, once mobile, acts as an enemy of the Conspiracy, avoiding capture and using a (natural) radiation-burst weapon in exactly the same way as the Conspiracy enemy in 'Fallen Angel' did. Thus, we can be fairly certain that we're dealing with a (very patient) representative of the Rebel Colonist faction here, appearing in its true form. The Cigarette-Smoking Man has seen the effects of the radiation burst before (presumably both during his investigation in the 1950s and following the events of 'Fallen Angel'), and seems worried about them, probably because, following hearing about the events of 'Fallen Angel', he puts two and two together and realises what he and his colleagues missed in the fifties. He presumably has the victims killed to stop further inquiry into the manner of their deaths. The craft the alien arrived in is one of the triangular ones piloted by Colonists and on loan to the USAF. The creature's ability to (partially) carry on pursuing Krycek's agenda while it inhabits his body also indicates (as does its ability to make human bodies walk and talk English) that it can access his memories. Colonists of both factions seem to thus have a way to access human memories, hence the high-quality information that their Shapeshifters have at their disposal. The Black Oil can clearly survive for fifty years with no food, water or air (that we're aware of). The groove in the craft seems to be a 'door' for the Oil to enter. The Oil was obviously able to traverse the sea bed during its time on Earth, so it must have chosen to enter the corpse in the Mustang in order to ambush the diver, having left its craft when the Conspiracy raised it. One wonders what it hopes to gain from re-entering its craft now: perhaps it's hoping to take off soon. The Conspiracy seem to regard this as a reasonable draw. (The craft is, after all, possibly radioactive, if we take the protective suits seen in 'Nisei' and the Grey craft in 'Max' as an indication.) They seal off the silo. (But Krycek's eventual escape might indicate that it's later opened, either to allow the Conspiracy to attack the Oil, or to reason with it if it's from the mainstream Colonists and simply unaware of whose side these humans are on. Its informed actions with Krycek would not really support that latter view, however, and would perhaps indicate that the two factions of Colonists form two separate hive minds, aware of all their hosts and activities at once.) The Conspiracy meet on New York's 46th Street. They view the Cigarette-Smoking Man as their 'associate' in Washington (presumably apart from Blevins). They've just discovered that he's prepared to lie to them. The Well-Manicured Man seems to want to frustrate and end the Cigarette-Smoking Man's violent activities. The Conspiracy used to keep UFOs at a base in Nevada (the famed Area 51?), but this place has recently become unviable (probably due to all the public attention). They now keep them in a disused missile silo site. The French action can perhaps be best explained if they have been excluded from the Conspiracy and, acting on Krycek's information, they want a slice of the UFO action now.

Continuity: The epitaph on Melissa's gravestone reads 'Melissa Scully, beloved sister and daughter, 1962–1995'. The man who shot her and Skinner was Luiz Cardinal, a Nicaraguan, formerly involved in the Iran/Contra scandal. (True to the Conspiracy's methods, he left an unregistered gun at the scene of Skinner's shooting.) There are continuity references to 'Colony', 'End Game', 'Paper Clip' (Krycek's attack on Skinner) and a possible oblique reference to 'Revelations' ('Other than a sign from God.' 'I've seen stranger things, believe me.').

The Truth: During World War II an alien craft was shot down as a 'Foo Fighter', almost certainly in the same incident which downed the Mustang. A submarine crew were sent to this area of the Pacific to recover what they were told was a Flying Fortress carrying a nuclear weapon. Instead, the captain was attacked by the Black Oil, and many of the crew died from radiation sickness. When the captain was locked away from the controls of the ship the Black Oil returned to the water, realising that it couldn't use the sub to get to the land. In 1953 Bill Mulder and the others investigated the fate of the submarine, and presumably failed to locate the alien craft. In 1996 the Conspiracy recovered the alien craft from this area. Later, the French vessel, also acting on information from the MJ Files, found the P-51 – and the alien. It was now inhabiting the 'dead' pilot of the P-51.

Trivia: The Conspiracy's phone number is 555 1012. (Can you imagine their answerphone message? 'Hello, Conspiracy. We're not here. We never were. Please leave the details of your alien experience after the beep and then forget about it.') The music at the Ice Rink is Strauss's 'The Blue Danube'.

The Bottom Line: PC: Isn't it odd that the Conspiracy say 'UFO' when they know exactly what these things are? It's good to see the Cigarette-Smoking Man telling his bosses that his pawn 'acted alone', one of many delights in a script that actually saves this two-parter completely, mainly through the refreshing device of throwing us some solid bits of information to hang on to. This idea of early closure as a remedy for the misty and intangible nature of the Conspiracy works quite well throughout the third season. In this case, we're quite surprised and pleased that Scully actually lays her hands on the man who killed her sister, a motif which looked like it would be with us for all time.

MD: The pre-title sequence is excellent (the chap who plays the young Cigarette-Smoking Man is staggeringly accurate, even down to vocal inflections), and much of what follows does not disappoint.

KT: 'You can't bury the truth.' Oh yes you can, matey. The 1950s RCA Victor tape recorder sets the tone for this marvellous episode: style, and astonishing attention to detail. One tiny point of query, however: the Assistant Director of the FBI is shot and only three agents turn up at the hospital, two seemingly very inexperienced, and the third (Scully) there only because he's gone out on a limb for her and Mulder so often. You would have thought the place would have been crawling with middle management eager for promotion.

66: 'Pusher'

US Transmission: 23 February 1996
UK Transmission: 25 June 1996 (Sky One)/
2 January 1997 (BBC1)
Writer: Vince Gilligan
Director: Rob Bowman
Cast: Vic Polizos (Agent Frank Burst),
Roger R. Cross (SWAT Lieutenant),
Steve Bacic (Agent Collins), Don MacKay (Judge),
Brent Sheppard (Prosecutor),
D. Neil Mark (Deputy Scott Kerber),
Meredith Bain Woodward (Defence Attorney),
Darren Lucas (Lead SWAT Cop)

Detective Frank Burst goes to Mulder and Scully about a man, Robert Modell, who calls himself 'Pusher', who has admitted to several 'suicide' killings, and escaped him. The agents track him to a golf range, where he makes a trooper set himself on fire, but they catch him. He's freed because of Mulder's testimony and Pusher's ability to convince the judge of his innocence. He walks into the FBI, and accesses private files, causing Skinner to be attacked by a secretary. It turns out that Modell is dying of a brain tumour. After he talks Frank Burst to death over the phone, Mulder corners him in a hospital, where he plays Russian roulette with the FBI agent. Scully, about to be shot by Mulder at Modell's request, pulls the fire alarm, breaking Mulder's concentration and allowing him to shoot Modell instead.

Don't Be in the Teaser: Modell sends a car carrying him, Burst and a deputy into a collision with a lorry. The deputy is killed.

How Did He Do That?: Mulder jumps at exactly the right magazine advert as being Modell's. Modell, for his part, instantly realises that Mulder and Scully aren't, actually, potential customers, but the FBI. Modell, despite his many gifts, isn't psychic, so how does he know that the oncoming truck is from the Cerulean Blue Hauling Company? Lucky guess? Coincidence?

Scully Here is a Medical Doctor: She gives Burst mouth-to-mouth resuscitation and assesses Modell's brain condition over a video link.

Ooze: Collins's self-inflicted burns.

Scully's Rational Explanation of the Week: 'Please explain to me the scientific nature of "The Whammy".' The circumstantial evidence is enough, in this case, to make Scully (eventually) agree with Mulder.

Phwoar!: Mulder looks gorgeously shaken after he shoots Modell. Scully sheds a tear when Mulder's about to shoot her, and they hold hands at the end, playing with each other's fingers. If they were ever close to going home and shagging like bunnies, this is the point. Mulder doesn't seem strong enough not to shoot Scully (after all, she's the one with the balls in this relationship), but there is a suggestion that Mulder subconsciously wants revenge for her shooting him.

Dialogue Triumphs: Modell: 'You must be Frank Burst? You know, I've got to tell you, you got the greatest name.'

Mulder: ' "Mango Kiwi Tropical Swirl"! Now we know we're dealing with a madman.'

Continuity: Mulder, doubtless thanks to the events of 'Nisei', now has a Japanese dictionary.

The Truth: Robert Modell was an army supply clerk who wanted to be in the special forces, an anti-authoritarian who wanted to be in authority. He failed the FBI psyche test several years ago (he should have waited: by the time of 'Lazarus' they were letting anybody in . . .) and, until a cancer developed in his temporal lobe, was a failure. The cancer brought on epilepsy, and the power to make people obey his will, but it was also killing him. Presumably the cancer is the result of a genetic flaw, since in 'Kitsunegari' we discover that Modell's sister seems to have developed it also.

Trivia: The *World Weekly Informer* is a tacky tabloid. As well as the headline FLUKEMAN FOUND WASHED UP IN MARTHA'S VINEYARD, it has further headings: DEPRAVITY RAMPANT ON HIT TV SHOW (with a photo of what must be two of the series' creators, one in suspenders), and GIRL RAISED BY SQUIRRELS FOR 15 YEARS FOUND BEGGING FOR PEANUTS IN PARK. There are apt references to *Yojimbo* and *Svengali*. Dave Grohl, of the Foo Fighters and formerly Nirvana, and his wife, Jennifer Youngblood-Grohl, make a cameo appearance as Modell attempts to enter the FBI building. (He should have been in last week's episode . . .) There's another example of Mulder's T.S. Eliot fixation when he (mis-) quotes 'The Hollow Men' with the phrase 'Not with a whimper but a bang'.

The Bottom Line: PC: I'd have preferred it if Mulder had had the mental strength to break Modell's control. He's a fabulous villain: a bulky, rude bully with 'Samurai' stylings so obviously fake that his use of them is obscene. Robert Wisden does an amazing job with the man's odd mix of charisma and ugliness. For him to be a discontented militiaman, with that outsider fascination for the things of government that such morons claim to hate, is very subtle characterisation. Mind you, the script does have its failings, such as none of our heroes even trying to defend themselves against a menace the nature of which they're all well aware. Earplugs would have helped, and couldn't Frank Burst just have held the phone away from his ear? Scully really should stop Mulder from telling so much of the truth in court, and his shooting of Modell at the end is probably grossly unlawful. Final proof, also, that actors just can't look natural shopping.

MD: I love the sequences with the fake pass, and the production team really seem to have it in for poor old Skinner this season (why him in a building full of hundreds of people?). The image of the chap setting himself on fire is terrifying, and much of the episode has a similar grotesquely hypnotic appeal.

KT: 'Bet you five bucks I get off!' Sometimes when I see lists of least favourite episodes on the Internet, I want to smash up my computer and resign from the human race in protest. A classic example of the age-old truism that, if you try to be daring in TV, the fans will spit at you. 'Pusher' is a masterpiece. It's about 'a little man who wishes he was big'. What does this remind us of? Poor Skinner gets maced and chinned by the local YTS-trainee. After being shot two weeks ago, somebody is clearly trying to tell him something. Excellent ending. In fact, excellent episode.

67: 'Teso dos Bichos'

US Transmission: 8 March 1996
UK Transmission: 2 July 1996 (Sky One)/
16 January 1997 (BBC1)
Writer: John Shiban
Director: Kim Manners
Cast: Vic Trevino (Dr Alonzo Bilac),
Janne Mortil (Mona Wustner), Gordon Tootoosis (Shaman),
Tom McBeath (Dr Lewton), Ron Sauve (Tim Decker),
Alan Robertson (Dr Carl Roosevelt),
Garrison Chrisjohn (Dr Winters)

The grave of a female shaman is found in Ecuador. The urn containing her body is taken to a museum in Boston, and becomes the centre of controversy as the Ecuadorians demand its return. Several academics vanish: one, having discovered a dead rat in his car, is identifiable only by his intestine, found in a tree. The curator's assistant, Bilac, falls under suspicion, seeming tired and washed out after taking Ecuadorian tribal drugs. His friend, Mona, finds the museum toilets full of rats, and then vanishes. Mulder and Scully read Bilac's journals and arrest him, but he disappears. The agents go into the sewers in pursuit, and find the bodies of all the vanished people, but, rather than the jaguar or the rats they expected, they're attacked by a horde of cats. They escape and the State Department decide to send the urn back.

Don't Be in the Teaser: Dr Roosevelt gets killed by something nasty and feline created by a nearby tribal ceremony.

How Did He Do That?: A human killer is the most obvious thing in the world, so Mulder opts for death by Ecuadorian jaguar spirit.

Scully Here is a Medical Doctor: She plays 'Whose Intestine Is It Anyway?' by examining its last lunch.

Ooze: Yahey, the Vine of the Soul.

Scully's Rational Explanation of the Week: Bilac is the killer, the rat climbed into the car to keep warm, lots of old buildings have rats . . . Mulder may have been drinking yahey.

Dialogue Triumphs: Mulder: 'If someone digs me up in a thousand years, I hope there's a curse on them, too.'

Scully to cop: 'Label that.' 'As what?' 'Partial rat body part.'

The Truth: The shaman's soul transmigrated into a host of killer cats.

Trivia: Dr Lewton is named after Val Lewton, who produced the movie *Cat People*. Scully: 'A possessed rat? The return of *Ben*?' Another example of her love for big-budget, tacky horror films (see 'Shadows', 'Miracle Man'). Gillian Anderson is allergic to cats. In the scene where she's attacked by one, a fur-covered pillowcase was used.

The Bottom Line: PC: What could have been a very routine episode is saved by a cool series of audience expectation bluffs as to the real nature of the killer, using media references to send us guessing this way and that. It consciously uses the 'cat-leaps-out' gag more than once, and Ecuadorian viewers will be pleased to find out (in a 'Fire' kind of way) that their countrymen all wear quaint native costume, with not a pair of Levi's in sight, but for what could be a filler episode, it's cracking. The script raids *Altered States*, Pharaoh's-curse movies and *The Rats* before settling on a riff from *The Uncanny*. I'll now make way for the others to make the obvious joke. Go on.

MD: Er, what joke would that be? This is a fair-to-middling episode, although the entire plot is so hackneyed and predictable that the viewer is left feeling 'Been there, seen it, bought the officially licensed poster magazine . . .' The silly ending is a bit of an added bonus, though.

KT: 'Invasion of the Killer Pussies . . .' Sorry, couldn't resist it. The body count in this episode is astronomical! The cats are brilliant (notably in their shocking first appearance). Anyone wanting to go to the toilet during, or immediately after, this episode . . . Well, think twice, that's all.

USELESS INFORMATION

Many previous books about *The X-Files* seemed to have no idea about what sort of information fans of the series would find interesting, and what they would regard as meaningless. It was as if somebody in the publishing business got the idea that 'fans like information', and decided that all information was equally valid. Some particularly funny instances of this syndrome include detailed summaries of every time Mulder and Scully have fired their guns, an obsession with numbers, including numberplates of cars belonging to incidental characters, and we have to mention *The Truth is Out There*'s box-out about how David Duchovny met his girlfriend. This syndrome reached its nadir with the release of the

USELESS INFORMATION

CD-Rom *Unrestricted Access*, which not only offered you one such dull factoid every time you switched on your computer ('Vernon Ephesian, leader of the Temple of the Seven Stars, had six wives') but allowed you to handle various dull props from the series, such as the urn from 'Teso dos Bichos'. The technology involved was fantastic, but *... why would anybody want to know or do these things?!* And the sound and video clips were chosen seemingly at random, and as for the pan around our heroes' offices . . . What's the point if you can't zoom in and look at anything?!

They know we're willing to buy the products. What they don't know is what we like about them.

68: 'Hell Money'

US Transmission: 29 March 1996
UK Transmission: 9 July 1996 (Sky One)/
23 January 1997 (BBC1)
Writer: Jeffrey Vlaming
Director: Tucker Gates
Cast: B.D. Wong (Detective Glen Chao),
Lucy Alexis Liu (Kim Hsin), James Hong (Hard-Faced Man),
Michael Yama (Hsin Shuyang),
Doug Abrahams (Detective Neary),
Ellie Harvik (Organ Procurement Organisation Staffer),
Derek Lowe (Johnny Lo), Donald Fong (Vase Man),
Diana Ha (Dr Wu), Stephen M.D. Chang (Large Man),
Paul Wong (Li Oi-Huan)

A Chinese man is found dead, burnt in a crematorium oven in San Francisco. With him is a fragment of hell money, ceremonial cash used to placate the dead. Chinese characters are painted on the door of his house, labelling it as a haunted house. Meanwhile, a man loses a secret lottery, and is buried in an as-yet-unused grave. Mr Hsin, a carpet layer, has lost an eye in that same lottery, trying to win to pay for his daughter's operation. Mulder and Scully's Chinese detective contact,

Chao, is attacked by the 'ghosts' who buried the earlier victim. Mulder and Scully track a rogue doctor to the place where the lottery is held, and also find Chao there. Mr Hsin has lost the lottery, and is due to forfeit all his organs. Chao was working for the game, but, sickened by it, he rebels, and shows that the game is fixed. Mulder and Scully save Mr Hsin, but nobody will talk about the lottery, and the perpetrators go free. Chao is killed for his transgression.

Don't Be in the Teaser: A kid on the run is ambushed by masked 'ghosts', who burn him in a crematorium oven.

How Did He Do That?: Mulder and Scully instantly suspect Chao, for no good reason.

Scully Here is a Medical Doctor: She does an autopsy on the burnt man, and on an organ donor who turns out to have a (living) frog inside him.

Scully's Rational Explanation of the Week: Ritual Triad killings.

Dialogue Triumphs: Scully: 'If I'm right this is one man who left his heart in San Francisco.'

The Truth: The losers of the lottery have certain body parts removed, which are sold by the lottery organisers. If we accept certain perceptual problems concerning the 'ghost' enforcers, then no supernatural elements are present.

Trivia: Mulder refers to *Ghostbusters* ('Who you gonna call?').

The Bottom Line: PC: Incredibly nihilistic, this episode upset me more than any number of Monsters of the Week could. No good is done, nothing is achieved, futility is all. I've always been disturbed by self-sacrifice, the tendency of people to form an orderly queue for the firing squad. At the centre of it is the way that the heroes' traditional foreknowledge of who the bad guy is (a cliché that a series as good as this shouldn't stoop to, and indeed makes a point of fooling with in the Conspiracy episodes) translates in this case into sheer (and, as it turns out, accurate) prejudice on the part of Mulder and Scully, as they harshly interrogate and suspect Chao, who, in terms of the plot, isn't acting suspiciously at all. Add to that the question of why, if nobody is ever seen to win this lottery, anybody still plays it, and what the frog was about, and you've got an alienated and disturbing evening's viewing. That might be good or bad: but I suspect this is scary for all the wrong reasons.

MD: I loved this episode – I don't think it's nihilistic so much as realistic, the acute poverty and the (real-life) trade in human organs being almost impossible to watch in a fantasy fiction about little green men. This central concept is strong enough to carry the episode, as long as we ignore possible cultural stereotyping and the unexplained frog (nice image, though, given its apparent symbolism in Chinese culture). I suppose it's a critique of all lotteries, with the majority paying to make a tiny minority grotesquely rich (and thus the ultimate parable of right-wing thinking), although it is indeed worrying that we get only one hint that anyone has ever been seen to win before. There's now two million dollars in the pot, for crying out loud! I have no problem with the ending: Chao saves Hsin and his daughter, and puts a stop to the exploitative game. The perpetrators go free – but then, as I say, life can be like that . . .

KT: 'It's definitely not Chinese food I'm smelling . . .' No, I don't like this one either. My main problem with the episode (which, as Martin notes, is full of terrific images) is exactly the same as Paul's – good people die (notably Chao), while evil seems to win (or, at least, get a fighting draw), which might be realistic, but in a series as life-affirming as *The X-Files* doesn't work at all well. And there are some very dodgy (if, no doubt, unintentional) racist attitudes on display.

69: 'Jose Chung's *From Outer Space*'

US Transmission: 12 April 1996
UK Transmission: 16 July 1996 (Sky One)/
18 December 1996 (BBC1)
Writer: Darin Morgan
Director: Rob Bowman
Cast: Charles Nelson Reilly (Jose Chung),
William Lucking (Roky Crikenson),
Daniel Quinn (Lieutenant Jack Schaeffer),
Jesse Ventura (Man in Black),

Sarah Sawatsky (Chrissy Giorgio), Jason Gaffney (Harold),
Alex Diakun (Dr Fingers), Larry Musser (Detective Manners),
Alex Trebek (Second Man in Black),
Allan Zinyk (Blaine Faulkner), Andrew Turner (CIA Man),
Michael Dobson (Sergeant Hynek), Mina E. Mina (Dr Hand)

Scully relates the story of one of her cases to the novelist Jose
Chung, whom Mulder has refused to see. Recently, Mulder
had a girl who was apparently the victim of an abduction
hypnotised, and she told the standard abduction story. But the
story of the boy who was with her was different: he said he
was imprisoned with an alien smoking a cigarette. A watching telephone engineer saw the aliens, and then had a series of
experiences with 'Men in Black'. Hypnotised again, the girl
remembered USAF men instead of aliens. Then a dead alien
was found: he turned out to be a USAF major in an alien suit.
Mulder met another USAF man who told him a tale of USAF
abductions, their men pretending to be aliens, but, according
to Chung's other interviewees, this interview did not take
place. Mulder and Scully met the 'Men in Black' in Scully's
hotel room, and one of them was revealed to be (or resemble)
a game-show host, Alex Trebek (later Scully is unable to
recall the meeting). Mulder and Scully were shown the
supposed crash of a secret USAF aircraft. Among the dead
was the pilot whom Mulder says he spoke to. Chung's
research finished, he is visited by Mulder, who asks him not
to go ahead with the book as it will make the whole business
look foolish, but *From Outer Space* is published, and everyone is left just as confused as before.

Don't Be in the Teaser: Two unconscious humans, two
freaked-out 'Greys' and . . . Lord Kinbote.

Scully Here is a Medical Doctor: She performs the 'alien
autopsy' and finds a zip. 'It's so embarrassing.'

Scully's Rational Explanation of the Week: The girl is
suffering from stress and sexual trauma, the hypnotist is
leading her on, hypnotism doesn't enhance memory (despite
her own experience to the contrary), the witnesses have
fantasy-prone personalities, and the abduction scenario is
now culturally entrenched. 'Mulder, you're nuts!'

Phwoar!: Scully's sober hero-worship of Chung is charming, and her fictional 'You tell anyone, you're a dead man!' just makes us want her to boss us about. And, of course, Mulder and Scully wake up in the same room, but Scully doesn't remember anything about the night before (which is a cool comment on the initial boy/girl problem). Mulder lying on a bed at the end certainly looks like a ticking timebomb of some sort. (The bed we see him on is, presumably, either in a hotel room, or forms part of Chung's readers' fictionalised representation of Reynard Muldrake's lifestyle. See 'Small Potatoes' for confirmation that Mulder has no bed.)

Dialogue Triumphs: Blaine's description of Scully and Mulder: 'One of them was disguised as a woman, but wasn't pulling it off, like her hair was red, but it was a little *too* red . . . And the other one – the tall, lanky one – his face was so blank and expressionless.'

Man in Black: 'Even the former leader of your United States of America, James Earl Carter junior, thought he saw a UFO once. But it's been proven he only saw the planet Venus.'

Roky: 'I'm a Republican!'

Manners: 'Yep, that's a bleeping dead alien body if ever I bleeping saw one!'

Pilot: 'You ever flown a flying saucer? Afterwards, sex seems trite.'

Scully: 'I know it doesn't have the sense of closure that you want, but it has more than some of our cases.'

The Conspiracy Starts at Closing Time: Memory loss after 'UFO' encounters is attributed by the USAF pilot to nerve gas or (as in 'E.B.E.') a sonic weapon. This is probably true in some ways, but not the whole story, since the pilot knows nothing of the Conspiracy's abduction scenario.

Continuity: Mulder may (or may not) like lots of sweet-potato pie. The Stupendous Yappi has hosted a video based on Blaine Faulkner's camcorder footage, entitled *Dead Alien: Truth or Humbug?* Scully never considered the paranormal much before working with Mulder. She thinks Chung's *The Caligarian Candidate* is one of the greatest thrillers ever written (Chung's *The Lonely Buddha* is also one of her favourite novels). Mulder also considers Chung 'a gifted writer'.

The Truth: 'How the hell should I know?' It goes against the whole spirit of the episode to do this, but . . . The USAF, disguised as aliens, has been systematically helping in the Conspiracy's abduction of American citizens. The abductees are subjected to memory erasure. (All this we've seen before in previous episodes.) The pilot's explanation to Mulder is new, however: that this is a test of new reconnaissance aircraft, and the folk myth of UFOs is being built up worldwide to ensure that these craft won't be shot at. However, this is revealed to be a very innocent point of view (for a start, it doesn't include any knowledge of human experiments). One might think that this level of the truth (just one level down from that which Kritschgau professes in 'Redux') is designed to counter the rumours concerning the Conspiracy that must abound in the USAF. Mulder's source and his source's fellow pilot were abducted from the scene of their latest abduction by 'Lord Kinbote', who resembles a Japanese comics character. This, like several turns of this story, seems to be a device to make sure that witnesses to weird events aren't believed, because their stories are too bizarre. That 'Lord Kinbote' is also a creation of the USAF or the Conspiracy in general is underlined by the fact that he appears from one of the triangular UFOs flown by them. (He might even be a Shapeshifter: it's cheaper than making a costume.) The pilot, on being found by his bosses with Mulder, says that he's dead meat, and refers to Lord Kinbote very casually, giving the impression that he's told the truth as far as he knows it, and that, rather than make him appear ridiculous, now that he's talked to Mulder, his superiors will have him killed. And they do. The sincerity of his story is underlined by the fact that the cook who would have witnessed this conversation tells Chung that Mulder just sat there alone eating sweet-potato pie all evening, asking him stereotypical questions about UFOs. (The cook presumably had his memory wiped and altered into a series of images taken from the media, in this case vaguely echoing *Twin Peaks*.) Chrissy's story of alien abduction is very similar to Duane Barry's and Scully's, and, indeed, has been carried out by the same forces. (She ought to check out the back of her neck.) Mulder and Scully encounter two 'Men in Black' who look like celebrities. But Scully seems very out of it during this encounter and later claims not to remember it all. At some point, then, we must assume that Scully's been got at by the memory-erasing device (in the form of a sonic weapon?) and forced to forget the encounter. (The best way to break the two of them up – or to have one doubt the other and thus expose them to the authorities – would be to cause the two of them to have different experiences of the same event, especially with one account being so ridiculous. This may, in effect, be the first attempt to do to our heroes what is later attempted with Skinner in 'Avatar', but since the Conspiracy seem to want Mulder active and vocal at this point, it's possible that his paranoia is just being stoked, and he's supposed to be alienated from Scully, his calming influence. At any rate, the side effect is to send Mulder further on the road to his belief state in 'Redux'.) It's also possible that Scully's been preconditioned not to be able to perceive these two Shapeshifters. They're carrying out a plan of making witnesses seem laughable that's much too subtle for the Cigarette-Smoking Man, but seems to be just the sort of thing that the Well-Manicured Man would think up. The hypnotherapy employed in this story, and the USAF's implied memory-wiping, act to make sure that virtually every version of the truth on show here is suspect. Chung's final book makes the whole field look ridiculous, but it's significant that he's become jumpy enough to draw a gun when he thinks he sees an alien. By the end of this episode, the Conspiracy are shown to be almost literally in control of the difference between truth and fiction, their policy of 'plausible denial' having taken on a life and culture of its own.

Trivia: The Mulder and Scully characters in Chung's book *From Outer Space* are called Reynard Muldrake and Diana Lydsky. There's a *Close Encounters* mashed potato allusion. At the end of the episode Roky goes to live in Ej Cajon, California, the town where Darin and Glen Morgan grew up. Blaine Faulkner wears a *Space: Above and Beyond* T-shirt (in an episode first shown on the night when David Duchovny guested on that show) and also has Mulder's 'I Want To Believe' poster. Alex Trebek hosts the American game show *Jeopardy*, the effect being rather like the sudden entrance of Bob Monkhouse. The other 'Man in Black' is the former

wrestler Jesse 'The Body' Ventura, also a famous face. Roky
Crikenson's name is a play on Roky Erickson of the 13th Floor
Elevators (his next band was Roky Erickson and the Aliens).
Klass County is named after Philip J. Klass, a UFO debunker
(and a great proponent of the Venus-as-UFO theory); Robert
Vallee, Jack Schaffer and Sergeant Hynek all have the sur-
names of UFO experts. Detective Manners is named after the
producer Kim Manners. Judging by his description of CIA
hypnosis experiments in the 1950s, Chung's *The Caligarian
Candidate* seems to be a close cousin of Richard Condon's *The
Manchurian Candidate*, and also includes a nod to *The Cabinet
of Doctor Caligari*. Mulder is seen watching the famous Bigfoot footage on TV. The opening, as with most of Darin
Morgan's stories, is pure *Star Wars*, but the Star Destroyer
turns out to be a phone engineer's crane. (This story all over.)
Lord Kinbote is named after David Kinbote, a character from
Vladimir Nabokov's *Pale Fire*. The novel concerns the way
people interpret experience to conform to their opinions.

The Bottom Line: PC: 'Roswell!' What an astonishing
script. This is the first script to deal with the fact that the
material Mulder and Scully investigate has become part of the
American psyche, and that the series itself is responsible for
shaping and projecting that material. (The 'alien autopsy'
footage is a brilliant pastiche, its musical score a rather obvious
take off of . . . 'Theme from *The X-Files*.') The story is
constructed like a series of Russian dolls: versions of the truth
buried inside one another. There's a powerful commentary on
the nature of subjectivity going on here: Scully edits the crude
detective's swearwords out of what she tells Chung; Blaine's
narrative is wildly at odds with her own (and it's fun to see
Mulder and Scully reconstructed into the 'Men in Black', that,
in the mythos, they would be cast as); Mulder won't even play
this game, he sees it as so treacherous. There are also numerous
delightful moments and catchphrases in a ferociously entertaining episode, from the mapping of the hypnotherapist and the
other humans into aliens, to 'Men in Black' lore recast as
wrestler braggadocio (underlining how what the world currently believes is, basically, what it sees on TV), to Mulder's
girlie scream when he sees the alien. That's a moment of

genuine feeling, though, as is the ending, when we see that natural emotion has been completely replaced by the conditioned responses and demands of television. That's the scariest *X-Files* episode for you. The funniest. And the best.

MD: 'I know how crazy this sounds ...' Just imagine that your first sight of *The X-Files* was that intentionally daft pre-titles sequence, complete with badly animated Ray Harryhausen-type monster! There are great things going on here – I especially liked the character of Blaine, desperate to get abducted to avoid having to find a job, who says he learnt a little something about courage from playing Dungeons & Dragons. The little flashes of reality are very enjoyable – from Mulder's mention of prison rape to Chung's interest in hypnosis as proving the power of mere words – and the Mulder-like summing-up at the end is brilliant. But . . . when I first watched this I thought it was by far the worst Darin Morgan script, the clever ideas and smart direction lost beneath a diabolically obscure narrative structure that was trying to be too clever by half. Now I'm not so sure. Maybe I'm just too thick to really enjoy Morgan's work.

KT: 'This is not happening!' Morgan, with this and his previous three scripts, has, effectively, taken the series to pieces, and reconstructed it as a parody of the original. But it's so much more than a mere clever pastiche; Roky's 'testimony', all that stuff about Venus being mistaken for UFOs, Mulder's reaction to the discovery of the 'alien' (positively the greatest single moment in the history of the programme), the 'alien autopsy' . . . There are many magical moments. Fantastic – in every sense of the word.

'JOSE CHUNG'S DOOMSDAY DEFENSE'

After his (all too brief) appearance in the fourth season of *The X-Files*, Darin Morgan became 'consulting producer' on the second season of *Millennium*. In November 1997, he wrote and directed a sequel to his greatest creation, with Charles Nelson Reilly reprising his role as the cynical, world-weary writer. In many ways 'Jose Chung's *Doomsday Defense*' is a critical summation of Morgan's four *X-Files* scripts, as Frank Black becomes involved with Chung after the writer has ventured into the shady world of a religious cult (Selfosophy) formed by one of his protégés, Juggernaut Onan Goopta. It's also hilarious, notably the anti-porn feminist lesbian sequence ('She was one of the sexy, good-looking kind'). There are many *X-Files* in-jokes on display (as in '*From Outer Space*', Chung renames the hero in his fiction, Black becoming Frederick Bloork). There's a Spotnitz sanitarium, a three-minute pre-title sequence entirely in voice-over, and, best of all, the tale of Bobby Wingood (who 'used to be an out of work actor, high on drugs, beating up paparazzi because they wouldn't take his picture' before joining the Selfosophists) represented in two movie posters (*Mr Ne'er Do Well* and *Operation: Box Office*) by David Duchovny! Chung says that Selfosophy institutes popped up throughout the country, but a map shows one on the east coast, and several hundred in California! Chung's cameo in a Cannes award-winning film looks like an excerpt from one of Frank Zappa's campy early seventies forays into film, while Onan Goopta's best selling trio of 'How To . . .' books, may be a subtle reference to Douglas Adams's Oolon Colluphid, and his trilogy of 'God' books in *The Hitch Hiker's Guide to the Galaxy*. We also learn more about Chung's career. His first novel (the title of which may be *So Lonesome You Could Die*, a reference to 'Heartbreak Hotel') was an autobiographical story of his circle of friends. Everybody loved it, except for the friends who never forgave him for writing about them. Other Chung novels mentioned include *A Lapful of Severed Tongues* (which he considers his worst book, but which Frank Black read many times in high school), *To Serve Man* (the book that ultimately gets him killed), and *Doomsday Defense*, published post-humously. He also wrote a short story (parody-ing Selfosophy) for the men's magazine *Playpen*. Goopta's dreadful literary work centres on the charac-ter of Rocket McGrain (played, with blond hair, by

Lance Henricksen) who continues to appear in many novels including *Dance on the Blood Dimmed Tide*, and *The Hacked-Up Hack* (despite the author's death in 1979). The Selfosophists send out their members to buy multiple copies of Goopta's work to keep it permanently on the best-sellers list, an idea Chung finds delicious. The juxtaposition of Chung writing his work longhand with one of the Selfosophists ghost-writing Goopta's next best seller on a PC ('My writing's really improved since I got this new software'), and the discussions on which author's work will still be read in the next millennium show Morgan's eye for the absurd, while the episode also contains one of the writer's finest lines of dialogue as Chung, asked by Black whether he believes in God replies: 'There have been times when I've been a devout believer, and other times when I've been a staunch atheist. And sometimes I've been both during the course of the same sexual act.' Whether the new millennium will bring (as Chung believes) 'a thousand more years of the same old crap' is debatable, but this episode is more than a mere footnote to 'Jose Chung's *From Outer Space*'. Sadly, Chung's death at the climax seems to negate the possibility of Morgan resurrecting his creation again to subvert other series (wouldn't you just have *loved* the idea of Chung turning up in something like *ER* or *Friends*?) but the episode's mantra ('Don't be dark') stands as an epitaph for this marvellous character.

70: 'Avatar'

US Transmission: 26 April 1996
UK Transmission: 23 July 1996 (Sky One)/
30 January 1997 (BBC1)
Writers: Howard Gordon, from a story by David Duchovny,
Howard Gordon
Director: James Charleston

Cast: Tom Mason (Detective Waltos),
Jennifer Hetrick (Sharon Skinner),
Amanda Tapping (Carina Sayles),
Malcolm Stewart (Special Agent Bonnecaze),
Tasha Simms (Jane Cassal), Stacy Grant (Judy Fairly),
Janie Woods-Morris (Lorraine Kelleher),
Bethoe Shirkoff (Old Woman)

Skinner wakes beside a dead woman, and claims to have lost his memory of the night before. He won't take a polygraph test. Mulder and Scully discover the woman was a prostitute, and go to see her madam, who says that Skinner paid for her. Skinner, meanwhile, is having visions of a mysterious old woman as he meets his (soon to be ex-) wife. He's being treated for a sleep disorder that prompts nightmares. Scully discovers a phosphorescent trace left on the dead woman's mouth. Skinner's wife is run off the road and badly injured. It turns out that the old woman Skinner is seeing saved his life during a near-death experience in Vietnam. Mulder finds the image of a man on one of the airbags in Skinner's wife's car: she was driven off the road deliberately. At a hearing, Skinner is dismissed. The madam is killed in a fall, but Mulder and Scully discover that the man whose face is on the airbag hired the prostitute. They set a trap for him, but it's obvious, and he prepares to spring it. Skinner goes to see his comatose wife, electing not to divorce her, and the old woman gives him a message. He arrives to shoot the man who injured his wife, thus clearing himself. He won't reveal the nature of the message.

Don't Be in the Teaser: Skinner gets his end away: the scariest thing we've ever seen in *The X-Files*. She turns into a hag, and he wakes up beside a woman with her head on back to front.

Scully Here is a Medical Doctor: She does the autopsy on Skinner's apparent victim.

Ooze: Luminescent traces on the woman's mouth and nostrils.

Scully's Rational Explanation of the Week: Skinner is suffering from REM sleep behaviour disorder.

Dialogue Triumphs: Mulder: 'At least they were having safe sex.'

Scully (on the sumptuous surroundings of the escort agency): 'Business must be booming.' Mulder: 'You mean banging.'

Skinner: 'I was no choirboy. I inhaled.'

The Conspiracy Starts at Closing Time: This is an attempt to frame Skinner, the Conspiracy having failed to kill him. (All this is presumably because his newfound resistance is putting a brake on all sorts of everyday stuff the Conspiracy would like to accomplish in the FBI via Blevins.) The stuff on the prostitute's face is presumably the chemical that wiped Skinner's memory. They probably take the sample of it from Scully's case. It may be just their good luck that Mulder gets off on his succubus riff, or perhaps they're aware of the nature of Skinner's dreams from the treatment that he's having, and have read enough of the sort of books Mulder reads to guess he'd start thinking this. At any rate, they nearly get Mulder and Scully fired as well as Skinner, which might not have been the aim.

Continuity: Skinner is trying to get a divorce, and now only has to sign the final paper. He and his wife Sharon haven't been together for eight months. Their wedding ring is inscribed 'Love forever, Sharon'. Skinner mentioned Mulder to her, saying that he respected him. Skinner drinks whiskey, and took drugs (probably marijuana) in Vietnam. His middle name is (incredibly) Sergei. The Office of Professional Conduct believe that Mulder has 'enchanted' both Skinner and Scully into believing his own wild theories. There's a mention of Mulder's sometime helper Danny (see 'Conduit', 'The Erlenmeyer Flask' and others).

The Truth: The old woman gives Skinner messages from some outside source, or perhaps (she being one of the archetypes, the wise old woman) from his own subconscious. (It's possible that, if Mulder and Scully are registering their investigation as they go, he could have logically followed them to the trap, the only subconscious cue being the idea that they might be in danger.)

Trivia: The scenes with Sharon in the red coat are taken from *Don't Look Now* (only, in this case, Sharon looks ridiculous in the coat). Jennifer Hetrick, who plays Sharon, also played Captain Picard's girlfriend Vash in *Star Trek: The Next Generation*. She must have a thing for bald, authoritative, telefantasy icons.

Scientific Comment: It's stated that sodium metal coats the interior of the airbag. Sodium is an extremely reactive metal. It should never be handled. So it's difficult to believe that it would be in an airbag even after it's been activated.

The Bottom Line: PC: A clever, complicated maze of a story, that tries to be a little too clever for its own good. If Skinner would tell anybody his weird story, it would be Mulder. And how, exactly, does he get off the charges against him? He's proved there's a plot going on, but the initial evidence is still rather damning. *X-Files* scripts often purposely confuse two different phenomena, which audiences, used to the straighter through-lines of regular US television, tend to initially see as one. In this case, Skinner's hag experience is overlaid upon the attempt to frame him, and the twists and turns of the plot mean that it takes quite a bit of thought to separate them out, especially when Mulder (the lead usually tells the audience the truth) muddies the ground between them still further.

MD: Poor Old Skinner (Part Whatever) – don't you just want to hug him at the beginning? No? OK. This is a fantastic little story, and I especially liked the scene with Skinner explaining his emotional coldness to his unconscious wife. But I just can't believe you can get an impression of a face from a discharged airbag . . .

KT: 'He's behaving like a guilty man.' Love Skinner's wedding photo – with such an obvious toupee that it takes on the quality of grand kitsch! More *JFK* imagery and dialogue and 'several questions remain unanswered . . .' To be honest, I lost the plot of this one quite early on and never really recovered. Not that it's bad, necessarily, just a little overcomplicated.

71: 'Quagmire'

US Transmission: 3 May 1996
UK Transmission: 30 July 1996 (Sky One)/
20 November 1996 (BBC1)
Writers: Kim Newton, Darin Morgan (uncredited)
Director: Kim Manners
Cast: Chris Ellis (Sheriff Lance Hindt),
Timothy Webber (Dr Faraday), R. Nelson Brown (Ansel Bray),
Mark Acheson (Ted Bertram), Peter Hanlon (Dr Bailey),
Terrance Leigh (Snorkel Dude), Murray Lowry (Fisherman)

Missing persons around Heuvelmans Lake, Georgia, which is associated with a monster, 'Big Blue', attract Mulder's attention. Dr Faraday, a biologist, denies that he killed a man who was sceptical about his work, and tells Mulder that the lake's frog population has declined. A half-eaten body is found, and, after further disappearances, the lake is 'shut down'. Scully's dog is snatched from her by something in the bushes. Mulder and Scully take a boat out onto the lake, and end up marooned on a rock, which turns out to be very close to shore. Mulder becomes convinced that the monster lives in the woods, and, hunting it, is attacked by a huge alligator, which he kills. But after the two agents leave, a real lake monster appears.

Don't Be in the Teaser: Dr Bailey, a 'frog holocaust' sceptic, gets dragged into the lake.

How Did He Do That?: Faraday asks the question for us, concerning Mulder's frog/food-chain leap.

Scully Here is a Medical Doctor: She puts a tourniquet on Faraday's leg.

Scully's Rational Explanation of the Week: Lake monsters are folk tales born of a collective fear of the unknown. It's a busy lake, people get killed, by boats and by drowning. One body's flies are undone, so he must have fallen in while relieving himself. The fish ate one of the torsos. As the Sheriff says, 'I'm not at all convinced we're dealing with an aquatic menace.'

Phwoar!: Scully's sadness over her dog makes you want to hug her, but Mulder just doesn't understand. Marooned on the rock, they manage some very charged small talk, prompting Mulder to ask, 'Scully, are you coming on to me?' But very obviously they don't attempt to keep each other warm. Mulder's stutter reappears as he reveals another small piece of his soul: that he'd prefer to have a handicap than an obsession, because a handicap would give him good cause to work hard and improve. Faraday arrives with 'Hope I'm not interrupting anything', and Scully's reaction is pure comedy guilt. They're able to talk now about the nature of their dispute earlier this season (does Mulder pursue the truth without reason?). And Scully comes to understand and accept him a bit more.

Dialogue Triumphs: Stoner: 'Dude, what's wrong with you? You made me drop my toad.'

Faraday: 'If you'll excuse me, I have some amphibians to release.'

Continuity: Scully has apparently lost some weight lately (as we all know . . .). Her father taught her to respect nature ' 'cos it has no respect for you'. She won't put her dog in kennels (problem solved) and can pilot a small boat. As a child, Scully was interested in the mysteries of the deep. Then 'I grew up, and became a scientist.'

The Truth: A big alligator has been eating people and frogs. But there is also (badly animated though it might be) a real sea serpent in Heuvelmans Lake.

Trivia: Tyler Labine and Nicole Parker reprise their roles from 'War of the Coprophages', still trying to open the 'doors of perception'. Big Blue is possibly a reference to IBM (after a man called Gates was the villain in Kim Newton's last script . . .). Heuvelman's Lake is named after Dr Bernard Heuvelmans, a cryptozoologist who was an expert on sea serpents. The Doors, Jimi Hendrix, Hole and Primus are referenced by the kids, along with the Discovery Channel and *Unsolved Mysteries*. There are visual references to *Jaws*, and an extended metaphor around *Moby Dick*, with Scully's little dog being called Queequeg (whose death Mulder, cast as Ahab, ignores in his obsessive pursuit). Interestingly (given what it was doing to its previous owner in 'Clyde Bruckman's Final Repose'), in *Moby Dick*, Queequeg was a cannibal. The scene between Mulder and Scully on the rock was written by Darin Morgan.

The Bottom Line: PC: This one resembles nothing more than one of those Vodaphone adverts starring Kyle MacLachlan. It's way cool, though, the cult of Darin Morgan having taken the two Kims for members. The series has started to demonstrate that what some newspaper critics have alleged (that fans watch the show believing it to reveal 'the truth') is nonsense. This episode is a case in point, as our gaze is invited to rest on such implicitly silly sights as Scully piloting a boat, and that first shot of her little dog, which has the viewers yelling, 'He's dead meat!' The sitcom direction holds everything in an ironic frame, recognising that, before the third season, our lead characters had so solidified as icons that seeing them doing ordinary things like washing dogs is hilarious, and that this trick can be played without damaging their credibility. (From the distance of season five, I'd say they've now used up all my goodwill on that point.) Mulder and Scully tracking monsters with a little dog in tow is wonderful to watch, and the viewers are smart enough to dig this stuff. The only problem with the script is that once we've started to recognise and enjoy the *Moby Dick* metaphor, Scully actually *tells* us it to make sure we all got it. And the mountains of Georgia were nice. Just when we're thinking it's refreshing to see such closure from *The X-Files* (there was a monster, and Mulder shot it), we get that final frame, which is cheesy, but yeah, in that it encapsulates the continuing search for mystery . . . is rather sweet.

MD: A wonderful monster story that's as comfortable as a pair of old slippers. Simple subversions – the fisherman catching a corpse (not the expected monster), the man in boots being chased by a similar-footed creature, the duck in the mist – are balanced by little elements such as Mulder and Scully's discussion of cannibalism. Not for the first time, though, I can't help but think that only sickos read their kids *Moby Dick* at bedtime.

KT: 'You slew the Big White Whale, Ahab.' I like this one a lot (especially Faraday's rant about pseudo-scientists chasing fairytales). The scene on the rock is another definitive *X-Files* moment.

PARODIES

An episode of the final season of *Spitting Image* in 1996 featured a clever parody of *Scooby Doo – Where Are You?* in which Mulder and Scully solved the case, much to the chagrin of a cheesed-off Velma who complains that *The X-Files* has done nothing more than rip off the cartoon series' plots. (We wonder if this was an influence on the *Rocky and Bullwinkle* references in 'Never Again'?) Mulder notes that *The X-Files* is 'grown up' and 'scary' but still gives his partner a 'Scully snack'! Another series to success-fully parody *The X-Files* is its Fox stablemate *The Simpsons*. In the episode 'Grampa vs. Sexual Inadequacy' (April 1994), Bart's UFO infatuation, combined with a spate of child abandonment in Springfield, leads Bart, Milhouse and their friends to speculate about an elaborate conspiracy involving 'the Rand Corporation' and 'the Saucer People'. When Lisa, playing a Scully-type sceptic, pours scorn on the idea, suggesting sarcastically that they should also include 'the Reverse Vampires', Bart apes Mulder by taking her seriously. It was perhaps inevitable that we'd end up with a direct cross-over, and in January 1997, 'The Springfield Files' appeared featuring Duchovny and Anderson. The episode (mostly narrated by Leonard Nimoy), con-cerns Homer encountering an eerie green creature in the woods. Mulder wants to investigate the case, leading to one of the all-time great Mulder/Scully dialogue exchanges: Mulder: 'There's been another unsubstantiated UFO sighting in the heartland of America. We've got to get there right away.' Scully: 'Well, gee, Mulder, there's also this report of a shipment of drugs and illegal weapons coming into New Jersey tonight.' Mulder: 'I hardly think the FBI's concerned with matters like that . . .' The episode is full of cool in-jokes for the fans (Bart's opening chalkboard lines are 'The Truth Is Not Out There'; The Cigarette-Smoking Man puts in a brief appearance during Homer's polygraph test; the picture of Mulder on his badge is a full-length study of him in his red swimwear!). It also includes some very subtle characterisation, as Mulder sits in Moe's Tavern allowing Homer to make a completely incompetent pass at Scully, and noting that the FBI's motto is 'invading your privacy for 60 years'. In a marvellous climax, the agents join Nimoy and Mr Burns in song (the *Hair* anthem, 'Good Morning Starshine'). A worthy addition to *The X-Files* canon, this story makes a lot more sense than several *proper* episodes! At the same time, American sitcom *Cybill* was parodying the series on a regular basis, as the titular heroine got the lead in the (often somewhat brainless) Grey aliens and flashlights show *Life Forms*. As well as sending up the motifs of *The X-Files*, there were nods to Cybill Shepherd's former series *Moonlighting*. Often, lampooning aesthetics can provide a critical summation of genuine problems. In a January 1996 issue of *NME*, the column 'Oi! Bullshitter! With Grant Mitchell' focused on Scully (or, rather, 'Bird off *The X-Files*'!). With many viewers expressing annoyance with Scully's lack of belief in *everything*, the *EastEnders* character notes: 'You reckon you're an FBI agent out to find out about UFOs and all that shit? Well, aintcha? What does it take, eh?' The rant continues with the memorable opinion: 'Every week Mulder rings up and says "Oi! Bird off *The X-Files*, I got a crashed spaceship/werewolf/vampire/ conspiracy ... and it's right here in New York/Philadelphia/The arse-end-of-nowhere." And what do you do? ... You get abducted ... get taken to Jupiter – and back again – then dumped ... with a tattoo on your head that says "Aliens have just had it off with me".' And yet, as 'Grant' says, at the end of every single episode she still ends up saying into her dictaphone, '"I think something happened, but it wasn't the paranormal." Mulder would be better off being partnered by Angus Deayton. At least he's not so bloody cynical.' The most infuriating aspect of this pastiche, is that it's *exactly* what many fans have been saying since Episode Two. Perhaps it's inevitable that a series like *The X-Files* should become such an obvious name to drop – TV programmes as diverse as *Brookside*, *2 Point 4 Children*, *Fantasy Football League* and *Jonathan Creek* have referred to it. Comedian Eddie Izzard made the comparison between the world's shock at the death of Princess Diana to what would have happened if they'd suddenly decided to end *The X-Files* with an episode at 2 a.m. one Monday morning. In early 1998, Britpop band Catatonia scored a top-five hit in the UK with a charming song called 'Mulder and Scully'. When the stage-set of Oasis's 1997 'Be Here Now' tour was described as '*X-Files*-like' by several magazines, the imagery didn't require much explanation. This is nothing new, of course. The media has always enjoyed nodding to its more esoteric flavours of the month – *The X-Files* has simply become the new subject of a series of jokes that used to finish with the line 'It's like something out of *Doctor Who*!' Indeed, the self-referencing extended to a British TV series of adverts for vodaphone featuring former *Twin Peaks* star Kyle MacLachlan that successfully captured the spirit and mood of *The X-Files*. But, when we hear about motorcycle, hi-fi and music magazines featuring Duchovny and Anderson on their covers, or the tenth newspaper this week to point out that Chelsea's Romanian full back Dan Petrescu looks uncannily like David Duchovny, we know we are dealing with something bigger in the public consciousness than a popular TV series. Full marks, though, to the football magazine *90 Minutes* who, in their 1996 calendar, were the first to spot the spooky resemblance Manchester United's Paul Scholes bears to Scully!

72: 'Wetwired'

US Transmission: 10 May 1996
UK Transmission: 6 August 1996 (Sky One)/
6 February 1997 (BBC1)
Writer: Mat Beck
Director: Rob Bowman
Cast: Colin Cunningham (Dr Henry Stroman),
Tim Henry (Plain-Clothed Man),
Linden Banks (Joseph Patnik), Crystal Verge (Dr Lorenz),
Andre Danyliu (County Coroner), Joe Maffei (Motel Manager),
John McConnach (Officer #1), Joe Do Serro (Jimmy),
Heather McCarthy (Duty Nurse)

Mulder gets a tip-off from someone he doesn't recognise concerning a man who's killed five people, thinking that they were all the same person. The killer taped cable news. Scully watches it, and finds mention of a Serbian war criminal on the nights of the killings. That night, she sees Mulder in conversation with the Cigarette-Smoking Man. Many other similar killings occur. Mulder pursues a TV engineer, and finds a strange golden attenuator in a cable TV box, which the Lone Gunmen explain sends signals between the frames of a TV picture. Scully gets more and more paranoid, and shoots at Mulder. The FBI begin to hunt her. Mulder is told she's dead, but it's not her. Mulder goes to Mrs Scully's house, and finds Scully hiding there, afraid, ready to kill him. Her mother persuades her not to. Mulder deduces that the doctor who examined the first killer is controlling this experiment: he's met with the Cigarette-Smoking Man. But just as Mulder tracks him down, X arrives and kills all involved. He and Mulder have a confrontation. X explains that he tried to let Mulder get to these people first, but he let himself be sidetracked by Scully. X meets with the Cigarette-Smoking Man, and tells him that the security leak has been closed: his position is still safe.

Don't Be in the Teaser: A poor chap kills two people, including his partner, thinking they're a war criminal.

Scully's Rational Explanation of the Week: Amphetamine abuse and too much TV-watching.

Scully's Irrational Explanation of the Week: That Mulder has sold them out to their enemies.

Phwoar!: Mulder's utter lack of visible reaction until he knows that isn't Scully's corpse. His kick at the car. Scully, armed and dangerous, is an extraordinary sight to behold.

Dialogue Triumphs: Scully has got so used to the Conspiracy stories by now that her first question to Mulder about his contact is: 'What does he want us to recover?'

Mulder: 'Yeah, but those studies are based on the assumption that Americans are just empty vessels, ready to be filled with any idea or image that's fed to them, like a bunch of Pavlov dogs.'

The Conspiracy Starts at Closing Time: X is the Cigarette-Smoking Man's lieutenant (these days, having probably been Deep Throat's beforehand), and his position is still secure, because his superior doesn't know he's leaking information. In this case, X leaked news of the television experiment to Mulder via a contact (whom he was then forced to kill to cover his tracks), and then found himself ordered, because of this breach of security, to kill the men running the experiment and clean it all up. He pursued them as slowly as he could, while encouraging Mulder to get to them first, but found that he couldn't help but win this race. Since the Cigarette-Smoking Man knows there's an information leak at a higher level, it seems that X's days are, from this point, numbered. A weapon which sends people crazy via their TV, and encourages them to, ahem, trust no one, would be a wonderful paranoia-causing weapon, useful to maintain 'plausible denial' and this seems to be why the Conspiracy are developing it. The ultimate aim – according to X – certainly transcends commerce or politics.

Continuity: Mulder is red/green colour-blind. He toys with a basketball, hinting at the skills we see in 'Paper Hearts'. He doesn't believe that cow flatulence is depleting the ozone layer, or that violence on TV causes real violence, which he thinks is 'political bunkum', making him rather left-wing, if politically innocent. (He's probably so pro-TV because it's been his constant companion for so long ... and he's not paranoid at all!) Scully's greatest paranoias are that Mulder may be working for the Conspiracy, and that her home is bugged (though both Mulder and Scully are by now used to the idea that their phones are sometimes tapped). Her final collapse is set off by stumbling into a scenario very like that of Melissa's murder. Mrs Scully has photos of herself and a baby and of both the Scully sisters by her bed. Special Agent Pendrell of the Sci Crime Lab is mentioned, as is Danny (see 'Avatar').

The Truth: The Conspiracy have developed a weapon that uses television signals to make viewers paranoid, fearful and violent.

Trivia: Two incredibly self-conscious girls with flowers walk down the hospital corridor, eyeing up Mulder. Whose nieces were those? One of the tapes Scully watches is labelled *Jeopardy*. *Die Hard* is on the TV as the cable man cuts the connection, which happens just before the line about needing a couple more FBI agents ...

Scientific Comment: The Lone Gunmen state that television is a rapid sequence of still pictures fired against the tube. At best this is a highly misleading description, at worst it's plain wrong. A standard 50 Hz TV picture is a set of lines with half of the lines repeating at 50 cycles/sec, and the other half also at 50 cycles/sec between these. The episode's description makes it sound like a very fast slide show. It's then stated that the subliminal messages are in the signal between the frames. If this was so, the messages would never be 'fired at the screen' (using their terminology) and so wouldn't be seen. To be seen, the subliminal messages would have to replace the picture itself.

The Bottom Line: PC: A non-Conspiracy Conspiracy episode which manages to bring a breath of fresh air to the activities of the Cigarette-Smoking Man by offering us another nice, solid bit of closure. We now know who X works for. And he really ought to stop leaving those cigarettes around. It's odd to find Mulder talking about pseudo-science and being the non-paranoid one, but it's great to see the series finally recognising that Mulder and Scully would, by now, be hiding in their houses with the wardrobe against the door. The TV effects are wonderful, though it's a little worrying to find that cable news (and shopping channels!) are the culprits, rather than action series (a bit too close to home?). Still, with another astonishing performance from Gillian Anderson, another routine episode gets the magical touch of season three.

MD: season three certainly ends with a fine clutch of stories. This is really rather good (though – I may as well be the first to say it – it is very like 'Blood').

KT: 'Television does not equal violence, I don't care what anyone says.' This *is* like 'Blood', but it has a wonderful anger of its own. Mulder's rant about those who use TV to make political points is particularly welcome.

73: 'Talitha Cumi'

US Transmission: 17 May 1996
UK Transmission: 13 August 1996 (Sky One)/
3 September 1997 (BBC1)
Writers: Chris Carter, from a story by David Duchovny and
Chris Carter
Director: R.W. Goodwin
Cast: Roy Thinnes (Jeremiah Smith),
Angelo Vacco (Doorman), Hrothgar Mathews (Galen Muntz),
Stephen Demopoulos (Detective), John Maclaren (Doctor),
Cam Cronin (Paramedic), Bonnie Hay (Night Nurse)

A gunman goes crazy in a burger bar. A man called Jeremiah Smith heals the victims, then vanishes from the scene. Mrs Mulder meets with the Cigarette-Smoking Man, who asks her to remember something. Mrs Mulder is then hospitalised, having had a stroke, and writes Mulder a note saying 'palm'. The Cigarette-Smoking Man finds Smith working at a social security office, and imprisons him. X shows Mulder photos of Mrs Mulder and the Cigarette-Smoking Man, telling

Mulder that the stroke happened after the man left. Smith, meanwhile, turns himself in to the FBI, and answers all questions blandly, essentially closing the investigation. Mulder searches his mother's beach house. 'Palm' turns out to be an anagram of 'lamp': inside a lamp is an alien-killing weapon that Mulder has seen before. The Cigarette-Smoking Man interviews Smith in his cell. Smith is a Shapeshifter, but one who wants to offer humans hope. He tells the Cigarette-Smoking Man that he's dying of lung cancer and it's implied that he cures the Cigarette-Smoking Man, who then frees him. Mulder and Scully find 'their' Smith, but he escapes by shapeshifting. The Shapeshifter Assassin arrives at the cell to kill Smith, but he's vanished. The Cigarette-Smoking Man visits Mrs Mulder in hospital, and tells Mulder that Smith has information about Samantha. X, seeking the alien weapon, meets Mulder. They fight, and back away from a stand-off. Scully is visited by Smith, who starts to tell her of a plan that involves Samantha. Mulder meets with them, and asks Smith to come and heal his mother, but the Shapeshifter Assassin arrives, intending to kill Smith.

Don't Be in the Teaser: Well, in this case, do, because everybody ends up OK despite four people being shot.

How Did He Do That?: Mulder makes a connection between the two palms – 'You think it's a leap?' – and gets it absolutely wrong, but he does work it all out in the end.

Scully Here is a Medical Doctor: She gives Mulder an update on his mum's condition.

Scully's Rational Explanation of the Week: Mrs Mulder's linguistic centres have been scrambled: correct!

That's a Mouthful: The Cigarette-Smoking Man: 'This becomes a responsibility. The thing I'm now called upon to put right, and put down.'

Phwoar!: Mulder sobbing at his mum's bedside just demands a warm towel and some cocoa.

Dialogue Triumphs: Smith to the Cigarette-Smoking Man: 'You live in fear. That's your whole life.'

Dialogue Disasters: That whole muddled and misty verbal duel between Smith and the Cigarette-Smoking Man. 'You talk!' shouts the Cigarette-Smoking Man. Indeed. We learn nothing and are simply bored by this undramatic mess of pseudery.

The Conspiracy Starts at Closing Time: The Cigarette-Smoking Man and the Mulders used to hang out together at the summer house. The Cigarette-Smoking Man knew the Mulders' children (as we see in 'Demons', Mulder needed therapy to recall their meeting, even though he was clearly old enough to remember, so maybe these details were taken from his memory in 'Deep Throat'). The CSM knew Mrs Mulder before Mulder was born. There's a hint that the Cigarette-Smoking Man and Mrs Mulder may have been lovers (and that suggestion is furthered by one of Mulder's memories in 'Demons', but it's still unclear if he's just the father of Samantha, or of both Mulder children). X called an ambulance for Mrs Mulder, and wants Mulder to know of her and the Cigarette-Smoking Man's acquaintance (knowing, certainly, that this would set Mulder even more against the CSM). He knows that something is stored in the beach house, but only after Mulder finds it does he know what. And then he immediately wants it. Perhaps X knows that, at the moment of truth, the weapon will be the proof he needs to show somebody in authority, or, more likely, he wants the only weapon that can kill a Shapeshifter for personal protection or for a planned assassination. Smith used to be one of the Conspiracy, a junior member, if his lowly but useful position in social security is anything to go by, but has now decided to give the humans 'hope'. He no longer believes in the 'greater purpose'. In effect, he wants to defect to the Rebels. His touch can not only heal wounds, but suck up blood and dematerialise bullets. It doesn't patch up clothes (so we're not talking about a trick with time here), but perhaps that would just be unnecessary work. This sort of matter/energy manipulation is just the sort of thing that a real shapeshifter would have to be able to accomplish, and, seeing as the Shapeshifter Assassin manages it in the next episode, presumably all Shapeshifters could do it if they wanted to.

This is the first sign that their powers can extend to other people (and, in addition, that they can possibly influence their thoughts, as Smith almost does right at the beginning). The Cigarette-Smoking Man knows all too well that only a blow on the back of the neck by an alien weapon can kill a Shapeshifter or a human/Colonist hybrid clone, so he summons the Shapeshifter Assassin to act as Smith's executioner. A date has been set for the Colonisation of Earth (we're betting it's 13 October!). To achieve this Colonisation, humans must, for some reason, lose their belief in everything but science (presumably because this will leave them vulnerable to the various perception-altering weapons of the Conspiracy). The Cigarette-Smoking Man wants to be a 'commandant', ruling over his own people (the image is of concentration camps) when the process (which he thinks is the transformation and mutation of humanity into slaves, rather than into Greys as revealed by the movie) begins. The elaborate plan, or Project, involving Samantha, may or may not be the Colonisation plan itself. (It's possible that Smith may only be about to tell our heroes about the whole Conspiracy abduction/breeding business, which, as a loyal Conspiracy drone, he discovered Samantha was present in the paperwork of, unaware that the CSM had rescued her from being a breeder.) Skinner used to know how to contact the Cigarette-Smoking Man, but, as we suspected he would after Mulder went to his house, the man's made sure that this is no longer true (they must get back in touch sometime before 'Memento Mori'). It's confirmed that he doesn't know the Cigarette-Smoking Man's real name. Smith transforms into Bill Mulder and Deep Throat during his conversation with the Cigarette-Smoking Man. This seems to amaze the CSM, as well it might if he thought that Smith was simply a hybrid clone, and not an actual Shapeshifter. (We've never seen the hybrids shapeshift, even when they've had great cause to do so, as in 'End Game'.) Presumably, this implies that Smith is more than your average hybrid clone, and has learnt to control the Black Oil in his system to shapeshift. He's unusual also in asserting his independence.

Continuity: After her divorce, Mrs Mulder vowed never to return to the summer house at Quonochontaug, Rhode Island. Bill Mulder was a good water-skier, but nowhere near as good as the Cigarette-Smoking Man. That wasn't all Bill was the lesser man at, he says.

The Truth: see The Conspiracy Starts at Closing Time above.

Trivia: 'Talitha cumi' (or 'talitha koum') is New Testament Greek for 'little girl, get up', and are the words used by Jesus when healing a child in Mark 5:41. (Both an apt reference for Smith's activities, an explicit reference to Mulder's desire to have his mother healed, and a nod in the direction of Samantha?) Angelo Vacco, a production assistant, appears as one of the healed gunshot victims. In real life, William B. Davis is a top veteran water-skier (what an extraordinary mental picture that conjures up . . .). The Smith/Cigarette-Smoking Man confrontation is a take on a scene from Dostoevsky's *The Brothers Karamazov*. The original has a returning Jesus arrested by church leaders, and told that he burdened mankind with too much freedom, which they took away, because people want to be led. So it's not only rubbish, it's unoriginal too.

The Bottom Line: PC: The solid feel of the Conspiracy stories in season three continues, with Diet Conspiracy, a firm, fast-paced story that doesn't try to lump in all the usual ingredients (Krycek, the Lone Gunmen, etc.) for the hell of it, but just gets on with it. Unfortunately, in the middle of all that is an empty dialogue that proves, once and for all, that Chris Carter has never quite got the idea that drama is about doing, not talking. It's actually insulting that such sound and fury signifying nothing is supposed to be lapped up by the fans as deep and meaningful. We've seen deep and meaningful, and it's in the so-called 'comedy' episodes of Darin Morgan. That apart, this is a fitting end to the best season of *The X-Files*, one that saw Scully empowered, a lot of clichés flattened, and some intelligent thought put into developing and solidifying the back story behind what was then the most subversive, high-quality and zeitgeist-surfing television series on the planet.

MD: A hugely enjoyable finale with some fantastic effects. The only dark cloud on the horizon is how much longer the (massive) invasion/subversion/world domination plot could be used without changing the entire tenor of the series. In that sense, the fact that the conclusion next season turned out to be such a crushing disappointment isn't really surprising at all.

KT: 'He's here to kill me . . .' A bit rambling in places (notably the thoroughly pretentious Cigarette-Smoking Man/Smith scenes which seems to go on *for ever* without any point), though I did enjoy Mulder's brawl with X. At the time I wondered if this wasn't a disappointing blind alley, taking the story-arc off at a tangent to little effect. And it's easy to get very tired of Smith, as he's played without much sympathy, and about a million miles from Architect David Vincent, by Roy Thinnes. And the cliffhanger is *tame* beyond measure.

Fourth Season

24 45-minute episodes

Created by Chris Carter

Associate Producer: Lori Jo Nemhauser
Consulting Producers: Ken Horton, Glen Morgan (74–86),
James Wong (74–86)
Co-Producers: Vince Gilligan, Paul Rabwin, Frank Spotnitz
Producers: Rob Bowman (74–92),
Joseph Patrick Finn, Kim Manners
Executive Producers: Chris Carter, R.W. Goodwin,
Howard Gordon, David Greenwalt (90–97)

Regular Cast: David Duchovny (Special Agent Fox Mulder),
Gillian Anderson (Special Agent Dana Scully, 74–93, 95–97),
William B. Davis (The Cigarette-Smoking Man, 74, 80–82, 87,
94), Ken Camroux (Senior Agent, 74[20]), Charles Cioffi
(Section Chief Scott Blevins, 97), Jerry Hardin (Deep Throat,
80), Scott Bellis (Max Fenig, 90, 91), Sheila Larken (Margaret
Scully, 87, 97), Tom Braidwood (Melvin Frohike, 80, 87, 93[21]),
Dean Haglund (Langly, 87, 93[22]), Bruce Harwood (John Byers,
80, 87), Mitch Pileggi (Assistant Director Walter Skinner,
74, 76, 78, 81–84, 87, 89, 91, 93, 94), Vanessa Morley
(Young Samantha Mulder, 83, 96), Steven Williams (X, 74),
Nicholas Lea (Alex Krycek, 81, 82), Michael David Simms
(Senior Agent, 74[23]), Christine Willes (Agent Karen E.
Kosseff, 95), Rebecca Toolan (Teena Mulder, 74, 83, 96),
Paul McLean (Special Agent Kautz, 94[24]), John Moore
(2nd Elder, 94), John Neville (Well-Manicured Man, 81,
82), Don S. Williams (Elder, 94[25]), Gillian Barber (Penny
Northern, 87), Brendan Beiser (Agent Pendrell, 74, 76, 81, 90,
91), Morris Panych (Gray-Haired Man, 74, 87, 94), Brian

---

[20] Credited as 'Second Senior Agent' in this episode.
[21] Voice only.
[22] Voice only.
[23] Credited as 'Senior FBI Agent' in this episode.
[24] Credited as 'Agent Kautz' in this episode.
[25] Credited as '1st Elder' in this episode.

Thompson (The Shapeshifter Assassin, 74), Laurie Holden (Marita Covarrubias, 74, 76, 81, 89, 94), Dean Aylesworth (Young Bill Mulder, 80, 96), Chris Owens (Young Cigarette-Smoking Man, 80, 96), Anatol Rezmeritsa (Commandant, 81,[26] 82[27]), Pat Skipper (Bill Scully, Jr., 97), Arnie Walters (Father McCue, 97)

74: 'Herrenvolk'

US Transmission: 4 October 1996
UK Transmission: 12 January 1997 (Sky One)/
10 September 1997 (BBC1)
Writer: Chris Carter
Director: R.W. Goodwin
Cast: Roy Thinnes (Jeremiah Smith),
Garvin Cross (Repairman)

Smith and Mulder escape, Mulder stabbing the Shapeshifter Assassin in the back of the neck with the alien weapon. Smith takes Mulder to see both the great plan . . . and his sister. They head for Canada, where they find a repairman killed by bees. The revived Shapeshifter Assassin forces Scully to find out where they're going and follows them. Meanwhile, the Conspiracy are aware of a security leak, and let X know that Mrs Mulder is under threat. Skinner has found five Smiths across the country, all compiling data. Scully manages to decipher that data: it's an inventory of protein tags put into humans as part of the Smallpox Eradication programme. Her superiors find that hard to believe. Mulder and Smith find covered fields of an unknown shrub and, working on the farm, many copies of his sister at the age she was abducted. The Shapeshifter Assassin arrives at the farm, and Mulder hides with Smith and 'Samantha' in a vast apiary. The Shapeshifter Assassin, badly hurt, chases Smith and leaves Mulder. Mulder returns to the hospital, where Scully, advised by X, has placed a guard on his mother. But there is no threat; it's a trick by the Conspiracy to test X's loyalty. He's

[26] Uncredited.
[27] Uncredited.

ambushed and shot, writing 'SRSG' in blood before he dies. That means: 'Special Representative to the Secretary General' of the UN. Mulder meets Marita Covarrubias, the assistant to that person, in New York and, while rebuffing all his claims about the farm, she covertly gives him photos of Samantha. The Cigarette-Smoking Man makes the Shapeshifter Assassin heal Mrs Mulder, saying that Mulder, who is important to the project, must always have something to lose.

Don't Be in the Teaser: A repairman is killed by bees.

Scully Here is a Medical Doctor: 'You show a twenty-letter code to any scientist and they immediately think "protein amino acid sequence code"!' She does a great job with the smallpox vaccination information.

Ooze: From the back of the Shapeshifter Assassin's neck, and on the face of the stung repairman.

Scully's Conspiracy Theory of the Week: Smallpox jabs plant a protein used as a tag, a genetic marker. This has been going on for fifty years. 'This sounds like something we might have expected from Agent Mulder,' one of the FBI men tells her.

That's a Mouthful: Smith: 'A flowering shrub, but its specific epithet can't be found on any of your taxonomic charts.'

Phwoar!: Mulder tells Scully that he needs her to know that he's OK. Scully holds Mulder by his mum's bedside. Pendrell gets all hot under the collar.

Dialogue Triumphs: X: 'Protect the mother.'
Marita: 'Not everything dies, Mr Mulder.'

The Conspiracy Starts at Closing Time: The human race, or at least the American public, are apparently being tagged and inventoried through fifty years of smallpox inoculations. (And at the same time not being inoculated, presumably, since the Conspiracy would want a proper large-scale test of their bee-based Black Oil dispersal system.) This must be the heart of Bill Mulder's Project. In 'Ascension' we see Scully's arm being scanned by a grid pattern of lights, presumably reading her tag. Those who have escaped from the Tunguska prison camp cut off their left arms, getting rid of the tag. Presumably, these tags contain a quick record of the genetic information of that particular individual, perhaps designed to allow attacking Black Oil to discover the exact nature of the body it's about to inhabit, and whether that person has been genetically biased towards any specific function. (We may now begin to see the number of 'genetic mutants' in the series, plus prodigies like Gibson Praise in 'The End', as being pre-planned creations, designed in the remote past by the Colonists to fulfil special roles once inhabited or bred within by the Black Oil. The otherwise slightly puzzling title of 'The Host' now becomes clearer.)

The New-York-based Special Representative to the United Nations (one of several) is part of the Conspiracy. The plan of the Colonists, at least the part involving the bee attack, is known as 'the Process'. Smith regards it as 'a new origin of species', by which, it turns out in the movie, he just means that the plants and bees are genetically engineered, the plants able to pass on either Black Oil virus or smallpox to the bees. The Colonists' agrarian workforce consists of serial ovatypes, clones who, in the case of these particular drones, can't speak. (These are presumably just a variation on the genuine human/Colonist clone hybrid that we meet on many other occasions.) Smith describes himself as a drone (which is probably more of a job description than a biological one). The farm worker drones and Smith are immune to the bee stings, so it's slightly odd that the Shapeshifter Assassin is troubled by them. Mind you, he doesn't succumb, and his face has returned to normal by the end, so perhaps it's just that he was acting aggressively and so got stung. (If these bees are carrying Black Oil rather than smallpox, his facial markings are the result of his system having to take onboard more Black Oil than usual.)

We see another early sign of what happens to some female abductees: the Samanthas are clearly the children of Samantha's ova and Colonist DNA, as were the ones in 'Colony'. Smith and the Shapeshifter Assassin both make big leaps, as we've seen Shapeshifters, human/Colonist hybrids and quasi-hybrids do in the past. All Colonists, it would be safe to conclude, since an assassin can do it, can heal wounds by touch. There is only metaphor to suggest that they are at all insect-like (but see 'Folie à Deux').

'Everything dies' is either a Conspiracy slogan which Marita has heard (perhaps it's something they've heard from their masters, and which they repeat to each other because of its worrying subtext), or her mentioning the phrase is sheer coincidence. The Cigarette-Smoking Man infers to the Shapeshifter Assassin that Mulder is important to the plan, but that's probably just him peddling his usual line to keep his old lover Mrs Mulder alive: when Mulder apparently dies a season later, the Conspiracy are seen to not particularly care.

The Truth: The Colonists have been preparing their bee attack apparatus on secret farms with UN backing. Scully's Conspiracy theory also appears to be true: Americans are being catalogued, tagged and inventoried by a government organisation.

Trivia: The title is German for 'master race'.

Scientific Comment: If someone shows a twenty-letter code to me I do *not* immediately think 'protein amino acid sequence code'. I tried this on a few other astrophysicists and a plasma physicist and it did not leap to their minds either. It probably does for biological scientists. You can't get an infinite number of variations from a fifteen-letter sequence.

The Bottom Line: KT: 'Don't unlock doors you're not prepared to go through.' Strange episode, this. Huge opening five-minute chase sequence with a debt to *Terminator* larger than the national debt of a third world country. Good music (particularly the industrial/techno stuff). *The X-Files* does *Swarm* with the (frankly baffling) bee metaphor plastered all over the episode. Despite the rambling narrative, and enough pretentious dialogue for a dozen episodes of *Millennium*, the ending is enigmatically brilliant ('You know how important Agent Mulder is to the equation').

PC: Some cool images, including insect-like conformity in farming pastureland, and some features very reminiscent of *Doctor Who* (the Sontarans' neck weakness, Dalek interior music for the Shapeshifter Assassin's chase scenes),

Quatermass II, and *The Invaders*, which could now almost be in the same canon as this show. It's good to see Scully using science as a tool to get to the truth, the demonstration of which the show's rationalist detractors often ignore. There is, however, more of that horrid 'poetic' dialogue. I'm not as disturbed by a lack of answers as I used to be. I've come to expect that, which may be a shame.

MD: Mulder finally gets to meet Jeremiah but, instead of getting him to tell everything he knows about the Conspiracy, they set off for a trek across country. And then, just when Jeremiah is about to spill the beans, the alien bounty hunter shows up. Oh, please! We aren't really told anything of significance during this depressingly routine episode. Although the ending is good, and the iconography memorable, 'Herrenvolk' is fatally flawed by bringing the alien killer back to life. Given that the thrust of this and previous stories is that they can be killed by the pointy gadget, to deny us that logical outcome is (like the lack of explanations) just plain silly.

75: 'Home'

US Transmission: 11 October 1996
UK Transmission: 19 January 1997 (Sky One)/
17 September 1997 (BBC1)
Writers: Glen Morgan, James Wong
Director: Kim Manners
Cast: Tucker Smallwood (Sheriff Andy Taylor),
Chris Nelson Norris (Edmund Creighton Peacock),
Adrian Hughes (Sherman Nathaniel Peacock),
John Trottier (George Raymond Peacock),
Karin Konoval (Mrs Peacock),
Sebastian Spence (Deputy Barney Paster),
Judith Maxie (Barbara Taylor), Kenny James (Radio Singer),
Neil Dennis (Catcher), Cory Fry (Batter),
Lachlan Murdoch (Right Fielder), Douglas Smith (Pitcher)

Mulder and Scully arrive in the small Pennsylvanian town, Home, after the grizzly discovery of a deformed infant body. Obvious suspects seem to be three retarded brothers who live close to the crime scene, though the local sheriff is sceptical about their involvement. Scully is shocked by the number of genetic defects displayed by the baby's body, suggesting inbreeding. The agents visit the Peacock farm and find evidence of a recent birth. Before they can be arrested the brothers murder the sheriff. Mulder and Scully, with a vengeful deputy, return to the farm where the deputy is killed. They find the men's mother, a helpless invalid, in the house and survive an attack from the men, killing two of them. The third escapes with his mother.

Don't Be in the Teaser: A newborn child is buried alive in a muddy field. Nice family entertainment there . . .

Scully Here is a Medical Doctor: She examines the dead child and is horrified by its numerous birth defects.

Ooze: Blood and mud. Urgh!

That's a Mouthful: Mulder: 'What we are witnessing, Scully, is undiluted animal behaviour. Mankind absent in its own creation of civilisation, technology and information regressed to an almost prehistoric state, obeying only the often savage laws of nature.' And several other similarly stilted rants. Good grief, it doesn't even sound like him!

Scully's Rational Explanation of the Week: The Peacocks kidnapped and raped some helpless girl and held her until she gave birth.

Phwoar!: Mulder comforts Scully after she is obviously upset by the state of the baby's body. He touches her back gently and asks whether her family has any history of genetic defects. She says they haven't and he tells her to 'find yourself a man with a spotless genetic make-up and a really high tolerance for being second-guessed, and start pumping out the little Uber-Scullies'! Now who on Earth could that refer to?! (Ironic, if the stuff about the Cigarette-Smoking Man and Mrs Mulder turns out to be true.)

Dialogue Triumphs: Scully: 'Mulder, if you had to do without a cellphone for two minutes you'd lapse into catatonic schizophrenia.'

Mulder (as he and Scully push the pigs around): 'Scully, would you think less of me as a man if I told you I was kind of excited right now?'

Continuity: Mulder used to play 'all-day pick-up games' of baseball with his sister in the vineyard of their home, which he fondly remembers, along with riding their bikes to the beach and eating baloney sandwiches. Mulder says he dreams of leaving the city behind and making his home in a small rural community like this. He's never thought of Scully as a mother. (Or so he says, but considering 'Kill Switch', etc. . . .)

The Truth: A straightforward tale of incest, infanticide and murder.

Trivia: Johnny Mathis's 'Wonderful' accompanies the murder of Sheriff Taylor. The episode title seems to be a (dark?) reference to Morgan and Wong's return to the show. The Peacocks are named after Glen Morgan's parents' neighbours. In the sickly sweet American TV series *The Andy Griffith Show*, Andy played the sheriff of Mayberry, named Andy Taylor. There is also a mention of Barney the dinosaur.

Scientific Comment: The chances of getting three different fathers for the baby even if the ovum is capable of accepting three sperm is at best only one in nine. There is nothing to stop three sperm of the same man being accepted rather than one from each of three men. To reach even a one in nine probability all three men would have to mate with the woman in very quick succession. It's a race between sperm after all. I am not convinced that you could tell there were three different fathers just by looking at the baby's DNA pattern. The alleles would come from four different parents but without a genetic map of all four for comparison you wouldn't be able to say where they came from. The process of meiosis would be interesting with three fathers. There would be four sets of DNA strands interacting instead of two.

The Bottom Line: KT: 'They're such good boys . . .' Sick. There's nothing redeeming in this dreadful waste of time and talent, just waves of repulsive images. Defenders of this episode have described it as a tribute to horror movies and accused me of being squeamish. Not a bit of it, if 'Home' had an ounce of originality behind the gore, then it might have still worked, but the episode is just a bunch of borrowed plot devices strung together for effect; echoes of *To Kill a Mockingbird* and *Psycho* at the beginning give way to a depressingly ugly series of set pieces taken from *The Texas Chainsaw Massacre* and *The Hills Have Eyes*. The US transmission contained a pre-titles warning of the carnage to come ('Due to some graphic and mature content, parental discretion is advised'). Pity they didn't include a warning about insulting the audience's intelligence, too. Only two things save it from complete disaster – the previously mentioned Mulder/Scully scene, which is charming, and Mulder's discovery of a newspaper from the day Elvis died. I can't believe the writers of 'E.B.E', 'Beyond the Sea' and 'Blood' wrote this abomination. Dreadful.

PC: The central, indeed, only, problem with this episode is that Mulder and Scully, who we've come to regard as ethical heroes, keep on wisecracking amongst the slaughter, concerned only with themselves as everybody else suffers. Perhaps it was thought that that would lighten the episode, but the effect is exactly the opposite: in a cruel world, our heroes are cruel also. The BBC edit for violence actually makes it slightly more scary.

MD: The direction has a certain brutal flair about it, but I'm glad that I saw only the sanitised BBC version. With a lot of the more gratuitous violence taken out, I actually think the episode has some merit, although the script is rather clumsy at times. There are some nice little dialogue nods to the insidious advance of the modern world (all this stuff about unlocked doors and the Sheriff's fears), and Mulder's absolute addiction to television is hysterical (he says he couldn't live anywhere that wasn't able to pick up New York Niks games, and ends up watching a fuzzy programme on jackals). The image of the brothers listening to syrupy MOR pap in their old car is something David Lynch would be proud of, as is the scene where the boys try to round up the escaped pigs, their arms flapping. Ultimately, the viewer is forced to ask what is it that is really horrifying about this episode? –

and it's not the violence, or the deformed brothers. It's the central idea of the grotesquely willing mother who has lost any sense of individual purpose. The execution is as crude as that of a horror comic, but the very idea strikes deep into our concept of motherhood and humanity.

> **HOME . . . ALONE?**
>
> 'Home' saw the return to *The X-Files* of writers Glen Morgan and James Wong after a year producing *Space: Above and Beyond*. Perhaps the bitterness and anger of dealing with the networks over the cancellation of their show had something to do with the extreme violence portrayed in the episode. Though it was apparently a relaxed shoot (Tucker Smallwood describing the experience as 'one of the happiest and most fun shows I've worked on'), the Fox network were nervous about the finished product, giving it a pre-episode caption warning of its 'mature content'. Since its initial transmission, 'Home' has never been repeated on the main Fox network, and is unlikely to ever be. At Thanksgiving 1997, however, the Fox cable station FX ran an all day repeat run of episodes chosen by viewers as the most popular, a poll that 'Home' won by some distance. But perhaps that's down more to rarity than quality.

76: 'Teliko'

US Transmission: 18 October 1996
UK Transmission: 26 January 1997 (Sky One)/
24 September 1997 (BBC1)
Writer: Howard Gordon
Director: James Charleston
Cast: Carl Lumbly (Marcus Duff),
Willie Amakye (Samuel Aboah),
Zakes Mokae (Minister Diabira),
Maxine Guess (Flight Attendant),
Bill Mackenzie (Bus Driver),
Bob Morrisey (Dr Simon Bruin),

Michael O'Shea (Lieutenant Madson),
Danny Wattley (First Officer)

Summoned to Skinner's office, Scully is asked her medical opinion on a recently discovered body. A man, an African-American, has undergone a dramatic change, losing all his skin pigmentation. Mulder's investigations (aided by Marita Covarrubias) lead him to the toxic thorn of a West African passion flower and Samuel Aboah, a recent immigrant. Aboah appears to have no pituitary gland. A minister from Burkino Faso blames the deaths on the legendary Teliko, evil spirits who drain their victims of life and colour. Mulder, however, comes to believe that the Teliko are nothing more than members of an African tribe, who hunt down other humans to steal hormones from the pituitary gland (which in turn leads to the change in skin colour of their victims). Aboah escapes the hospital and, while pursued, uses a thorn to immobilise Mulder. Scully rescues her partner, shooting the African before he can finish Mulder off.

Don't Be in the Teaser: An African turns white and dies in an aeroplane toilet.

Scully Here is a Medical Doctor: She performs several medical tests and an autopsy on Owen Sanders, the fourth black man to go missing.

That's a Mouthful: Scully: 'Not everything is a labyrinth of dark conspiracy. And not everybody is plotting to deceive, inveigle and obfuscate.'

Phwoar!: Pendrell seems crushed when he hears that Scully has a date.

Dialogue Triumphs: Mulder: 'There's a Michael Jackson joke in here somewhere, but I can't quite find it.'
  Mulder, on why Aboah left his own country: 'Free cable?'

Dialogue Disasters: Mulder: 'Hey, I heard you were down here slicing and dicing. Who's the lucky stiff?'

The Conspiracy Starts at Closing Time: Marita is presumably aware of what's happening here more because weird stuff just naturally gets passed to her than because the Conspiracy are interested. Although maybe their interest in the human gene pool has led them to an interest in all manner of genetic abnormalities. Perhaps they're even aware that their Colonist masters take a special interest in such things, eyeing up their future property, as it were?

Continuity: This is Scully's 74th journal entry, and the 76th episode. So we might assume that she's written one entry for every story apart from '3' and 'One Breath'? Bit too neat, isn't it?

The Truth: The members of a lost African tribe have no pituitary gland and thus no dark pigmentation. In order to survive, they must extract the melanin and hormones they need from (unwilling) donors. Aboah's apparent contortionism, and his ability to swallow and regurgitate a long blow pipe, might be unique to that individual, or another genetic modification typical of his people.

Scientific Comment: At the rate Aboah gets through victims any African tribes living near the Teliko would have been wiped out. Such behaviour would not be a good evolutionary characteristic for the Teliko. I don't believe that an institution like the CDC (Centre for Disease Control) would ever ask a non-practising doctor like Scully to try to identify a new disease. The CDC would have access to full-time, top medical researchers and all the latest equipment. They might ask for an autopsy, but they'd do the rest themselves. It seems unlikely that destruction of the pituitary gland would cause the skin to turn white so fast. Melanin production might be stopped but the existing melanin would not be destroyed.

The Bottom Line: KT: 'I had hoped if I closed my eyes it would go away this time.' A speed-written reworking of 'Squeeze'. Some interesting pieces of African tribal culture, but it's all been done before. A further example of *The X-Files* running on the spot at a time when the series seemed to have become a victim of its own success.

PC: Some episodes you just can't find anything to write about. This is just . . . functional. It exists, OK?

MD: 'Aboah. What the hell kind of name is that?' Great

central idea, though perhaps the story would have more resonance if the whiteness of the black men was seen more metaphorically in the context of what amounts to white superiority in the West. (One only has to think of old soap adverts, with gollywogs scrubbing themselves clean, to see what's bubbling beneath the surface here.) Still, there aren't many programmes that would even attempt anything as borderline as this, though it's interesting to see how PC Mulder is (wondering if it's all just a PR exercise because black men have gone missing and the perception is that the police aren't doing anything). I'm uncomfortable with the implication – put into the mouth of the black immigration expert – that once Aboah gets US citizenship then he can bring his entire extended family over with him. Sounds more like a KKK preconception than actual reality. Bad bits: The fact that it turns into a mindless rehash of 'Squeeze' about half-way through (and the way Aboah is tracked to his lair is very contrived). Good bits: the scene with Aboah and the immigration man, who eventually switches on the light, which is almost a parody of the usual darkness of the show. The mind-blowing incidental music. There's no real fantasy content – even in the drug-influenced scenes. (Compare with something like 'Eve', where the supernatural content is purely a result of direction that cheats.) Best of all is the poster with the words 'It is a small world after all' at the bus stop. So underplayed, it had me in hysterics.

77: 'Unruhe'

US Transmission: 27 October 1996
UK Transmission: 9 February 1997 (Sky One)/
1 October 1997 (BBC1)
Writer: Vince Gilligan
Director: Rob Bowman
Cast: Pruitt Taylor Vince (Gerald Thomas Schnauz),
Sharon Alexander (Mary Louise LeFante),
Walter Marsh (Druggist), Angela Donahue (Alice Brandt),
William MacDonald (Officer Trott),
Ron Chartier (Inspector Puett),

Michael Cram (Officer Corning),
Christopher Royal (Photo Technician),
Michelle Melland (ER Doctor), Scott Heindl (Billy)

Traverse City, Michigan: a young woman has a passport photo taken and then disappears, while her boyfriend is killed. The developed photo shows the woman screaming, surrounded by ghostly images. Soon the woman is found, having been the victim of an amateur lobotomy. Another woman is abducted in similar circumstances. While Scully follows up a possible lead concerning a construction company, Mulder takes photos from the two crime sites to Washington for enhancement. Finding hidden clues within the photo he calls Scully, who arrests a man, Gerry Schnauz, a former mental patient. Schnauz is haunted by his sister's suicide and his attack on his father, blaming both on 'the howlers', evil spirits living within people's minds. Lobotomisation is his attempt to cure the women. He escapes and captures Scully, intending to perform the same treatment on her, but Mulder arrives in the nick of time and kills him.

Don't Be in the Teaser: Mary Louise LeFante is drugged and kidnapped. Her boyfriend, Billy, is stabbed in the head.

How Did He Do That?: One of Mulder's finer leaps, guessing the presence of 'thoughtographs' on the film in Mary's camera.

Scully Here is a Medical Doctor: She graphically describes Mary's 'ice-pick lobotomy'.

Scully's Rational Explanation of the Week: Heat damage to the film, which is also out of date. Or the photographer was involved in the kidnap. 'All right, so what's *your* theory?'

Dialogue Triumphs: Mulder: 'That was a bad year. What else happened in 1980, Gerry?' 'Well, John Lennon got shot. Where the hell are you going with this?'

Continuity: Scully took German in college.

The Truth: Schnauz, traumatised by personal demons, has (seemingly) developed an elaborate scheme to 'save' the women he is attracted to from their own demons ('the howlers'). He can affect the development of photographs, making them show either something of the future, or the 'howlers' that haunt people (or, perhaps, the contents of his own mind).

Trivia: The title means 'unrest' in German, but the inspiration for this episode came from a Time-Life book on psychotic killers, read by Vince Gilligan, which included an article on mass murderer Howard Unruh.

The Bottom Line: KT: 'Let's talk about "the howlers".' Scary. Again, loads of obvious roots are visible, including *The Silence of the Lambs* and *The Legend of Hell House*, as well as really clear debts to two of the series' own episodes, 'Shadows' and 'Grotesque'. But for all that, this is three-quarters of the way towards a really good episode – the first sign that season four had picked up from its frankly disappointing start. The ending, however, is awful. It's sad that, given Scully's stated empathy with Schnauz in the concluding scene (a mirror-image of Mulder's descent into hell in 'Grotesque'), she still has to be tied to a dentist's chair and slavered over before Mulder comes charging in. The empowerment of much of season three seemed at the time of this episode to have gone, along with Darin Morgan.

PC: Rather wonderful, with some outstanding images (the approaching attacker seen through the umbrella) but didn't we get rid of Scully being strapped to chairs last season?

MD: Battle ye not with monsters, lest ye become a monster . . . It could almost sum up the whole series. Anyway, I found this rather engrossing, and, like 'The Field Where I Died', it's an interesting examination of the essential difference between Mulder and Scully (the former wants to know the truth, even when they fail to save the woman's life, whereas Scully's obligation is to other people, and she thus doesn't have the stomach for the quest in isolation from that). In defence of 'Unruhe', I'd like to point out that Scully has already partly released herself before Mulder shows up. I wonder how Pruitt Taylor Vince made his eyes flicker like that?

78: 'The Field Where I Died'

US Transmission: 3 November 1996
UK Transmission: 16 February 1997 (Sky One)/
8 October 1997 (BBC1)
Writers: Glen Morgan, James Wong
Director: Rob Bowman
Cast: Kristen Cloke (Melissa Riedal Ephesian),
Michael Massee (Vernon Warren/Ephesian),
Anthony Harrison (FBI Agent Riggins),
Doug Abrahams (Harbaugh), Donna White (Therapist),
Michael Dobson (BATF Agent)

The FBI raid the farm owned by the religious cult The Temple of the Seven Stars in Apison, Tennessee, searching for a cache of weapons. Preventing the suicide of the charismatic leader Vernon and his six wives, Mulder and Scully interrogate one of the wives, Melissa, who appears to regress to previous lives, including one in which she and Mulder were lovers. While Scully investigates possible links in the past, Mulder undergoes regression hypnosis. As the FBI continue to search for the weapons, the cult members are released and, under Vernon's instructions, commit suicide, Melissa among them, Mulder arriving just too late to save her.

Don't Be in the Teaser: . . . Or you'll have to suffer Mulder chanting Robert Browning at you!

Scully's Rational Explanation of the Week: Multiple Personality Disorder (spot on – see The Truth).

That's a Mouthful: 'At times I almost dream I too have spent a life the sage's way and tread once more familiar paths. Perchance, I perished in an arrogant self-alliance an age ago. And in that act of prayer, went up so earnest . . .'

Phwoar!: Mulder and Scully's heart-to-heart over their passage through time together is amazingly touching. Their friendship even survives Scully's anger at Mulder's casual use of Melissa to (hopefully) find answers about himself.

Dialogue Triumphs: Mulder: 'Souls come back together.

Different, but always together. Again and again.'

Continuity: Scully says she wouldn't have changed a day of her and Mulder's four years together (although she could have 'lived without that flukeman thing' – see 'The Host').

The Truth: Melissa and Mulder discover under hypnosis that they seem to have lived past lives as Sarah Kavanaugh and Sullivan Biddle, two Confederates during the civil war in November 1863. Mulder's claim that souls come together again and again (Scully was the sergeant of his platoon) is interesting. But rubbish. During another regression he claims he was a Jewish woman in a Nazi concentration camp and that Scully, Samantha and Melissa were related to him. Fine. Possible. But then he goes and spoils it by claiming that The Cigarette-Smoking Man was a Gestapo guard. Despite the fact that The Cigarette-Smoking Man, in *this* incarnation, would have been *alive* during the years of Nazi terror, and yet, being conceived just two months into the war (if we take the birthdate given in 'Musings of . . .' as true, or even already born if we adjust for the fictional nature of that text and make him old enough to be working for the government in 1953 as seen in 'Apocrypha'), not old enough to participate. Ooops. So we're backing Scully's theory about Multiple Personality Disorder. And Mulder is susceptible enough to Melissa's fantasies to place himself into them.

Trivia: There are lots of biblical quotations, most seeming pretty accurate (despite his scepticism in 'Revelations', Mulder seems surprisingly well versed in the last book of the Bible). In real life, a Civil War soldier named Sullivan Ballou wrote a now famous (and very moving) letter to his wife, Sarah, in which he assured her that his love for her was 'deathless' and that even though he might be killed in the war, he would always be with her, he would wait for her, and that 'we shall meet again'. One week after writing the letter, Ballou was killed in the First Battle of Bull Run. Mulder's soliloquy at the beginning and end of the episode is from the Robert Browning poem 'Paracelsus'. Vernon Ephesian, the character likened to David Koresh, bears Koresh's real first name.

Scientific Comment: How did Scully call up that biblical quote so rapidly on the computer? It must already have been in a Bible database routine.

The Bottom Line: KT: Now this is better! Apart from the one walloping great continuity error (that throws the intended reincarnation/regression concept out of the window, and would be built on in 'Musings of . . .' Careless!), this is a virtually flawless script aided by a series of astonishing performances (Duchovny and Kristen Cloke are especially electric). A couple of subplots (the child abuse one, chiefly) get lost in the maelstrom, but this script has a cohesion and focus altogether missing from those shown previously in the season. This season's 'Beyond the Sea' (although, again, it's a bad dialogue fan's dream).

PC: This is silly! Very well done, but operatic fan fiction tosh all the same. One of those areas of weirdness that I have no interest in, though, so that affects my judgement. I'm all for Robert Browning normally, also, but using verse out of context as a sort of meaningless seasoning of supposed intellectualism . . . It cries out for being made central to the text: why are we being asked to watch Mulder quote unconnected poetry?

MD: There's some good stuff here, but it doesn't quite hang together. Frankly, if we cared about the cult members at all, the ending might have been moving. Mind you, I'd love a black jacket with 'FBI' on the back. That would be so cool.

REVELATION(S) AND THE TEMPLE OF THE SEVEN STARS

The Temple's 'logo' – a seven-horned, seven-eyed lamb – is as described in Revelation chapter 5. The seven stars (Rev. 1:20) are the angels of the seven churches written to in Revelation chapters 2 and 3. When Vernon attempts to quote from the letter to the church in Smyrna (Rev. 2:8–11), Mulder says that his understanding was that the Temple modelled themselves on the church in Ephesia (silly boy, he means Ephesus (Rev. 2:1–7)). (Odd, too, that Vernon's surname is Ephesian. Interestingly, the church at Ephesus is criticised in Revelation for having lost its ability to love, which seems a fair criticism of the Temple of the Seven Stars.) Mulder talks of Revelation 12:17 describing the devil's army (when actually it talks of a dragon waging a war on God's people). Scully (who really should know better) then mentions Revelation*s* (note the erroneous plural), describing a Christian army defeating the devil, which isn't a summary most readers would recognise. Mulder then gets in on the act, also calling it Revelation*s*. Arghh! Vernon's own grasp of the Bible, as one might expect of people like David Koresh, is about as loose as his morals. He claims to have been with John Mark when he delivered his message of the apocalypse (in other words, Revelation). Wrong John: John Mark is believed to have been the author of Mark's gospel, whereas Revelation is generally considered to have been written by John, son of Zebedee, a different bloke altogether. Indeed much of what Vernon says is entirely extrabiblical.

79: 'Sanguinarium'

US Transmission: 10 November 1996
UK Transmission: 23 February 1997 (Sky One)/
15 October 1997 (BBC1)
Writers: Valerie Mayhew, Vivian Mayhew
Director: Kim Manners
Cast: Richard Beymer (Dr Jack Franklyn),
O-Lan Jones (Rebecca Waite, RN),
Arlene Mazerolle (Dr Shannon),
Gregory Thirloway (Doctor), John Juliani (Dr Harrison Lloyd),
Paul Raskin (Dr Eric Ilaqua), Andrew Airlie (Attorney),
Marie Stillin (Dr Sally Sanford), Norman Armour (ER Doctor),
Martin Evans (Dr Hartman)

Greenwood Memorial Hospital, and Mulder and Scully investigate the claims of a doctor who has recently killed a patient while, he says, undergoing an out-of-body experience. Mulder is convinced the doctor was possessed and finds evidence of a pentagram in the operating theatre. Suspicion falls on a nurse who attacks another doctor. He fights her off and she dies, having ingested hundreds of needles. The deaths at the hospital continue and provide links to a series of deaths ten years ago. Mulder concludes that Dr Franklyn, another medic, is responsible – killing patients born on sabbats in a bizarre ritual to gain a new identity. The nurse, a white witch, was trying to fight him. Franklyn fools Mulder and Scully with a false lead, completes his plan, and turns up at a hospital in Los Angeles wearing a new face.

Don't Be in the Teaser: Dr Lloyd liposuctions a patient to death.

Scully Here is a Medical Doctor: She's really at home in a hospital, reminding an entire operating theatre of her credentials. ('I'm an FBI agent . . . I'm a doctor!') She says that in medical school she saw 'some weird stuff' concerning objects being swallowed, and she's clearly disapproving of the Managed Health Care policy which allows cosmetic operations at the expense of other medicine.

Ooze: Blood. Tonnes of it!

Scully's Rational Explanation of the Week: Medical malpractice. Lack of sleep. Drug use. And lots of guff about bizarre medical conditions. All of which are much easier to swallow than witchcraft.

Dialogue Triumphs: Scully: 'There is magic going on here, Mulder, only it's being done with silicon, collagen and a well-placed scalpel.'

Scully: 'If it's that simple, why don't you put out an APB for someone riding a broom and wearing a tall black hat?'

Continuity: Mulder seems to spend the episode thinking about having a nose-job.

The Truth: Black Magic. Dr Franklyn (formerly Dr Cox) has the ability to transport objects into people's bodies. He is also able through means unknown to use the deaths of people born on the four sabbats in a ceremony to cut off his own face and (seemingly) grow a new one. He can also levitate.

Trivia: Mulder again shows off his biblical knowledge, in this case quoting from Ecclesiastes ('Vanity, all is vanity'). The address 1953 Gardner Street is probably named after Gerald Gardner, who founded his own form of witchcraft, the Gardnerian, in 1953, when laws against the practice were revoked. Nurse Rebecca Waite's name may be a conflation of Rebecca Nurse (one of the Salem witches) and Arthur Edward Waite, a famous writer on medieval witchcraft and the co-creator of the modern tarot deck.

The Bottom Line: KT: 'I think this patient is finished.' Wow, this is nasty! There's a lot of good characterisation on display, the switching of suspects is clever and the bathroom sequence is suitably shocking. But, really, this is nothing more than a lot of old horror clichés thrown about without much imagination (and how many times have we said *that* about this season?). And the lack of explanations gets very annoying by the end. In a definite throwback to 'GenderBender' we're given a series of things happening and absolutely no idea why they happen (other than the fact that the occult is at work).

MD: The first couple of minutes lead you to expect a witty and shocking discussion about cosmetic surgery and self-image; instead, 'Sanguinarium' is full of mindless gore and hopeless dead ends. There is no real interaction with other characters, no investigation, no dramatic progression. It's just a series of gross set pieces (although, for me, nothing was more stomach-churning than the pre-title sequence of the doctor scrubbing his hands). Only nice bit: Mulder's hilarious reaction to Scully's quip about the APB.

PC: I really liked this. Great to see a positive portrayal of a Wiccan in the series (though the nature of her belief system and her foe's are both glossed over), even if she is just there to stop the viewer taking one look at the awesome Richard Beymer and being immediately certain he's guilty. (Weird bits: her bothering with a bath of blood to attack Franklyn; the nods towards making us believe that a coven is at work (Franklyn must have bought the hospital that meeting table) and the astonishing coincidence of the victims' birthdates being suitable.) It's different, but I like the ghoulish wonder of it.

80: 'Musings of a Cigarette-Smoking Man'

US Transmission: 17 November 1996
UK Transmission: 9 March 1997 (Sky One)/
22 October 1997 (BBC1)
Writer: Glen Morgan
Director: James Wong
Cast: Morgan Weisser (Lee Harvey Oswald),
Donnelly Rhodes (General Francis), Dan Zukovic (Agent),
Peter Hanlon (Aide), Paul Jarrett (James Earl Ray),
David Fredericks (Director), Laurie Murdoch (Lydon)

The Cigarette-Smoking Man enters a building opposite the Lone Gunmen's offices with a rifle, and eavesdrops electronically on a conversation between Mulder, Scully, Byers and Frohike in which the latter says he knows who the Cigarette-Smoking Man is, and who he wants to be. We see various significant moments in the Cigarette-Smoking Man's life, including his assassinations of John F. Kennedy and Martin Luther King, and an occasion on which he and Deep Throat encountered an alien. He could easily kill Frohike, but decides not to.

That's a Mouthful: Young Cigarette-Smoking Man: 'You've enough plausible deniability to last the rest of your nine lives.' Later: 'Sure, once in a while there's a peanut butter cup or an English toffee, but they're gone too fast, the taste is fleeting. So you end up with nothing but broken bits filled with hardened jelly and teeth-shattering nuts.'

Dialogue Triumphs: Mulder: 'No one would kill you, Frohike. You're just a little puppy dog.'

Young Cigarette-Smoking Man: 'I'd rather read the worst novel ever written than sit through the best movie ever made.'

Concerning the assassination of JFK: 'Is there a cover story?' 'Tell them it was done by men from outer space!' (Now that's surely a dig at *Dark Skies*, in which that happens!)

The Cigarette-Smoking Man: 'I work very hard to keep any President from knowing I even exist.'

And: 'Once again, tonight, the course of human history

will be set by two unknown men standing in the shadows.'

'Life is like a box of chocolates. A cheap, thoughtless, perfunctory gift that nobody ever asks for!'

THE JACK COLQUITT STORY

The nature of truth in this episode is complex, as there are two possible sources for the narrative. Are we watching the Cigarette-Smoking Man's memories, or the tale Frohike is telling, which consists of the CSM's fictionalised account of his own life, altered even more towards the sensational by the editor of *Roman a' Clef* (sic)? There are some clues. For a start, we know that the CSM was working for the government in 1953 ('Apocrypha'), a few years too early for the given birthdate, so we might take it that he's vainly made his alter ego younger, or put his hero's birthdate on the date of a famous assassination for dramatic irony. We're presented with an establishment that knows nothing and cares nothing about aliens throughout the sixties, with Roswell as a pure smokescreen, when we know that the Conspiracy's Colonist-backed abduction programme had been in operation for at least twenty years then and the CSM and Deep Throat were investigating alien ooze in 1953. (So, in effect, this piece of fiction is backing up one of the Conspiracy's big lies, that the standard Grey aliens of myth have just arrived and the government is fighting them using what little knowledge they have. The story even portrays the countries of the world as vying to discover alien knowledge, instead of being part of a pan-national Conspiracy.) The story also gives us a Bill Mulder who's a lowly intelligence captain in 1962, hardly already in control of the Project that bears his name that began in the 1940s. So we can take the whole JFK/MLK assassination story as being either true or false, but the CSM's running of every modern conspiracy as fictional. (One of his aides in that sequence regards the fall of the USSR as meaning that there are 'no more enemies'. The CSM should know, considering that he's given his daughter Samantha up to some, that there still are! Unless we're looking at an 'outer conspiracy' here, the people who *think* they run the USA from an office in the CIA, and yet know nothing of Colonists, etc., then this point, and also the very clichéd nature of this sequence, makes it likely to be pure fiction.) We might even think that we can see some of the CSM's thought processes in operation in the fiction: taking Deep Throat's Hanoi alien killing story and redressing it as the first meeting between US agents and the aliens in 1991 (although he keeps the detail of the Grey's toxic green blood, a detail which his superiors might find fault with him using in public), and inserting himself pining for Mrs Mulder in 1968, then giving up all thought of her after the MLK assassination. (We do know, however, that there was an 'alien assassination' in the CSM's own draft, before the magazine editor altered it, so perhaps the editor did him a favour by moving that part out of Hanoi and presenting it as a new dramatic turn . . . It's even possible that the magazine is being used by the Conspiracy to stop the CSM leaving and/or to stop his desire to let some of the truth get out in fictional form. If he let certain details out, surely he'd worry about his personal safety after his resignation?)

However, there are strange details present in the narrative that would surely jar in a work of fiction. The naming of Bill Mulder, as in 'a living alien could advance Bill Mulder's Project by decades' (which is simply untrue in the real world: these people *know* real aliens on social terms), and the numbering of the UN resolution concerning killing crashed aliens give away checkable details right at the heart of the Conspiracy's plan. Either the CSM's fictional version of Bill Mulder has some already-revealed Project concerning the government's secret battle with aliens, and that's not the UN resolution's real number (or Deep Throat gave a standard lie to Mulder about that resolution in 'E.B.E') or we're hearing the CSM's memories from Hanoi intrude on to Frohike's narrative. So, altogether, it seems here that the CSM's book portrays Diet Conspiracy, a picture of an invidious organisation that are doing all the things the American public expects it to be doing ('Who fixes every Oscar night? We do!' as the Stonecutters sang in *The Simpsons*), but is also heroically battling the alien menace. Do you think the CSM could get anyone interested in doing it as a TV series?

The Diet Conspiracy Starts at a Dramatically Apt Time: According to the fiction, the Cigarette-Smoking Man was born ('appears') on 20 August 1940 in Baton Rouge, Louisiana (on the same day that Trotsky was assassinated). His father was a Soviet spy who was executed for passing information on America's entry into World War II to the Nazis. His mother (a smoker) died of lung cancer (which would explain his early disinterest in cigarettes ('I never touch 'em'), and his reaction in 'Talitha Cumi' to being told that this is how he too will die). He was thus orphaned while still a baby, and became a lonely child who read extensively. Then, according to Frohike, he disappeared until October 1962. At this stage he appears to have been a captain in the US military, at 22, a very young one, specifically at the Center for Special Warfare, Fort Bragg, serving alongside Bill Mulder. He denies having been involved in covert action in Central America in 1961 (but then, he would, wouldn't he?). By 1968, the fictional Cigarette-Smoking Man is in such a position that he treats J. Edgar Hoover as subservient (as he, and perhaps his alter ego, presumably continued to do with every FBI chief thereafter). He respected Martin Luther King ('an extraordinary man') and supported his stance on civil rights, but suggested, and carried out, his murder because of his perceived communist leanings. The 'departmental projects' he is overseeing on Christmas Eve 1991 include the

Anita Hill case, the moving of the Rodney King trial, Bosnian independence ('America couldn't care less,' he says perceptively), and the Oscar nominations. The fixing of the Superbowl (for reasons unknown, the Cigarette-Smoking Man doesn't want to see the Buffalo Bills win the trophy as long as he's alive), and his rigging of the 1980 Olympic Ice Hockey final (in which the USA unexpectedly beat the USSR), thanks to the drugging of the Russian goaltender, indicate that the Cigarette-Smoking Man and his cohorts may control everything in the world. He says he'll call Saddam Hussain back! He intends to keep a personal eye on Fox Mulder, who has managed to get himself assigned to the X-Files, presumably in order to keep his know-nothing aides off Mulder's back. (Another detail from the book that rings true: perhaps in the novel he ends up killing Mulder, the son he could never acknowledge? There are further hints that Mulder is his son – why else would he constantly carry a photo of Mrs Mulder and the baby Fox?) His discussion with Deep Throat is full of astonishing pieces of information. Roswell 'was concocted to keep everyone looking the wrong way'. He lies to Deep Throat, saying that he's not killed before, and it wouldn't be at all surprising if he made use of a loaded coin. It is implied that Deep Throat was the Conspiracy's chief propagandist, being in charge of 'deadly lies', and certainly that sounds like the real version. The plaster the CSM is wearing looks like a nicotine patch. But all the above is probably fictional.

Fictional Continuity: Fox's first word, according to his father, was 'JFK' (as this is in October 1962, he would have been eleven months old). We get another glimpse of Scully's senior thesis on Einstein's twin paradox (University of Maryland, dated 15 May 1988). In this fictional, ultimately paranoid version, if you look closely, the thesis contains a discussion on and references to MJ-12, the organisation who in UFO lore are responsible for crashed alien craft, so this Scully is obviously a plant set up to get on Mulder's good side from day one. (The fact that the CSM can quote dialogue from Mulder and Scully's first meeting, however, indicates that he really did have Mulder's office bugged –

and Mulder now knows that, so has probably done a bit of DIY by now.) The Cigarette-Smoking Man seemingly didn't smoke until November 1963. His lighter in the fiction is inscribed 'Trust No One' (is that a guilty reference to his author alter ego's part in Deep Throat's death?). He writes under the (probable) pseudonym Raul Bloodworth. His stories concern a secret agent named Jack Colquitt. Two novels specifically referred to in this episode are *Take a Chance*, which was brutally rejected by publishers in 1968, and *Second Chance* from the early nineties, which is the story we see, serialised in the (salacious) magazine *Roman a'Clef* (sic), but rewritten.

Continuity: In addition to *The Lone Gunman*, Byers, Langly and Frohike seem to publish another newsletter, *The Magic Bullet*. (In fact, they appear to have appropriated their original magazine's title for themselves, the plaque on the door reading 'The Lone Gunmen'.) Frohike believes the Cigarette-Smoking Man is trying to kill him, much to Mulder's amusement (but he's actually quite correct). Byers states that no electronic surveillance device can cut through the (aptly named!) CSM-25 Counter-Measure Filter (he's wrong!).

The Truth: ?

Trivia: The episode includes five captions at the beginning of the episode and subsequently at the start of each act:
' "For Nothing can seem foul to those that win." *Henry IV, Pt 1*, Act 5, Sc. 1.'
'Part I: "Things really did go well in Dealey Plaza." '
'Part II: "Just down the road aways from Graceland." '
'Part III: "The most wonderful time of the year!" '
'Part IV: "The X-Files." '
Bill Mulder and the Cigarette-Smoking Man discuss *The Manchurian Candidate*. There are overt visual and dialogue references to *Apocalypse Now* (the scene in which the Cigarette-Smoking Man denies that the Bay of Pigs operation happened), *JFK* and *Forrest Gump*. Lee Oswald calls the Cigarette-Smoking Man 'Mr Hunt', presumably a reference to Howard Hunt, the CIA agent involved in Watergate and, allegedly, the Kennedy assassination (see Anthony Summers'

The Kennedy Conspiracy for the full story). All of the 1992 scenes featuring Scully come from footage from the pilot episode. The CSM knows the Aeschylus poem Robert Kennedy quotes at the funeral of Dr King. On the news stand where the CSM buys his magazine is a journal called *End Credits*, the headline of which is: 'Where the hell is Darin Morgan?' (Where indeed?) Jack Colquitt is the name of a marine from the *Space: Above and Beyond* episode 'Who Monitors the Birds?' Closed captioning reveals that the Cigarette-Smoking Man calls Deep Throat by the name 'Ronald'! (But, of course, in a novel the character would have to be referred to by a name. We really wish we could say for certain that it's also true in the 'real life' of the series!)

Scientific Comment: The alien is kept in an area which requires humans to wear breathing apparatus. Presumably, the outer chamber is designed to be used as an airlock. But Deep Throat walks straight through it without waiting for any air exchange to take place.

The Bottom Line: KT: 'I can kill you whenever I please. But not today.' A remarkable piece of work; a triumphant, stylish mixture of thirty years of American conspiracy theory, and a load of clever, very funny in-jokes. Love the Countermeasures Filter and the symbolic first cigarette after Lee Oswald's arrest. One of the best bits of the episode is the sequence in which the Cigarette-Smoking Man buys his colleagues (probably the closest thing he has to friends) identical ties as Christmas presents. The very idea that he's a sad, lonely, bitter man who only wants to be a writer and would quit his job in an instant to fulfil his dream (and then turn up in *The X-Files*' equivalent of The Village, no doubt!) is one of the best jokes the series has ever done. The twitchy, if sympathetic performance of William Davis is a great bonus too, giving the audience a genuine puzzle as to whether these events are real or not (apparently this confusion extended to the production staff with Morgan and Wong believing they were doing a genuine Cigarette-Smoking Man origin story, while Carter and crew allowed the episode to go ahead by framing the whole thing as a combination of Frohike's overactive imagination, and a series of CSM dream sequences). And it's *lovely* for all of those reasons and many more besides (who else but these guys would take on *Forrest Gump* and do it so badly!). I think if I ever got a publisher's rejection letter that included the words 'frankly crap', I'd turn into a cold-hearted killer too! Are you listening, publishers?

MD: A pretentious shaggy dog story, full of good jokes, but utterly unbelievable. This man who's killed more people than I've had hot dinners is really just a big softie who's had one novel too many rejected? No, I don't buy that for a moment. I was cringing with embarrassment at the garbage dialogue William B. Davis was given in the scene with the tramp (if his novels are anything like that, no wonder he's always getting turned down). *The X-Files* has always featured vast tracts of non-naturalistic dialogue, but in 'Herrenvolk' and in this story, it's getting way out of hand. What's worse, the show is becoming gorged on its own importance, desperate to pull in every paranoid aspect of the post-war American mythos (JFK? That was the Cigarette-Smoking Man. MLK? Yeah, that was the Cigarette-Smoking Man, too). Oh, and the Conspiracy find the time to rig major sporting events. I'm sure Keith will be telling me soon that's why Newcastle lost the Premiership a couple of years ago.

PC: Oh my God: he killed Kennedy! I'm glad that such an awesome episode wasn't prevented because it clashed with continuity so much. The Cigarette-Smoking Man has become a figure out of American mythology, and this episode is the one that roots him into that tradition (albeit rather forcibly). On reflection, I think it's nice that, in terms of the rest of the series, we don't believe a word of it, because I think this is one of those television episodes that might become the basis for quasi-factual bar room stories, about both the episode and its subject matter. The sheer balls that it takes to take on every little bit of American paranoia and say 'we made this' takes this story into the realm of joyous laughter, and past that, into pure legend. Wonderful.

81: 'Tunguska'

US Transmission: 24 November 1996
UK Transmission: 4 May 1997 (Sky One)/
29 October 1997 (BBC1)
Writers: Frank Spotnitz, Chris Carter
Director: Kim Manners
Cast: Fritz Weaver (Senator Sorenson),
Malcolm Stewart (Dr Sacks), David Bloom (Stress Man),
Campbell Lane (Chairman), Stefan Arngrim (Prisoner),
Brent Stait (Timothy Mayhew),
John Hainsworth (Gaunt Man),
Olesky Shostak (Bundled Man),
Jan Rubes (Vassily Peskow),
Robin Mossley (Dr Kingsley Looker),
Jessica Schreier (Dr Bonita Charne-Sayre),
Eileen Pedde (Angie), Lee Serpa (Swarthy Man)

Mulder has been sent evidence suggesting the existence of a major terrorist cell. When he and an FBI team set a trap for the revolutionaries, he captures Alex Krycek, who says that he leaked the information to Mulder. He wants revenge on the Cigarette-Smoking Man. His clues send Mulder and Scully to the airport where they intercept a courier bag containing a piece of rock, which turns out to be a meteor fragment. Mulder takes Krycek to Skinner's apartment, then visits his UN contact, who arranges for him to follow the trail to Russia. As Krycek speaks the language Mulder takes his former partner with him. The rock seems to contain the alien oil substance, and Scully investigates the deaths of several people who came into contact with it. She and Skinner are ordered to appear before a Congress investigation into the death of the courier, killed by Krycek in Skinner's apartment. Meanwhile, in Siberia, Krycek and Mulder find a slave labour camp, and are captured. Mulder is drugged and wakes up to find himself being sprayed with the Black Oil.

Don't Be in the Teaser: A 'flash-forward' as Scully addresses the Congress investigation committee and refuses to reveal

Mulder's whereabouts. The real teaser follows this, as a customs officer becomes the latest victim of the Black Oil.

How Did He Do That?: How did Krycek manage to hang from a seventeenth-storey balcony by a pair of handcuffs and remain unharmed? Mulder's geography is astonishing: he recognises a small town in Russia and knows where it is.

Scully Here is a Medical Doctor: She and Pendrell get into toxicity protection suits to investigate the apparent death of the scientist investigating the rock.

Ooze: Alien oil. Again.

That's a Mouthful: The Cigarette-Smoking Man: 'Our necessary and plausible denial is intact.'

Phwoar!: The way that Scully, dressed in black combat gear, cocks that gun at the start sends a shiver down the spine. And that helmet's a bit too big for her. Mulder under the chicken wire isn't actually very flattering.

Dialogue Triumphs: Mulder: 'You're full of crap, Krycek. You're an invertebrate scum-sucker whose moral dipstick is about two drips short of bone dry.'

Mulder: 'I'm leaving the window rolled down. If I'm not back in a week, I'll call Agent Scully to come by and bring you a bowl of water.'

The Conspiracy Starts at Closing Time: The Well-Manicured Man spends some of his time at a horse farm in Charlottesville, Virginia ('because there are no phones'). The Conspiracy are well aware of the experiments going on in the Siberian gulag, and have arranged for a sample of some four-billion-year-old Martian rock that landed as a meteorite in Antarctica to be shipped to them. (They're, as always, eager to get hold of any Black Oil the Colonists aren't aware of.) Marita, without the Conspiracy's knowledge, slips Mulder documents to get him to Russia (which, like all her actions, seems to be because she's genuinely on his side). Krycek claims that he loves his country, and wants revenge on the CSM (presumably for trying to have him killed). He's telling the truth, but Mulder didn't ask which country.

Continuity: Skinner has recently moved apartments (after the irredeemable break-up of his marriage, despite the events of 'Avatar'?), and now lives on the seventeenth floor of an apartment block. When he meets him nearby, the Cigarette-Smoking Man implies that he knows Skinner's new abode. Skinner gets his own back on Krycek over the former agent's attack on him in 'Paper Clip'. ('We're not even yet, boy, but that's a start!') Krycek's parents were Russian Cold War refugees.

The Truth: Some of the Black Oil inhabits Martian rocks that are four billion years old. Some of this rock landed on Earth as a meteorite in the Antarctic, and some as the meteorite that caused the 1908 Siberian explosion. (Of course, it's possible that these meteorites simply uncovered deposits of the Black Oil left behind when the Colonists' expedition left Earth in distant prehistory.) The Russians are now mining rock from this meteorite and experimenting on prisoners to try and develop a vaccine against its effects.

Scientific Comment: Finding poly cyclic aromatic hydrocarbons in or on a rock of unknown origin is not surprising. These are very common, e.g. 5 per cent of petrol is made up of aromatic hydrocarbons. Benzene is also an example, and that shows up even in mineral water. Thus you could not say that because these are similar to the ones seen in the Mars meteorite the rock must therefore be from Mars. The discovery of hydrocarbons *inside* a meteorite that was known to come from Mars was exciting because the material came from inside the rock and must therefore have originated on the planet. No contamination of the inside of the rock by organic molecules on Earth could have occurred. Mulder and Scully have no reason to think the rock is from Mars and even if it was it's been lying around on Earth long enough to be contaminated on the outside. I don't see how the oil could manage to get inside a viral protective suit. Exobiology is research into the possibility of life on other planets. There is no Department of Exobiology at NASA GSFC at Greenbelt, as was shown in this episode. However, some groups at GSFC are trying to move that way. They do have an Astrochemistry branch in the Laboratory for Extraterrestrial

Physics at Greenbelt. NASA's institution at Ames, California, is the NASA centre with the greatest interest in exobiology.

The Bottom Line: KT: 'Whatever's in that rock, it seems to be lethal.' Dull and confusing at the start, this improves as it goes along with Mulder's casual and probably very illegal abuse of Krycek being quite amusing in places. It's a Conspiracy story only in so much as the Cigarette-Smoking Man and the Well-Manicured Man turn up for a couple of largely perfunctory sceenes. The best bit of the episode, by far, is the end.

MD: Topical (Martian life in Antarctic rocks) but dull. There's not much wrong with this episode – although the scene in which Mulder discovers Krycek can speak Russian is absolute pants – but there's not much enjoyment to be had, either.

PC: It gives us a few crumbs to be going on with, but it's still a victory of images over story.

82: 'Terma'

US Transmission: 1 December 1996
UK Transmission: 4 May 1997[28] (Sky One)/
5 November 1997 (BBC1)
Writers: Frank Spotnitz, Chris Carter
Director: Rob Bowman
Cast: Fritz Weaver (Senator Sorenson),
Stefan Arngrim (Prisoner), Jan Rubes (Vassily Peskow),
Brent Stait (Timothy Mayhew), Malcolm Stewart (Dr Sacks),
Campbell Lane (Chairman),
Robin Mossley (Dr Kingsley Looker),
Brenda McDonald (Auntie Janet), Pamela MacDonald (Nurse),
Eileen Pedde (Angie), Jessica Schreier (Dr Charne-Sayre),
John Hainsworth (Gaunt Man), Olesky Shostak (Bundled Man)

A former KGB man is sent to the USA and murders the Well-Manicured Man's physician. Mulder and Krycek escape

---

[28] As part of a movie format double-length episode with 'Tunguska'.

from the camp in Russia. Krycek has his arm amputated by the escapees to save him from the 'tests'. Scully is questioned by the Senate Select Sub-Committee on Intelligence and Terrorism, and is briefly imprisoned for contempt of Congress. Meanwhile the Russian assassin kills the scientist infected by the alien 'black cancer', and steals the Tunguska rock. Mulder returns to the hearing, and he and Scully set off after the meteorite fragment, but an explosion sends it deep into the ground, and the Russian escapes.

Don't Be in the Teaser: A 'mercy killing' in Florida goes horribly wrong.

Ooze: We glimpse a 'nest' of squirming microscopic worm-like creatures in the infected scientist, but thankfully are spared the full glory of Krycek's arm being amputated.

That's a Mouthful: Skinner breathlessly explains the plot for viewers who missed the first episode: 'You owe me some answers, Agent Scully: answers I don't have to questions I'm being asked about this missing diplomatic pouch, the pouch presumably being carried by the man who was allegedly pushed off my balcony, and whose connection with a known felon I harboured in my house against all good sense I'm going to have to explain to avoid perjuring myself before a Senate sub-committee tomorrow, which, I might remind you, is a very serious crime in itself, is it not, Agent Scully?' Phew, an eighty-five-word sentence!

Phwoar!: The scene in which Mulder and Scully are reunited is extremely charged. They indulge in a very public hug, and Mulder tells her how good it feels to put his arms around her.

The Conspiracy Starts at Closing Time: The Conspiracy's Dr Charne-Sayre (one of their six most important members, as she was one of the six who knew that this covert investigation into a rebellion against the Colonists was going on) was experimenting on old folk in Florida in an attempt to develop a vaccine against the Black Oil, which many participants in this story believe (at least in terms of this batch) comes from Mars. (It's entirely possible the Colonists could have left some there too.) The Black Oil, under the name of 'the black cancer', is used as a biological weapon by the likes of Saddam Hussein. Presumably the Oil simply decides to inflict a comatose condition on its victims when used as such. The Colonists would naturally be delighted with the idea of humans deliberately throwing the stuff over each other! (If the CSM has ever really had a phone call from Saddam, like the fictionalised one we hear about in 'Musings of . . .', this is what it might have been about.) Charne-Sayre also had a sideline in forcing through the decision to destroy the last sample of smallpox, which might be in order to slow down a large-scale response to the testing of the bee-borne virus delivery system using smallpox. (The events of 'Zero Sum' being relatively minor: we haven't seen a full-scale test of the system yet.) She has also tended Presidents. The Russian attempt to develop a vaccine has proved successful (within limits, as we see in 'The Red and the Black'), the orange substance injected into the back of the neck (a relevant point perhaps, considering the emphasis human/Colonist hybrids put on this area) preventing the Black Oil from staying in a host body and attaching itself to its pineal gland. Having gained this lead, they send an assassin to wipe out the Conspiracy's experiments in this area, presumably with no further intent than to be the only nation with both this biological weapon and its antidote. The Cigarette-Smoking Man seems to imply that the Conspirators having sex (with each other, or in general?) will endanger the whole project, but he's obviously just being cautious about the way secrets get exchanged in bedrooms. Even the Well-Manicured Man cannot call off the Senate's investigation (which he wants to do, presumably in order not to tip off the Russians that the Conspiracy have also got a sample of the Black Oil), which seems an honestly motivated enquiry, albeit wilfully blind. This whole affair may have been an attempt by Marita to get Mulder a sample of the Black Oil (Krycek wasn't freed by militiamen but by someone else), a mission she continues later in the series. She may already be Krycek's lover by this point, since his mission, on orders, to expose the American Conspiracy and destroy their rock samples, seems to be parallel to hers.

Continuity: Dr Charne-Sayre was the Well-Manicured Man's lover, as well as his personal physician. He owns the stables. We discover that Krycek has been a KGB agent. Was he thus reporting back to his country throughout his association with the Conspiracy? It was certainly a very successful infiltration, and the Russians must now know about the abduction scenario. (And, if 'Patient X' is anything to go by, resent it happening on their territory.) By the end of the episode he is missing his left arm, amputated by Russian escapees from the prison camp who explain: 'No arm, no test.' This suggests that the 'inoculation scar' in the left arm inserted by Bill Mulder's Project contains information that can be accessed by the Russians in their experiments: perhaps it's therefore a record of a person's medical history and identity. The Russians may, early on, have tested the Black Oil on a genetic mutant of some kind and found the results alarming (perhaps the Oil couldn't help but blow its cover as a biological weapon, and hatched into a full grown Grey?). Since then, they've started using the data on genetic identity in exactly the same way as the Colonists possibly will, to determine who's potential Black Oil fodder and who's something more special.

The Truth: Both the Russians and the Conspiracy are trying to create an immunity to the Black Oil. Krycek had prepared two bombs to destroy the two rock samples in the USA.

Trivia: The tag line, 'E Pur Si Muove', is Italian for 'And still it moves', Galileo's whispered defiance of the Inquisition concerning his insistence that Earth moves round the sun. (This may be a reference to Mulder's insistence on the reality of alien life in front of a disbelieving band of inquisitors.) The 'honorable men' lines spoken by the Well-Manicured Man are almost directly quoted from Shakespeare's *Julius Caesar*.

The Bottom Line: MD: This seems ridiculously complex, with lots of elements (hacked-off arms, Krycek's involvement with militiamen) and hoary old adventure show set pieces thrown into the mix with little thought or precision. The Russian gulag stinks of Cold War clichés, and the sequence with Mulder almost literally getting on his soapbox towards the end had me cringing. 'Tunguska' and 'Terma' form the worst multi-part *X-Files* Conspiracy story so far seen. Chris Carter's name might be on the script, but it is as if his attention had switched to *Millennium*, and, for all our occasional criticism of his stilted dialogue, the programme that brought him to prominence had begun to suffer as a result.

PC: I'm as concerned as the American journalist who raised this point that Mulder, once a humane and thoughtful hero, bullies Krycek so violently all through these episodes, and generally acts like a boor. He was to get even worse with regards to anger management. What a crap speech by Mulder at the end! What a ridiculously inconvenient moment for the brakes on a truck to fail, just for dramatic effect! What an awful two-parter! Only good thing: the odd *New Avengers* character, Peskow, and his crap cover story for crossing the border.

KT: This is one of the worst episodes in *The X-Files*' history. Stupidly over-complicating their job by adding in about a dozen additional plot elements all over the place. (Imagine the script meetings before this: 'Hey, Frank –' 'Yes, Chris?' 'How about something on euthanasia?' 'OK . . . How many minutes do you reckon we've got left to fill?') Conspiracy episodes work best when they have a definite aim, and a *big* revelation that changes our perception of the story-arc we thought we knew by adding something unusual to it. All 'Terma' does is bore the pants off the audience by giving them far too much to think about. Over-ambitiousness isn't the worst crime a television series can commit, but pretentiousness is!

83: 'Paper Hearts'

US Transmission: 15 December 1996
UK Transmission: 16 March 1997 (Sky One)/
12 November 1997 (BBC1)
Writer: Vince Gilligan
Director: Rob Bowman

Cast: Tom Noonan (John Lee Roche),
Byrne Piven (Frank Sparks), Jane Perry (Day Care Operator),
Edward Diaz (El Camino Owner),
Sonia Norris (Young Mother), Carly McKillip (Caitlin Ross),
Paul Bittante (Local Cop), John Dadey (Local Agent)

In a dream, Mulder follows a red laser light to a girl's body. The next day, with the help of a forensic team, he uncovers a corpse in the location revealed to him while asleep. Mulder knows that the girl was killed by John Roche, who murdered thirteen eight- to ten-year-olds between 1979 and 1990 (this discovery brings the total to fourteen). Roche cut a heart shape from the dress of each victim. Mulder's profile helped capture the man, a vacuum cleaner salesman, but, although Roche was imprisoned, the pieces of fabric were never recovered. The corpse is identified as that of Addie Sparks, who went missing in 1975 (and was, therefore, Roche's first victim). Did he kill anyone else? Mulder discovers the cloth hearts inside a copy of *Alice in Wonderland* – there are sixteen of them. Mulder confronts the man in prison, who initially refuses to co-operate. Then, after Mulder dreams of Samantha's abduction – this time, with Roche kidnapping her – Roche claims that he was in Martha's Vineyard in 1973, and that he sold the Mulder family a vacuum cleaner. Mulder finds just such a cleaner at the family home, but the body that Roche directs him to is not that of Samantha. Mulder illegally springs Roche from jail and takes him to his parents' home, which Roche claims to remember from his kidnapping of Samantha: however, it is the house they moved into after Samantha's disappearance. Roche later escapes from Mulder, and goes after a girl he spotted on the plane to Boston. Mulder tracks down Roche, and shoots him to save the life of the girl, still unsure as to the source of Roche's knowledge.

Don't Be in the Teaser: Mulder finds the corpse of a girl, buried in a park.

Scully's Rational Explanation of the Week: She thinks that Mulder knew all about the other bodies, and simply processed the information subconsciously. (She quotes Mulder in 'Aubrey': 'A dream is an answer to a question we haven't learned how to ask.') She also says that Roche knows about the precise circumstances of Samantha's abduction because the prison library affords him Internet access.

Phwoar!: Mulder embraces Scully at the end, and watches her go with a look that says volumes about how much he couldn't do without her.

Continuity: Mulder was brought on to the case by Reggie Purdue in 1990. We again see Mulder's ankle gun ('Nisei'). Roche's description and Mulder's dream feature many of the key elements of Samantha's abduction: It's 27 November 1973. Watergate is on TV, Fox wants to watch Bill Bixby in *The Magician*; he and his sister are playing Stratego. Mulder has been left in charge, while, extraordinarily, considering what they know is about to happen, Mr and Mrs Mulder have merely popped next door to see the Goldbrandts. (It's probable that they took their neighbours out for a drive to stop anyone seeing the bright lights! But telling young Fox that he's 'in charge' when they know his sister is going to be abducted is the sort of offhand *faux pas* that can cost a parent years of therapy bills.) In this version, Mulder attempted to get his father's gun and shoot at the intruders (echoing his actions in 'Little Green Men' – perhaps under Conspiracy influence, his attitude towards the 'alien abductors' has become more and more aggressive. But then, Roche has been messing with Mulder's memories). Samantha broke her collar bone when she was six, playing on a swing in the back yard. Scully doesn't believe in the Samantha/alien scenario, but by now this must mean that she's convinced that abductions are purely human in origin. Mrs Mulder has recovered from her stroke. Some of Mulder's past cases include those of Douglas Redmond and Sivias Rivas. That old house of the Mulders still hasn't been sold or even refurbished: does it have more secrets hidden inside? Mulder is a pretty good basketball player.

The Truth: Given what we later come to know of Samantha's disappearance, she cannot have been abducted and killed by

Roche. (Indeed, in Mulder's visions her dress doesn't match
the fabric of the heart.) However, Roche's knowledge, and the
presence of a 1973 vacuum cleaner in the Mulder household
('He had a really hard time choosing', Roche says of Bill
Mulder) is puzzling. Mulder believes that his attempt to
get into Roche's mind via psychological profiling created
a 'nexus', which allows Roche to see his thoughts and
memories (and vice versa). (The only other explanation – that
somehow Roche was involved in the Conspiracy's abduction
of Samantha – does not explain Mulder's insight into the
murders.)

Trivia: Mulder finds Roche's old car in Hollyville, Delaware,
named after writer Vince Gilligan's girlfriend, Holly Rice.

The Bottom Line: MD: 'Thirteen sounds more magical.' *The
X-Files* meets *Millennium* in an involving story that's like a
nod back to some of the more conventional first season
stories. There's a certain similarity to 'Beyond the Sea', and
the ending (though engrossing) is something of a cop-out. In
the final analysis, this might have worked better if it made no
reference to Samantha's disappearance at all. For all that, it's
still a very enjoyable piece of work. Oh, and I wonder how
many times they had to shoot the basketball scene.

PC: I can't tell you how moved I was by this. Mulder and
Scully as ethical heroes on a heartfelt quest: Gilligan can do
gorgeous pathos as well as comedy. Here they're far removed
from the cartoons they were to become in the next season,
showing sorrow for the victims they encounter, awareness of
their own humanity, and grace such as the wonderful moment
with the basketball. And they don't go to the other mawkish
extreme either: the dialogue is crisp and efficient, and it's left
to David Duchovny to make us care with perhaps his finest
performance as Mulder. His body language when intuiting
here is almost autistic. The only use of the series' continuity
is as a red herring, and perhaps, as Marty said, in making us
realise that this is a perfect reflection of my other favourite,
'Beyond the Sea'. It doesn't even fall into the most obvious
trap: the child killer is dull and non-charismatic, and contempt is shown for the glamorisation of his business. Perfect.

KT: 'Tell me about this dream.' Another cracking Vince

Gilligan script, with a claustrophobic air and clever use of set pieces (Mulder's basketball shot!). There are many great scenes, like Mulder and Scully's emotional visit to the father of the murdered girl, and Skinner's angry confrontation with Scully. But it's Mulder's episode, focusing on the horrifying quality of obsession within him. Like 'Young at Heart' and 'Grotesque' (to which this episode is almost the completion of a beautifully scripted trilogy), we get beneath the sometimes shallow exterior of Mulder. Betrayed, humiliated and hurt, you just want to hug him as much as Scully does at the end of the episode, particularly in his confessional 'It's not your fault, it's mine'.

84: 'El Mundo Gira'

US Transmission: 12 January 1997
UK Transmission: 23 March 1997 (Sky One)/
19 November 1997 (BBC1)
Writer: John Shiban
Director: Tucker Gates
Cast: Rubén Blades (Conrad Lozano),
Raymond Cruz (Eladio Buente),
José Yenque (Soledad Buente), Simi (Gabrielle Buente),
Lillian Hurst (Flakita), Susan Bain (County Coroner),
Robert Thurston (Dr Larry Steen),
Michael Kopsa (Rick Culver), Markus Hondro (Barber),
Janeth Munoz (Village Woman), Pamela Diaz (Maria Dorantes),
Fabricio Santin (Migrant Worker), Jose Vargas (INS Worker),
Tony Dean Smith (Store Clerk)

In a migrant workers' camp in southern California, a young woman is found dead after an explosion and a flash flood of yellow rain. Some of the locals blame the event upon El Chupacabra, a mythical vampiric creature. However, Soledad Buente tells Mulder and Scully that his brother, Eladio, is responsible: both of them were in love with the dead woman. Scully discovers the girl's body is covered in a fungal growth, and speculates that Eladio is a carrier for an enzyme that accelerates the growth of natural fungus. Eladio escapes from custody, and is almost killed by his brother, who is seeking revenge. Local policeman Conrad Lozano uses Soledad to force Eladio into the open. However, despite the attendance of a bio-hazard team, the brothers escape, both having now succumbed to the enzyme, and travel towards Mexico.

Don't Be in the Teaser: Maria Dorantez (and a goat) succumb to El Chupacabra . . . Allegedly.

Scully Here is a Medical Doctor: 'I'm a medical doctor,' she tells the pathologist. She performs at least two autopsies.

Ooze: Yellow rain. Fungus. Urgh.

Scully's Rational Explanation of the Week: 'Two men. One woman. Trouble!' Maria died naturally from a fungal infection, her immune system weakened by pesticides in the soil, or by an enzyme exuded by the Buente brothers. They have an abnormally high tolerance to this enzyme themselves, thanks to an 'anti-enzyme gene', and anybody they touch with the enzyme falls victim to natural fungi (death by Athlete's Foot!) and/or the new one the brothers carry. She's close to the truth.

Dialogue Triumphs: Scully: 'Mulder, I know you don't want to hear this, but I think the aliens in this story are not the villains, they're the victims.'

Mulder: 'Scully, I've been thinking – I know that's dangerous, but just bear with me.'

Dialogue Disasters: Soledad: 'Come out like a man so I can split open your face, bastard!' (Sounds so much better in Spanish.)

The Conspiracy Starts at Closing Time: This whole scenario looks familiar. A community of the dispossessed, exposed to dangerous chemicals (an enzyme and a new species of fungus in this case), who as a result start to look like Greys, and whose biology is associated with immune system problems. That 'bolide meteor' might just as easily have been an artillery shell. Perhaps the American military are still using some remnant of Colonist DNA to conduct little operations like this? (And thus perhaps those who come to clean up afterwards work for the Conspiracy?)

Continuity: Mulder's Spanish has improved a touch since 'Little Green Men'.

The Truth: It's like Scully says it is, with the addition of a new (alien?) kind of fungus, also carried by the brothers, which may have come from a meteor that landed in water nearby, throwing up a blast of the yellow rain. But see The Conspiracy Starts at Closing Time. The legend of the Goatsucker is a fairly modern phenomenon among Latin American communities, and it might be a useful protection against a real threat if such communities are the focus of Conspiracy experiments. The old woman's tale of aliens coming in a flash of light is clearly highly subjective, especially as Mulder and Scully give a rational explanation in the arrival of the bio-control team.

Trivia: The title means 'The World Turns' in Spanish. As there are several references to the plot of this episode being 'a Mexican soap opera', the title is probably a play on the popular American daytime soap opera *As the World Turns*. There's a great in-joke when Scully opens the body bag containing the fungus-ridden corpse of Maria Dorantez: for once, before Scully can say 'Oh my God!', somebody else gets in first (in this case, the pathologist). This is the first time Mulder mentions a 'Fortean event' in connection with the cases he and Scully investigate (but he's a little wide of the mark in defining it as a purely meteorological classification). Mulder thinks (in response to Scully's pun) that 'Purple Rain' (by Prince) is a 'great album' but a 'deeply flawed movie!' Scully quotes from Leonard Bernstein's 'Maria', from *West Side Story*. Eladio's cry of 'I am the Chupacabra!' echoes Dr Frankenstein's similar acceptance of his nature in *Young Frankenstein*. Erik Estrada, of *CHiPs* fame, is mentioned.

Scientific Comment: A bolide is a large, exceptionally bright meteorite that often explodes – and might well look like what occurred in the episode. Mulder's theory of the bolide hitting a lake, superheating it (and hence evaporating it) causing instantaneous rain is also valid, though I think he should do a little checking to see if there is a nearby lake and if its water level has suddenly got low. This kind of behaviour is called a steam explosion (and is a worry for water-cooled nuclear reactors).

The superheated steam undergoes a rapid phase transition (RPT) when it gets into the cool air, turning instantly into liquid. You should see fog, however, along with the rain. As for the yellow colour, I suppose if the alien material were well mixed with the steam in the explosion that could happen. Solar system dust is the source of zodiacal light and it is estimated that this dust adds a few million tons of mass to Earth each year. Thus Mulder's quote of '2000 tons of extraplanetary material falling to Earth every day' is actually a pretty good estimate. Large chunks of rock hitting Earth are far less common, of course.

The Bottom Line: KT: 'It was a terrible thing . . .' A perfectly awful episode with a heavy-handed, clod-hopping attempt at social comment that hardly sits well with the themes on display in the rest of the episode (presenting Mexicans as a race of superstitious, vengeful, and ignorant peasants is another aspect of *The X-Files'* annoying habit of stereotyping the third world with rather atypical American cultural cynicism). Badly plotted, too. The worst episode of the season by a distance.

PC: A gorgeous meditation on where modern legends come from, and the need for fantasy they fulfil in places where the real world is too awful and there's no institutionalised system of blame. The monster is the systematic abuse of these people, as the sly little fade from the graffiti of a Grey to Skinner, the symbol of Anglo law, illustrates. Probably the only reason why he's in the episode. Unfortunately, while grandstanding about the whole problem of immigrant abuse, John Shiban allows Mulder and Scully a couple of racist moments themselves. We return again to the unreliable narrative, the place of genuine myth where the storytelling desire of the series hits slap bang into its nature as series television. In this case, it works. It's just a pity the actual nature of the brothers' plight becomes so confused.

MD: 'Look . . . The rain is strange.' A clever fusion of political comment and nasty-lurgy-on-the-loose-type thriller. Much of this story – especially the exchange between Eladio and the barber ('How long have you been in this country?') – shows the dirty underbelly of the American dream in particular and national capitalism in general. As Paul says, there's much here about the making of myths ('You got your own stories, too,' Lozano tells Mulder) and the unreliability of single-perspective narrative (much more simply handled here than in 'Jose Chung'). And the ending is glorious, doing something similar to Neil Gaiman's *Neverwhere* in turning the invisibility of the oppressed into the literal truth of fantasy. As Mulder says, 'The truth is, nobody cares.'

85: 'Leonard Betts'

US Transmission: 26 January 1997
UK Transmission: 30 March 1997 (Sky One)/
26 November 1997 (BBC1)
Writers: Vince Gilligan, John Shiban, Frank Spotnitz
Director: Kim Manners
Cast: Paul McCrane (Leonard Betts),
Marjorie Lovett (Elaine Tanner),
Jennifer Clement (Michele Wilkes), Bill Dow (Charles Burks),
Sean Campbell (Local Cop), Dave Hurtubise (Pathologist),
Peter Bryant (Uniformed Cop), Laara Sadiq (Female EMT),
J. Douglas Stewart (Male EMT), Brad Loree (Security Guard)

Leonard Betts, a thirty-four-year-old paramedic, is decapitated when the ambulance he is riding in crashes. Later, a morgue attendant at the Monongahela Medical Center is attacked, and Betts's headless corpse disappears. Video footage of the incident is inconclusive, and when Scully attempts a post mortem on the head, the eyes and mouth spontaneously open. Later analysis shows that the entire head was riddled with cancer – Betts should have been dead long before the accident. Betts's fingerprints find two matches in the FBI database: Betts himself, and one Albert Tanner. Tanner's mother, Elaine, is adamant that her son was killed in a car crash six years previously. Meanwhile, Betts's former partner Michele Wilkes comes to the conclusion that he is alive and working at another hospital. Frightened of being found out, Betts kills her, but is handcuffed to a car by a security guard. He escapes by pulling his hand through the metal cuffs, tearing off his thumb. Betts kills a man with lung cancer, leading Mulder to postulate that he needs cancerous tissue to aid his regeneration. He and Scully trace Betts to a garage: when Betts tries to flee in a car, the agents fire at him, and the vehicle explodes. Although they recover a body from the wreckage, Mulder is convinced that Betts is even able to regenerate an entire body, which is how he survived the car crash that 'killed' Albert Tanner. Betts operates on his mother Elaine, removing a cancerous growth from her to eat. Scully finally confronts him at the hospital. He attacks her, telling her that she has something he needs, but she is able to use a pair of defibrillation pads against him. Betts, apparently, dies, and Scully is left pondering her own condition.

Don't Be in the Teaser: There's a sixty-two-year-old man suffering a cardiac arrest, a decapitated Emergency Medical Technician, and a morgue attendant attacked by a headless corpse. *Casualty* never starts like this.

Scully's Rational Explanation of the Week: It's body snatching for profit, owing to a shortage of cadavers at medical school (as Mulder quite rightly queries, why steal one *sans* head?). The movement in the disembodied head is a post-death galvanic response, and the multiple deaths of Betts have been staged by someone.

The Conspiracy Starts at Closing Time: If the Conspiracy and/or the US government were interested in the work of Ridley ('Young at Heart'), they're going to love Betts! However, there is nothing to indicate that they are aware of him, and certainly, besides the fact that the human gene pool has been fiddled with, his unique regenerative ability seems to be natural and not the result of experimentation.

Continuity: When Mulder takes a slice of Betts's head to Dr Charles Burks to have its aura photographed, Scully's disdain for complementary medicine is apparent. Danny is mentioned again; this time, he checks on Betts's fingerprints. Betts tells Scully: 'I'm sorry, but you've got something I need,' and later she awakes with a nose bleed, the first indication that she has cancer.

The Truth: Leonard Betts is an evolutionary leap, able to heal himself by rapidly growing new cells. To aid this, he must ingest cancerous tissue. He has also developed an uncanny ability to detect and diagnose cancer in others. He also seems to be immune from disease. His shed skin seems to possess enough of a vestigial brain to drive a car (because it manages to make a very sharp turn!).

Trivia: This episode bears some strange coincidental similarities to the American *Doctor Who* television movie. In both, an apparently dead body violently breaks out of a morgue drawer while an attendant is watching something appropriate on television while listening to headphones, and walks off complete with toe-tag. The 'No way!'/'Way!' exchange occurs in both these shows concerning non-human ambulance drivers, female doctors and the concept of regeneration! The man with lung cancer in the bar is called John Gillnitz, a composite of the three writers of this episode, a name which was later re-used for the doctor who ran Scully's DNA analysis in 'Christmas Carol', and was used previously in 'Wetwired' for the man who was shot in his hammock. Gillian Anderson seems to have trouble calling Dr Burks by his name: she prefers 'Burns'. Reference is made to American cinema critics Siskel and Ebert.

The Bottom Line: MD: The theme of matriarchal protection and sacrifice from 'Home' reappears, and there's some lovely interplay between Mulder and Scully (Mulder's glee at the very idea of a headless, walking corpse; his later distaste at having to investigate the hospital's offal bin; Scully's discomfort (almost embarrassment) when telling Mulder about the head blinking at her). I like the way this episode takes a really stupid, pulpy, central idea, and does something reasonably fresh and interesting with it.

KT: 'You think Leonard Betts regrew his head?' This is a terrific episode – featuring a new 'Cancer Man' for Scully and Mulder to worry about! Lyrical, nasty, yet with a sympathetic central theme, some great moments (Mulder's reaction to having to look into the hospital incinerator) and the hilarious scene with Chuck Burks. Plus the first hint of Scully's cancer – the main plot arc of the rest of this season. Loads of roots are evident – *The Dead Zone*, *Scream and Scream Again* (Leonard handcuffed to the car) and *The Silence of the Lambs* (Betts hiding on top of the ambulance); but this is much more than a generic patchwork. Top quality.

PC: It's a pity that Leonard kills his former partner purely in order, in terms of the drama, to justify Mulder and Scully pursuing him, because it would be very interesting to explore some of the issues raised by a monster who helps people, who our heroes get to talk to! A clever way to start the cancer arc, though.

86: 'Never Again'

US Transmission: 2 February 1997
UK Transmission: 13 April 1997 (Sky One)/
3 December 1997 (BBC1)
Writers: Glen Morgan, James Wong
Director: Rob Bowman
Cast: Rodney Rowland (Edward Jerse),
Jodie Foster (Voice of Betty), Bill Croft (Comrade Svo),
Jay Donohue (Detective Gouvela), B.J. Harrison (Hannah),
Jillian Fargey (Kaye Schilling), Jan Bailey Mattia (Ms Hadden),
Igor Morozov (Pudovkin), Ian Robison (Detective Smith)

In Philadelphia, recently divorced Edward Jerse gets drunk in a seedy bar and decides to get tattooed. Soon afterwards he begins to hear a woman's voice taunting him, urging him to kill his neighbour, which he does. Scully, in town on what she feels is a fruitless assignment, meets him and they become attracted. She also gets tattooed. Later, she discovers the red dye used in the tattooing contains a harmful parasite. Jerse attacks Scully, the voice urging him to incinerate her, but at the last moment he rebels, holding his arm in the flames to burn off his tattoo.

Don't Be in the Teaser: One of the series' scariest, even if nobody dies. Ed Jerse arrives home and collapses as the camera closes in on his tattoo . . . which is no longer winking.

Scully Here is a Medical Doctor: Something she tells Jerse (twice), and once to a pair of detectives investigating the neighbour's disappearance.

Phwoar!: A sexually charged episode with a few genuinely erotic scenes: the tattooing; the perhaps-kiss. Scully doesn't go in for one night stands, though: Ed wakes up on the couch after whatever happens, happens. Mulder and Scully tiff about her not being interested in his work, or, subtextually, in him, any more.

Dialogue Triumphs: Scully: 'Your contact, while interesting in the context of science fiction was, at least in my memory, recounting a poorly veiled synopsis of an episode of *Rocky and Bullwinkle*!'

Mulder: 'Congratulations for making a personal appearance in the X-Files for the second time!'

Continuity: Mulder hasn't taken a day off in four years ('Loser!') and has been told that he must have at least a week off. He says he is going on a 'spiritual journey', which turns out to be to Elvis's home Graceland in Memphis. When Scully was thirteen, she went through 'a phase' of sneaking out of the house and smoking her mother's cigarettes. On her last date, she went to see *Glengarry Glen Ross* (1992). Assuming a long arthouse run, then, this might be the date seen in 'The Jersey Devil'. If 'the characters had a much better time', that was a hell of a date: the movie is about salesmen driven to the point of breakdown. She says she always ends up with an authority figure in her life, enjoys the approval, and then rebels. She cites her father, and mentions there were others. We might add Jack Willis ('Lazarus') to the list (they went out to seedy bars, too), but is Mulder even Scully's type? And if he isn't, is that a bad thing? Scully gets an ouroboros tattooed somewhere on her back. Nobody else but Scully features in more than one X-File. Mulder and Scully always stay at the same hotel when they're working in Philadelphia. The bureau there know nothing of the X-Files.

The Truth: Both Scully and Jerse have been exposed to a chemical: $2C_{15} H_{15} N_2 CON - (C_2H_5)$, a psychoactive drug containing an ergot parasite found in certain grasses, and in rye, which the tattooist explains he uses in his red dye. However, Mulder subsequently states that there wasn't enough of the drug present to induce the kind of psychotic paranoid hallucinations that Jerse had.

Trivia: Once again, this episode saw the departure of Glen Morgan and James Wong. The title reportedly indicates the likelihood that they'll be back for a third time. The tattoo 'Betty' was voiced by Jodie Foster, whose portrayal of Clarice Starling in *The Silence of the Lambs* was, of course, one of the main inspirations for the creation of Scully. The questions 'Where is Scully's desk?' and 'Why isn't her name on the door?' are regularly asked on the *X-Files* internet newsgroup, alt.tv.x-files. Mulder and Scully are sometimes referred to as 'Moose and Squirrel' on alt.tv.x-files, after someone pointed out the similarities between the pair and *Rocky and Bullwinkle*. When Scully connects to the Web, the list of search engines seen onscreen include 'Magella', 'Excited', 'Infosunk' and 'Yahoots' – all parodies of genuine search engines. The Web site Scully contacts is http://fbi.lab.rl.fns.gov/FORENSICS/chem/haluc.drugs.html which doesn't exist (believe us, we've tried . . .) and isn't actually a valid address anyway. Jerse's ex-wife is called Cindy Savalas in honour of *Kojak* actor Telly Savalas. Scully's tattoo is an ouroboros, a mythical serpent eating its own tail (a symbol of the unending cycle of destruction and re-creation). This is an appropriate symbol for Dana who tells Jerse that she has 'always gone around in this circle'. The ouroboros is also the symbol, in *Millennium*, of the Millennium Group, mystical crusaders (or freelance profilers, depending on how commonplace you want to be) on a quest to save humanity. Since Morgan and Wong left to take over production on that series, and that, at least through Jose Chung, the two series share a continuity, it's possible that the tattoo sets Scully up for a guest appearance in that show. The 'crummy bar' visited by Scully and Jerse is called the 'Hard Eight Lounge', a reference to Hard Eight Pictures, Inc., Morgan and Wong's production company. The name of Jerse's neighbour, Kaye Schilling, alludes to Mary Kaye Schilling, the senior editor on the November 1996 *X-Files* issue of *Entertainment Weekly*. (Morgan and Wong were alleged to be annoyed with the ratings some of their episodes received in that issue.) Ms Schilling is seen using an issue of *Entertainment Weekly* to line her bird cage, which seems to belabour the point somewhat! The headline of that issue is

'The Wisest Man in Hollywood' and the picture is of producer Bob Goodwin. Mulder's list of people for Scully to investigate includes Yakov Smirnoff (a popular Russian comedian), Vladimir Nabokov (the author of *Lolita* and *Pale Fire*) and Vsevolod Pudovkin (Soviet experimental filmmaker of the 1920s). The two people who call at Jerse's apartment are described as Jehovah's Witnesses by the tattoo, but since the magazine they carry is *Faith Today* (and not *Watchtower*, or *Awake!*) they must be from some other religious group. The scene in which the camera backs out of Jerse's apartment as the door closes is a direct lift from Hitchcock's *Frenzy*, and Jerse's psychosis is rather like that displayed by Norman Bates in *Psycho*. Film director Quentin Tarantino (*Reservoir Dogs*, *Pulp Fiction*) originally expressed an interest in directing this episode, but was prevented from doing so by not having a Television Directors Guild union card.

The Bottom Line: KT: 'All this because I didn't get you a desk?!' This is a great episode, if rather odd. Duchovny is hilarious in his Memphis sojourn (*love* the Elvis sunglasses, and the kung-fu moves!), but it's Anderson who really shines here – giving a magnetic, sensual performance. The episode is unnerving and weird in all the right places and the very fact that virtually nothing happens makes its success all the more surprising. The final scenes prove what a selfish git Mulder is!

PC: A beautiful, heartfelt episode from the time when the series still did 'heartfelt'. Once again we see Mulder's work as decadent compared to the real life horrors that have laid Ed low. (There's something ultimately crass about 'virtual gambling'.) Scully needs to connect with the real world again, and in doing so, connects with a man she could probably have saved, were they not both stuck in their respective circles. The despair of Mulder finding a supernatural element in Scully's private life, turning her real life adventure into an X-File, is horridly perfect. 'Two steps forward and three steps back.' Is that Morgan and Wong's commentary on where the show was heading, as we speculate in the box below? Either way, this is a tragedy, one of my favourite episodes, and the ending is perfect: an absolute denial of closure.

MD: Not nearly as interesting as it sounds, and almost ruined by the unusually cheap-sounding music during the Scully/Jerse fight (a first for the otherwise flawless Mark Snow). Unless it was *supposed* to sound awful, and I've just missed the point. Wouldn't be the first time. Anyway, not a bad story as such, just very, very boring.

TWO STEPS FORWARD, THREE STEPS BACK

In *The X-Files*, the usual certainties of popular television drama no longer apply when it comes to minorities, Native Americans apart. Health workers and the mentally ill may be the bad guys, as in the real world. (Which is why it feels so strange when, in odd episodes like 'Hell Money', Mulder and Scully display the TV hero's traditional immediate distrust of this week's hidden villain.)

This real life uncertainty extends to the Conspiracy episodes, where there are *no* signifiers or dramatic indicators: characters lie and our heroes are mistaken without us being able to tell when this is happening. These episodes thus have to be shaped into drama in quite a radical way: their circular nature. The same sorts of things keep happening in every Conspiracy episode: the majority of the Conspiracy act behind the back of one of their number; Mulder returns from the dead; a prominent Conspiracy member is seduced by Mulder's honesty into coming over to his point of view and is assassinated. Even little motifs recur, like the driver of a truck stopping to kill the thing that he's got in the back. It's the drama of the recurring nightmare, the one way in which the (now bureaucratic and dull) everydayness of the Conspiracy episodes live any more in the same dreamland as the rest of the series.

In its refusal to ground the audience in certainty and comfort them, this new form of TV drama could be seen as a very positive trend, akin to Brecht's theatre of alienation. Unfortunately, now we've seen this promising experiment in popular television in action, it turns out that, at least in the way that it's done at the moment, it's also a crap way to treat your audience. This might be Morgan and Wong's complaint in 'Never Again', that the show is going round in circles, now unable to deliver any sort of realism because of its refusal to disclose at the right time the plot points that would give the viewers the information they need to follow it as real drama. (And if the makers of the series thought that viewers would be attending every tiny detail and feverishly theorising, they must be disappointed, as the efforts to do so seem (sadly) to be mostly confined to this volume.) The possibility still exists (as seen in more successful forays into the Conspiracy such as 'Christmas Carol') that *The X-Files* could become a *working* new model for a TV series, with no history and no signifiers, schizoid and gleaming, but it's going to need more experimentation to make it happen. After the Conspiracy arc is complete, perhaps those in charge will just say 'never again'.

87: 'Memento Mori'

US Transmission: 9 Feb 1997
UK Transmission: 20 April 1997 (Sky One)/
10 December 1997 (BBC1)
Writers: Chris Carter, Vince Gilligan, John Shiban,
Frank Spotnitz
Director: Rob Bowman
Cast: David Lovgren (Kurt Crawford),
Sean Allen (Dr Kevin Scanlon), Julie Bond (Woman)

Holy Cross memorial hospital, Washington DC: Scully tells Mulder she has cancer. Together, they travel to Allentown, to meet the MUFON group of women abductees that Scully met last year. Only one, Penny Northern, is still alive, the rest having apparently died from the disease. Scully undergoes chemotherapy while Mulder searches for a cure, eventually discovering links to a secret government research facility. Together with the Lone Gunmen, he breaks in and finds a number of hybrids who tell him that the women are being used as baby machines by the Conspiracy. They are attempting to subvert the process and save the women – their mothers. Scully decides that she will fight the disease and Mulder rings Skinner to thank him for his advice not to do a deal with the Cigarette-Smoking Man, just as the assistant director seems to be in the process of doing that very thing.

Don't Be in the Teaser: ... or you'll suffer another dose of 'The Field Where I Died' syndrome. This time Scully has two minutes and eight seconds of almost entirely unintelligible dialogue, without a pause for breath.

How Did He Do That?: The discovery of the computer password from a snowglobe is signposted by the biggest 'white arrow' in history.

Scully Here is a Medical Doctor: Scully says she has a 'nasal-pharyngeal mass' (a small growth on the wall between the superior concha and the ethmoidal sinus). It's not operable, and to all intents and purposes untreatable.

Ooze: Loads of green blood when 'Crawford' is killed.

That's a Mouthful: 'For the first time, I feel time like a heartbeat, the seconds pumping in my breast like a reckoning ...' Whatever it is that Deep Throat, the Cigarette-Smoking Man, and Mulder have got, it's contagious, because they've given it to Scully ... There are another couple of examples in the episode, too (though neither, thankfully, as long or breathtakingly gibberishesque as the above), in the form of a letter written from Scully to Mulder. 'I'd decided to throw it out,' she says.

Phwoar!: Mulder's stunned reaction to Scully's announcement. The penultimate scene in the hospital, where Mulder hugs Scully and kisses her forehead. Aaaaah!

Dialogue Triumphs: Mulder: 'The truth will save you, Scully. I think it will save both of us.'

Dialogue Disasters: Mulder: 'Pick out something black and sexy and prepare to do some funky poaching.'

The Conspiracy Starts at Cloning Time: Scully's name, along with those of the other MUFON women, is held on a file directory for a federally operated fertility clinic, connected to Lombard Research, who seem to be one of the Conspiracy's cover companies. The Cigarette-Smoking Man says he always thought of Skinner as Fox Mulder's 'patron'. Having advised Mulder against offering the Cigarette-Smoking Man a swap of help for information, Skinner bravely enters into such a deal himself. (See 'Zero Sum'.) The abductees were all denied state or federal health care. Scully's blood contains unwound, branched, mutable, active DNA, doubtless the result of her having kept at least one Colonist/human hybrid in her womb. Records are presumably kept to keep track of the success rate of the birthing programme and the results on the abductees. (It must suit the Conspiracy that they all have their blood-controlling microchips removed. Maybe they were encouraged to do so.) The Cigarette-Smoking Man knows about Scully's illness (presumably the Conspiracy were aware that the chip had stopped functioning). Penny tells Scully that human compassion isn't something that their abductors had, so presumably she saw Greys (either Conspiracy hybrids or men in Grey suits). But what was that drill bit (assuming it's real) for? (Perhaps Scully was swiftly turned over, and it was used on the back of her neck?)

Continuity: An almost direct sequel to 'Nisei', the episode contains a flashback to that story. Scully has never had a major illness before. A scene cut from the broadcast version introduces us to her brother Bill for the first time and reveals that her other brother is called Charles. Scully's ova sample is dated 29th Oct 1994 (during her abduction). Betsy Hagopian's sample is dated 11th Nov 1994, so they certainly could have been part of the same group.

The Truth: Conspiracy agent Dr Scanlon was actually hastening the deaths of his patients (who have had the chips in the backs of their necks removed, as we saw in 'Nisei'). The twelve abducted women from the MUFON group, first seen in 'Nisei' (including Penny Northern and Betsy Hagopian), all die within a year of each other, all of identical brain cancer. A high amplification radiation procedure caused them to ovulate multiple times, making them barren. One of the hybrids muddies the issue by saying that the process caused their cancer also, but the part of the process that perhaps did so is actually bearing one of the children produced by mating these ova ('one half of the raw materials') with Colonist DNA. (If they don't actually carry a child, why was Scully's stomach seen so enlarged and why is her bloodstream contaminated with that DNA?) Also, the hybrids refer to the women as their 'birth mothers': they actually gave birth to these hybrids. Presumably, Scully was part of a different 'batch', ones who gave birth to many clones of Emily. Post-birth, some hybrids (those even weaker than the Emily type, or is it just a question of apparent age required?) are perhaps grown to full size in tanks full of what may be the same green blood as is in their veins. (The visual similarities between these hybrids in their tanks and the quasi-hybrids of 'The Erlenmeyer Flask' may be down to the fact that both types need much the same kind of support to survive.) These particular hybrids have been conducting research to try and save their mothers (so the Conspiracy's ideal of passive drones doesn't always work out) and may still be plotting against the Conspiracy from within from another location (the facility presumably having been relocated after Mulder saw it).

Trivia: The title is Latin for 'reminder of death'. The 'snowglobe' that contained the password alludes to the town of Vegreville in Alberta, Canada (did one of the Conspiracy visit while going to see the farm run by the Samantha clones?) where there is (appropriately) an egg monument.

Scientific Comment: In statistics, the chances of an event occurring are never zero. They can approach zero, but never attain it.

The Bottom Line: KT: 'You can't ask the truth from a man who deals in lies.' A mixed bag, beginning with a load of right old award-seeking tosh (Pretentious? Tu? Oui . . .) and then settling down once the first alien bounty hunter seen for the best part of half a season turns up (because, like, one of them is usually good for a laugh, right?). From there onwards, despite a bewilderingly difficult to follow plotline (what else do you expect from an episode written by *four* people?!) things get better, and the end of the episode is a peach with a real classic of a final scene. Mulder's escape from the Lombard Research facility (despite a debt to *Edge of Darkness*) is one of the highlights of the season.

PC: You can hear the four writers each pitching in with their bits in sequence, leading to a script that jerks along by such odd movements as Mulder leaving 'Crawford' alone with the evidence without a word. It's more like a list of plot points than a drama, a condition which all the Conspiracy stories attempt to alleviate in the same two ways: action set pieces and touching human sentiment. The latter here, unfortunately, is mostly provided by Scully's horrid narration, so this thing falls apart even more than usual. Gillian Anderson's sincere performance and contained emotion do something to save it.

MD: Scully's opening narration is staggeringly grotesque. I'm not even sure it counts as English. From here on, things do improve, with some good thriller sequences with the Gunmen, and a dash of genuine emotion in Mulder and Scully's scenes together. A bit all over the place, but not without its moments.

88: 'Kaddish'

US Transmission: 16 February 1997
UK Transmission: 27 April 1997 (Sky One)/
17 December 1997 (BBC1)
Writer: Howard Gordon
Director: Kim Manners
Cast: Justine Miceli (Ariel), David Groh (Jacob Weiss),
David Wohl (Kenneth Ungar), Channon Roe (Derek Banks),
Harrison Coe (Isaac Luria), Jonathon Whittaker (Curt Brunjes),
Timur Karabilgin (Tony), Jabin Litwiniec (Clinton),
George Gordon (Detective),
Murrey Rabinovitch (1st Hasidic Man),
David Freedman (Rabbi)

Isaac Luria, an Orthodox Jew, is murdered by three racists. Later, one of the killers is strangled and Luria's fingerprints are found on the body. The two remaining racist killers try to exhume Luria's body, but one of them is murdered. Mulder and Scully find a mystical book under the corpse's head, which bursts into flame. The book belongs to Jacob Weiss, Luria's fiancée's father, who is arrested at the site of a third murder, and confesses. But then the leader of the anti-Semitic group is killed, and an image of Luria caught on video. Mulder discovers that a golem with the appearance of Isaac Luria has been created by Ariel, his fiancée. She meets with the creature on what would have been their wedding day, and the golem nearly kills Jacob. Ariel wipes the first letter of the sacred word off its hand, reducing it to dust.

Don't Be in the Teaser: Following Isaac Luria's funeral, a golem is made in the graveyard.

Ooze: Animated mud.

Scully's Rational Explanation of the Week: It's a resurrection hoax, the corpse shows post-mortem lividity, contaminated water leaked into the book to make it flammable, the video was made by the hoaxers. She seems very interested in pursuing this hoax, very pro-active, perhaps motivated by the fact that this seems to be a case from the X-Files that she herself has decided they should take on.

Dialogue Triumphs: Mulder to the racist Brunjes on resurrection: 'A Jew pulled it off two thousand years ago.'

Continuity: Despite the quote above concerning apparent Christian belief (not something he usually displays outside of a mocking context), his willingness to joke about a sacred text, and the fact that he refers (specifically to this Hasidic community?) as 'a people' as though he wasn't part of them, Mulder may possibly reveal his Jewish ethnicity during this episode. He keeps very up to date with news of anti-Jewish violence, smiles ironically when Brunjes says he looks Jewish, and leaves him with 'Bless you'. However, he states that he doesn't speak *any* Hebrew, so we're still uncertain.

The Truth: Using a mystical book, Ariel Weiss animated a golem in the shape of her husband-to-be, to revenge his killing and to say goodbye to him.

Trivia: Detective Bartley is named after John Bartley, sometime cinematographer on the series. Mulder mentions Caspar the Friendly Ghost. A kaddish is a prayer – the Mourner Kaddish, which we hear at the beginning and end of the episode, is said at every funeral – and is also the title of a poem by Allen Ginsberg. Strictly speaking, Ariel, as a woman, shouldn't be saying it, and wouldn't be sitting Shiva for a man she hadn't yet married, either. As the story indicates, in Old Testament law, an engaged couple are considered already married. The word written on the hand of the golem is Emet, truth, from which Ariel wipes away the E to produce Met, death, thus destroying the creature. Ariel's line 'I am to my beloved as my beloved is to me' is a quotation from Song of Solomon 6:3. A caption at the end of the episode reads: 'In loving memory of Lillian Katz' (producer and author Howard Gordon's recently deceased grandmother). Gordon originally wanted the episode to feature black anti-Semitism, but this was seen as too controversial. Rather wonderfully, in an episode about grey areas, the original Isaac Luria (1534–1572) was a Jewish dualist sage, who believed the world could be divided into absolute good and evil. (This detail found in *The Devil – A Biography*, by Peter Stanford, a text which also includes a detailed look at the Nephilim story (as featured in 'All Souls'), indicating, once more, that we might have stumbled on the production crew's reading matter.)

Scientific Comment: Scully's spontaneously combusting book theory, though very unlikely, is actually possible. There could be moisture in the coffin containing arsenic compounds and this might get into the book. An arsenic compound such as arsenic sulphide could then react with the water to create arsene gas (AsH_3), which is highly combustible. When Mulder removes the book from the coffin and is holding it, if he disturbs the pages so that the gas in the book suddenly comes into contact with the oxygen in the air it could spontaneously combust.

The Bottom Line: PC: Ordinary, in as much as we all know how this is going to go, but lush, contemplative, and with a truly wonderful musical score, especially the theme for the golem.

KT: 'Very Old Testament.' *The X-Files* usually has problems in presenting a story set in a different ethnic community, but Howard Gordon's angry focus on anti-Semitism is something else altogether. A beautiful, almost Shakespearean revenge-tragedy at the beginning, it suffers from becoming a variant on *The Monkey's Paw* as the episode progresses, but it's still got some breathtaking moments, and great dialogue.

MD: Sometimes this tired hack needs reminding what a splendid series this is, and then, along comes 'Kaddish'. Utterly brilliant in every respect; this is becoming one of my very favourite episodes.

89: 'Unrequited'

US Transmission: 23 February 1997
UK Transmission: 11 May 1997 (Sky One)/
7 January 1998 (BBC1)
Writers: Howard Gordon, Chris Carter, from a story by
Howard Gordon
Director: Michael Lange
Cast: Peter Lacroix (Nathaniel Teager),
Scott Hylands (General Benjamin Bloch),
William Taylor (General Leitch),
William Nunn (General Jon Steffan),
Larry Musser (Denny Markham),
Lesley Ewen (Renee Davenport),
Ryan Michael (Agent Cameron Hill),
Allan Franz (Dr Ben Keyser), Jen Jasey (Female Private),
Mark Holden (Agent Eugene Chandler),
Don McWilliams (PFC Gus Burkholder)

When a vanishing assassin kills a general, suspicion falls on the Right Hand, a militia group, whose leader identifies the killer as Nathaniel Teager, previously considered as missing in action. While Mulder finds that he may not be missing,

Scully finds a floating 'blind spot' in the eyes of a woman who encountered him. Although a security camera detects the presence of the assassin within the Pentagon, he easily evades capture and kills his second target. His next one is going to be at a veterans' rally. Mulder meets with Marita, who tells him the government is using Teager. At the rally, Mulder and Scully corner Teager, who is killed by another agent. They find the whole affair has been hushed up.

Don't Be in the Teaser: Huh? A sample from the main show, like *The Outer Limits* used to do. Did a planned sequence fall through? The first caption in the main show, which says 'twelve hours earlier', doesn't do much to limit the confusion.

How Did He Do That?: Why doesn't Mulder assume there's an invisible assassin standing beside him in the general's office? He's already got his theory worked out, after all. Wouldn't his gun and mobile phone set off the security alarm? On a grander scale, this is one episode where, whichever way you look at it, the motivations of those setting this whole thing up make no sense at all. See below.

Scully's Rational Explanation of the Week: The general's driver is lying, Mrs Davenport has a sub-conjunctival haemorrhage. She's not even sure she saw Teager.

Dialogue Triumphs: Mulder: 'I found his story compelling, but then again, I believe the Warren Commission.' (If he's telling the truth, then he (correctly?) didn't believe what he heard in 'Musings of a Cigarette-Smoking Man'.)

Dialogue Disasters: Skinner: 'I've already seen more dead soldiers than I ever want to see!'

The Conspiracy Starts at Closing Time: Mulder meets Marita at the Lincoln Memorial. She tells him that the generals who are being killed were those who disavowed knowledge of South Vietnamese guerrillas working for the US, left behind enemy lines (we learn that Teager's personal reason for revenge was that the same generals left him and his comrades behind, too). The government wants to silence these generals before they face charges and admit their deeds, thus increasing the level of reparation payments to Vietnam, and presumably causing a scandal. Therefore, they've given protection of the generals over to the FBI. (Which is hardly a death sentence in itself: maybe they've purposefully given the job just to Skinner's overstretched command, which is fairly stupid of them, since it contains the one man who might consider the possibility of an invisible soldier!) It's weird that Marita knows about non-Conspiracy conspiracies, and Mulder equates this matter with a Conspiracy plot, thinking that this is an attempt to discredit him, Scully and Skinner. (Presumably he assumes that they'd be mocked for blaming their failure on an invisible killer.) He also seems to blame the Conspiracy for the soldiers still missing abroad. But that doesn't sound like the sort of thing the Conspiracy care about. Perhaps they've simply assured the federal government that what Teager is doing is possible, as their advisers on matters of weirdness. (Markham says that Teager evaded US commandos that boarded the Right Hand's aircraft that was bringing him back to the USA, so perhaps the Conspiracy at some point wanted him as one of their super soldiers (see 'Sleepless').) Perhaps they actually secured his services, but his motivations here seem purely personal. Markham, far from distrusting the federal government as he claims to, is smug enough to mock the general who interrogates him, as if certain of rescue, and finally helps in the cover-up over Teager's presence (although it could be that, as Mulder says, he's forced to do that), so is probably working for some covert part of the establishment.

Continuity: Is Scully's eagerness to be sent to bring in Markham just her usual promotion-friendly competence, or indicative of her personal politics? It's strange, also, that Mulder doesn't empathise with Markham's attitude towards a corrupt establishment. Perhaps he's aware of the difference between the rest of the militiaman's beliefs and his own.

The Truth: Nathaniel Teager has learnt, from his Viet Cong captors, how to cause blind spots in those who try to see him.

Trivia: General McDougall was named for editor Heather

MacDougall. When Mrs Davenport sees Teager, two of the names you can see on the wall behind her are Jesse R. Ellison and Harlan L. Hahn. Harlan Ellison is a sci-fi writer, while Jessica Hahn was at the centre of a scandal involving a preacher and eventually posed for *Playboy*. We suppose that those two names were just the first that came to the prop person's mind.

The Bottom Line: PC: Ugh. What could have been (and probably was) a very straightforward suspense story is complicated by an apparent desire to pin the 'MIAs are still out there' slur on the US government. So in come Marita, the Conspiracy behaving out of character, and the kind of tacked-on developments that indicate desperate rewriting to make the final tottering structure … well, I would say 'work', but it just doesn't make sense. All for the sake of polemic.

KT: 'Maybe the war isn't over?' What a right load of old cobblers! More post-Vietnam guilt on display in a story that tries to take all of the best bits of 'Sleepless' and 'The Walk' and fashion something interesting from them. And fails, miserably. More insider nods on display – *Apocalypse Now* (the Death's Head cards) and *JFK* (Mulder and Marita at the Lincoln Memorial) – but little imagination. Mulder gets a few good lines, but his rant at the end is just plain embarrassing, and Scully's hardly given anything to do. Ordinary.

MD: Almost good, but completely hamstrung by the pre-titles sequence (that renders the next thirty minutes or so just about pointless) and a lack of imagination. The militia plot makes a little more sense here than in 'Tunguska', and there are one or two effective moments. The ending isn't too bad, either.

90: 'Tempus Fugit'

US Transmission: 16 March 1997
UK Transmission: 18 May 1997 (Sky One)/
14 January 1998 (BBC1)
Writers: Chris Carter, Frank Spotnitz
Director: Rob Bowman
Cast: Joe Spano (Mike Millar),
Tom O'Brien (Corporal Frish), Chilton Crane (Sharon Graffia),

Greg Michaels (Scott Garrett),
Robert Moloney (Bruce Bearfield),
Felicia Shulman (Motel Manager),
Rick Dobran (Sgt. Armando Gonzales),
Jerry Schram (Larold Rebhun), David Pálffy (Dark Man),
Mark Wilson (Pilot), Marek Wiedman (Investigator),
Jon Raitt (Father)

Scully's birthday dinner at a pub is interrupted by Sharon Graffia, who claims to be Max Fenig's sister. She's obeying Max's last wishes by bringing them in to investigate the air crash which killed him. Mulder believes the aircraft was forced down, and finds a familiar nine-minute time loss on victims' watches. Sharon is abducted from her motel room, and one of the two military air traffic controllers who observed the incident on radar is killed. The other USAF man, Frish, comes to Mulder and Scully, in fear of his life. He tells them that the commercial jet was intercepted by a fighter. Mulder, Scully and Frish are pursued from the Air Force base. Sharon returns, found by the incredulous accident investigator Millar, who witnesses a UFO searching for another crash site. Scully waits with Frish at the pub, only for Garrett, a Conspiracy agent, to enter and, intending to silence Frish, shoot Agent Pendrell. Mulder decides that a second craft involved in the incident plunged into the Great Sacandaga Lake. He dives to find the craft, and the corpse of a Grey. But suddenly lights shine down from above . . .

Don't Be in the Teaser: Max Fenig and the 133 other passengers and crew of Flight 549 all have a close encounter with a UFO, swiftly followed by one with the ground. Our highest ever pre-titles bodycount.

How Did He Do That?: Mulder *knows* that Max wasn't in the crash. This time, he's completely wrong.

Scully's Rational Explanation of the Week: Max opened the fissile plutonium he was carrying; the aircraft suffered a complete systems malfunction. On seeing the trashed motel room, Mulder says to her: 'OK, Scully, hit me with your best shot.'

Phwoar!: A thudding lack of any sexual tension in Mulder and Scully's supposedly intimate birthday dinner. Nice to know, however, that even after being up for thirty-six hours, Scully is willing to run over to Mulder's room if he calls.

Dialogue Triumphs: Scully to Mulder after his wince-inducing speech to the crash investigators: 'You sure know how to make a girl feel special on her birthday.'

Her birthday present is: 'An alien implant?' 'Two actually, I made 'em into earrings.'

The Conspiracy Starts at Closing Time: See 'Max'.

Continuity: This episode establishes that Mulder, Scully and Pendrell patronise a pub (called The Headless Woman in the scripts) that's a regular gathering place for FBI agents. (You'd have thought they'd have chosen somewhere with a serious door policy.) Mulder has never remembered Scully's birthday in the four years he's known her. He gives her an Apollo Eleven key ring. Mulder makes reference to 'the missing nine minutes' once more. Max's alias was Paul Gidney.

The Truth: See 'Max'.

Trivia: Larold Rebhun is named after the series' soundmixer, who pronounces it differently.

Scientific Comment: The estimate that statistically you could fly every day for 26,000 years before having an accident is about right. I can see no reason why exposed fissile plutonium would cause a plane to crash. It must be foggy (as usual in this series) as you can see the light beam coming down from the UFO.

The Bottom Line: PC: A satisfying number of seemingly vastly budgeted set pieces (and thus one very low-budget visit to a military base) gives one a clue as to why this more-obscure-every-day series managed to get into the top ten: it's produced, in terms of money use, better than any other show. Big images abound, such as the roomful of body bags and the chicken run with a plane. Joe Spano and the quietly wonderful Tom O'Brien turn in great performances. Unfortunately, it's harmed by Mulder's continuing bonkers refusal to tone down the public pronouncement of his beliefs, and a truly awful performance from David Duchovny, who seems to be saving the strength in his face muscles for later episodes.

KT: 'Do you remember the last time you were missing nine minutes?' Possibly the most unexpected episode to have a sequel done to it would have been 'Fallen Angel', so I'm delighted to report that this is a little classic. Beautifully plotted from beginning to (cliffhanging) end, with many shocking moments (Pendrell's shooting), a genuinely great performance by Joe Spano (one of my favourite actors), and one huge mother of a car chase. Best bits: Mulder's annoyed expression when Scully completely kills one of his pet theories with some hard evidence; Millar and the stealth aircraft (or is it a UFO?); and the climax.

MD: Some excellent thriller sequences and a story that goes somewhere. The cut from (poor) Pendrell to the underwater scene is very effective.

THE MISSING MISSING TIME

There is no consistent treatment of the 'missing time' effect throughout the series. In the pilot, Mulder and Scully lose nine minutes of time without their watches being affected at all: Mulder simply checks his watch before and after the event, and notes that they have both lived through nine minutes of which they have no memory. The watches are keeping time as normal. In 'Tempus Fugit', time does indeed fly, the crash occurring at 7.52 while the watches of the passengers have stopped at 8.01. That is, they have *gained* nine minutes, presumably having had time accelerated for them, and all the watches having been stopped by the crash. In the next episode, 'Max', the very opposite happens: Mulder's watch on being returned from his alien experience says 10.47 compared to Skinner's 10.56. That is, he has actually been taken out of time for nine minutes, or had his watch stop for that length of time and then restart. We may take it that the Rebel Colonists who abduct people like this can alter time either way, in 'Tempus Fugit' to stage a swift snatch and grab (which any survivors of the crash possibly would have remembered), in 'Max' to switch off the memories of all those involved (outside of time) in order to quietly take one person. That they don't bother to do this in the pilot is either a sign that they did something different to Mulder and Scully and erased their memories some other way; that they simply knocked them out and brought them around nine minutes later; or that that attack was done by a USAF craft with a sonic weapon (in order, perhaps, to activate the whole 'Mulder as believer' stalking horse plot).

91: 'Max'

US Transmission: 23 March 1997
UK Transmission: 25 May 1997 (Sky One)/
21 January 1998 (BBC1)
Writers: Chris Carter, Frank Spotnitz
Director: Kim Manners
Cast: Joe Spano (Mike Millar),
Tom O'Brien (Corporal Frish),
Chilton Crane (Sharon Graffia),
Greg Michaels (Scott Garrett), John Destrey (Mr Ballard),
Rick Dobran (Sgt. Armando Gonzales),
Jerry Schram (Larold Rebhun), David Pálffy (Dark Man),
Mark Wilson (Pilot)

Mulder inspects the Grey craft, and is captured by the military. The killer, Garrett, escapes from the scene of the shooting while Scully tends to Pendrell. When Mulder is released, he learns the agent is dead. Sharon Graffia turns out not to be Max Fenig's sister, but an unemployed, disturbed aeronautical engineer. Mulder and Scully search Fenig's trailer, and discover his video accusing the military of copying alien technology. Mulder uses Max's undelivered mail to find the location of one of the three pieces of an alien power source that Max and Sharon had stolen. Mulder takes the item onboard a flight to Washington, but is pursued by

Garrett, whom he confines, only to experience missing time just as Garrett breaks out. When the aircraft lands, Garrett has vanished, abducted along with the item.

Don't Be in the Teaser: Mulder is chased and captured by soldiers.

How Did He Do That?: Is even an FBI agent allowed to carry a gun aboard a commercial airliner?

Scully Here is a Medical Doctor: She tends to Pendrell.

Scully's Rational Explanation of the Week: A control tower error.

That's a Mouthful: Scully, on Mulder's present: 'I think you appreciate that there are extraordinary men and women, and extraordinary moments when history leaps forward on the backs of these individuals . . .' and so on for five minutes. To which Mulder replies, for all of us who can't stand this sort of trite substitute for dialogue: 'I just thought it was a pretty cool keychain.'

Phwoar!: Mulder looks trim in his wetsuit. He expresses some nice touches of affection to Scully, whose understated reaction to the death of Pendrell is very real. Scully describes Mulder and Max's lifestyle thus: 'Men with spartan lives, simple in their creature comforts, unwilling to allow for the complexity of their passions.' Which sounds like she's given the matter a lot of thought. She turns her back while Mulder is changing.

Dialogue Triumphs: Mulder to Scully about her visiting a mental hospital: 'I'd go with you, but I'm afraid they'd lock me up.' 'Me too.'
   On Garrett's abduction: 'I think he got the connecting flight.'
   Mulder also impersonates Homer Simpson.

The Conspiracy Starts at Closing Time: Cummings Aerospace is one of the military contractors with connections to the Conspiracy, utilising a stolen Rebel Colonist power source (which, since they kept it in three parts, they've presumably copied rather than use it directly). This power source must be something peculiar to the Rebels (since we've never definitively seen the mainstream Colonists bending space and time: perhaps this is the source of that ability), as they're eager to get it back, and don't assume their foes would be able to give the humans something similar. The Conspiracy have powerful influence right up to the Joint Chiefs of Staff, and still use triangular USAF craft to search for the crashed Rebel Colonist ship. The Conspiracy abduct Sharon Graffia here (and maybe have been all along), who perhaps keeps tabs on Max for them. It seems likely that, to track him so much, the Rebel Colonists are probably the ones who've been abducting Max. (And he's gone from his former ignorance to being aware of this.) Colonist craft are radar-invisible (as the stealthy shapes of the USAF versions suggest: the one seen on radar in 'Fallen Angel' was obviously damaged in some way before it crashed). Garrett tells Mulder that a few deaths are worth it to save 'the lives of millions'. Perhaps he believes that the Conspiracy are standing against an alien invasion? Or is this his rationalisation for giving Earth to the Colonists, because they could just destroy the world otherwise? The radioactive Rebel Colonist power source (they seem to have a great tolerance to radiation) comes in three pieces, each of which has three circular pieces inside (although that isn't a good description of what we see on the X-ray: and why wasn't it fogged by the radiation?). They can accelerate time for at least nine minutes (so the fighter pilot must have been a good shot to get a missile lock on to them during what was, presumably, a supernaturally fast approach run at the airliner). This obsession with threes is a direct take from Whitley Strieber's version of the Greys in *Communion*. The power source may make use of cold fusion, over-unity energy, or be a source of anti-gravity, such as is being studied by Finnish scientists (in real life). This episode is the first indication that Greys definitely exist in some form other than a decayed version of the Conspiracy's Colonist/human hybrids.

Continuity: Scully didn't know Pendrell's first name (so, despite a few interested looks, they never got on intimate terms). When Mulder takes a flight with the alien device, is he (consciously or otherwise) hoping to get abducted? He receives radiation burns from the Rebel Colonist craft. Mulder wears a Swiss army watch.

The Truth: Max had stolen a piece of Rebel Colonist technology from the Conspiracy. They wanted it back, but so did the Rebel Colonists, resulting in their craft intercepting Flight 549, speeding up time, and taking Max from the aircraft. However, the Conspiracy had been shadowing the airliner with a USAF F-15 Eagle fighter, presumably in case just this sort of thing happened. The fighter shot down the Rebel Colonist craft, which crashed in a nearby lake. This had the (unforseen, or are they that ruthless with the lives of their agents?) effect of depressurising the airliner and making it crash. Mulder is subsequently used by the Conspiracy to locate the third missing piece of the device, but this time the Rebel Colonists manage to get it back, taking Garrett with them (and Mulder logs another nine minutes of missing time).

Trivia: Max has *Songs in the Key of X* in his trailer, the track playing being 'Unmarked Helicopters' by Soul Coughing. Immediately before this episode was shown on BBC1, *Harry Enfield and Chums* ended with an interview with Julio Geordio, Tyneside-based footballing import from South America: 'Maybe watch *The X-Files* tonight, like.' 'I've never seen it myself,' replies the commentator. 'But they tell me it's very good, Barry.' The question the Conspiracy agent asks Mulder is similar to that asked of Joseph Cotton by Orson Welles in *The Third Man*: 'What if one of those dots down there stopped moving?' Mulder mentions a piece of *Sesame Street* merchandise, the Tickle Me Elmo doll. Actor Steve Guttenberg is also mentioned.

Scientific Comment: Radiation burns from Alpha and Gamma sources look just like other burns, they can't be easily identified as such. Beta particle radiation penetrates more deeply and might be recognisable. Great offhandedness is shown in the handling of radioactive material: everybody involved with the alien object would be in danger.

The Bottom Line: PC: The best 'mythology' two-parter so far, one which actually has a satisfying dramatic shape, a lot of action, and doesn't strangle itself with the story arc (though the motivations of Joe Spano's character go all over the place, and him being so good an actor just underlines that). Good to see an incidental character like the trailer park owner caring about Max's fate, when the lazy cliché would be for him not to. Good, also, to see Mulder's crusading zeal when he finally gets close to his enemies. This episode even makes dramatic use of Pendrell's death, as he and Max are compared to Scully and Mulder, the latter two being made to ponder the mortal danger of their quest. (Scully even has a nosebleed as Pendrell dies.) Scully's (awful) closing speech indicates that Carter has his own thesis on the Marxist view of history, that individuals have to fight against a manifest destiny: these thoughts continue into the movie. It's just a pity that Max himself isn't given more to do in an episode named after him.

KT: 'All I know is this plane seems to be killing people as it sits there on the ground.' Carter and Spotnitz paint their masterpiece, as this virtually flawless two-parter just gets better and better. Densely plotted, clever, and intricate, the episode is made by some marvellous dialogue (Scully's comparison between Max and Mulder), top-notch support acting, and that really cool ending. Great music, quality direction, and a plot that made sense first time around. I rather liked this one, as you can probably tell!

MD: Wow, a two-part Conspiracy story that replaces the usual beginning, muddle and end with something dramatically satisfying! And with loads of sympathetic dialogue and excellent set pieces thrown in for good measure. The flashback to the plane crash is perhaps the most frightening thing I've ever seen on *The X-Files* – precisely because we know the passengers don't survive.

92: 'Synchrony'

US Transmission: 13 April 1997
UK Transmission: 8 June 1997 (Sky One)/
28 January 1998 (BBC1)
Writers: Howard Gordon, David Greenwalt

Director: James Charleston
Cast: Joseph Fuqua (Jason Nichols),
Susan Lee Hoffman (Lisa Ianelli),
Michael Fairman (Elderly Man), Jed Rees (Lucas Menand),
Hiro Kanagawa (Dr Yonechi),
Jonathan Walker (Chuck Lukerman),
Alison Matthews (Doctor), Norman Armour (Coroner),
Patricia Idlette (Desk Clerk), Brent Chapman (Security Cop),
Terry Arrowsmith (Uniformed Cop),
Aureleo Di Nunzio (Detective)

Two MIT scientists, Jason Nichols and Lucas Menand, are
approached by an old man who predicts that Menand will die
at 11.46 under a bus. This, indeed, happens and Nichols is
blamed for the death after it is discovered that Menand was
threatening to expose errors in his cryogenic work. Nichols'
fingerprints are also found on the body of the security guard
who arrested the old man. Later, the old man kills a Japanese
scientist, Yonechi, with a lethal injection of a rapid freezing
agent that Nichols and his girlfriend, Lisa, are developing, but
that is still several years from completion. The old man stalks
Lisa but is unable to kill her. Mulder deduces that the old man
is actually Jason, back from the far future and attempting to
alter history. Lisa is saved from a frozen death by Scully but
Jason dies, along with his older self, in a fire, the old man
describing the horror of a world forty years in the future
'without history, without hope'. Ominously, Lisa is set to
continue their work.

Don't Be in the Teaser: Four characters appear in this, and
none survive the episode. Two (Menand and the security
guard) don't even survive the teaser!

How Did He Do That?: Mulder's 'logical' leap to time travel
on the strength of a photograph is extreme even by his
standards.

Scully Here is a Medical Doctor: She examines Menand's
corpse, and uses knowledge gained during the unsuccessful
attempt to resuscitate Dr Yonechi when saving Lisa's life.

Scully's Rational Explanation of the Week: She suggests that the frozen death of the security guard may be due to ingestion of a chemical refrigerant, though she admits this is a complete guess.

That's a Mouthful: Mulder: 'If Lucas Menand never gets hit by that bus, his complaint gets heard before the grand committee, Jason Nichols loses his funding and he never gets to collaborate on his research with Dr Yonechi. Therefore, this photograph never gets taken because this celebration never happens.' Scully: '. . . And, if your sister is your aunt, and your mother marries your uncle, you'd be your own grandpa!'

Dialogue Triumphs: Mulder: 'The security officer who's now in the morgue has a body temperature a little south of Frosty the Snowman.'

Continuity: Scully wrote her thesis on Einstein when she was twenty-three. Mulder twice quotes from it ('Although common sense may rule out the possibility of time travel, the laws of quantum physics certainly do not' and 'Never is a very long time. Although multi-dimensionality suggests infinite outcomes in an infinite number of universes, each universe can produce only one outcome') which suggests he has memorised it. Could it be that Mulder (like us) thinks there's something fishy about a woman who goes around rewriting the laws of physics? (Not to mention using such populist prose in a physics thesis!) He suggests she was a lot more open-minded when she wrote it.

The Truth: Time travel becomes a scientific reality sometime between 2007 and 2037, the technology having derived from the ability of tachyons to travel faster than the speed of light while at absolute zero. Scully suggests that its discovery is inevitable, and that even Nichols' death cannot change that (which is in direct contradiction to the spirit of 'Clyde Bruckman's Final Repose'). Mulder might take heart from the idea that, if there is only one universe to travel back and forth in, then in 2037 Earth hasn't been Colonised, proving that his side wins in the end.

Trivia: The iconography of the opening scene (notably the clock) mirrors various aspects of *Back to the Future* and its sequels.

Scientific Comment: In most US universities postdoctoral fellows are unable to apply for their own grants. I doubt that ingesting liquid nitrogen would completely freeze you as Scully's theory would suggest. It's a long way from your stomach to your feet. She could test her theory by looking for a temperature gradient versus distance from the stomach. NMR (nuclear magnetic resonance) is usually called MRI (magnetic resonance imaging) these days to avoid frightening people with the word 'nuclear'. However, a chemical under analysis would probably not be very scared. The scientists say they need to solve the vitrification problem during freezing. 'Vitrification' means to change into a glass-like (i.e. non-crystalline) substance, so the problem is really *lack* of vitrification, i.e. they want vitrification to occur rather than getting crystals in the cells as freezing occurs. It is not physically possible to get down to absolute zero. Nothing in the universe is that cold, although physics experiments have got close. The temperature the frozen corpses got down to (8 degrees Fahrenheit) is an awful long way from absolute zero (−459°F).

The Bottom Line: KT: 'Puts a whole new spin on being your own worst enemy.' Ohmigod, this is a total and utter bloody mess! Time travel, when it's done well, as pure science fantasy (H.G. Wells, *Doctor Who*, *Quantum Leap*) is a thrilling sub-genre in which the only limits are the viewers' imaginations. Here, in attempting to put a logical context around it, *The X-Files* reduces the idea to something midway between ignorant dismissal and selfish bravado.

PC: The ice killings are well done, but where's the atmosphere that would have made this work? I think you'd need sheer gall, rather than this episode's painstaking care not to tread on its own toes, to pull this off.

MD: 'The iceman cometh.' Few flaws, but not much to commend it, either, barring the fantastic scene where Yonechi bursts into flame.

93: 'Small Potatoes'

US Transmission: 20 April 1997
UK Transmission: 15 June 1997 (Sky One)/
4 February 1998 (BBC1)
Writer: Vince Gilligan
Director: Cliff Bole
Cast: Darin Morgan (Eddie Van Blundht),
Christine Cavanaugh (Amanda Nelligan),
Lee de Broux (Fred Neaman), Robert Rozen (Dr Alton Pugh),
Paul McGillion (Angry Husband),
Jennifer Stirling (Angry Wife), David Cameron (Deputy),
Forbes Angus (Security Guard),
Peter Kelamis (Second Security Guard),
P. Lynn Johnson (Health Department Doctor),
Carrie Cain Sparks (Duty Nurse)

The birth of five babies all with tails in a small town in West Virginia sparks Mulder's interest. The culprit turns out to be Edward Van Blundht ('The H is silent') and not Luke Skywalker as one of the impregnated women claims. Van Blundht is a janitor with the unusual ability to change his facial appearance at will. Mulder and Scully discover the corpse of Eddie's father, complete with tail. Imprisoning Mulder, Eddie returns to Washington to take the agent's place. Getting Scully drunk on red wine they are about to kiss when the real Mulder returns. Eddie is imprisoned, but not before he has given Mulder some advice on how to run his life.

Don't Be in the Teaser: Amanda Nelligan gives birth to a healthy baby girl. With a tail. ('Good Lord, not *another* one!')

Scully Here is a Medical Doctor: She does the autopsy on the mummified corpse of Eddie the Monkey Man, discovering that he died of natural causes, and that a 'thin stratum of voluntary muscle tissue' (a 655th muscle, unique in her experience) underpins the 'entire dermal layer of his skin', a genetic defect which Mulder believes Van Blundht passed on to his son.

Scully's Rational Explanation of the Week: Foetuses have caudal appendages. The coccyx enlarges to contain the spinal fluid and then it shrinks as the child develops. Occasionally it doesn't. When Mulder points out that it's happened five times in three months in a town with a population of less than 15,000, Scully agrees it's odd, but thinks it should be the local Health Department investigating, not them. Other theories include a date-rape drug as a possible cause of the impregnation, and a linked-gene birth defect to explain Eddie's father's tail.

Phwoar!: After Scully has agreed with one of Mulder's assessments, he says, astonished: 'Should we be picking out china patterns, or what?' They're really getting on at the start of the episode, Mulder teasing out that Scully would like to be Eleanor Roosevelt (so she'd like to be secretly in charge?), and Scully anticipating his latest theory. 'Even educated MDs do it', he says, making reference to the Noël Coward song 'Let's Fall in Love'. It's cute when he ducks to fit under her umbrella. Seeing as how it's Friday, Scully will be spending the evening writing a monograph for the *Penology Review* on diminished acetylcholine production in recidivist offenders (PC: the sexiest thing she has *ever* said! God, I adore that calm exterior!). We should also mention her pullover at this point. Scully is (probably) about to kiss Van Blundht while he impersonates Mulder (because, drugs apart, Mulder seems to be actually paying attention to her life, needs and interests for once!), so this is something that is only *this far* from happening with the real Mulder and Scully (see the movie). She seems to try and open up this territory at the end, assuring Mulder that he isn't a loser, but his bitchy (and jealous?) reply assures both her and us that this is the real Fox once again. More's the pity.

Dialogue Triumphs: Mulder (after Amanda has claimed the baby's father comes from another planet): 'Were you abducted?' Amanda: 'No, he dropped by my apartment one day and one thing sort of led to another . . .'

Mulder: 'If you're waiting for my usual theory as to what's going on, I don't have one.'

Scully: 'What are you saying, that Van Blundht is an alien?'

Mulder: 'No. Not unless they have trailer-parks in space.'

Eddie, in Mulder's apartment: 'Where the hell do I sleep?'

Eddie: 'I was born a loser, but you're one by choice ... You should live a little. Treat yourself. God knows, I would if I were you.'

Continuity: Scully tells Van Blundht about her prom night with a boy named Marcus, her twelfth-grade love, and how the actions of her friend Sylvia and 'her idiot prom date' caused them to get a lift with the fire department. Mulder makes an oblique reference to Shapeshifters ('We've both seen something like this before'). Mulder's address is flat 42, 2630 Hegal Place, Alexandria, VA 23242. (The correct number for the real house in York Avenue, Vancouver. Did they know we were going to be able to see that zipcode?) His driving licence number is 123–32–132, and it expires on 31 March 1999. In Mulder's flat, Eddie finds two messages on the answerphone. One is from Langly and Frohike ('Geeks for friends,' notes Van Blundht); the second is for 'Marty' (an alias Mulder previously used in '3') from a lady called Chantelle, which turns out to be an advert for a (probably salacious) chat-line. Mulder really *does* sleep only on his couch!

The Truth: Eddie Van Blundht has a genetic defect that allows him to change his appearance. With the help of a drug, he impregnated four women by pretending to be their husbands, and one by appearing to her as Luke Skywalker. There is the vague possibility that Eddie may have been subject to previous experimentation by the Conspiracy's Japanese scientists to give him his shape-changing abilities. Maybe Mulder's suggestion that muscle relaxants would stop him from being able to 'make faces' was something Mulder picked up during his dealings with the Shapeshifters. But it's unlikely – that would give Eddie's life an importance that it, frankly, could never have.

Trivia: The latest issue of *World Weekly Informer* (see 'Pusher'), in addition to revelations about this case, also includes a story concerning MICHAEL JACKSON HELD CAPTIVE BY EXOTIC PETS, and in the bottom right corner, we see that the issue also features the Stupendous Yappi. The other headline, ETAP BIGSHOT BUSTED, refers in the *X-Files* universe to the chief of ETAP, an organisation who make various items seen in close-up in the series. The fact that they're all the product of Prop Master Jim Pate means this is probably a reference to some behind-the-scenes happening, the truth of which we will perhaps never know. Scully mentions 'McGruff, the Crime Dog', a police public information cartoon once brilliantly parodied by *The Simpsons*. Eddie does the mirror 'You lookin' at me?' scene from *Taxi Driver* in Mulder's apartment. Amanda claims that Luke Skywalker fathered her child. He sang her John Williams' *Star Wars* theme during the liaison and she says that she has seen *Star Wars* 368 times. (One nice little homage is the TIE-fighter-like musical sting between the first two scenes.) There's a drawing of (Darin Morgan as) the flukeman from 'The Host' on Mulder's office wall. Van Blundht, like David Duchovny, has a silent 'h' in his name: the 'h' falls off his father's door, much as Duchovny's father dropped the 'h' from the spelling of his name. Despite his goofy behaviour, we might assume that (in the deepest of double bluffs) that's actually the real Mulder in the autopsy scene: he's wearing Mulder's tie, which is the only difference between the doubles.

Scientific Comment: Mulder would swiftly learn not to touch a corpse covered with quicklime with his bare hands. Eddie appears to be able to change his mass and bone structure as well as his muscle and hair (!) structure.

The Bottom Line: KT: 'I said, "Son, you ain't much to look at, you ain't no athlete and you sure ain't no Einstein. But at least you got that tail. Otherwise you're just small potatoes." ' The only episode to feature Darin Morgan's bum-crevice (out of which, as this episode demonstrates, the sun shines). Not only does he put in a towering, genuinely sympathetic performance as Eddie, but Vince Gilligan's stunning script is clearly influenced by Morgan's previous work on the series. And David Duchovny acts his socks off in the sequences when playing Eddie-playing-Mulder. The action is by turns hilarious (the bit where Mulder snaps the tail off the corpse and tries to hide the evidence from Scully), and thought-provoking ('You're a damn good-looking man'). Eddie's disgust at Mulder's waste of his opportunities ('This is where my tax dollars go') and his own inability to spell 'Federal Bureau of Intelligence' twice (!) are other brilliant moments. If nothing else this is an example of what *The X-Files* has become since Darin Morgan first got his hands on it – a series that *has* no rules any more except that there *are* no rules. Easily the best episode of the fourth season.

PC: This is excellent, a quiet exploration of whether a person is made by personality or appearance. It's a pity about the date-rape drug, which seems only there to muddy the waters of Eddie's night with Scully, since we really want to like him. It's not hard to believe that he makes a more satisfying and attentive Mulder than Mulder does. Duchovny excels, particularly in his creation of a 'Darin Morgan face', and suggests that Mulder is actually envious of Van Blundht throughout. And a nod to Lee de Broux for his wonderful little turn in two roles also. Deeply thoughtful.

MD: Glorious, simple, clever and downright funny. Its humour isn't at the expense of drama or suspension of disbelief, which makes a pleasant change for *The X-Files*.

94: 'Zero Sum'

US Transmission: 27 April 1997
UK Transmission: 22 June 1997 (Sky One)/
11 February 1998 (BBC1)
Writers: Howard Gordon, Frank Spotnitz
Director: Kim Manners
Cast: Nicole Nattrass (Misty),
Fred Keating (Detective Ray Thomas),
Allan Gray (Entomologist),
Addison Ridge (Bespectacled Boy),
Lisa Stewart (Jane Brody), Barry Greene (Dr Emile Linzer),
Christopher J. Newton (Photo Technician)

A postal worker, taking a break from her work, is killed in suspicious circumstances. Skinner, having brokered a deal with the Cigarette-Smoking Man which he hopes will save Scully's life, deletes key files from Mulder's computer and impersonates the Special Agent in order to clean away the evidence. Skinner swaps a phial of blood taken from the woman, and incinerates the body. However, he is confronted by the police officer who sent Mulder the information, but Skinner tells the man that there is nothing to investigate. To Skinner's shock, the police officer is later shot. When he returns to the delivery company, Skinner finds the remains of a beehive behind the wall where the woman was killed. He takes some honeycomb to an entomologist, who finds a living larvae within. The scientist is later killed by a swarm of killer bees. Mulder finds out about the dead man, and is told that he was killed by smallpox. A swarm of bees attacks children at a school in South Carolina, and Mulder discovers that it was Skinner who impersonated him. Skinner confronts the Cigarette-Smoking Man, but cannot kill him. The Cigarette-Smoking Man instructs Marita Covarrubias to lie to Mulder if he investigates further.

Don't Be in the Toilets: Jane Brody is attacked by killer bees while smoking in the toilet.

How Did He Do That?: Why is there still so much of this evidence around for Skinner to remove? Mind you, somebody's already taken the bees (unless they're homing bees, too!), further indicating that this is just a test designed to see how much the CSM can use Skinner.

Phwoar!: We ought to mention Skinner's Y-fronts.

The Conspiracy Starts at Closing Time: Mulder speculates that the bees are being used as carriers of 'a disease that has killed more people throughout history than any other contagion known to mankind', viz. smallpox (variola). The virus has been mutated to shorten the usual eight-day incubation period, and the bees have apparently been genetically engineered to breed incredibly fast out of a mix of larvae and royal jelly. They also appear to have been trained to attack and escape afterwards. This is the Conspiracy's chosen method of distributing the Colonist virus, a method which they elect to test using smallpox. This would demonstrate the potency of the delivery system instantly, especially since children aren't vaccinated against smallpox in the USA any more. (Paranoid sidenote: is that why Bill Mulder or the CSM changed Samantha's birthdate in their records, so it wouldn't look strange if she didn't have a smallpox inoculation scar, and was thus saved from having her ova taken through the abductee extraction technique? Perhaps. But the ages probably aren't right: Scully has a vaccination scar, and she's roughly the same age as Samantha.) The Cigarette-Smoking Man tells the Elder that the trial run has already begun (it seems that either the bees were not supposed to have been tested yet, but, given that some have escaped, their success will be monitored, or Marita is feeding Skinner a lesser level of the truth when she tells him of the damaged package, the latter being the more realistic possibility since the Conspiracy sent seven packages to the area very deliberately). When Marita Covarrubias investigated the farm in Canada (see 'Herrenvolk'), she says she found nothing there, but that's probably a lie too. When she meets Skinner, she initially tries to discover the depth of his knowledge of the Conspiracy, and what he's told Mulder, then quickly encourages him to speak out about what he knows. (Indicating, as we later learn, that she's on the side of the good guys.) The CSM instructs her, at the end of the episode, to tell Mulder 'what he wants to hear' about whether Skinner was privy to this whole plan (which is presumably letting Skinner off the hook by having Marita minimise the description of his involvement). This is, in the end, a test of Skinner's loyalty to the CSM, possibly an audition to become the new X and do what he used to do. An audition Skinner fails. Though immediately saved by the CSM's sense of drama, this leaves Skinner open to plots against him such as that seen in 'Redux'. Skinner doesn't think he's gotten anything out of the bargain (his aid for Scully's life), but the CSM eventually (in 'Redux') gives Mulder the information to save Scully. He says here that he saved her life before, presumably meaning that he was instrumental in having her abducted rather than killed, and returned more quickly than the Conspiracy were expecting. This, together with his sleight of hand involving Samantha, indicates he's close to that part of the organisation which organises the abductions, that is, the Japanese/Nazi war criminal section! This could explain why his own son (?)

might possibly be an abductee ('Patient X'). If that's true, he wants his whole lineage to survive, even in the form of hybrids.

Continuity: Mulder came to the forensic entomologist 'about six months ago' with evidence of the unique bees he found in 'Herrenvolk'. Skinner mentions his advice to Mulder concerning not doing a deal with the Conspiracy ('Memento Mori'), noting that he didn't follow his own advice. Interesting to note that Mulder feels he's on close enough terms with his boss to pop in to see him at home at four in the morning. (Or perhaps Mulder's just like that with everybody.) Skinner once more is aware of the Cigarette-Smoking Man's home address and phone number, which indicates the degree of self-discipline he must use every day in not giving it to Mulder.

The Truth: As part of the Conspiracy's 'trial run', seven packages (containing the smallpox-carrying bees) were sent from the Canadian farm to a PO Box in South Carolina. One was (inadvertently) stored at a routing centre in Virginia, the bees escaping to create a hive in the wall.

Trivia: Gillian Anderson doesn't appear in this episode, Scully undergoing cancer tests. The episode has an on-screen dedication 'In Loving Memory of Vito J. Pileggi' (Mitch Pileggi's father, who died in 1993).

Scientific Comment: I would have expected an entomologist to be able to identify a bee from its larva without having to wait for it to turn into an adult. Some types of anaemia are treated with folic acid. I don't think bee venom contains folic acid (as ant venom would) so it could not be argued that the lack of a folic acid deficiency was due to the bee stings.

The Bottom Line: MD: I'm a sucker for Skinner, and this near-solo episode works well, by dint of being understandable and logical, though it runs out of steam and just . . . ends. And it's a shame that even *The X-Files* can rarely bring itself to kill its (fictional) children: having only the teacher fall under the swarm smacks of sentimental artifice.

KT: 'I suggest you keep your voice down, Mr Skinner,

unless you want your neighbours to know the hours and company you keep.' Mitch Pileggi's finest forty-five minutes in an *X-Files* sweat-shirt. An episode full of horrific images (the pre-titles, the bees attacking the school), and some marvellous 'two-men-in-a-room' scenes (Skinner and the murder victim's best friend, and, especially, the closing Skinner and Cigarette-Smoking Man sequence – one of the finest in the series). A direct sequel to 'Herrenvolk', and one of the better stand-alone Conspiracy episodes that manages to balance the complexities of the developing story arc with carrying the story forward. It's only after it's finished that you realise Scully wasn't in it, and (uniquely) she wasn't missed.

PC: Congratulations to Bee Wrangler Debbie Coe for having the best job description in the series. This episode includes a developing TV cliché: morgue attendants always watch TV. Apart from that, it's mostly ho hum, with the bee attacks the only real fun to be had, and Mulder's superhuman instincts for once utterly failing him when the truth is under his nose. He must respect Skinner a lot to trust him after this one! Mitch Pileggi is, at least, charismatic enough to carry the episode on his own.

95: 'Elegy'

US Transmission: 4 May 1997
UK Transmission: 29 June 1997 (Sky One)/
18 February 1998 (BBC1)
Writer: John Shiban
Director: James Charleston
Cast: Steven M. Porter (Harold Spueler),
Alex Bruhanski (Angelo Pintero),
Sydney Lassick (Chuck Forsch), Nancy Fish (Nurse Innes),
Daniel Kamin (Detective Hudak), Lorena Gale (Attorney),
Mike Puttonen (Martin Alpert),
Ken Tremblett (Uniformed Officer)

Washington DC: A series of murders of young women seem to be accompanied by ghostly apparitions nearby, and the phrase 'She is Me' being reported as the victims' final words.

Investigations lead to an autistic man named Harold Spueler, a voluntary patient at a nearby psychiatric hospital, who Mulder believes made a call to the police after one of the murders. While at the hospital, Scully also experiences a vision of a dead girl seconds before Mulder informs her of the discovery of another victim. The murders are subsequently revealed to be down to a nurse working at the hospital whose violent impulses were increased by drugs she stole from the patients, but Mulder is more concerned with Scully's unwillingness to trust him with what she thought she saw.

Don't Be in the Teaser: There's the discovery of the body of a young woman with her throat cut, and some spooky goings-on with her ghost.

How Did He Do That?: Mulder's barmy theory about the dying being able to see the recently dead. What is he *on*?! The trick with the cola on the bowling alley is also pretty amazing.

Scully Here is a Medical Doctor: 'Agent Scully's a doctor,' Mulder tells the psychiatric home manager. It's a pity he doesn't ask 'What sort of doctor, exactly?'

Ooze: Blood, lots of it!

Scully's Rational Explanation of the Week: The murderer is suffering from an excessive form of an obsessive-compulsive disorder characterised by the drive to organise.

That's a Mouthful: Mulder: 'What is a death omen, if not a vision of our own mortality? And who among us would most likely be able to see the dead?'

Phwoar!: No other series could manage to make the simple act of its heroine putting on a pair of bowling shoes in the immediate post-titles scene into an auto-erotic moment. Dangerously sexy! Scully says she relies on Mulder's passion and strength and is frightened of letting him down.

Continuity: Mulder can bowl (pretty well on the strength of one attempt!). Scully visits the departmental psychologist from 'Irresistible' again.

The Truth: 'You're saying that what this man saw was the victim's ghost?' 'Sounds more like a disembodied soul.' 'Which is just another name for a ghost.' Scully speculates that her witnessing of the ghosts of the fourth victim, and of Harold, are just auto-suggestion caused by stress, but that doesn't explain how she was able to see the dead girl before Mulder had told her about the murder. Like her vision of her father in 'Beyond the Sea', this suggests some latent psychic ability in Scully.

Trivia: The episode's two working titles were 'Tulpa' and 'Revenant'. In Tibetan mystic practice, a Tulpa is a ghostly manifestation. A revenant is someone who comes back following a lengthy absence or returns from the dead. An elegy is a poetic epitaph. The scenes in the psychiatric home are reminiscent of *One Flew Over the Cuckoo's Nest* (Sydney Lassick, who plays Chuck Forsch, also appeared in the film in the memorable role of Charlie Cheswick). Scully holds up a copy of *TV Guide* in the psychiatric home with Jay Leno on the cover, and he is immediately identified as the murderer by many of the inmates!

The Bottom Line: KT: 'Working with these people, it starts driving you crazy, too.' A pretty good little episode, heavily indebted to previous forays into this kind of world ('Roland', 'Excelsis Dei', and especially 'Irresistible'), with a smashing, and completely unexpected twist in the form of the murderer's identity. Once again, Scully's scenes with her analyst are a highlight of the season – in fact, this could be Gillian Anderson's finest ever episode – she's simply brilliant, with a depth to her emotions that drags the viewer down a few dark roads with her. The climactic scene between Mulder and Scully where the bond they have shared is as good as severed is both gut-wrenching and yet strangely satisfying, because at last the cards are fully on the table. The final scene is a beauty, too.

PC: Very scary ghosts. Mulder leads Harold on in a completely unprofessional manner. The Mulder and Scully faith-testing sequences (and this episode should really have seen the end of Scully's scepticism) are a lovely distraction from an ordinary story featuring a very inadequate murder motive.

MD: Excuse the pun, but this is a bit of a dead end story. It's well acted and scripted, but I'm not sure it really goes anywhere. In its own way, it's probably more downbeat than either 'Hell Money' or 'Roland', and so leaves a slightly stale taste in the mouth. Best bit: Scully's nosebleed on to the bowling alley sheet, a gentle echo of the pre-titles sequence.

96: 'Demons'

US Transmission: 11 May 1997
UK Transmission: 6 July 1997 (Sky One)/
25 February 1998 (BBC1)
Writer: R.W. Goodwin
Director: Kim Manners
Cast: Jay Acovone (Detective Joe Curtis),
Mike Nussbaum (Dr Charles Goldstein),
Andrew Johnston (Medical Examiner),
Terry Jang Barclay (Imhof), Eric Breker (Admitting Officer),
Rebecca Harker (Housekeeper),
Shelley Adam (Young Mrs Mulder),
Alex Haythorne (Young Mulder)

Following a vision from his childhood of his parents fighting, Mulder wakes in a motel room, bloodstained and with no memory of how he got that way. Scully discovers that his gun's been fired, and the agents journey to a cottage belonging to David and Amy Cassandra, where that couple's corpses are found. It's their blood on Mulder's shirt. Mulder is arrested, but it's discovered that he, and Amy, both have traces of Ketamine in their blood. A police officer, a believer in UFOs and another of the Cassandras' circle of alien abductees, commits suicide. Mulder is cleared through forensic evidence, and the agents meet Dr Goldstein, who had been treating the Cassandras for memory loss. Mulder has a vision of his mother embracing the young Cigarette-Smoking Man. He goes to his mother's house to confront her, but she won't tell him anything. Mulder then makes Goldstein finish the treatment that he began on Mulder, resulting in Mulder holing up in his parents' summer house in Quonochontaug, seized by visions, a gun to his head. Scully manages to talk him down.

Don't Be in the Teaser: Mulder wakes up in a motel, covered in someone else's blood.

Scully Here is a Medical Doctor: She diagnoses Mulder, follows another medic's autopsy, and shouts 'I'm a doctor!'

Scully's Rational Explanation of the Week: Mulder's had a 'serious cerebral event' and is suffering from an acute physiological disturbance brought on by Goldstein's treatment. Spot on. But she also doubts the truth of Mulder's recovered memories.

Phwoar!: When Mulder is naked in the shower, Scully allows her gaze to drift down a little. She has huge faith in Mulder here, knowing he wouldn't shoot her, and certain of his innocence (a lovely moment when she grabs Dr Goldstein by the collar). At the end, she lays her head on his shoulders. She must find that woeful 'little lost puppy' look that Duchovny adopts throughout moving.

Dialogue Triumphs: Mulder mimics classic *Trek*: 'You're a doctor, not a lawyer.'

'Do the words Orenthal James Simpson mean anything to you?'

On his subconscious: 'The truth is in there, recorded, and I've gotten access to it.'

The Conspiracy Starts at Closing Time: Mulder's recovered memories, which may or may not be accurate, suggest that the Cigarette-Smoking Man forced Mrs Mulder to choose Samantha to be abducted (knowing that he could get his own daughter out the other side of the Conspiracy's net and thus keep her safe, or wanting his genetic line to continue after the destruction of humanity), resulting in a row between him and the Mulders. (Mrs Mulder yells 'Not my baby!' at one point. Does this mean that Fox isn't?) The image of the Cigarette-Smoking Man lies behind the image of Samantha in the flashbacks (indicating her true parentage?).

Continuity: We once more visit the Mulders' summer house at Quonochontaug ('Talitha Cumi'). Mulder's memories of the abduction confirm the game of Stratego, and Samantha floating out of the window (which isn't beyond the Conspiracy technology we've seen), and agree with the 'Little Green Men' version of events, but without aliens. (Was the stickman at the door inserted when Mulder's memories were tampered with by the Conspiracy in 'Deep Throat'?) If the row was on the same night as the abduction, then the Mulders were given very little time to make their decision. Scully is still in denial about the efficacy of recovering memories ('Nisei'), aggressively telling Goldstein 'I know what you do.' Scully starts to wonder about Mulder's sanity here, leading into the following three-parter.

The Truth: Mulder contacted abductees David and Amy Cassandra (interesting name: Cassandra was a prophetess of doom, and although nobody believed her predictions, she was always correct, which rather sums up the plight of an abductee in this series) and joined in with the Ketamine-assisted memory recovery treatment provided by Dr Goldstein. A side-effect of this drove Amy to kill her husband and then commit suicide, using Mulder's gun. (Mulder was presumably tripping in his memories at the time.) Mulder may have gone for help and then forgotten the events, and thus headed to his motel, or been smuggled back there, unconscious, by Goldstein.

Trivia: Were the Cigarette-Smoking Man's favourite brand named after the actor who plays the young Samantha, Vanessa Morley, or was it the other way round? The BBC1 broadcast was proceeded by a warning about flashing light sequences.

The Bottom Line: PC: A sudden change of direction half way, a struggle to produce a dramatic climax, promised revelations that never materialise. An ugly dull thing with nothing inside it. An episode crushed in the wake of a story arc that it doesn't even contribute to.

KT: 'The rest of the narrative is far too convenient and suspect.' Starting with one of the series' best pre-titles, this has pretty much *everything* (flashbacks-within-dreams!). A story of exorcising demons, Mulder's memories (or, are they dream-sequences – the plot never seems able to be definitive) are incredible, a real trip. The story snakes along with a few moments that stretch the imagination, but the scene with Mrs Mulder seems largely perfunctory. The references to 'Dostoevsky syndome' provide a link to Mulder's other heart of darkness, 'Grotesque'. Interestingly (as with one or two of the other Conspiracy stories) an apparent throwaway line (concerning the sleeping habits of Mrs Mulder) would be followed up in later stories.

MD: I'm writing this having only just watched it, and I can barely remember what happened. Absolutely lacking in tension or interest. File under: 'Ditchwater, dull as'.

CHRIS OWENS

Chris Owens appears as the young Cigarette-Smoking Man in 'Demons' and 'Musings of . . .' (the first actor to have played the part (uncredited), in 'Apocrypha' being Craig Warkentin) and as the Great Mutato in 'Post-Modern Prometheus'. He was, at the time of British broadcast of 'Demons', rumoured to be replacing David Duchovny as the lead in the series, playing a character called Spencer, Mulder's half-brother. This turned out to be a false rumour started by American DJ Howard Stern. Strangely, much of that rumour then started to come true, Owens being cast as Spender in 'Patient X', who might just turn out to be Mulder's half-brother.

97: 'Gethsemane'

US Transmission: 18 May 1997
UK Transmission: 13 July 1997 (Sky One)/
4 March 1998 (BBC1)
Writer: Chris Carter
Director: R.W. Goodwin
Cast: John Finn (Michael Kritschgau),
Matthew Walker (Arlinsky), James Sutorius (Babcock),
John Oliver (Rolston), Steve Makha (Ostelhoff),
Nancy Kerr (Agent Hedin), Barry W. Levy (Vitagliano),
Rob Freeman (Detective Rempulski),
Craig Burnanski (Saw Operator)

Mulder is apparently dead, the body identified by Scully, who is also rubbishing his beliefs in front of an FBI committee chaired by Section Chief Blevins. In flashback, we see how two anthropologists discovered the apparent frozen corpse of a Grey alien on a Canadian mountain. They called Mulder, who took Scully away from a family party to meet with one of the scientists, Arlinsky. The alien is supposed to be over two hundred years old: Arlinsky gives Scully ice core samples to study. Meanwhile, the party on the mountain are attacked by an assassin, Ostelhoff. Scully tussles with Kritschgau, a Pentagon staff member who stole the ice core samples, and arrests him. But he pleads not to be jailed: those who gave Scully her cancer will kill him. Mulder and Arlinsky rescue the alien body from the mountain and aid the survivors of the attack. They conduct an autopsy on the alien, but Mulder is called away to listen to Kritschgau's story: he says the alien corpse is a fake, part of a vast government hoax. Mulder storms out, and finds Arlinsky dead and the corpse missing. Scully tells him that she thinks she was given her cancer to help convince him of the hoax. End of flashback. Scully tells the FBI panel that Mulder shot himself.

Don't Be in the Teaser: Mulder hasn't really had his face blown off, but Carl Sagan died an untimely death . . .

Scully Here is a Medical Doctor: 'I am a medical doctor,' she affirms.

Ooze: The chimera 'alien' body.

Scully's Rational Explanation of the Week: Scully tells Blevins and co. that Mulder is 'a victim of his own false hopes, and of his belief in the biggest of lies', which is absolutely true, but she doesn't mean the lie they think she means. (And, on rewatching, she gives an ironic little curl of her mouth, pleased that she's put one over on them.)

Phwoar!: Scully's dark look when she goes after Kritschgau. A nice shot of Mulder sobbing over his beliefs fades in to Scully pondering hers at the same angle.

Dialogue Triumphs: Mulder: 'If someone could prove to

you the existence of God, would it change you?' Scully: 'Only if it had been disproven.'

Bill berates Scully: 'You think you can cure yourself!' And two episodes later, she does.

Mulder: 'I refuse to believe that it's not true!' Scully: 'Because it's easier to believe the lie!'

Dialogue Disasters: More of a plot hiccup. 'Why come to me now?' Mulder asks Kritschgau, but he hasn't, he's been dragged there by Scully. Perhaps Mulder means why come begging for sanctuary from their side after so many years working for the enemy.

The Conspiracy Starts at Closing Time: The chimera 'alien' body has three fingers and a thumb on each hand and a three-toed foot, is 147 cm tall, and weighs 24 kg. Its skin is grey, elephantine, hairless and covered in pustules. Its eyes are lidless, black, and covered by a membrane. It has human-like heart and lungs, but also a white, stringlike tissue inside its body. The chimera body is probably not specially created, but is simply that of one of the Conspiracy's Colonist/human hybrids, dead after having mutated into something resembling a Grey, the way these hybrids do. The lack of toxic blood is rather puzzling, but perhaps the Conspiracy have done something to the body after death to remove this obstacle to ease handling.

Continuity: Scully finally delivers her report on Mulder, commissioned four years ago by Section Chief Blevins. Her brother Bill, a naval man like his dad, once fell over her going downstairs. He remembers Scully's birthday 'once every ten years'. (Maybe she's one of those people who doesn't tell anybody about it?) He objects to Mulder's dangerous and extreme place in Scully's life. Father McCue is the Scully family priest. Mulder has known Arlinski, of the Smithsonian, for four years. Mulder's suicidal state at the end of this episode may be a direct result of the drug he was given during 'Demons': Scully presumably monitored him for a while, but the pursuit of the alien kept his state of mind upbeat enough for her not to suspect he was prone to collapse.

The Truth: What Kritschgau believes: the whole concept of alien life on Earth is a lie conceived by the Department of Defense's agitprop arm to distract public attention from the establishment's misdeeds. He knows about memory erasures, Conspiracy-run abductions (including that of Samantha), and that UFOs are USAF aircraft. He thinks that Scully was given cancer to make Mulder believe the abductions are carried out by aliens. (How exactly? Is the idea that her disease was supposed to be a radiation-induced consequence of being onboard an alien ship? Or is it that peril to his partner would make Mulder act more boldly and think less?) In short, Kritschgau has been given access to the same level of the truth as the USAF pilot in 'Jose Chung's *From Outer Space*'. This isn't, of course, anything like the whole truth (see the next two episodes).

Trivia: Considering his campaign against superstition and credence, it's grossly unfair to use an out-of-context 1972 clip of Carl Sagan to apparently support Mulder's alien theories. (Indeed, it seems to be all that's keeping Mulder's faith going at that point.) Certainly, through Scully, *The X-Files* continues to support rationality alongside Mulder's extreme beliefs, and this episode particularly warns against over-credulity, but it's still one hell of a liberty. Viewers of *Doctor Who* will wonder at the coincidence of a story about finding a traitor at the highest levels of power featuring an FBI agent called Hedin (the name of said traitor in the story 'Arc of Infinity').

Scientific Comment: I don't think you can get a 360-degree test from two parallel ice cores. There seems to be a very lax use of medical masks in this episode: everyone gets really close to the alien body without the masks at some point. Since the helicopter doesn't take them all the way up the mountain I assume this means it can't fly to that height. How, then, did they get the body down – by sledge? After a journey of several hours you'd expect the ice block to have melted on the outside and look wet but it doesn't. Did they have a refrigerated truck?

The Bottom Line: PC: A nice collision of faiths between Mulder and Scully, in which his obsession once more seems decadent in the face of her cancer, joins with another fine use of budget and a pleasingly straightforward script to produce a satisfying cliffhanger. We get another serious take on an alien autopsy, Scully unwilling to be a victim, even to her family, and the illusion of mountain locations. On the negative side are Arlinski's weird (supposedly Canadian?) accent, Scully watching Kritschgau take the ice core, and the worrying discovery that Chris Carter's awful 'poesy' isn't the stuff of fourth-draft diary entries, but our hero's voiced thoughts!

MD: This goes over old themes and set pieces – an investigation into Mulder, snowy wastes, an alien autopsy – with such a verve the end result is really quite engrossing. For instance, though we're used to *The X-Files* doing 'cold' and 'mountainous' well, the scenes in the ice cavern are extraordinary. Best of all is the convincing treatment of Scully's cancer. Her reaction – that it's personal to her – is frustrating and believable in equal measures. Similarly, Bill's response is both understandable and detestable. Having watched someone battle (unsuccessfully) against breast cancer, I found this episode hugely powerful, but it's a tribute to Carter that the visceral content never careers out of control.

KT: 'Is it easier to go on believing the lie?' A confusing mess at first, this episode does actually benefit from repeated viewing. It contains some lovely moments (the Scully family meal), and the alien autopsy is well handled. But there is a sense of too much padding, particularly the over-long explanatory scenes of Scully at the FBI inquiry (which get irritating after the first couple).

MULDER'S MOMENT OF DOUBT

In the New Testament, Gethsemane (the word is derived from the Aramaic for 'olive oil press') was a garden where Jesus frequently went to pray. It was here that he was betrayed by Judas and arrested by the secular and religious authorities. The use of this word as a title is a little more confusing than Carter's utilisation of 'Talitha Cumi' in the previous season. It's not as if Mulder is betrayed by those close to him (true, the alien seems to be a hoax, but those who brought the information to his attention were genuine). One could argue that the FBI panel, assessing Mulder's life and work, is an equivalent to those who tried and sentenced Jesus, but this takes us beyond Gethsemane and towards Golgotha (how about that as a title, Mr Carter?). According to the biblical narrative it was in Gethsemane that the enormity of the impending crucifixion threatened to overwhelm Jesus, and so it is in this story that Mulder has his moment of greatest doubt. He is haunted by the possibility that everything he has believed in has been a lie. Rather like the very human Messiah of Kazantzakis' *The Last Temptation*, the thought that he has suffered in vain is almost too much to bear. With this in mind, the interchanges between Scully and the overeager family priest, and between Scully and Mulder on the possibility of or need for 'proof' in a world of pure belief (be it in God or in extraterrestrial life), spring more sharply into focus. To deny Mulder proof is to make him believe more strongly: to take away his faith is to leave him with nothing to cling to. Small wonder he seems prepared to end his life.

A recurring motif in *The X-Files* is that there is an investigation into Mulder's character, which is affected by the news that he's dead. But he returns triumphantly to confound his oppressors. Those on the opposing side (Deep Throat, X, the Cigarette-Smoking Man) start to follow Mulder's cause, as if converted by his idealism, and die as a result. It's like the Truth attracts the bad guys to its cause. They start out using Mulder as a stalking horse, but end up as martyrs for him, the Mulder/Christ metaphor writ large.

Fifth Season

20 45-minute episodes

Created by Chris Carter

Consulting Producer: Ken Horton
Co-Producers: Lori Jo Nemhauser, John Shiban
Producers: Joseph Patrick Finn, Kim Manners, Paul Rabwin
Supervising Producer: Vince Gilligan
Co-Executive Producer: Frank Spotnitz
Executive Producers: Chris Carter, R.W. Goodwin

Regular Cast (118 indicates the *X-Files* movie): David Duchovny (Special Agent Fox Mulder), Gillian Anderson (Special Agent Dana Scully, 98, 99, 101–111, 113–118), William B. Davis (The Cigarette-Smoking Man, 98, 99, 111, 117, 118), Ken Camroux (Senior Agent, 98, 99), Charles Cioffi (Section Chief Scott Blevins, 98, 99), Jim Jansen (Dr Heitz Werber, 110, 111), Sheila Larken (Margaret Scully, 99, 103, 104), Tom Braidwood (Melvin Frohike, 98–100, 108, 117, 118), Dean Haglund (Langly, 98–100, 108, 117, 118), Bruce Harwood (John Byers, 98–100, 108, 117, 118), Mitch Pileggi (Assistant Director Walter Skinner, 98, 99, 105, 109, 111, 115, 117, 118), Steven Williams (X, 100), Nicholas Lea (Alex Krycek, 110, 111, 117), Melinda McGraw (Melissa Scully, 103), Megan Leitch (Samantha Mulder, 99), Brian Thompson (Rebel Leader, 110, 111), John Moore (2nd Elder, 110, 111, 117), John Neville (The Well-Manicured Man, 110, 111, 117, 118), Stanley Walsh (Other Elder, 118[29]), Don S. Williams (Elder, 98, 99, 110, 111, 117, 118), Julia Arkos (Holly, 98), Robert Wisden (Robert Modell, 105), Brian Thompson (The Shapeshifter Assassin, 111), Laurie Holden (Marita Covarrubias, 110, 111), Dean Aylesworth (Young Bill Mulder, 112), Anatol Rezmeritsa (Commandant, 110), Pat Skipper (Bill Scully Jr., 99, 103, 104), Arnie Walters (Father McCue, 114), Willy Ross (Quiet Willy, 98[30], 99, 110, 111), Lauren Diewold (Emily Sim, 103, 104, 114), Chris Owens (Special Agent Jeffrey Spender, 110, 111, 117), George Murdoch (3rd Elder, 111, 117, 118), Michael Shamus Wiles (Black-Haired Man, 117, 118)

[29] Credited as '2nd Elder'.
[30] Uncredited.

98: 'Redux'

US Transmission: 2 November 1997
UK Transmission: 1 March 1998 (Sky One)
Writer: Chris Carter
Director: R.W. Goodwin
Cast: John Finn (Kritschgau), Steve Makaj (Ostelhoff),
Barry W. Levy (Vitagliano)

Mulder confronts Ostelhoff, the man who was surveilling his apartment, and kills him in a struggle, discovering that the FBI itself, perhaps via Skinner, is implicated in the Conspiracy. Scully identifies Ostelhoff's faceless body as Mulder's. Mulder uses Ostelhoff's ID to infiltrate the Defense Advanced Research Projects Agency, where he finds Kritschgau. Kritschgau tells him that the whole business of alien life is a lie, designed to hide the government's bio-weapon research on its own citizens. Scully compares her DNA to the ice core samples, and finds a match, which she thinks proves she was given her cancer by deliberate exposure to the chimera genetic material. In the government complex, Mulder discovers alien bodies, comatose pregnant women, a vast card index (with cards for Scully, Kritschgau, and a blank one for Kritschgau's son), and a vial that might contain the cure for Scully's cancer. As Scully begins explaining the nature of the Conspiracy to the FBI panel investigating Mulder, she is taken ill. The Cigarette-Smoking Man arranges Mulder's escape from the government complex. The Lone Gunmen analyse the contents of the vial: it's just de-ionised water.

Don't Be in the Teaser: Mulder, driven to paranoid collapse by the idea that Scully's cancer is his fault, is about to top himself. Until he's told he's being spied on. He's then apparently shot by Ostelhoff. Except that the reverse is true.

How Did He Do That?: Mulder finds the chip in all those miles of filing.

Scully Here is a Medical Doctor: 'I am a medical doctor.' She investigates her own blood chemistry.

That's a Mouthful: 'I have held a torch in the darkness to glance upon a truth unknown . . .' And on and on and on for virtually the whole episode.

Phwoar!: Scully continues the worrying trend of actually getting her kit off. 'I have never seen her integrity waver or her honour compromised,' Mulder says of her. He's certain she would have saved him from promoting the fake alien. 'Why are you sitting in my bedroom in the dark?' asks Scully.

Dialogue Triumphs: The Cigarette-Smoking Man: 'I created Mulder.'

Mulder: 'I will not allow this treason to prosper. Not if they've done this to you.'

Dialogue Disasters: Is 'surveilled' a word?

The Conspiracy Starts at Closing Time: The Conspiracy have a holding facility connected by an underground tunnel to the cellars of the Pentagon, where they keep important items, as seen in the pilot episode. The Cigarette-Smoking Man is shocked to discover that Mulder-related plans are continuing without his knowledge. He didn't know Mulder was being bugged by the Conspiracy's operation within the Department of Defense (the Defense Advanced Research Projects Agency). The Conspiracy are fooled by Mulder's apparent death, but the Cigarette-Smoking Man isn't. Level four security clearance allows access to the biological quarantine wing of the Department of Defense, where vast quantities of DNA, from virtually every American born since 1945, are kept. (Kritschgau believes that the government have been testing bio-weapons on their own people, which is, as we know, true as far as it goes, but what he doesn't know is that it wasn't a Conspiracy-sanctioned operation. The Conspiracy seem to have 'come home' to the DoD and are now almost certainly running the operation.) Mulder also finds a roomful of Grey corpses (presumably those of Colonist/human hybrids) and another room full of comatose women with inflated, pregnant abdomens (exactly as happened to Scully in 'Ascension'), presumably incubating Colonist/human hybrids, so this facility now takes them from birth to grave. Scully discovers Colonist/human 'chimera' cells in her own blood (presumably via bearing the hybrid child Emily). This script's careful reference to 'an alien race . . . or races' is the first indication that the Colonists may not be the only ones concerned with Earth. It's interesting to note that Colonist/human cells can be grown in bovine serum (so the kids in 'Red Museum' were presumably being injected with Colonist DNA already inserted into human cells, a more reasonable form of gene therapy than utilising the plant/Colonist material contained in the 'Purity Control' flask, which may have been a misunderstood use of the Conspiracy's technology to put Colonist cells into plants to transfer them to bees). There is also the matter of the blank index card for Kritschgau's son, who is, Kritschgau thinks, dying due to having been exposed to toxins in the Gulf War. A blank card may indicate that he's already 'dead', having been infected with the 'black cancer', or, as we know it, the Black Oil. It might be simply that he's being kept alive by the Black Oil just until Kritschgau has primed Mulder with his story, then will be killed instantly.

Continuity: Holly in communications knows Scully on first name terms (see 'Pusher'). Samantha was abducted twenty-three years ago.

The Truth: Kritschgau has a security clearance (and presumably a knowledge of the truth) that is less than level four. Level four allows access to the Conspiracy's vault, which might mean that this clearance assumes knowledge of everything. (One is reminded of Ian Watson's *Alien Embassy*, where the number of pens one has in one's pocket indicates the version of the truth one has access to.) Mulder now believes that the whole alien abduction thing is a military/FBI hoax, and that there's a plot to weaken his faith and maybe drive him to suicide, that the 'very existence of a cure' for Scully means he's believed the lie. He thinks that the Conspiracy wanted Scully dead before he could go public about the alien menace, so she wouldn't be able to stop him being so foolish. But he should really read The Truth box for the next episode.

Trivia: Scully's file is indexed under 'SCU-SCV'. How many names are there going to be that begin 'SCV', and couldn't they have squeezed 'SCW-SCX' in there as well? Mulder now has a photo of the 'face on Mars' on his wall (so has he been doing some thinking about the events of 'Space'?). Mulder's comment 'Keep going, FBI woman' is perhaps a reference to a similar line in similar circumstances in *Butch Cassidy and the Sundance Kid*. Both the dialogue and the visuals during the Mulder/Kritschgau sequence are highly influenced by the Garrison/X sequences in *JFK*.

The Bottom Line: PC: Possibly the worst opening episode of a TV drama season ever, this monotonous exploration of the voice-over as the enemy of drama simply drains one's will to watch. The director resorts to splicing in stock footage to try and liven things up. Nice touches, such as the Cigarette-Smoking Man's fond look at a photo of Mulder and Samantha, and blood from Scully's nose falling on the evidence, can't distract from the fact that the middle part of this trilogy has only one thing of dramatic note to say: Mulder and Scully come to believe, to some degree, in each other's beliefs. And why are the Lone Gunmen in it?

MD: An almost completely empty exercise in thesaurus-regurgitation (how many more synonyms and descriptions of 'truth' and 'belief' can we expect in one single episode?), and the dramatic equivalent of running-on-the-spot. The budget seems to have run out right at the start of the season (a far cry from the impressive 'Gethsemane'), and so does the imagination. A piece of grit in a sandwich of delight.

KT: 'There's a dead man on the floor of my apartment and it's only a matter of time before he starts to stink the place up.' Oh dear, *what* a disappointment. A 'That's a Mouthful'-fest of *obscene* proportions (the scene in which Mulder and Kritschgau wander the corridors filling in the last fifty years of American history for anybody who missed it, over random stock footage in emulation of *JFK* is such a wasted opportunity) with an 'everything but the kitchen sink' feel to Chris Carter's script. I (genuinely) fell asleep during one viewing of the episode.

99: 'Redux II'

US Transmission: 9 November 1997
UK Transmission: 8 March 1998 (Sky One)
Writer: Chris Carter
Director: Kim Manners
Cast: John Finn (Kritschgau),
Robert Wright (Dr Zeckerman), Brent Sheppard (Doctor)

Mulder finds Scully comatose, and is taken by Skinner to see Blevins. The Cigarette-Smoking Man is castigated by the Conspiracy for allowing the evidently alive Mulder to escape. Scully suspects Skinner of being the mole in the FBI, but Mulder doubts that. The Cigarette-Smoking Man tells Mulder that the vial contains a microchip that will save Scully's life. Scully insists, despite family resistance, on having it implanted. The Cigarette-Smoking Man introduces Mulder to his sister, Samantha: she is the CSM's daughter. She flees on hearing Mulder's version of the night they parted. She's safe, with a life of her own. The Cigarette-Smoking Man tries to use his newfound trust with Mulder to bring him into the Conspiracy, but Mulder turns him down, even at the cost of losing his sister again. Seeing Skinner at a Congressional hearing into human cloning, the Elder decides it's time to be rid of him. Blevins tries to force Mulder into implicating Skinner as a mole, using the killing of Ostelhoff as a lever. Mulder won't agree. He names the mole as Section Chief Blevins. Conspiracy assassin Quiet Willy attempts to kill the Cigarette-Smoking Man. Blevins is also attacked, his death made to look like suicide. The body of the Cigarette-Smoking Man is not found. Scully's cancer, through the insertion of the microchip and/or prayer, goes into remission.

Don't Be in the Teaser: Scully contemplates death.

How Did He Do That?: How did Mulder know that Blevins was at fault? 'I didn't,' he confesses. 'I just guessed.' He also instinctively knows that Skinner is innocent (and the events of 'Zero Sum' make that a very unlikely instinct), and manages to make everybody forget that he killed Ostelhoff. (We might assume that Skinner fixed the pathology evidence.)

Scully Here is a Medical Doctor: She enforces her own course of treatment (having the chip put back in) and thus saves herself, as her brother denied she was going to be able to do.

Scully's Rational Explanation of the Week: Not this time. 'Isn't that a miracle?' she asks, concerning recovery from the edge of death.

Phwoar!: Mulder cries beside the sleeping Scully, and kisses her cheek and hand. He's passionate in his desire to find her when she falls ill. Scully offers to take the blame, post-mortem, for Mulder's execution of Ostelhoff. When Skinner says to Mulder that he's looking pretty good for a dead man, he replies, clearly thinking of Scully's condition, 'I'm only half dead.'

Dialogue Triumphs: Mulder to the Cigarette-Smoking Man: 'You murdered my father, you killed Scully's sister, and if Scully dies I will kill you. I don't care whose father you are: I will put you down.'

The Conspiracy Starts at Closing Time: One of the many companies who are infiltrated by or allied with the Conspiracy is Roush, a congressional lobbying firm who partly fund Kritschgau and Blevins. Blevins was the Conspiracy's 'man in the FBI', who the Elder orders killed when he's been exposed after his unsuccessful attempt to frame Skinner. The Cigarette-Smoking Man claims to be Samantha's father, which Samantha believes to be true (assuming this is the real Samantha). He told Samantha that 'something had happened' to her brother on the night of the abduction. Her memories gone (presumably wiped), she was placed with foster parents. Later, she was introduced to her real father. (So his loneliness in 'Musings of . . .' seems to be at least somewhat part of the fiction.) Mrs Mulder also seems to have known about Samantha's fate. Samantha says she was abducted by 'men', but has always refused regression therapy. The Cigarette-Smoking Man told Samantha that he'd only just found Mulder. She didn't know that her mother was alive, and now has children of her own. Presumably, the Cigarette-Smoking Man made the Mulders select Samantha as the child who would be taken into 'the Project' knowing that he'd set up an escape route for her into anonymity. (Her fertility indicates that she at least hasn't been used as an ova-donator, which is incredible, considering that there are clones of her throughout the Colonist/hybrid establishment. Presumably, either the CSM was able to set up some one-off cloning of Samantha that didn't involve ova-stealing – and her change of birth date on the paperwork might have allowed that – or her children are adopted.)

The Senate Subcommittee on Human Cloning seem to have no knowledge of the Conspiracy's activities (but the Elder keeps tabs on them just in case, and orders Skinner framed when he sees him investigating this area). The Cigarette-Smoking Man is apparently assassinated because of the well-founded suspicion that he'll actually do anything to keep Mulder alive and free, which isn't really that much of a priority for the Conspiracy. They may also resent his part in saving Scully's life (without her, Mulder would be unrestrained by logic and moderation, the thinking probably goes) and his increasing distance from the Conspiracy.

Continuity: Kritschgau's son dies during this episode. The Cigarette-Smoking Man has lost too much blood to still be alive, so we hear, but there's no body, so we weren't entirely surprised by the end of 'The Red and the Black'.

The Truth: The Cigarette-Smoking Man refers to Kritschgau's version of the truth (that the whole alien thing is a cover story) as 'beautiful lies', saying that Mulder has seen 'scant pieces of the whole' and offers him the real truth in return for coming over to his side. (Judging from his comments in 'Post-Modern Prometheus', Mulder may still prefer Kritschgau's version.) The Conspiracy's plan in this trilogy seems to have been for Mulder to go public about the chimera 'alien', thus discrediting him (possibly leading to him being dropped by the FBI) and adding to the morass of public belief and disbelief in matters alien. (The public would never believe in all the official explanations, leading to even more public paranoia with a rogue Mulder as its biggest prophet.) The chimera corpse was to be snatched away before Mulder could display it: its biology would raise too many questions to have it officially examined. To the Conspiracy's surprise, the reformed Kritschgau told Mulder as much of the truth as he knew, resulting in Mulder understanding the truth about Conspiracy abductions, but also believing (somewhat oddly, given that he knows all we do) that there were *no* real aliens, leading to his unanticipated suicidal state. The Conspiracy don't really want Mulder to die, but, while Mulder's paranoid encouragement of all things spooky may suit the Conspiracy's plans, he's not vital to them. None of them seem too worried by news of his death. If Mulder thinks things through, he'll realise that Kritschgau was at least mistaken about Scully's cancer being deliberate: she unwittingly caused it herself by having the microchip in her neck (one function of which is to restrain the cancer that the mothers of hybrids suffer from) removed. (The other abductee mothers also had theirs removed, causing their own deaths; though, as we see in 'Emily', the Conspiracy wasn't unhappy about that.) Although this episode started a lot of magazine reviewers saying, 'So there are no aliens!' that isn't the truth.

Trivia: The name Rousch is perhaps a nod to *USA Today* writer Matt Rousch, who's written many favourable pieces on the series. www.rousch.com gets one not to the Conspiracy's home page, but that of the Pillsbury company, they of the home-bake dough products. Realising the connection, Pillsbury changed their adline on the page, for a while, to 'Believe the Pie'.

The Bottom Line: PC: A vast reformatting of the series sees Mulder become a genuine mythic creation, as he's brave enough to sacrifice his initial goal (the search for his sister) in order to continue his pursuit of the Truth. He's unwilling to be compromised in the slightest, even if it means losing the thing he used to desire most. In effect, he becomes a pure Hero, on a pure Quest. The hope made manifest in this episode extends to Scully saving herself and redemption for the Cigarette-Smoking Man (whose life is saved (?) by the reflection in a photo of his child) through enabling her to do it. Rather huge and mythic, and with some real heart.

MD: This is more like it. Pivotal events (the seeming return of Samantha, the deaths of Blevins and the Cigarette-Smoking Man, the remission of Scully's cancer) and genuine drama. Thankfully, there is no explicit explanation for Scully's 'cure': a brave step, but one in keeping with real life and (I think) a nod to the sophistication of the viewer. Each one of us can decide exactly what this episode means – if, indeed, it means anything at all.

KT: 'You believe all this crap, don't you?' Better, though not by very much. At least a few answers are on show. There is a feeling of Carter having got stuck at one point and thinking 'I know, I'll kill off a semi-regular, that'll surprise them . . .' It would have if he hadn't done exactly the same at the end of seasons one and two and the start of seasons three and four. That apart (and a big 'Boo' to the rather perfunctory way Scully's cancer is cured), there's some good stuff on offer.

100: 'Unusual Suspects'

US Transmission: 16 November 1997
UK Transmission: 15 March 1998 (Sky One)
Writer: Vince Gilligan
Director: Kim Manners
Cast: Richard Belzer (Det. John Munsch),
Signy Coleman (Susanne Modeski),
Chris Nelson Norris (SWAT Lieutenant),
Glenn Williams (Officer),
Stuart O'Connell (1st SWAT Cop),
Ken Hawryliw (Himself)

May 1989. Baltimore, Maryland. At a computer fair, Federal Communications Commission public relations officer John Byers meets a woman who tells him she is trying to find her child, kidnapped by a psychotic ex-boyfriend named Mulder. Enlisting the help of two hackers, Frohike and Langly, they discover the woman is actually a chemist, Susanne Modeski, wanted by the FBI for murder and sabotage. Modeski tells them that she has been set up by government forces involved in a sinister conspiracy involving testing a nerve gas on the public. At a warehouse, the group are apprehended by Agent Mulder, but when other unidentified men attempt to arrest Modeski, there is a gunfight, and Mulder is covered in the gas. After Mulder has verified their story, and after they have seen Modeski taken away by X, the now politically literate trio befriend Mulder and begin to tell him of 'the truth' they have discovered . . .

Don't Be in the Teaser: A SWAT team find a semiconscious naked Mulder and three suspicious characters lurking in a warehouse. And lots of blood, but no bodies. 'They're here!'

That's a Mouthful: 'Security risks are being attenuated. Dr Modeski's team has been processed and plausible denial constructed.'

Phwoar!: Mulder's response to getting covered in paranoia gas is, of course, to rip his shirt off.

Dialogue Triumphs: Frohike: 'Me and the nark have a proposition to put to you!'

Modeski: 'No matter how paranoid you are, you're not paranoid enough.'

The Conspiracy Starts at Closing Time: Susanne Modeski worked for the Defense Advanced Research Projects Agency (the same branch of the Conspiracy that employed Kritschgau: they have their own web system, the arpanet) in New Mexico as an organic chemist creating E-H (Ergotimine Hystamine: ergot is a natural hallucinogenic fungus) gas, a substance that produces anxiety and paranoia in those exposed to it (cf. 'Never Again'). She says the government intend to test it on the population in the Baltimore area, the gas being hidden in asthma inhalers. This may form part of the Conspiracy's ongoing experiments with mind control as seen in 'Blood' (where something very similar may have been used) and 'Wetwired'. Once she had quit the project, she was accused of planting a bomb that killed four people (three from her research team – she suggests that the 'processing' mentioned in the encrypted file means they were killed to give the

Conspiracy an excuse to capture her). MPs turn up when
Byers hacks into the Defense Department systems, but that
may be just the standard response to such a hack. The
FBI (in the shape of Mulder) are interested in Modeski for
criminal activity (presumably set on her trail by Blevins),
while the two gunmen who attempt to capture Modeski at the
warehouse (and are killed by her) are probably working for X,
who turns up with his sanitisation team soon afterwards. X
seems to be working for Deep Throat's branch of the Conspiracy at this point, cleaning up the evidence and capturing
Modeski in a very underplayed fashion in the middle of a
crowded street. He knows enough about Mulder to state 'no
one touches this man'. (So the CSM had given standing
orders about Mulder and, presumably, set up his 'stalking
horse' plan to keep him safe long before the pilot episode.)
Seemingly the Conspiracy is able to initiate twenty-four-hour
surveillance on people by all sorts of means. In the case of
Modeski, her dentist (Michael Kilburn) implanted a device in
her tooth. (Is her tale of bugs in hotel Bibles also true?)
We see in this episode possibly Mulder's first encounter
with Conspiracy agents. His being bathed in the paranoia-
inducing gas (which is very close to being a superhero
origin for him!) results in a change of character, and in
him (appropriately, given the preceding episodes) seeing the
Conspiracy agents as Greys. That vision is perhaps informed
not only by Samantha's abduction, but also by the stalls he
investigated at the computer fair (one of which offered alien
abduction insurance). He gets his cry 'They're here!' (the
adline for Whitley Streiber's book *Communion*, as well as a
memorable line from both *Poltergeist* and *Invasion of the
Body Snatchers*) from a sign on one of the stalls. However, if
these Conspiracy agents are Shapeshifters or Colonist/human
hybrids then, ironically, Mulder's newly paranoid perspective
is letting him see the exact truth. At the end, X doubtless
lets the Gunmen go in order to spread paranoia about his
unprovable actions.

Continuity: Scully is absent from this episode. Mulder's career
rundown in his FBI personal history is closely modelled on
what we learn about him in the pilot episode. He was at Oxford

from 1983 to 1986, came top of his class at Quantico in 1988 and has been assigned to the violent crimes unit in the year since. He's supposed to be 6 foot tall and weigh 170lbs (which sounds underweight for his height). He takes a call (on a very clunky late-eighties mobile phone) from Reggie (his AOC Reggie Purdue, see 'Young at Heart'). John Fitzgerald Byers was born on 22 November 1963 ('Before the assassination, my parents were going to call me Bertram!'). He worked for the FCC up until the events of this story, and his meeting with Melvin Frohike and Langly (a Middle Earth Role Playing devotee), two computer hacking and electrical experts who run their own companies (Frohike Electronics Corp and Langly Vision). Mulder is wearing a wedding ring in this episode, indicating that (and we have no further information) he was married in 1989. (It's there again in 'Travelers'.) Langly's name is said in many sources to be revealed in this episode as 'Ringo', but there's no indication of this onscreen.

The Truth: The Conspiracy's Engineered Biological Operation on the general public seemingly began in 1989 (the defection of Modeski is said to be a 'blow to the programme' but the 'timetable remains unchanged'). Mulder is exposed to the paranoia gas, but it's possible that Byers, Frohike and Langly are also. It's interesting to note, though, that EBO could also stand for Extraterrestrial Biological Organism, and that the former being a cover for the latter is just what Mulder ran into in the previous episode. Maybe the paranoia gas lets him see the truth in many ways.

Trivia: The title (and aspects of the plot) are derived from the film *The Usual Suspects* (1996), which contains an unreliable narrative, a questionable character making up a story from objects he/she sees around the room, jail scenes, and a hard-to-explain beginning that is revisited later as a flash-back-within-a-flashback. Byers' co-worker Ken is played by prop man Ken Hawryliw (the end credits list him playing 'himself'!). The name had previously been used for characters in 'D.P.O.' and 'Pusher'. Richard Belzer appears in the role of Lt. John Munsch of Baltimore homicide, the same character he played in NBC's *Homicide: Life on the Streets*, a series that Vince Gilligan was heavily involved in. Detective

Munsch's line 'Do I look like Geraldo to you? Don't lie to me like I'm Geraldo. I'm not Geraldo,' is a reference to an early *Homicide* episode (where Munsch's line was 'Do I look like Montel Williams to you?'). Frohike's 'Your kung-fu is best' line is a reference to famed computer hacker Kevin Mitnick, who left the voice mail message 'My kung-fu is best' to tease federal investigators. When Suzanne first meets Byers, she tells him her name is Holly, borrowing it from a packet of Holly Sugar on the table. It's also a nod to writer Vince Gilligan's girlfriend, Holly Rice, the name Holly cropping up in several Gilligan episodes including 'Pusher' and 'Paper Hearts'. The references to Amtrack and the Susan B. Anthony dollar may be lost on non-US viewers. Both are objects of ridicule to many Americans: the former is the country's rail service, while the latter was a dollar coin introduced in the late 1970s in a bid to replace the dollar bill. It spectacularly failed to grab the popular imagination (to such an extent that many retail outlets in America will not recognise the coin as legal tender!). This episode was filmed first in the fifth season, to allow Gillian Anderson time to complete her scenes on the *X-Files* film.

Scientific Comment: A 'breadboard', as mentioned by Frohike and Langly, is a term for a plastic circuit board with contact strips, upon which you mount electronic components to test designs. When the testing is finished, the final device is then constructed on printed circuit boards. Breadboards are very delicate and should never be sold: they'd fall apart. The Lone Gunmen manage to get their printout of the hacked file on to an unconnected computer to decode it. Were they able to scan in a complete printout?

The Bottom Line: KT: 'Dallas. 1963. Hello . . .!' Quite possibly the best *X-Files* episode, for its wit. A labyrinthine, dark, and wickedly funny plot that drags together loads of strands in a neat bunch. As with 'Musings of a Cigarette-Smoking Man', it takes a brave series that will do an episode virtually without either of the lead characters (Mulder's only on-screen for about five minutes in total). There are great performances, notably from Signy Coleman, and Harwood, Braidwood and Haglund have loads of fun doing all of the cool detection stuff. One of my favourite bits is the wonderful subversion of that standard mystery cliché where characters witness a murder, then later return to the crime scene to find all of the evidence has vanished – here we see X's team going in with vacuum cleaners and scrubbing brushes to physically remove it! Some fans apparently regard this as an apocryphal story in the same vein as 'Musings of . . .' but the episode is clearly designed to be a direct prequel to 'E.B.E', and a 'Year One' story for both the Lone Gunmen and Mulder, who (albeit still something of a klutz) is very different from the character we later come to know. Another *cracker* from Vince Gilligan.

PC: I loved it too. With a much smaller setting than most episodes (mostly two buildings), Duchovny's excellent young Mulder (who's offhand, relaxed and unparanoid) with astonishing hairdo, Byers' Flandersish surprise at anti-government paranoia (there's a gamekeeper turned poacher!) and comic book 'origins' for both Mulder and the Gunmen, this is the new, campy *X-Files* at its best.

MD: 'I heard it was a lone gunman.' Lovely, simple, charming and thrilling. The scenes at the computer fair are marvellous, and it's great to see X again. Best bit has to be Langly playing a Middle Earth equivalent of D&D. The Lone Gunmen could certainly carry a programme on their own – perhaps Carter should look to them for a lighter follow-up to *Millennium*?

101: 'Detour'

US Transmission: 23 November 1997
UK Transmission: 22 March 1998 (Sky One)
Writer: Frank Spotnitz
Director: Brett Dowler
Cast: Colleen Flynn (Michele Fazekas),
J.C. Wendel (Stonecypher), Scott Burkholder (Kinsley),
Merrilyn Gann (Mrs Asekoff), Anthony Rapp (Jeff Glaser),
Alfred E. Humphreys (Michael Asekoff),
Tom Scholte (Michael Sloan),
Tyler Thompson (Louis Asekoff),
Simon Longmore (Marty Fox)

On their way to a team seminar in Florida, Mulder and Scully stumble upon a police investigation. Three men have disappeared in the forest, which has been earmarked for development, the only clue being inhuman footprints found at the scene. After the wife and son of one of the missing men are attacked in their home, Mulder and Scully search the woods, with the help of Michele Fazekas, a local police officer, and Jeff Glaser, who uses infra-red equipment to try to track the aggressors, who are almost invisible to the naked eye. Fazekas and Glaser are attacked by the creatures, and disappear, leaving Mulder and Scully to fend for themselves overnight. The next morning, Scully falls into the subterranean lair of the predators, and kills one with her pistol, rescuing the missing people.

Don't Be in the Teaser: Two surveyors are killed by a barely visible forest creature with glowing red eyes.

Scully's Rational Explanation of the Week: She attributes Louis Asekoff's tale of an invisible creature to a late-night viewing of *The Invisible Man* (1933) on video. Later she says that there 'has to be a scientific explanation for this', but none is forthcoming.

Phwoar!: Scully behaves incredibly flirtatiously and perkily throughout this episode, bringing cheese and wine to Mulder's hotel room and mentioning offhandedly that she's breaking regulations in doing so (she *has* changed since her recovery from cancer), seeming to regard this 'detour' as a chance to renew their acquaintance. She goes so far as to tell Mulder that if it was raining sleeping bags he might get lucky during the incredible forest scene, with a feverish Mulder talking about preserving heat by sharing a sleeping bag with someone else (preferably naked). Now, that's basically 'Come and get it', but all Mulder can mumble is: 'I don't wanna wrestle.' Either he's just *missing the damn point*, or they've been at it for years without telling us. Scully is left to frustratedly chat with him about *The Flintstones* (Scully identifies with Betty, but would never have married Barney), and sings Three Dog Night's 'Joy to the World'. Poor Scully. No wonder she's gone off him by the time of 'Bad Blood'.

Dialogue Triumphs: Mulder to Scully, after listening to agents Stonecypher and Kinsley dribbling on about team-building seminars: 'Kill me now.'

When asked if he has ever been to such a seminar before: 'No, unfortunately around this time of year I always develop a severe haemorrhoidal condition.'

Dialogue Disasters: Just about everything that the 'tree hugger' spouts at the beginning is pretentious in the extreme.

Continuity: Mulder says he was in the boy scouts, but perhaps he's joking. He does, however, seem to know what he's talking about when he examines some footprints. His knowledge of animal behaviour comes, he says, from watching *When Animals Attack* on the Fox network.

The Truth: The forest contains two (or more) semi-human creatures that can become almost invisible. They are protecting their territory against further encroachment, capturing people and tying them to posts bearing the Latin inscription 'Ad Nostrum' ('For our purpose'). This leads Mulder to speculate that there might be a link to the Spanish conquistadors, led by Ponce de Leon, who came to the area in 1521, searching for the fountain of youth. The conquistadors tied native Americans to posts bearing this same inscription as a warning to others; it is not clear from this whether Mulder means that the creatures were indigenous then, and are now reflecting the behaviour of the conquistadors, or whether the invisible creatures are the strange descendants of the original Spanish invaders. In addition, these 'predators' may or may not be connected to the X-File logged thirty years ago, when people in Point Pleasant, West Virginia, complained of seeing primitive-looking 'moth men' with piercing red eyes.

Trivia: Aspects and dialogue of this episode recall both the *Predator* and *Aliens* movies in a way that we thought the series had stopped doing in the first season. It's also all rather like Charles Grant's *X-Files* novel *Goblins*.

The Bottom Line: MD: It's rarely frightening enough to make you forget how predictable and familiar the material is. The message is as subtle as a day-glo brick, but the worst crime it commits is that, apart from one or two clever effects, it's just plain boring. Of course, I'd rather watch *The X-Files* doing 'boring' than, say, *Trek*, but that's hardly the point.

KT: 'They take the strongest first'. A strange episode that, on the surface, seems to be little more than a remake of 'Darkness Falls'. The pacing is hopeless, with a false ending thirty-eight minutes into the episode (the *deus ex machina* arrival of Agent Kinsley), then a rather annoying (albeit scary) coda. And yet, for all that, Frank Spotnitz's script, with its beautiful Mulder/Scully sequences (the night scene in the forest bringing to mind 'Quagmire'), is tight and effective. It's nice to see them out in the open again, just like back in season one. Only when one examines the plot does it all start to come to pieces in your hands – and the agents are only in the story because of coincidence, anyway.

PC: This is crap. We have the most non-atmospheric woodland possible, the soundtrack going into overdrive to try and compensate, David Duchovny utterly absent from his character, especially during the exposition, which he reads like a shopping list, and the sort of quoting of somebody else's text which involves using the word 'predator' every few minutes in case we missed the crass point. Not only that, but 'Home' syndrome reappears, as the leads are made so cute and camp that they're oblivious to the fate of every other character, and uncaring about anything beyond their own characterisation. If this script had been done in the second season, it would at least have been done with conviction.

102: 'Post-Modern Prometheus'

US Transmission: 30 November 1997
UK Transmission: 29 March 1998 (Sky One)
Writer: Chris Carter
Director: Chris Carter
Cast: John O'Hurley (Dr Pollidori),
Pattie Tierce (Shaineh Berkowitz),
Stewart Gale (Izzie Berkowitz), Chris Giacoletti (Booger),
Chris Owens (The Great Mutato), Dana Grahame (Reporter),
Jean-Yves Hammel (Izzie's Friend), Tracey Bell (Cher),

Lloyd Berry (Postal Worker),
Miriam Smith (Elizabeth Pollidori), Xantha Radley (Waitress),
C. Ernst Harth (Huge Man), Vitaliy Kravchenko (J.J.),
Jerry Springer (Himself)

'Somewhere in the land, a monster lurked . . .' Eighteen years ago Shaineh Berkowitz has an 'experience' in her home, and subsequently found herself pregnant with her son, Izzie. Now, it has happened again. Her description of her attacker matches that of a comic-book character her son has created, 'The Great Mutato'. Izzie tells Mulder and Scully that many local people have seen this creature. Investigations lead to a scientist, Dr Pollidori, involved in genetic research, the creature being a product of his demented experimentation. The townsfolk seek out the monster in their midst but, having initially wished to destroy him, they are charmed by his gentle manner and instead accept him, accompanying him to a Cher concert, and appearing on the *Jerry Springer Show*.

Don't Be in the Teaser: Shaineh Berkowitz, while watching the *Jerry Springer Show* on TV, meets a visitor with two mouths . . .

Scully Here is a Medical Doctor: 'I'm a scientist,' she tells Pollidori.

Scully's Rational Explanation of the Week: 'I think what we're seeing here is an example of a culture for whom daytime talk shows and tabloid headlines have become a reality against which they measure their lives. A culture so obsessed by the media and a chance for self-dramatisation that they'll do anything in order to gain a spotlight.' It's all a hoax, the mob making a monster instead of blaming themselves. 'Is there anything that you don't believe in, Mulder?' she asks.

That's a Mouthful: Mulder: 'When Victor Frankenstein asks himself "Whence did the principle of life proceed?" and then, as the gratifying summit to his toils creates the hideous phantasm of a man, he prefigures the post-modern Prometheus, the genetic engineer whose power to reanimate matter, genes, and to life, us, is only as limited as his imagination is.' (Which doesn't actually make grammatical sense.)

Pollidori: 'That repulsive physiognomy is the vilest perversion of science.' Mulder: 'Created by whom?' Pollidori: 'A pale student of my most hallowed arts whose life was taken by that which he gave life.' (And again.)

Phwoar!: Mulder and Scully dance at the climax. They've been through everything together, survived each other's emotional nightmares, helped one another to see clearly, and been there for each other when they most needed a friend. If the series had ended here, with this final image, there could have been no better way to remember it.

Dialogue Triumphs: Mulder: 'Scully, do you think it's too soon to get my own 1–900 number?'

Scully: 'Peanut-butter sandwiches?' Mulder: 'You think baloney would be more effective?!'

Pollidori on why he created a fly with legs growing out of its mouth: 'Because I can!'

Jerry Springer: 'Is it hard to love these babies?' Mrs Berkowitz: 'What's not to love?!'

Continuity: Mulder tells Mrs Berkowitz that he isn't sure if he believes in alien abduction any more (see 'Gethsemane' and 'Redux': but he doesn't say whether or not he still believes in aliens themselves, and we'd love to know what he thinks happened in 'Tempus Fugit'). A former case of Mulder's – 'Delores – Gave birth to a Wolf Baby' – appears on the *Jerry Springer* TV show. Mulder seems to have been specifically named on the episode, as Mrs Berkowitz was able to write to him telling her story (she even knows he is alleged to be an 'expert on alien abduction'). No wonder Mulder empathises with the creature . . . his dad was a mad scientist, too.

The Truth: Twenty-five years ago, Pollidori created a hideous monster as part of his research into the homeotic-haux gene. Pollidori's father, a simple farmer, loved the child and raised him as his own son. In attempting to create a mate for the boy, he used animal tranquilliser on the townswomen and inseminated them with the semen of various farm animals. The attempts ended in failure, with the birth of (relatively) normal children like Izzie, his friends, and the girl reporter. The Mutato used the periods while the townsfolk were knocked out by a gas to learn about the world from their books, records and 'home media centers' (!).

Trivia: The title is a homage to Mary Shelley's *Frankenstein; or the Modern Prometheus*. Prometheus was the Titan demigod who stole fire from Mount Olympus and taught mankind its use. Dr Pollidori was named after John Pollidori, the personal physician of Lord Byron, at whose Lake Geneva villa during a weekend in 1816, Percy and Mary Shelley, Claire Godwin, Pollidori and Byron amused themselves with a competition in writing horror stories – the source of *Frankenstein*. Pollidori's wife, Elizabeth, shares her name with the bride of Victor Frankenstein. The episode is also a homage to James Whale's two classic Universal films *Frankenstein*, and *The Bride of Frankenstein*, as well as spoofs *Young Frankenstein* and *The Man With Two Brains* (Pollidori looks very like Steve Martin!). Amongst the numerous allusions to these are: the torchlight procession of the villagers searching for the creature, his quest for a mate, and the references to Ingolstadt University (where Victor Frankenstein first had the idea of 'creating' a human). It's a pity that Mulder has to lumpenly mention the allusions, and get the ending of the book wrong! The 'chicken lady' reporter may be a classic freak via *The Kids in the Hall* and Tod Browning's *Freaks*. Three songs by Cher ('The one who was married to Sonny!') are heard: her version of the Walker Brothers' 'The Sun Ain't Gonna Shine Anymore', 'Gypsies, Tramps and Thieves', and 'Walking in Memphis'. The Monster's love of Cher seems to stem from her noted performance in Peter Bogdanovitch's *Mask* in which she plays a mother whose son has a rare deforming disease. Indeed, just as Frankenstein's Monster related to Milton's *Paradise Lost* as a metaphor for his life, so the Mutato found *his* truth in *Mask* ('Cher loved that boy so much . . .').

Scientific Comment: Hypertricosis means 'overtly hairy'!

The Bottom Line: KT: 'Goodnight, Dr Frankenstein.' Undoubtedly the strangest episode of the series – and one that, with effort, is one of the most rewarding. Framed as a comic-book narrative ('The Great Mutato! Collector's Edition!'), filmed in black and white (furthering the James Whale/*Frankenstein* links), and with much self-aware dialogue ('This is not how the story is supposed to end . . . I want to speak to the writer!'), the episode is one guaranteed to divide fans down the middle. That it's clever is not in doubt, but I can see why some fans would hate this episode, playing, as it does, with the series' sense of 'reality'. I love it. The tinkling music, the very subtle hint of bestiality (now *that's* got to be a first for TV *anywhere*!), Mulder's horrified little rant against genetic engineering (mirroring a similar scene in 'Humbug' in which Mulder was the target) . . . And most of all I love Mulder and Scully dancing which, if it's the only reason for the episode's existence, is enough.

PC: Until the (postmodern) ending, I would have written this off as a continuation of Carter's fascination with the success of Darin Morgan's style (there are no lighting concessions to the black and white filming, which thus only really works for the show in Pollidori's laboratory, besides helping the creature's make-up along). But the central ethical message of the episode (the mob really *is* the monster), and the transcendence of Mulder being able to cry, 'I want to speak to the writer!' (which sums up his whole quest) and thus create joy out of 'gritty realism' led me to revise my opinion swiftly. That release is a summary of everything Mulder and Scully do, of the show itself. And the dance (to a song about grace, one that, considering Mulder's holiday destination in 'Never Again', might mean a lot to him) is a fine celebration.

MD: Knowing my aversion to some of Darin Morgan's work, Keith *dared* me to like this one, thinking I'd hate it. I tried to prove him wrong and like it, dear reader, truly I did. But I can't: 'Post-Modern Prometheus' is tedious, bland rubbish. The tone of the thing is wrong, its tongue so firmly in cheek it's barely capable of coherent speech. We're only a beat away from Scully turning to the camera in the middle of one of Mulder's syntax-shredding expositions and pulling an Oliver Hardy-style long-suffering face.

PC: We're only seven episodes away from that, actually.

MD: I think it's the mention of the University of Ingolstadt that did it for me: another pointless reference that's only there to show us the colour of the author's research. And why, for instance, the flaming torches at the end? They exist only because generic convention demands it. I don't know why Carter didn't go the whole hog and transport Mulder and Scully bodily to the cod Europe of Universal and Hammer. It's all very well being postmodern and allusive, but when handled like this, drama goes out of the window. Things aren't helped by the dull and bland cinematography, more grey than monochrome. There are one or two good bits – the photograph of Izzie with a pig ('That's him there'), and Scully and Mulder's heads appearing in the doorway when Izzie is questioned – but, frankly, if I want to be reminded that I'm watching a piece of fiction, I'd rather go and watch Frankie Howard in *Up Pompeii!*

BEYOND THE TRUTH

Who called Scully in the first place in 'Christmas Carol'? We might romantically assume that it was the ghost of her dead sister, asking her to help an otherwise helpless sibling. But wait: this is a series that deals in looking into inexplicable events, experiencing them, and, through rationality, at least starting to explain them. There are some phenomena the series covers, however, those phone calls included, that the series places in a coy box marked 'Ah, well . . . What indeed?' The messages of Scully's dreams in this two-parter, the phantom nurse who watches over her in 'One Breath', the dead spirits who communicate with Mulder in 'The Blessing Way' . . . even, one might say, the presence of a cross (where Mulder can't see it!) in Mulder's computer-created hallucinations in 'Kill Switch' . . . All point to there being a further level of the supernatural in the series' reality, beyond the one that our heroes investigate. There's definitely an afterlife: 'Beyond the Sea', 'Lazarus', 'Born Again', etc.; and its inhabitants (those that stay there, anyway) are generally on our heroes' side. If we take it that 'The Field Where I Died' has it right, and the

BEYOND THE TRUTH

same opponents meet many times, then those like Deep Throat who are off the wheel of eternal suffering may indeed feel that they ought to help those who remain on it. Or maybe the whole thing simply represents a fuzzy populist idea of grace, and hasn't been properly thought through. We'll probably never find out.

103: 'Christmas Carol'

US Transmission: 7 December 1997
UK Transmission: 31 May 1998 (Sky One)
Writers: Vince Gilligan, John Shiban, Frank Spotnitz
Director: Peter Markle
Cast: Karri Turner (Tara Scully),
John Pyper-Ferguson (Detective Kresge),
Rob Freeman (Marshall Sim),
Gerard Plunkett (Dr Calderon),
Patricia Dahlquist (Susan Chambliss),
Eric Breker (Dark-Suited Man #1),
Stephen Mendel (Dark-Suited Man #2),
Walter Marsh (Pathologist),
Rebecca Codling (Young Melissa Scully),
Joey Shea (Young Dana Scully),
Ryan Deboer (Young Bill Scully, Jr)

Scully and her mother join Bill Jr and his pregnant wife Tara for Christmas. Scully takes, and traces, a call from a woman who sounds like Melissa saying 'She needs your help'. She goes to the scene of a suicide, the dead woman leaving a husband and a small daughter whose appearance startles Scully. Scully admits to her mother that since her abduction she can't have children. Another call comes, and Scully re-opens the local police's investigation into the open and shut suicide. The young girl, Emily, is revealed to have a genetic compatibility with Melissa: is she her daughter? Transgen Industries, a pharmaceutical company, have been paying the girl's father. Dr Calderon, for Transgen, explains that Emily was participating in a clinical trial. The dead woman had wanted to cease this. Emily's father confesses to murdering her mother, and is forcibly hanged in his cell. Scully's attempt to adopt Emily is discouraged. On Christmas morning, Scully gets a shock: DNA tests reveal that it's she herself who is Emily's mother.

Don't Be in the Teaser: Scully gets a call from her dead sister.

Scully Here is a Medical Doctor: 'I know you're a trained physician.' She does an autopsy on Mrs Sim (against a pathologist who, in the anti-Fortean tradition, is willing to 'damn' any evidence which doesn't fit with his prejudged results).

Ooze: Stomach contents.

Phwoar!: Scully's oh-so-ironed pyjamas. And she gets to be all motherly.

Dialogue Triumphs: Det. Kresge on Scully's return to his office: 'It's been, what, four hours? I was getting worried.'

The Conspiracy Starts at Closing Time: Transgen Pharmaceuticals are one of the companies working for or infiltrated by the Conspiracy's hybrid-breeding project.

Continuity: The Scully family were in Japan in 1966 (if it was the Mulders, we'd be suspicious). Dana has never had a long-term relationship (which redefines what we thought we knew about her and Jack Willis, see 'Lazarus'), because, she thinks, she was afraid of death. Now she feels more able to connect (as we saw in 'Detour'?). She only realised she wanted a child when she found that she couldn't. But her job counts against her adopting. Her father thought she was making a mistake going into the FBI. She felt wrong in med school. She doesn't believe in fate, but in making one's own way. (Or that was her philosophy as a youth.) When she was very young, her brother Bill searched for a rabbit, which she'd hid in an airtight tin, killing it. (The memory in the dream has a nice dream logic to it: 'The rabbit died' is an old euphemism for 'I'm pregnant'.) She was an Eagles fan as a teenager. She and Melissa both got crosses the same Christmas from their mother, who'd got one from her mother when she was about the same age. (Scully gives her cross to Emily.) Mrs Scully talks about seeing her dead husband ('Beyond the Sea'). Four years ago (1994), Melissa travelled for a while up and down the West Coast of the USA. Bill Scully always used to put the angel on top of the Christmas tree. Scully's badge number is 2317616. She makes a call to Danny at FBI HQ. While Scully is looking over the case file in the Sim investigation, she reviews a report on Robert Modell (from 'Pusher' and 'Kitsunegari'). The report includes information such as an education in general studies at 'Our Lady of Perpetual Motion' and a degree in philosophy from 'Bubba's Community College'. His work experience lists 'Caddy – Fairfax Driving Range' and a comment at the bottom of the report reads 'Modell has excellent dental hygiene'.

The Truth: See 'Emily'.

Trivia: Mulder appears for a moment only, wearing a Santa hat. Commercials played during this episode in the San Francisco area included ones for flashlights and mobile phones. References to the Dickens title include having Scully visited by a spirit and having visions of Christmases past, and the name 'Sim', as in Alistair Sim, who starred in the 1951 film version. (It's also what the non-people of computer game *Sim City* are called.) John Gillnitz, who did the DNA analysis, is a combination of the authors' names. He's also appeared as the lung cancer victim in 'Leonard Betts' and the man in the hammock in 'Wetwired'.

Scientific Comment: I thought a much more likely explanation for the dated photo of a non-pregnant Melissa was that the date was wrong, since Scully's suggestion of *in vitro* fertilisation would still leave Melissa pregnant (unless there was also a surrogate mother). And wouldn't Emily's alien DNA have shown up in the test? It's also unlikely that a DNA test could have discovered whether Dana or Melissa was the mother, since their DNA would be so similar, and any minor changes could be attributed to the unknown father.

The Bottom Line: PC: Not having Mulder around cuts reams of dialogue, which is a welcome relaxation. For once the Conspiracy arc opens up the space for an immensely mature episode about the alienation of someone who addresses her family with jargon, can't make it to a Christmas celebration because of her criminal investigations, and gets a package of evidence as a present. Little things like Bill's shock at the nasty details that Scully has got used to allow us to empathise with Scully's loneliness. And John Pyper-Ferguson is fab. Altogether magnificent.

MD: This is a superb piece of work, a Christmas ghost story that proves to be nothing of the sort. The flashbacks are well handled (particularly the maggot-infested rabbit, and the gift of the cross), and the cliffhanger (though predictable) is an absolute belter.

KT: 'A lot of people check themselves out around Christmas.' A bewilderingly confusing, shallow mess of a story, with a decidedly mawkish edge. The overpowering music doesn't help either. Liked the dream sequence featuring 'Little Dana – Rabbit Murderer', however. Surprisingly, the lack of Mulder hampers Anderson's performance, giving her little chance to employ the emotion that the story really requires. Good cliffhanger.

NARRATION

Chris Carter has certainly developed a unique writing style for many of his *X-Files* episodes, one that other writers are beginning to copy. Trouble is, as the opening to 'Emily' shows, it's a style that is as likely to have you hurling something at the screen as jumping for joy. The opening montage of images – especially Scully turning to sand – is simply startling. This sort of surrealism – exemplified by 'One Breath' – can work well, and is certainly to be applauded. Television, for all its power to excite with image and vision, can be depressingly mundane. The trouble seems to come when the writers strive to find a verbal equivalent for this visual dreaming state. It just comes across as bad sixth-form poetry – pretentious, in every sense of the word. This narration is crammed full of clever turns of phrase and intriguing wordplay, but ultimately it seems to signify nothing. It's interesting how in

'Christmas Carol' we are more prepared to accept dialogue from Melissa about fate than we would in a voice-over of purple prose. But the fact of the matter is that most people just don't talk like this: witness Deep Throat in 'The Blessing Way' (we might just excuse him because he's dead), or that entire, empty semantic exchange in 'Talitha Cumi'. Drama is about conflict and tension: such juddering chunks of self-indulgence qualify only as anti-drama. It's possible that Carter is influenced by the poetic dialogue of the wonderful 1960s anthology series *The Outer Limits*, but not only was the poetry of writers such as Joseph Stefano much better than his own, but the series in which it featured was consistently directed and designed as a dream narrative, where over the top speeches were to be expected. In a series noted for its realism, unreal dialogue simply looks bad. The actual nature of the voice-over/narration that frames many of the episodes has changed. We're far beyond the early episodes where we hear Scully's summary of the case, or Mulder's messages for Scully in 'Little Green Men'. In 'Gethsemane' and 'Redux' we listen in to the (babbling!) minds of the characters as they are at this moment, rather than reflecting on lessons learnt later in time (as in 'Colony' and 'End Game', for instance). Any critic should applaud thought-provoking, challenging dialogue and voice-over. But the opening words of 'Emily' are so opaque they may as well not be there. Such emptiness is not cleverness: it is the emperor with no clothes. Footnote: In a recent issue of *Movieline* magazine (July 1998), David Duchovny is interviewed, and is revealed to be a sweet, thoughtful and refreshingly grown-up actor. The poem printed with the interview, however, sounds very familiar in style. Frighteningly familiar. Is it possible that Chris Carter is rather too enamoured with his lead's poetic talents?

104: 'Emily'

US Transmission: 14 December 1997
UK Transmission: 31 May 1998[31] (Sky One)
Writers: Vince Gilligan, John Shiban, Frank Spotnitz
Director: Kim Manners
Cast: Karri Turner (Tara Scully),
John Pyper-Ferguson (Detective Kresge),
Bob Morrisey (Dr Vinet), Gerard Plunkett (Dr Calderon),
Patricia Dahlquist (Susan Chambliss), David Abbott (Judge),
Sheila Patterson (Anna Fugazzi),
Eric Breker (Dark-Suited Man #1),
Stephen Mendel (Dark-Suited Man #2),
Tanya Huse (Medical Technician)

Mulder arrives, with the news that Emily's mother is recorded as being one Anna Fugazzi. Scully asks him to speak for her at a hearing concerning the custody of the girl. Emily develops a cyst on the back of her neck, which, during a biopsy, spurts deadly green Shapeshifter blood. Dr Calderon refuses to transfer Emily's medical records to her new doctor, and Mulder assaults him. The two dark-suited men kill Dr Calderon using a Shapeshifter weapon, and, being Shapeshifters themselves, assume his form. One of them injects Emily with a green fluid. Mulder finds the real Anna Fugazzi in a retirement home. She gave birth to Emily a few years earlier, having received hormone injections. Emily's condition deteriorates, and something is seen moving beneath her skin. Mulder discovers cylinders containing embryos floating in green fluid. He takes a sample, but is mistakenly ambushed by Kresge. They are, in turn, attacked by one of the Shapeshifters, and Kresge falls victim to its blood. Emily dies, and her body is taken. All Scully is left with is the cross she gave her.

Don't Be in the Teaser: Scully is lost in the desert in a dream. But even more scary . . . it's the return of the meaningless poesy narration!

---

[31] As part of a movie format double-length episode with 'Christmas Carol'.

Scully Here is a Medical Doctor: 'I am a medical doctor.' She oversees Emily's treatment.

Ooze: Green Shapeshifter blood.

Phwoar!: Mulder calls Scully 'Dana' when addressing the judge. His extraordinary rage on her behalf is touching (if making him, as it has begun to do with repetition, look rather nerdish, as impotent as a school bully: it doesn't help that he ends his thuggery with 'I'll be back!'). And 'Are you two the parents?' is sweet.

Dialogue Triumphs: Scully in the pre-title sequence sums up her life: 'Alone. As ever.'

Scully introduces Emily to Mulder: 'I'd like you to meet a friend of mine. His name is Mulder. Remember I told you about him?'

The Conspiracy Starts at Closing Time: Shapeshifters need no prior knowledge of their subject: they can copy on sight.

Continuity: Mulder didn't tell Scully about (all) the events of 'Memento Mori'. Mention is made of the ice bath used to save toxic blood victims in 'Endgame'. Scully's passing of her cross echoes 'Ascension'. Bill Scully's newborn son is called Matthew.

The Truth: When she was abducted, all Scully's ova were taken, and she was rendered unable to bear children. The ova of all the abductees were used (presumably with Colonist DNA) to produce foetuses (such as the one Mulder finds in a tube like that featured in 'The Erlenmeyer Flask', although this one looks slightly more human, presumably indicating either a random variation or a progression of technology). These foetuses must spend some time inside the abductee, but then are taken and grown in the green toxic blood solution in flasks, then implanted in hormone-treated old women in old people's homes (and in government establishments as seen in 'Redux'), where they're presumably grown to something approaching full term. (Old folk in general are abused by the Conspiracy, also being part of their attempts to immunise humans against the Black Oil, as seen in 'Terma'. Presumably the same doctors handle both procedures with their captive audience.) Once born, hybrids such as Emily (who have toxic blood) are placed with adoptive parents (perhaps to give them some feeling for normal human behaviour) while treatment continues on their weak constitutions: Emily, at least, has auto-immune haemolithic anaemia (and we met a hybrid who had haemoraggic fever in 'Nisei'), controlled through injections of the toxic blood into the cyst in the back of her neck. (Perhaps if a suitable chip to control her nervous system was fitted there when she grew up, she'd be OK. And the condition seems to affect the arms particularly. Is this one of the things the Conspiracy's smallpox scar procedure is a record of, so the Black Oil would quickly recognise any hybrid it attacked as being on its own side?) It's unlikely that hybrid clones like Emily can shapeshift. (If they could, why couldn't the cloned Samanthas in 'Endgame', and the series' other threatened groups of clones, just hide? Jeremiah Smith must have been a special case.) Emily's adoptive mother wanted to take her away from Transgen Pharmaceuticals' influence, so she was killed. When Emily dies, the Conspiracy presumably steal her body to remove the evidence.

Trivia: Mulder does a rather good impression of Mr Potato Head. Mention is made of Michael Crichton. The video release of 'Christmas Carol' and 'Emily' has the surreal opening sequence moved from the start of the latter to the start of the former episode.

Scientific Comment: Medical scanners are usually designed not to make a scary machine-gun-like noise. Would a live foetus be happy in a fridge? They usually like a nice warm body temperature. Perhaps the alien part likes cold (or perhaps, since the alien blood is rendered inactive by cold, it's designed to keep it in suspended animation) but then it would not like being transplanted into a surrogate mother.

The Bottom Line: PC: How refreshing to find a Conspiracy two-parter that tells you what's happening as it goes (little informative notes being planted in all the right places), that surprises you with its use of the back story (that little moment we're given to remember continuity and realise the danger of Emily's blood) and that satisfies by communicating the feeling that suddenly, this production is absolutely in control of the message it's conveying. Nice to see Mulder realising that his testimony can be damaging: can't the man even use a euphemism once in a while? There are neat moments along the way, like a transition between Scully contemplating her virgin (ahem) birth to the Madonna in stained glass. I'm starting to really dislike Mulder's righteous rage, though. It makes character sense, but I want him to be above that, not to be so pathetic. And did anybody else see this as a powerful pro-choice polemic, with Scully controlling the destiny of her ovum? Thought not.

MD: I loved this episode, and 'Christmas Carol'. But I'm perhaps not the most objective of viewers here: my eldest daughter is called Emily, and as I write she's about the age of the girl in this story. Now, watching a blonde girl in hospital probably should make for depressing viewing – but somehow it doesn't. This story tackles important issues about the treatment of pain (and treatment at any cost), and seems to me to be more about redemption than sorrow. But I could be wrong. It's certainly a second episode that doesn't entirely disappoint, which is a novelty in itself. Perhaps 'Emily' works because it's so different from part one: from nowhere, this story becomes a Conspiracy thriller, effectively retreading the past in a way that 'Redux' singularly failed to do. Oh, and Mulder's much more in it, too, gaining a number of cracking scenes (most notably beating up the nasty doctor!). Well acted, sensitively written – an unparalleled delight.

KT: 'If you can show me a legal precedent for this case, I'd like to see it.' The staggeringly pretentious (and annoying) Chris Carter-like pre-titles (voice-over, meaningless dialogue) leads into another disappointing episode. Don't you just want to punch Bill Scully's lights out at every given opportunity? Duchovny's Mr Potato Head impression is a highlight, as is the initial alien-blood sequence. The ending is both needlessly complicated and terminally dull. Thank the Lord the little girl dies, seeming to kill off this blind alley of the Conspiracy arc.

THE BACK OF THE NECK

There may be an organ in the back of a Shapeshifter or a hybrid's neck that controls their green toxic blood. Pierce it with a Shapeshifter weapon (the length of which would indicate that, to be fatal, the blow must pierce right to the throat) and control of

THE BACK OF THE NECK

the blood is lost, the Shapeshifter swiftly dissolving from the inside, attacked by their own bloodstream and reduced to green goo. Humans who have been exposed to small amounts of Shapeshifter blood by bearing a hybrid child can have a microchip implanted that simulates the action of this organ, protecting them from the cancer-causing properties of the poison. Since refrigerating the blood kills it, one could also possibly kill a Shapeshifter with cold. (It's possible, though, that Shapeshifters and stable human/Colonist hybrids also make use of back-of-neck microchips, and that a neck blow destroys them simply by destroying that chip.)

105: 'Kitsunegari'

US Transmission: 4 January 1998
UK Transmission: 5 April 1998 (Sky One)
Writers: Vince Gilligan, Tim Minear
Director: Daniel Sackheim
Cast: Diana Scarwid (Linda Bowman),
Colleen Winton (Therapist), Scott Oughterson (Old Orderly),
Ty Olssen (Young Orderly), Donna Yamamoto (Female Agent),
Kurt Evans (Sports Store Employee),
Stuart O'Connell (First Cop), Jill Krop (Television Reporter),
Michelle Hart (Trace Agent), Michael Dobson (US Marshal),
Richard Leacock (Second Cop)

Lorton Penitentiary, Virginia: Robert Patrick Modell, the 'Pusher', lures an orderly into his cell, and escapes. Modell's physiotherapist tells Mulder that his only regular visitor was a nun. Modell telephones Mulder, and tells him he has something important to discuss. The body of the prosecutor who helped convict Modell is discovered, drowned in cerulean-blue paint. Surrounding the body is the Japanese symbol 'kitsunegari', or 'fox hunt'. The prosecutor's wife, Linda Bowman, seems to be Modell's next target, but Pusher's seeming reluctance to kill anyone (even Mulder) when given the opportunity causes Mulder to suspect that Linda is more than a grieving widow, much to Scully and Skinner's annoyance. Mulder believes that the nun who visited Modell was Linda, but before the therapist can identify the nun, she receives a phone call and electrocutes herself in front of Mulder. Modell finds Linda, but is shot by Skinner and taken to hospital. Linda uses mind control to get past Mulder, making him believe she is a nurse. When Modell regains consciousness, Linda wills his heart to stop beating. Pursuing the woman to an address, Mulder finds Scully waiting. Scully claims Linda is controlling her mind and appears to shoot herself. Moments later, Linda appears, but claims she is Scully, and that Linda is alive and in the room. Scully shoots Linda whom she discovers was Modell's twin sister.

Don't Be in the Teaser: A young orderly ignores the advice of his older partner about Robert Modell, and suffers accordingly. 'He had to go.'

How Did He Do That?: Mulder guesses Linda's involvement in her husband's death surprisingly quickly and on very flimsy evidence (chiefly her use of the words 'paint' and 'brush'). Linda manages to convince Mulder that she's Scully without telling him that she is.

Ooze: Ingested blue paint.

Scully's Rational Explanation of the Week: 'That's one hell of a plan, Mulder. A serial killer makes us believe that he's guilty in turn diverting the suspicion away from the real-estate lady. Well, he had me going!'

Dialogue Triumphs: Scully: 'How you feeling?' Mulder: 'Aside from the utter grinding humiliation that comes from knowing I let our suspect go, pretty good . . .'

Mulder, on seeing the paint-covered victim: 'I'm going to take a wild stab here, and guess this is a clue.'

Continuity: We learn that Mulder's mother is called Teena. The time scale of this episode in relation to 'Pusher' is a bit mixed up. Those events took place in 1996, as did Modell's trial, and sentencing, but it's stated that Modell was in a coma for at least six months after Mulder shot him (at which point he simply 'woke up'). Therefore, unless he was tried *in absentia*, a prosecution must have been mounted in something like two or three months, making it one of the fastest in US legal history. Mulder states Modell is a serial killer responsible for 'at least seventeen murders'.

The Truth: Linda Bowman is Bobby Modell's twin sister. They spent most of their lives separated from each other. She has exactly the same ability as Modell, presumably as a consequence of having the same type of temporal lobe tumour, though this isn't mentioned in the episode.

Trivia: Larry Cohen's *It's Alive* and Clint Eastwood are referenced by Pusher in his phone call to Mulder. He calls Skinner 'Mel Cooley' after the bald producer of *The Dick Van Dyke Show*. The end credits on the original US showing listed Donna Yamamoto playing both 'Female Agent' and (the male) 'Young Orderly'.

Scientific Comment: It would be fatal just to be completely painted. You wouldn't also need to have ingested the paint.

The Bottom Line: KT: 'You think you can hold me?' Further proof that nobody knows better what makes *The X-Files* tick these days than Vince Gilligan. Bringing back his best creation is a clever move – making him into an abused anti-hero is inspired. Another *brilliant* performance by Robert Wisden (a mixture of thuggish intelligence and animal cunning) and top-notch performances from the regulars (love Mulder's reaction when told by Modell's physio that his shot to the head did a lot of damage).

PC: I've also become a fan of Gilligan's fan fiction episodes. This one is played fast, and nearly straight too, against the run of the season in general. Still, it bothers me that Mulder is still talking tough, yelling and making threats. At least he looks guilty about shooting Modell.

MD: This is an illogical mess of an episode. We're asked to accept that a bullet wound to the head has suddenly turned Modell into a nice guy. Yeah, right. I like the bit where Modell watches Mulder and Scully on the news, and the blue

paint job is visually arresting, but even the ending is a pale
shadow of the (far superior) original.

106: 'Schizogeny'

US Transmission: 11 January 1998
UK Transmission: 12 April 1998 (Sky One)
Writers: Jessica Scott, Mike Wollaeger
Director: Ralph Hemecker
Cast: Chad Lindberg (Bobby Rich),
Sarah-Jane Redmond (Karin Matthews),
Katharine Isabele (Lisa Baiocchi), Bob Dawson (Phil Rich),
Cynde Harmon (Patti Rich), Laurie Murdoch (Coroner),
Myles Ferguson (Joey Argentino), Kate Robbins (Lisa's Aunt),
George Josef (John Ramirez), Gardiner Millar (Mr Baiocchi),
Christine Anton (Teacher)

Mulder and Scully come to Coats Grove, Michigan to investigate a man who drowned in the muddy ground of an orchard.
At first it seems that Phil Rich was killed by his stepson
Bobby, possibly with the help of an accomplice. However,
when Bobby's mother and Karin Matthews, the boy's coun-
sellor, each give wildly different versions of his domestic life,
Mulder becomes convinced that the boy is innocent. Bobby is
friendly with Lisa Baiocchi, and her father is killed after an
argument about Bobby. It appears that Eugene Baiocchi was
pushed through an upstairs window, but Mulder finds forensic
evidence that indicates that the man was *pulled* through. An
autopsy reveals a fragment of live wood in the corpse's neck,
and John Ramirez, who tends the trees, says that a blight
affected the orchard soon after the death of Karin's father.
Karin has imprisoned Lisa in her cellar, and later Bobby and
Mulder are attacked by the trees that are an expression of
Karin's own childhood abuse. They are saved by Ramirez,
who decapitates Karin with an axe.

Don't Be in the Teaser: Bobby's stepfather is sucked into the
ground by an unseen force.

Scully Here is a Medical Doctor: She performs an autopsy on Phil Rich, and over twelve pounds of mud is found in the man's stomach and lungs.

Ooze: Lots of wet soil at the autopsy, and elsewhere. 'Is it possible that he took the term "mud pie" literally?' wonders Mulder.

Scully's Rational Explanation of the Week: Bobby killed his stepfather by digging a hole in the ground, and an accomplice helped hold Phil Rich under the mud. Alternatively, the hole might have been created by the death of the hazelnut tree roots, and Phil might have sucked in the mud as he struggled to breathe. Mulder just smiles nicely at her.

Dialogue Triumphs: Mulder, as he climbs a tree: 'Hey, Scully, is this demonstration of boyish agility turning you on at all?'

Continuity: Mulder says he can relate to Bobby and the difficulty he seems to have in creating relationships. He admits to the problems with anger that he starts to manifest this season.

The Truth: Karin Matthews' abuse at the hands of her father was ended by the trees that sucked her father to his death, just as some years later they turned on Bobby's stepfather. (The corpse of Karin's father was pulled by the tree roots into the cellar where she was abused as a girl.) Karin projected her own anguish on to the teenagers she counselled, encouraging them to stand up to their fathers. In turn, the trees killed Phil Rich, Mr Baiocchi and Lisa Baiocchi's aunt. (Rather pleasingly, Mulder comes up with no pat explanation for all this: we're just asked to accept the 'monster', and move on.)

Trivia: At the beginning, Bobby is playing the computer game *MDK*. There's a long overdue use of the phrase 'psycho killer', which may or may not be a nod to Talking Heads. The origin of the title is a little unclear, but it could be translated as 'split generations', hence 'generation gap'. Scully's line about the town getting 'four hundred inches of rain a day' is a quote from David Duchovny, asked about Vancouver on *Late Night with Conan O'Brien*. Here Mulder is made to respond 'Now that's a bit of an exaggeration, don't you think?'

Scientific Comment: Six inches of rain is considered to be a lot . . . 400 inches is 33 feet of it, higher than a house! Talk about exaggeration . . . Scully's suggestion about the victim's oesophagus syphoning mud into his lungs is also pretty unbelievable.

The Bottom Line: MD: Once we get beyond the hackneyed pre-titles sequence (Bobby Price seems just like Harry Enfield's listless, sulking teenager), this is really rather good, a fantasy-tale-as-familial-horror-story that knows exactly what's required of it. At first the viewer is encouraged to think that it's going to be a story about false memory syndrome, and that it will show the distance between the UK, where child abuse is now a grim fact of life, and the States, where apple pie virtue might still be in evidence. But then we get glimpses of the real exploitation that underpins the events. It's a shame that the story runs out of steam towards the end, killing people for no logical reason, and lopping off poor Karin Matthews' head only because no other closure could be envisaged.

KT: Beginning as an almost carbon copy of 'D.P.O', this develops quickly into a throwback to the first season – a small town American Gothic with something big-and-scary in them-there woods. It's ironic that this episode was shown before one co-written by Stephen King, since it's to his novels that 'Schizogeny' and many other episodes owe a huge conceptual debt (in this case, one could note *Carrie* as a direct influence). Features another rotten attempt at getting Generation X right ('I am an outsider' . . . somebody get these writers away from their Nirvana CDs and back to reality). There's also a couple of dreadfully sick jokes, and a ridiculous *Psycho* style denouement that turns the whole thing into a parody. The initial murder sequences are horrifyingly effective.

PC: This is the kind of thing Morgan and Wong used to do, a nice-looking episode with a serious tone and realistic dialogue that Duchovny especially seems to appreciate. It suffers from Mulder and Scully persecuting a character they have every reason to believe is innocent, as in 'Hell Money', and Mulder once more shows extraordinary disregard for evidence (grave robbing!), but it clicks along amiably enough. With this title, though, shouldn't it be a joint sequel to 'Syzegy' and 'Synchrony'?

107: 'Chinga'/'Bunghoney'

US Transmission: 8 February 1998
UK Transmission: 19 April 1998 (Sky One)
Writers: Stephen King, Chris Carter
Director: Kim Manners
Cast: Susannah Hoffmann (Melissa Turner),
Larry Musser (Jack Bonsaint),
William MacDonald (Buddy Riggs),
Jenny-Lynn Hutcheson (Polly Turner),
Henry Beckman (Old Man), Carolyn Tweedle (Jane Froelich),
Dean Ray (Rich Turner), Gordon Tipple (Assistant Manager),
Harrison R. Coe (Dave the Butcher), Ian Robinson (Ranger),
Elizabeth McCarthy (Shopper), Tracy Lively (Clerk),
Sean Benbow (Customer)

Scully, on vacation in Maine, comes across a shopful of people who have clawed at their eyes and a grisly apparent suicide. She narrows down the suspects to Melissa Turner, who locals believe to be a witch. Melissa tells a local lawman, Riggs, how, before the occurrence, she saw visions of violent death, and he recommends she get out of town. All this is observed by her daughter, Polly, and her doll. They get upset with a shop assistant, and, seconds later, her hair is pulled into an ice-cream-making machine. Mrs Froelich, one of those who's accusing Melissa, slits her throat with a broken record. Tormented by visions of death, Melissa finds she can't successfully escape town, and is unable to stop Riggs beating himself to death. Meanwhile, Scully finds an old man who tells her that Polly's father found her doll while checking lobster pots. Then he died. Melissa starts sealing up her house, terrified of Polly and her doll, and sees a vision of her own death. Scully breaks into the house, and as Melissa grabs a hammer to beat her own brains out, throws the doll into the microwave and roasts it. Later, another lobster fisherman finds the doll.

Don't Be in the Teaser: Everybody at the Supersaver gouges at their eyes, and Dave the Butcher kills himself.

Scully Here is a Medical Doctor: But you notice she doesn't say that when she's introduced to a shopful of bleeding people and she's on holiday.

Mulder's Rational Explanation of the Week: St Vitus's dance; a viral infection transmitted by touch; the kind of talking doll that has a pull string in its back . . . 'Maybe we need to keep our minds open to extreme possibilities,' says Scully.

That's a Mouthful: Scully hasn't seen 'evidence of conjury or the black arts, or shamanism, divination, wicca, or any kind of pagan or neo-pagan practice, charms, cards, familiars, bloodstones, or hex signs, or any of the ritual tableaux associated with the occult, santorea, vodoun, macumbo, or any high or low magic'. To which Mulder replies: 'Marry me!'

Phwoar!: Scully charmingly can't dress in civvies, and we get to share a long relaxing bath with her.

Dialogue Triumphs: Mulder: 'It sounds to me like that's, er, witchcraft, or maybe some sorcery that you're looking for there.'

Continuity: Scully is on vacation in Maine. All Mulder has in his fridge is some juice dated October 1997. Mulder got his 'I Want to Believe' poster at an Elm Street head shop about five years ago. Mulder is watching 'The World's Deadliest Swarms' on video, so perhaps he's thinking about killer bees? ('Zero Sum'.)

The Truth: Autistic Polly Turner, descendant of witches, is using/being used by her fetish doll to make people she doesn't like hurt themselves. Her mother's magical bloodline allows her to see who just before it happens.

Trivia: Mention is made of the Salem witch trials and Chucky, monster of the *Child's Play* movies. Stephen King is a best-selling horror novelist. Elements of this story echo King's own *Carrie* and *Firestarter*, as well as the *Twilight*

Zone movie. Much of King's fiction is set in Maine, and Mark Snow's music certainly takes on a King-like feel, but the attitude to the locals here owes more to the Coen Brothers' *Fargo*. (Perhaps there's a Coen nod in: 'You know, with the hook?') A 'chinga' is a hex symbol, or (and this may be accidental or a deliberate piece of sabotage from one of the authors) a Mexican Spanish slangword roughly equivalent to 'fuck' and in very common usage. That could be why the episode, prior to its British broadcast, was officially retitled to 'Bunghoney' (which doesn't sound rude at all . . .), a unique case of the first audience seeing an episode under one title and then it being altered (which is why we kept the first title). One American listings magazine listed the episode as 'Bunghoney' from the first, which makes one wonder just how and where this 'mistake' occurred . . . The teenage daughter of 'Kill Switch' writer Tom Maddox appears in this episode: a birthday gift from Chris Carter. The boat 'Working Girl' has the same name as one of David Duchovny's movies. The book Scully is reading is *Affirmations for Women Who Do Too Much*, which, after 'Bad Blood', she really ought to lend to Mulder.

The Bottom Line: PC: The now-familiar overripe style undermines the horror in a script that doesn't sound much like King. However, it did make me jump in shock a few times (which the series doesn't do to me often), and it has a truly great ending, with Scully using the microwave to destroy the doll. Nice to see how lost and anal Mulder is on his own.

KT: 'I was on vacation, just getting out of my own head for a few days.' Given the influence on modern American folklore (of which *The X-Files* is merely a very recognisable part) of the novels of Stephen King (see 'Schizogeny'), an *X-Files* episode from the writer would seem a logical step for both parties. What is surprising is that just as the film version of King's *The Shining* suffered because director Stanley Kubrick failed to understand that he was using standard horror-movie clichés for his set pieces, this very ordinary episode is weighed down with a plot that could have come from the pen of any old hack imitating Stephen King's Maine Gothica. Badly. (Devil dolls, yeah, *that's* original!) Where

'Chinga' works, and works well, is in the Scully/Mulder phone scenes (Chris Carter's contributions to the script?) which are downright hilarious (it's impossible not to snigger at the contents of Mulder's fridge, or the *World's Deadliest Swarms* bit). The structure neatly recalls 'War of the Coprophages', with the roles reversed (though, significantly, Scully gets through the episode without needing Mulder to be there in person).

MD: 'Like I said, the eyes play tricks.' Typically visceral direction from Kim Manners goes some way to disguising the fact that, at its worst, this is more like the film *Maximum Overdrive* than, say, the original novel of *The Shining*. That is, crass and obvious, rather than startling and engrossing. Still, I enjoyed this much more on second viewing: it's so far short of being original it's almost delightful for that very reason. There are many great bits in this episode: the Mulder and Scully scenes, of course (I love the sequence with Mulder and the pencils), but also much of the doll material is actually very well handled. Melissa's attempt to set the house on fire ('Don't play with matches!') is fantastic, with the daughter for once frightened, and the self-inflicted hammer blows are very nasty indeed. It's great to see the daughter becoming afraid of the powers of the doll, with the violence inflicted on the mother being very much the turning point.

108: 'Kill Switch'

US Transmission: 15 February 1998
UK Transmission: 26 April 1998 (Sky One)
Writers: William Gibson, Tom Maddox
Director: Rob Bowman
Cast: Kristen Lehman (Esther Nairn),
Kate Luyben (Nurse Nancy), Peter Williams (Jackson),
Rob Daprocida (Bunny), Patrick Keating (Donald Gelman),
Jerry Schram (Boyle), Steve Griffith (1st Paramedic),
Ted Cole (2nd Paramedic)

Washington DC: Mulder and Scully investigate a massacre at a diner. One of those killed is Donald Gelman, a computer genius. Enlisting the help of the Lone Gunmen, Gelman's last e-mail is intercepted from 'Invisigoth' which states 'David missing. Fear the worst'. Following a lead, Mulder and Scully go to a dockside storage unit and find 'Invisigoth', a maverick hacker named Esther Nairn. She tells them that she was involved in the creation of an Artificial Intelligence and that it is trying to kill her, using defence satellite weapons. Fairfax County, Virginia: Mulder finds the access terminal to the AI and is captured by it, entering into a nightmare world of computer-created hallucinations – in which his limbs are amputated. He is saved by the timely intervention of Esther and Scully. Esther joins her former lover in the consciousness of the machine.

Don't Be in the Teaser: Bloodbath at the Metro Diner!

How Did He Do That?: How did the AI *start* building its corporeal base? (Maybe Markham began it in order to be uploaded?) And why does the AI send the people it's about to zap images of them being homed in on? And why is every readout in its base designed for *people* to understand? And why, being already in the know about virtually every aspect of the AI's plans, didn't Mulder just cut the T3 line?

Scully Here is a Medical Doctor: 'Call my doctor . . . Call Dr Scully,' Mulder tells Nurse Nancy.

Scully's Nearly Fatal Rational Explanation of the Week: 'You believe this load of crap?!' Invisigoth managed to blow up her home with a pre-set charge.

That's a Mouthful: Invisigoth: 'The primordial slime, the ooze out of which all life evolved. Except this time, it's artificial slime. Artificial life. One man alone achieving the equivalent of Copernicus, Magellan and Darwin.' Scully: 'What was your role in all this? Were you the bass player?!'

Phwoar!: Even Mulder's nightmares feature several nurses rubbing his body in a suggestive manner! But at least one of them wears Scully's cross, with a big version over the bed. When Scully comes crashing in like Emma-Peel-on-Acid, kung-fuing villains left, right and centre, some sort of series high point is reached. Dig the way she puffs her hair back. Mulder's internal vision of Scully (and let's face it, the AI knows her only from his thoughts) is as a saving, nurturing, tremendously strong and dominating presence. Nothing Oedipal about that at all.

Dialogue Triumphs: Scully (on the laptop Mulder has stolen): 'Mulder, that's evidence!' Mulder: 'Gee, I hope so.'

Invisigoth: 'You want my address? It's T-O-A-S-T!'

'Are you going to take off these cuffs, or do I have to do this with my tongue?!'

The Conspiracy Starts at Closing Time: There exist secret Warbird grade (maybe, and a nice touch of authenticity if so, the guys who built it were *Trek* fans?) orbital weapons platforms run by the Department of Defense that can zap anything on the ground. Useful if you're planning an invasion, eh? And indicative that they're apparently in geosynchronous orbit above the USA. A car CD player doesn't access data, so the fact that the disc affects the car (along with similar leaps across technologies in 'Duane Barry' and 'Blood') indicate that the Conspiracy might be making use of some alien technology, and that this has got out into the wider market.

Continuity: Scully reads the latest issue of *The Lone Gunman* with the headline 'Infrared Technology – Who's Monitoring Us Now?' In previous episodes, the magazine resembles a fanzine, but now it's become a broadsheet newspaper, indicating that the Lone Gunmen have got some serious money behind them now. (And thus that X was right to let them go at the end of 'Unusual Suspects': their paranoid speculations are obviously proving very popular and more and more mainstream.) Mulder suspects the drug dealers entered the Metro 'for the pie'. Is he pondering sweet potato pie again? ('Jose Chung . . .') Did he ever? And when Mulder loses his left arm first, is he subconsciously echoing what happened to Krycek? Mulder breaks the rules over interfering with evidence ('Grotesque'), this time for real and casually. He is getting to be a loose cannon these days. The AI's file on Mulder lists the usual details established elsewhere, plus the fact that he graduated from Oxford University (not mentioning his actual college) with an 'AB' (!) in Psychology (nice to know the series is keeping up its attention to detail as far as British culture is concerned) and that he signed on at Quantico in 1984. Intriguingly, it lists him as 'unmarried', rather than divorced (but is that an option?).

The Truth: Donald Gelman ('inventor of the Internet') created a new type of Artificial Intelligence and set it loose on the web, in the hope that it would grow into a new life form. His protégés, Esther Nairn and David Markham, planned to upload their own consciousness into the AI and become part of it, but the virus ran out of control and began trying to kill them before they could operate the kill switch they had developed to destroy it. Mulder's knowledge allowed the AI to prepare itself to receive the kill switch. Judging by the message left on Byers, Langly and Frohike's computer at the end, Extropian Esther seems to have achieved her goal of immortality.

Trivia: Gelman's nonsensical email address is gelman@com. The song used for the kill-switch is The Platters' 'Twilight Time' (1958). Reference is made to *King Lear* and Esther's make-up recalls *Blade Runner*. William Gibson is the author of *Neuromancer* and the doyen of Cyberpunk. Tom Maddox is a fellow contributor to the *Mirrorshades* anthology and SF novelist. It takes twenty-three seconds to upload Esther's consciousness: a T3 line transfers at 45 Mb/sec (Lone Gunmen statistic). Therefore, a human consciousness is held in data just 1035Mb big – just over a gigabyte. Most people could have one at home!

Scientific Comment: A computer maven could probably arrange to hide a program on a CD with a song on it, either after the song or in the places that the CD would treat as a recoverable error. However, I don't believe it would get the car to flash its lights in time to the music! As for 'One man achieving the equivalent of Copernicus, Magellan and Darwin', since this achievement was the creation of an evolving lifeform, I don't see the relevance of Copernicus (an astronomer) or Magellan (an explorer).

The Bottom Line: KT: 'Upload!' Magnificent. A sublimely simple story (despite the technobabble trappings) of the quest for immortality, and exploring Mulder's darkest corners. Influenced (obviously) by Gibson's own 'Johnny Mnemonic', with nods to *A Clockwork Orange*, Lindsay Anderson's *Oh, Lucky Man* and *The Avengers*. We first saw this episode in Los Angeles, which was an astonishing experience. Great performance by Kristen Lehman whose Uma Thurman looks and delivery give her character a touching edge. And as for those dreams of Mulder . . . !

PC: Fabulous stuff. Not often does a name author work for a TV series and do an episode that's very them and very him at the same time. Lovely to see Scully portrayed as a Gibson heroine, utterly capable, rescuing Mulder for once. And the zaps are brill.

MD: The glossy surrealism somewhat obscures the fact that, in many ways, 'Kill Switch' is about as predictable and clichéd as 'Chinga': just compare and contrast the wonderfully obvious endings of both serials. Where 'Kill Switch' exhibits originality, it's in those areas which mark it out as being a world apart from 'The Ghost in the Machine', *The X-Files*' first take on artificial intelligence. For instance, the 'brain' is transplanted from a state-of-the-art building (hoary cliché) to a little caravan in the middle of nowhere (clever juxtaposition). The organic-synthesised music echoes this cleverness, as does the almost Lynchian use of the Platters song over the final sequences (cf. 'Home', 'Post-Modern Prometheus', etc.).

109: 'Bad Blood'

US Transmission: 22 February 1998
UK Transmission: 3 May 1998 (Sky One)
Writer: Vince Gilligan
Director: Cliff Bole
Cast: Luke Wilson (Sheriff Hartwell),
Patrick Renna (Ronnie Strickland),
Forbes Angus (Funeral Director), Brent Butt (Coroner)

Mulder and Scully discuss their (vastly different) recollections of a recent case in Chaney, Texas before a meeting with Skinner at which they will explain why the FBI is being sued by the family of Ronnie Strickland for 446 million dollars, because Mulder apparently staked him, believing him to be a vampire. The meeting is postponed, however, because Strickland's corpse has walked out of the morgue. Investigating, Mulder and Scully discover that Strickland, his folks, indeed everybody in the town, were vampires. The vampires leave, and Mulder is cleared, but left none the wiser.

Don't Be in the Teaser: A classic chase sequence through the woods, as Ronnie Strickland is cornered by Mulder, and staked through the heart. Of course, the false teeth are a surprise. ('Oh, sh . . .')

Scully Here is a Medical Doctor: She does an autopsy on Dwight Funt ('who is arguably having a worse time in Texas than I am, but not by much!') and, later, the second victim, Paul Lombado.

Ooze: Heart, lungs, and, euw, intestine, all weighed. Twice.

Scully's Rational Explanation of the Week: Leaving aside the fact that the entire first third of this episode is *all* Scully's Rational Explanation of the Week, we have references to 'satanic cults', delusional behaviour and 'haemotodypsia'. 'You really know your stuff, Dana!'

That's a Mouthful: Scully's moment of pure shrewishness: 'What do you mean you want me to do another autopsy? And why do I have to do it right now? I've spent hours on my feet doing an autopsy, all for you. I do it all for you, Mulder. You know I haven't eaten since six o'clock this morning, and all that was was half a cream cheese bagel, and it wasn't even real cream cheese, it was light cream cheese, and now you want me to run off and do another autopsy?!'

Phwoar!: 'Erotic? Yeah!' Scully on a vibrating bed. Mulder in vest and pants (the scene of him kicking his wastepaper bin to smithereens is packed with the Phwoar! Factor). Scully straightening Mulder's tie before their date with Skinner is awkwardly matrimonial! Their visions of each other are startlingly waspish, albeit informed by their current (terminal-seeming) predicament. She sees him as an uncaring, selfish, and overdramatic rotten elder brother, who just walks into her room, orders her around, and gets in the way of her relationships. He sees her as critical and undermining, but interestingly, he looks sillier in his own version than hers, always talking too much and fumbling around her. Very insecure. It's nice that, by the end, they're reconciled, as parts of both their narratives turn out to be true, and Mulder feels confident enough to leave Scully with the Sheriff (even though it might be because he finds him too goofy to be competition). They're getting to be like a very married couple.

Dialogue Triumphs: Mulder: 'Prison, Scully. Your cell mate's nickname is gonna be Large Marge. She's gonna read a lot of Gertrude Stein.'

Mulder: 'Sheriff, do you have an old cemetery in town, off the beaten path, the creepier the better?'

Coroner, removing the shroud from Ronnie, with the stake still in his chest: 'Probable cause of death? Gee, that's a tough one . . .'

Plus: 'We staked out the cemetery', 'They pulled up stakes . . .'

Continuity: There are references (in both versions of the story) to El Chupacabras, 'that Mexican Goat-sucker' (see 'El Mundo Gira'), but Mulder still seems to believe in a physical version of the beast, which has four fangs and preys on goats. Mulder's tantrum with the wastebasket is evidence of his steadily rising level of anger.

The Truth: Ronnie Strickland is a vampire, and all of the other inhabitants of Chaney are also. But they don't have fangs, having to provide their own artificial incisors and drugs to quiet their victims. There is no evidence that the other townsfolk/vampires kill humans – indeed, when they have the perfect opportunity to do so with Mulder and Scully, they do not. The Sheriff's comments about Ronnie ('He makes us all look bad') indicate that these vampires prefer not to kill people but probably get their blood from animals without all of the ritual rubbish that Ronnie is interested in. (Compare '3'.)

Trivia: The town's name is a reference to legendary horror actors Lon Chaney Jr and Sr, both of whom played vampires (in *The Son of Dracula* and *London After Midnight* respectively). Ronnie delivered for AB Pizza (also the company of Jack Hammond in 'D.P.O'). It's a very appropriate name for a pizza firm in a town full of vampires. Ronnie's middle name was LaVelle. Curiously, this is also the middle name of the character Xander Harris in *Buffy the Vampire Slayer*. The references the Sheriff makes to vampires leading ordinary lives, even 'paying taxes', is similar to a line used in several episodes of *Forever Knight*, another series concerning a vampire policeman. Mulder quotes several lines from Isaac Hayes's 'Theme from *Shaft*'. Allegedly. He is also familiar with the film *Rain Man*. The idea of doing an episode with the same story repeated from two points of view is reminiscent of the *Moonlighting* episode 'The Dream Sequence Always Rings Twice' (although the story here is, of course, entirely original). Is it possible the producers might have screened that episode to investigate the business of filming an episode in black and white, as they were preparing to do for 'Post-Modern Prometheus'?

Scientific Comment: Chloral hydrate is a crystalline solid and really is used as a sedative. I guess you really could sprinkle it on pizza!

The Bottom Line: KT: 'I don't want to jump to any hasty conclusions . . .' This is *brilliant*, Gilligan again proving that he's the most consistent writer on the show, post-Darin Morgan. And the funniest. Basically what we have here is a twenty-minute episode, told twice, from different perspectives. Scully's story is Lisa Simpson-on-autopilot; clinical, exact, portraying Mulder as a kind of maverick older brother, wild and uncontrollable. Mulder, on the other hand, sees Scully as a cynical, shrewish, and domineering (a situation he seems to tolerate with a passive, almost masochistic acceptance). That this is hilariously funny characterisation is obvious, but it also adds a cunning second layer to our perception of the characters when we know what they secretly think of each other. And we've got other classic moments, like the Sheriff's Dwayne Dibbley teeth, the changing of the locale caption when Mulder corrects Scully in voiceover, and just about every scene involving Anderson and Duchovny together, the pair of them giving the lie to the idea that they can't do comedy.

PC: The best bit of writing on the show in years, with Gilligan setting himself a vast 'get out of that' and pulling it off with style. An awesomely designed script, exploring, once more, the concept of the unreliable narrative, and giving us great character insight (like what all those offhand autopsies really involve). It's true, however, that the level of reality on display is akin to that of *The Simpsons*. Can this series still do heartfelt or scary on a regular basis, or is that reserved for the 'important' Conspiracy episodes?

MD: The cleverness and wit of this episode does, unfortunately, give rise to an ending almost entirely lacking in tension. Still, this is *The X-Files* as Roman Polanski (in *Dance of the Vampires* mode) would have done it: witness Mulder's attempt to read Ronnie his rights, or the cross made out of bread sticks. Favourite bit: the Sheriff's musings on the lack of birdsong in the graveyard.

110: 'Patient X'

US Transmission: 1 March 1998
UK Transmission: 21 June 1998 (Sky One)
Writers: Chris Carter, Frank Spotnitz
Director: Kim Manners
Cast: Veronica Cartwright (Cassandra Spender),
Alex Shostak Jr (Dmitri), Ron Halder (Dr Floyd Fazio),
Kurt Max Runte (Ranger), Raoul Ganzeen (Guard),
Max Wyman (Dr Per Lagerqvist),
Barbara Dyke (Dr Dominique Aleqin)

In Kazakhstan, a group of people waiting for a UFO are killed by fire. The only survivor is a teenage boy. The next morning, he is discovered by Krycek and some Russian soldiers. Krycek confronts Marita Covarrubias and her UN troops.

Mulder, meanwhile, meets his old hypnotherapist Dr Werber at a conference where Mulder has denounced alien abduction as a cover story. Werber introduces him to his best subject, Cassandra Spender. Meanwhile, Krycek has the boy exposed to the Black Oil, sews his orifices shut, and abducts him to the USA on a freighter. The Conspiracy regard the initial burning attack as an assault on their plans. Krycek calls them and offers to exchange the witness for their research into a vaccine against the Black Oil. At the FBI, Cassandra's son, an FBI agent, is irritated by Mulder's interest in his mother. Scully discovers that Cassandra was abducted at Skyland Mountain, and that she also has a neck implant. She visits her, and finds out that they've both felt a sensation of being 'called'. A group of people waiting at Skyland Mountain are destroyed by fire. Marita meets with Krycek: they're lovers, and plotting together. But Marita betrays him, taking the boy in order to introduce him to Mulder. But the Black Oil escapes the boy and attacks her. The Well-Manicured Man surprises Krycek, asking him where the boy is. Scully is 'called', as if asleep, and travels to Ruskin Dam, where Cassandra, the boy, Conspiracy assassin Quiet Willy and a group of people are waiting. Suddenly, a UFO appears overhead, and then faceless men appear, and start to set the crowd ablaze.

Don't Be in the Teaser: Forty-one people are biochemically frazzled, and two Russian boys get ambushed by a faceless man.

Scully Here is a Medical Doctor: 'But not a practising one,' she tells Cassandra.

Ooze: The Black Oil.

Mulder's Rational Explanation of the Week: It's all just the military, covering up its bio-weapons research. 'A conspiracy, wrapped in a plot, inside a government agenda' to make people believe in aliens so much they question nothing.

Phwoar!: Marita and Krycek have a very physical relationship going on. But it seems she's just having sex with him to further her plans. Some sacrifice. It's cute when Mulder draws a beard and moustache on his own picture.

Dialogue Triumphs: Scully to Mulder: 'I'm done here. You seem to have invalidated your own work. Have a nice life.'

Mulder: 'Do I look like I'm having fun?' Scully: 'You look constipated, actually.' Mulder: 'That would make sense. I've had my head up my rear end for the last five years.'

The Conspiracy Starts at Closing Time: The Conspirators who meet at East 46th Street, New York, are humans who work for alien Colonists, doing the preparation work for 'the final phase' of (presumably) the invasion. The timetable they have been given says that this phase will begin in about fifteen years, and that large-scale group abductions will begin to occur around that time. (Presumably the Colonists will gather together all those they can control to form a beach-head of Black Oil subjects, passively ready for infestation.) Chapter seven, articles 39 and 42 of the UN Charter allow UN peacekeepers to either attend disaster sites to help or intervene in alien attack scenarios, depending on how honest Marita is being.

Continuity: Mulder is a visiting lecturer at Massachusetts Institute. His participation in the Duane Barry case made the newspapers and made him a hero to Cassandra Spender. He doesn't question the value of hypnotic regression, just the nature of what he remembered as his sister's abduction. He hasn't seen Dr Heitz Werber for almost five years. Dr Werber has met Scully before, but not in a professional capacity (as we see at the end of the pilot episode). Mulder's phone line at the FBI is a secure one. Skyland Mountain is the abduction site from 'Duane Barry'. Marita speaks fluent Russian. Special Agent Jeffrey Spender is the son of abductee Cassandra Spender. Cassandra knows Scully, probably from their abduction experiences.

The Truth: Abductees such as Scully, who have microchip implants in their neck, are being summoned to 'lighthouse' sites such as Skyland Mountain. There, they are slaughtered by blank-faced attackers using heat weapons (one of whom is similar in build to the Alien Bounty Hunter, but is not him. We assume that, since he's a vital member of the Rebels, he's probably the individual we met in 'Colony'). These killers are enemies of the Conspiracy, and they have presumably found a way to activate the Conspiracy's microchips at will. These are, obviously now, Rebel Colonists. Cassandra Spender has been being abducted for thirty years. Since she's had a foetus taken from her, and has an implant, at least some of those abductions have been undertaken by the Conspiracy and their scientists. However, she professes a great love for her alien abductors, and speaks of other forces at work, and there being 'war among alien nations', so possibly she's been abducted by the Rebel Colonists also. Krycek, with the aid of Marita, brought Dmitri, witness to the attack of the Rebel Leader, to New York to swap him for the Conspiracy's latest research into the creation of a vaccine against the Black Oil. (He hopes to 'rule the world' with the vaccine.) He has brought a sample of the Russians' rather more successful attempt at a vaccine along as well. As becomes clear next episode, he's infected the boy with the Black Oil as a defence against anyone interrogating him without his say-so, having already had the boy vaccinated against such infection (which is why the boy's had his eyelids sewn up, because the Black Oil will thus leave him at the first opportunity). However, Krycek must regard the Russian vaccine as lacking in some way (since it doesn't succeed in freeing Marita from the Oil, we might assume that it only works pre-infection, and isn't a cure after the fact), because he wants the Conspiracy's research in the first place. Unfortunately for Kryeck, in the next episode the Conspiracy learn all they need to know about the burnings without his help, and Marita is revealed to have betrayed him, in order to have Dmitri tell Mulder about the burnings. However, Marita didn't know about Dmitri containing the Black Oil, and was thus infected by it. If Marita is the dangerous woman we think she is, it's possible that her 'first meeting' with Krycek really was just that, rather than a play put on for the watching troops, and that their relationship developed very swiftly. (Though that would mean parties unknown freed Krycek from the silo.) Krycek knew all about her and her place in the Conspiracy. Scully feels the call of the summoning to her mass gathering on seeing the constellation Cassiopeia from her window, the same constellation that Cassandra draws on her own window. (Perhaps they've had a star in Cassiopeia pointed out to them during their abduction experiences? If such a star is the home sun of the Colonists, and if it's one that forms the shape of the constellation, then Alpha, Beta, Delta or Epsilon Cassiopeiae are the main candidates, since Gamma is a double star.)

Trivia: This episode went out with a graphic and mature content warning. The name 'Cassandra' again occurs for an abductee, once more a possible textual warning against believing their testimony (see 'Demons'). Krycek refers to the Conspiracy's phone as 'the Batphone'. (Maybe because it's a number only he knows: they're shocked when it rings.) Cassiopeia, in Greek mythology, was placed in the heavens by Neptune but was condemned to sit on her throne for all eternity (much like Cassandra Spender must sit in her wheel-chair). Dr Lagerqvist was played by Max Wyman, the book review editor for the *Vancouver Sun*. The constellation image echoes the 'star map' that was reportedly shown to famous abductees Barney and Betty Hill.

Scientific Comment: The constellations shown at the start aren't that close to each other in reality. Leo and Cassiopeia are nine hours of Right Ascension apart.

The Bottom Line: PC: Nice to see UNIT in *The X-Files*. Mulder is a real git without his faith, his new characterisation being painful and true. Starting off a lot of new plotlines when there are still plenty of old ones to resolve is a worry. Still, the sudden revelations of this episode give one a giddy feeling of delight. If the second episode pays off, one thinks, then this is going to be great! So it's a pity that the second episode is the most terrible load of . . .

KT: An attempt to cross-reference just about every previous conspiracy story as far back as 'Duane Barry' (and maybe beyond) that is, for the most part very successful. Mulder's angry disbelief in *everything* in the aftermath of 'Redux' is startling, and it's always nice to see Krycek, Well-Manicured Man, et al. There are some superb performances, too: the always impressive John Neville, Veronica Cartwright and Chris Owens, subject of much contemporary rumour that he'd be taking over from Mulder if Duchovny carried out a threat to quit (see box on p. 367). The plot is complex, but understandable with a bit of work and a decent grounding in the series (what the hell a first-time viewer would make of this is another matter but, seriously, is there any such thing as a 'first time *X-Files* viewer' these days?). This is one of the best conspiracy episodes simply for its verve and some shocking revelations. And the climax is amazing.

MD: The sequence with Mulder and the fruit-cake professors talking about ontological shock is fantastic, and the parallel between the warring aliens and Greek gods battling it out in the heavens is an interesting one, but overall this is a bit of a mess.

111: 'The Red and the Black'

US Transmission: 8 March 1998
UK Transmission: 28 June 1998 (Sky One)
Writers: Chris Carter, Frank Spotnitz
Director: Chris Carter
Cast: Veronica Cartwright (Cassandra Spender),
Alex Shostak Jr (Dmitri), Chapelle Jaffe (Dr Patou),
Michal Suchanek (Young Jeffrey Spender),
Klodyne Rodney (Medic), Jenn Forge (Nurse),
Derek Thomas Versteeg (MP), Jack Finn (Young Boy)

Skinner and Mulder find Scully, alive, among blackened bodies, including those of the boy and Quiet Willy. Scully has no memory of the events, and Cassandra is missing. The Well-Manicured Man, meanwhile, having seen to helping the comatose Marita, offers Krycek his freedom in return for the successful vaccine against the Black Oil, the possible existence of which animates him: resistance to the aliens is possible! A triangular craft crashes at Wiekamp Air Force Base, and a faceless alien survives the landing. The Conspiracy recognise him: he's a resistance fighter against the alien colonists. The Elder wants him to be turned over to the Colonists, but the Well-Manicured Man wants to resist them now, if the vaccine they've injected into Marita works. The Elder's view prevails when Marita fails to recover. Mulder

discovers that all the people at the dam had implants. Scully
is hypnotised by Dr Werber, and recalls conflict between two
alien ships, one of which abducted Cassandra. Spender tells
Mulder and Scully how, as a child, he became part of his
mother's abduction fantasies. Krycek surprises Mulder in his
apartment and tells him about 'lighthouses', beacons that call
abductees *en masse* to particular sites, and about the alien
rebels who are performing the burnings. He tells Mulder
where to find the alien rebel, and that he's going to be killed
and must be rescued. Mulder and Scully head for Wiekamp
AFB, and encounter the Shapeshifter Assassin, who has
kidnapped the Rebel Leader in a truck. Just as the Assassin is
about to kill the Rebel Leader in front of him, Mulder is
caught in a whiteout as another faceless alien arrives bent on
rescue. He's left without answers or short-term memory.
Meanwhile, Spender returns unread a letter sent to him by
someone who's very fond of him ... the very much alive
Cigarette-Smoking Man.

Don't Be in the Teaser: A father writes to his son at the FBI.
We're supposed to be following closely enough to be 'teased'
by this.

Mulder's Rational Explanation of the Week: The government made Scully's chip to monitor her immunity to biological weapons. Scully has a false memory of a powerful, staged
experience. Git.

Phwoar!: Krycek passionately kisses Mulder on the cheek in
what's either a Russian expression of good wishes, or the
result of pressure from the fan fiction lobby. Scully's 'Oh my
God!' memory retrieval is rather orgasmic, and Mulder holds
her hand all the while. His slow-motion search for her on the
bridge is also charming.

Dialogue Triumphs: Skinner: 'Extraterrestrial phenomena is
frankly the more plausible explanation.'
    Mulder's reply to Krycek's boast about beating him with
one hand: 'Isn't that how you like to beat yourself?' He adds:
'If those were my last words, I can do better.'

The Conspiracy Starts at Closing Time: Since the Well-

Manicured Man believes that, with a vaccine against the Black Oil, resistance to the alien Colonists is now possible, it follows that the Conspiracy are only helping the aliens because they thought it impossible to fight them and win in the past. They debate whether or not to join with the Rebel Colonists in this episode, but decide (behind the Well-Manicured Man's back) to tell the Colonists where the blank-faced Rebel Leader (as we call him, seeing as everybody refers to him as being vital to the Rebel cause) is being held. We assume that this individual is the same one who destroyed several Conspiracy hybrid-manufacturing centres in 'Colony' and 'End Game'. The Well-Manicured Man, in response, very probably frees Krycek and sends him to encourage Mulder to find the Rebel Leader before the Shapeshifter Assassin does. The planned invasion will begin at 'lighthouse' sites such as Skyland Mountain. The Rebel Colonists seem to be against the invasion of Earth. The fact that their leader is similar to the Shapeshifter Assassin must be sheer coincidence, since we've seen them change faces to match a stranger's instantly in 'Emily', unless, of course, the 'Alien Bounty Hunter' shape is a specific, functional design, like the Shapeshifters' version of a classic car frame. Their agents these days change their features so that there are no entry points for the Black Oil, but can see just as well. (Presumably, they must only be afraid of enemy Black Oil, since they play host to their own. Alternatively, it's possible that the Shapeshifters are a naturally occurring species, rather than humanoids who have had their skins 'melted' by the Black Oil (as the movie hints at), and that only one faction of them has been infected by the Oil, the others thus feeling the need to keep it out of their orifices.) Both factions of the Colonists are confirmed as using triangular craft. The Conspiracy now know that Marita's first loyalty is to Mulder, and have her under wraps, still a victim of the Black Oil. Three intramuscular injections of the Russian vaccine haven't helped her, and increasing the dose probably won't help either. (Perhaps Krycek was hoping that the Conspiracy had been working on a post-infection solution, and combining their work would make him the only possessor of a complete defence against this biological weapon.) It seems that, by the movie, research has moved on somewhat.

Continuity: Conspiracy assassin Quiet Willy is killed by the Rebel Leader in this story. His features form part of the Shapeshifter Assassin's repertoire of faces (presumably learnt from associating with members of the Conspiracy in the past). Skinner has been persuaded by Mulder's point of view over the last five years. Spender had heard of Mulder's office on the level of FBI myth: 'It really *is* in the basement!' He made up, or so he now believes, the story of his own and his mother's abduction when he was a child. But since his father is the Cigarette-Smoking Man (who's alive, living in Canada, and sending his son letters), it's probable that he was selected for abduction for the same reason Samantha was, so that the Cigarette-Smoking Man's line would continue. The Cigarette-Smoking Man left Cassandra Spender when Jeffrey was young. (Let's hope Spender gets the family photos out to show Scully at some point.) The Cigarette-Smoking Man seems to still have influence in the FBI, since he can be a 'patron' to Spender without Skinner knowing who that patron is. (Presumably he's still getting his underlings to attach positive notes to Spender's reports, a phenomena Skinner recognises through experience as being the result of such attention.) However, Spender doesn't know of the Cigarette-Smoking Man's patronage, though he must know there's somebody helping him, and is resentful of the fact: he returns the letter unread. The Cigarette-Smoking Man's letter mentions a Navajo legend of twin war gods coming to their father for aid to destroy a monster . . . Does this indicate anything about Mulder's parentage? Mulder starts an X-File on Spender's mother.

The Truth: On this occasion, a mainstream Colonist craft arrives at the site of the mass abduction, and uses a heat weapon to wound the blank-faced Rebel Colonists as they apparently 'beam up' to their own craft, resulting in them crashing their ship soon afterwards at a USAF base. The Colonists then settle for abducting Cassandra once more. Scully remembers nothing of the experience (before her hypnosis) from the point of being 'called' to the bridge. She's left with first degree burns (from radiation or the heat weapons?) and scorching. The microchips presumably led the survivors of the bridge away to shelter in a nearby wood. Having been tipped off by the Conspiracy as to the Rebel Leader's location, the Colonists send the Shapeshifter Assassin to kidnap him. He presumably elects to kill his quarry when Mulder arrives, but is prevented from doing so by the arrival of another blank-faced Rebel Colonist, who levitates into the back of the truck in a beam of light, armed with a flame weapon. Mulder presumably has his memory of the next few moments erased, so we don't know the result of the fight: only that all the participants left. (The incident echoes other abduction experiences Mulder's had, confirming for the first time that all abductions in the series are carried out using the same form of alien technology. The only difference here is that the silhouette in the brilliant light is distinctly chunky rather than stickmanlike: a Shapeshifter rather than a Grey, which, as we learn in the movie, are just different containers for the Black Oil.)

Trivia: The title may refer to chess pieces or a roulette wheel, or (thematically) to Stratego (albeit not necessarily to red and black colours). Alternatively, it could be a reference to Stendhal's *Le Rouge et Le Noire*. The main character in that book (Julien Sorel) is an angry, self-made man who hates the rich people who don't accept him because he was born poor. The book follows his life as he manipulates and connives to advance his career and his status in life. The title of the book relates to two life-choices that were available to Sorel: the army or the priesthood. Eventually, the character's past comes back to haunt him, and he loses everything. This could be the story of almost any of our characters. A US government propaganda film of the 1950s also bears the title of the episode, depicting the Cold War as a clear conflict between good and evil. (And we see from the next episode that the production office have been researching that time period.)

The Bottom Line: PC: . . . bollocks.

KT: 'Resistance is possible!' It would have taken a work of crass incompetence to screw up the potential of this after 'Patient X' and, thankfully this isn't quite that bad (though it's touch and go for a while). Aside from the glorious bit of overacting from the doctor treating Marita, and the weak, inconclusive end to the sequence with Mulder and the bounty hunter, this isn't a bad episode, though it tries to pack in even more ideas than the first part and, in doing so, hardly gives the viewer a moment to consider what is actually going on. Things finally kick into gear with the Mulder/Krycek scene (a truly *key* sequence), and Scully's hypno-regression to the scenes on the bridge are worthy of considerable praise. Still, if for no other reason than the major spoiler in the final scene (yes, we *knew* it was coming . . .), this one will be memorable.

MD: '. . . a struggle for heaven and earth, where there is one law – fight or die – and one rule – resist or serve.' This features just about the stupidest pre-titles sequence I've ever seen, and the world's quickest recovery from first degree burns. The sightless, mouthless killers are the one genuine shock in an otherwise lumpen mishmash, with all the best bits either happening in flashback or off-screen.

112: 'Travelers'

US Transmission: 29 March 1998
UK Transmission: 10 May 1998 (Sky One)
Writers: John Shiban, Frank Spotnitz
Director: Bill Graham
Cast: Fredric Lane (Young Arthur Dales),
Garret Dillahunt (Edward Skur),
Brian Leckner (Hayes Michel), David Moreland (Roy Cohn),
Darren McGavin (Agent Arthur Dales),
Eileen Pedde (Mrs Skur), David Fredericks (The Director),
Mitchell Kosterman (Sheriff), Roger Haskett (Coroner),
Jane Perry (Dorothy Bahnsen), J. Douglas Stewart (Landlord),
Cory Dagg (Bartender), Eric W. Gilder (Old Edward Skur)

1990. Edward Skur dies in a house with a body with the internal organs removed. His last word is 'Mulder'. Mulder visits a retired FBI Special Agent, Arthur Dales, who worked on a series of murders Skur committed in 1952, after which he vanished. On a tip from Dales, Mulder watches footage of the McCarthy anti-Communist hearings, and sees his father there. Mulder visits Dales again, and we flashback to his story in 1952. Dales had arrested Skur for Communist activities, only to have him apparently hang himself. Then Dales ran into Skur again, and saw a spiderlike creature emerge from his mouth. Dales was told to censor his report. Then, upon attending the murder scene of a German doctor, his body hollowed out, Dales was given a tip-off to meet a contact in a bar: that man was Bill Mulder. He tells Dales that Skur is a patriot whom the government have experimented on, one of three such men: he wants the truth to be known. He warns Dales that Skur thinks he's one of his enemies. Skur attacks Dales' partner, and the spider creature enters him and eviscerates him. Dales' protests about the lack of autopsy are silenced when he's threatened with being labelled as a Communist. Dales, led there by a clerk, searches the X-Files of unsolved cases and finds a reference to the German doctor. He has an autopsy done on one of Skur's fellow experimental subjects, and kills the spider creature he finds inside him. It's been grafted in. Dales is escorted to a meeting with Skur by Bill Mulder: it seems Mulder was just using Dales to find Skur. It also seems that Dales is being set up to be killed by Skur. The men struggle, and Dales secures Skur for arrest. Back in 1990, Mulder asks what Skur's dying words meant. Dales doesn't know. Back in 1952, we see Bill Mulder release Skur, giving him his freedom, it's implied, in order that, one day, the truth will out.

Don't Be in the Teaser: A Sheriff shoots Edward Skur, who keeps a sucked-out corpse in his bathroom.

Ooze: Alien spiders sutured into human bodies.

Proto-Scully's Rational Explanation of the Week: The sceptical pathologist thinks the German doctor was forced to ingest acid.

Dialogue Triumphs: Dales to the clerk, concerning the X-Files: 'Why don't you file them under "u" for unsolved?' 'I did,' she replies, 'until I ran out of room.'

The Conspiracy Starts at Closing Time: It's probably a safe assumption that the German doctors who implanted the (alien?) creatures into the volunteers were brought to the USA by Operation Paper Clip. J. Edgar Hoover, the director of the FBI at the time (and according to the fictionalised events of 'Memoirs of . . .', very much a Conspiracy stooge), is, by implication, aware of the whole project, wanting to use every possible tool against the Communists (which he may, at this point, genuinely regard as the real threat). So this would seem to be a very early example of the Conspiracy's super-soldier programs, at a time when their agenda had to appear to be very similar to that of the USA. (Later they became multinational in emphasis and started to limit the US government's use of 'their' alien materials.) The spiders (which may, considering the events of 'Tunguska', 'Space', etc., be from Mars!) appear to drive their human hosts to kill, and then enter the body of the victim to eat their innards. Skur says that's made him into a 'killing machine', but since no super-human abilities seem conferred on the subjects, it's easy to see why this particular direction wasn't followed up in the modern era. The origin of the spiders is unknown, but there's no reason why they couldn't be another form of vehicle for the Black Oil, injecting it internally into their victims to liquify their innards and thus, if required, passing on an infection of Oil. (This all seems very primitive compared with something as efficient as a Shapeshifter, however.) The older Dales hints that the House Un-American Activities Commission knew that they weren't hunting Communists but covering up for the activities of those like Bill Mulder, and his presence at the hearings seems to bear that out. (It's as if the Communist witch-hunts were the direct ancestor of the 'biological weapons' explanation that Mulder is fed in 'Redux'.) Bill Mulder is part of the project that developed them, working at this point with Deep Throat and the CSM in the State Department. It's interesting to see him develop the strategy of setting up an idealistic FBI agent to pursue 'the truth', under the guise of being an altruistic source, and then using them to flush out the information he himself is seeking. (Perhaps Deep Throat was simply playing out a well-established strategy.) But Bill Mulder is here shown to have something of a conscience: he wants to save Dales, and lets Skur go free, though the impact of that decision is a grey area in itself.

Continuity: Mulder, seen here after the events of 'Unusual Suspects', and thus twitching about every tiny clue to weird happenings, is still a profiler with the Behavioral Sciences Unit in 1990. This may be the point at which he decides the X-Files are worth checking out. He's still wearing his wedding ring, smokes, and wears his glasses more often than these days. (He may have got contacts recently.) He and his father 'don't really speak', presumably a relic of his parents' divorce, and maybe aggravated by him going through something similar (he seems to live in his current bedless apartment. Did he never want to sleep in a bed again if he couldn't share it with her?). The creation of the X-Files seen here, with a secretary filing unsolved mysteries under 'X', contradicts the version of events recalled in 'Shapes', with J. Edgar Hoover starting the files in the 1940s. However, if we assume that Hoover simply ordered unsolved cases to be kept on file, and the secretary put them under 'X', when, as she says, she ran out of room in 'U', then both versions can be true.

The Truth: Xenotransplantation, the grafting of one species into another. In this case, aggressive (and possibly Black Oil-carrying) alien spiders into human beings, turning the latter into innard-hungry predators.

Trivia: The episode makes passing references to *Citizen Kane*, with Dean Aylesworth looking and dressing like a young Orson Welles, the matter at hand being the puzzling last words of a dying man and the moral character of the Welles figure. (Mind you, the result of that enquiry, 'I haven't the faintest idea', sounds more like Darin Morgan!) The whole thing is also very *Dark Skies*, but that's perhaps unavoidable. 'Fellow travellers' was a nickname for Communist sympathisers in the McCarthy era. Darren McGavin was the star of *Kolchak: The Night Stalker*, a series Chris Carter has referenced as being an influence on *The X-Files*, and an actor he'd been trying to cast for a long time. The version of 'Lily Marlene' we hear was recorded by 'Paula Rabwini' (a female version of Producer Paul Rabwin), on the ETAP label, ETAP being a commonly used brandname in the series, a reverse of the name of prop master Jim Pate. Frank Spotnitz and John Shiban had a teacher at the American Film

Institute called Howard Dimsdale. Dimsdale was blacklisted during the McCarthy era, the source of much of this episode's committed anti-McCarthy stance.

Scientific Comment: I don't think that being force-fed a corrosive agent would make you lose the soft tissue in the whole of your body, e.g. arms and legs.

The Bottom Line: PC: Nice to see the series (whose politics are sometimes a little murky) come out so strongly against the nightmare of HUAC. But the characters are so deadly dull and the pace so slow one has to ask: if you've got Darren McGavin, why not give him something to do?

KT: 'See, you're a patriot again.' What was all *that* about? A pocket movie, beautifully put together but ultimately hollow (and very nasty). Shiban and Spotnitz's script is full of nice moments and lines, but has little substance. The J. Edgar Hoover cameo is interestingly over-the-top. A great guest slot from Darren McGavin.

MD: 'You keep digging through the X-Files and they'll bury you, too.' Glorious. It's nothing like a 'normal' episode but, whereas deviations from the usual template function by reminding you of the fictional nature of the narrative, this swamps you with the power of its storytelling. I kept having to remind myself that I was supposed to be watching this critically, and I didn't miss Scully and (for most of the time) Mulder at all. It's beautifully shot, sensitively scripted and acted, and, frankly, it's about time *The X-Files* had a go at HUAC.

113: 'Mind's Eye'

US Transmission: 19 April 1998
UK Transmission: 17 May 1998 (Sky One)
Writer: Tim Minear
Director: Kim Manners
Cast: Lili Taylor (Martie Glenn), Richard Fitzpatrick (Gotts),
Blu Mankuma (Detective Pennock),
Henri Lubatti (Dr Wilkenson), Peter Kelamis (ADA Costa),
Joe Pascual (Examiner), Colin Lawrence (First Cop),

Jason Diablo (Angry Man), Veronica Stocker (Sexy Woman),
Dalias Blake (Second Cop)

When a drug dealer is murdered, blind woman Martie Glenn
is found cleaning up at the scene of the crime. She's arrested,
but released when Mulder ascertains her blindness to be real.
Tormented by visions seen from the killer's point of view, she
observes him kill again, finds the body, and bogusly admits to
both crimes. She then warns off the killer's drug buyer by
phone and sends the police to the location of his drugs. When
genetic tests prove her guiltless, she finally gives in to
Mulder's insistence of her innocence: he has discovered that
the killer is her father. Martie distracts Mulder and Scully, and
sets the killer up to find her, so she can kill him and free
herself from his point of view.

Don't Be in the Teaser: Martie Glenn witnesses a murder
mentally, and is caught at the scene of the crime.

How Did He Do That?: The word 'see' in a polygraph test
provides Mulder with his whole theory.

Scully's Rational Explanation of the Week: Martie can see,
but isn't aware of it. 'Don't make me state the obvious,' she
says.

Phwoar!: Does Mulder have more than an admiration for
Martie? Certainly, at the end, he's looking at her with that lost
puppy expression of his.

Dialogue Triumphs: Mulder on the dead drug dealer: 'I have
the same pair of pants.'
    Det. Pennock: 'You are one sceptical guy, Agent Mulder.'

The Truth: Martie Glenn lost her sight in the womb when her
mother was murdered, and gained an insight into the vision of
her father, the killer. Her other sensory skills are natural.

Trivia: O.J. Simpson's glove is mentioned.

Scientific Comment: Martie is cleared by a PCR test. PCR
tests are a less stringent test than actual DNA testing (though
they use the same principles). They can only single out a

person to one in about 4000. Even the stringent DNA tests are not 100 per cent reliable. They could pick out a person to one in several million. This means that if a DNA match is found for a British person there could statistically be about fifty random people in the UK that would also match the test sample. For the PCR test this would be many more. Also close relatives have very similar DNA and if one is a positive match it's likely that many of them would be. So if the real murderer and suspect are closely related, as they are here, it is very likely that both of them would show a positive match. So Martie is incredibly lucky!

The Bottom Line: PC: The lack of formulaic set-up or any subtext make this a refreshing, if entirely inevitable, trip back to season one. Good shock moments with Martie walking into the street and seeing herself through Gotts's eyes. Great performance from Lili Taylor, and good to see Mulder being sweet again, but Scully's hardly in it.

KT: 'You just leave her alone. I'm watching you.' Interesting idea, though in places it's frustrating and cliché-driven (the killer is the girl's father). There's a strange and unsatisfying ending, too. Good points: Mulder is terrific – touchingly angry in this episode, and with a neat line in self-deprecating irony (the 'sceptic' scene). The killer is repulsive – he's got the most abnormally evil sneer I think I've ever seen. One major minus point: the killer was jailed in 1970 for aggravated assault and only paroled 'three weeks ago'. It must have been some assault for him to get twenty-eight years plus for it . . . Maybe it was the sneer.

MD: 'So, I'm all ears.' Brilliantly conceived and acted, this sensitive and not-at-all patronising look at apparent disability would indeed not be out of place in the first or second seasons. And I mean that as a compliment.

114: 'All Souls'

US Transmission: 26 April 1998
UK Transmission: 7 June 1998 (Sky One)
Writers: Frank Spotnitz, John Shiban from a story by
Billy Brown, Dan Angel

Director: Allen Coulter
Cast: Glenn Morshower (Aaron Starkey),
Jody Racicot (Father Gregory), Emily Perkins (Dara/Paula),
Joseph Patrick Finn (Priest), Patti Allan (Mrs Kernoff),
Erick Keenleyside (Lance Kernoff),
Lorraine Landry (Pathologist Vicki Belon),
Tracy Elofson (Four-Faced Man)

Scully emotionally recounts a case we see in flashback. She is asked by her priest to help comfort the parents of a girl with congenital deformities, who'd died in a praying position, her eyes burnt, after walking for the first time and going out to meet a stranger. The death of a girl who proves to be the girl's natural sister leads Mulder and Scully to the conclusion of the involvement of Father Gregory, an unorthodox priest who was trying to adopt the second girl. Gregory insists he was trying to protect her. Later, while examining Paula's body, Scully experiences a vision of her own dead daughter, Emily. Mulder uncovers a third sister. With the help of Aaron Starkey, a social worker, he traces her to an abandoned building, but she is already dead. Gregory is there, and is arrested. The priest insists that he tried to protect the girls' souls from the Devil. He warns that the fourth sister must be located, but he is killed (by Starkey) while Scully and Mulder are out of the room. Scully has a visitation from a figure whose head rotates, revealing four faces. She seeks out Father McCue, who recognises Scully's description as that of a seraphim, an angel who fathered four children by a mortal woman. According to apocryphal literature, God sent the seraphim after the four children – Nephilim – to save them from the Devil. Starkey tells Scully that the fourth girl is at Gregory's church, but Scully sees in his shadow the image of a demon. Scully finds the girl, and releases her (after she takes on the form of Emily) into a blinding light, much to the anger of Starkey. The fourth girl dies.

Don't Be in the Teaser: Dara Kernoff has her eyes burned out and dies in the rain to full-on *Exorcist* music.

How Did He Do That?: Mulder's mindset this week is as

offhand and incredulous as he only ever gets in one of these 'role-reversal' episodes. Gregory, on the other hand, divines Scully's Catholicism simply from the fact she wears a cross.

Scully Here is a Medical Doctor: She performs the autopsy on Paula Koklos. 'I'm a scientist,' she asserts.

Mulder's Rational Explanation of the Week: Father Gregory is a religiously motivated psychotic killer. 'You know, they say when you talk to God, it's prayer, but when God talks to you, it's schizophrenia.'

Phwoar!: Mulder's scepticism really alienates the two of them. She ought to have given him a good slap when he starts going on about personal issues clouding her judgement. For some Special Agents we could mention, that's a career.

Dialogue Triumphs: Mulder on Gregory: 'He thinks he's doing God's laundry.'

Continuity: Is Mulder's extreme anti-religious position and ignorance the attitude of someone who's in denial about his Jewishness? Most Forteans, after all, have a vast, albeit distanced, interest in religion. Scully carries a picture of Emily with her, and believes herself to be 'angry at God' for her death, though she now regularly goes to Mass. These events take place 'several months' after those of 'Christmas Carol', according to Scully: since that was Christmas, and this takes place at Easter, it's actually about four. Scully also says it's 'several months' since her last confession, which presumably means she's had at least one since 'Revelations' (two years ago). She believes in an afterlife. She correctly blames herself for the death of the girl at the end of this episode, but believes she's been helped through a stage of grief in the process. Mulder's supposed to be trailing a suspect when he talks to Scully on the phone, but he then heads into a cinema showing what appears to be a season of porn movies ('A Decade of Dirty Delinquents'!).

The Truth: Satan in the shape of a social worker pursued the four Nephilim children, perhaps seeking to have them join his own host, but one of the Seraphim arrived on Earth and saved them by hunting them down and killing them horribly. Or is it all a visionary experience on Scully's part, brought on by her repressed grief process?

Trivia: Mulder makes reference to *Secret Squirrel* (or is it another Moose and Squirrel gag?) and *Jesus Christ Superstar*. Various musical tags recall *The Exorcist*. All Souls Day is 1 November (not when the episode is set), a Christian gloss on the pagan festival of the dead, the start of the year, which follows the sheltering from evil that occurs on Samhain, the night before. For these two days, this world and the next are united, and on 1 November the dead can be safely met. Which Scully manages here. The Christian Easter festival, shown here, is also a celebration of Resurrection. Mulder's usual knowledge of the Bible deserts him: he mentions a mote in an eye, the eyes being the window to the soul, and an eye for an eye, and says that these phrases are from 'ancient scripture . . . maybe even the Bible'. Well, it's difficult to imagine the Mulder of 'Die Hand die Verletzt' and 'Revelations' not being more sure of this (just for the record, the first and final phrase are biblical). Still, Father McCue's knowledge is even more off-whack, and he's got no excuse. Joseph Patrick Finn, the series' producer, appears as the priest Scully confesses to, but, oddly, is only credited in prints of the episode sent abroad, not being so on the original run. (This is Finn's second appearance as a cleric in the series, the first being as a prison chaplain in 'The List', but since there's no proof that these are the same person, we haven't put him in the regular cast.)

VICARISH ALL SORTS

The creature that Scully sees in this episode has four faces, namely human, eagle, lion and bull. When she describes this to Father McCue, he calls the creature a seraphim. Wrong! He means cherubim, the creatures set to guard the Garden of Eden after the Fall (Genesis). Two golden carvings of cherubim were placed on the arc of the covenant (Exodus), and Ezekiel describes them in a vision as four-winged, four-faced 'living creatures who were shaped like humans', the faces in question being human, lion, ox and eagle. (In addition, 'seraphim' is a plural word: McCue should really talk of 'a seraph', but then, the King James Version of the Bible makes this mistake as well, so perhaps we should excuse him.) Seraphim, in fact, only appear in Isaiah chapter 6, and are celestial beings with six wings. Cherubim and Seraphim could both (loosely) be called angels, as McCue does. McCue then goes on to describe how a seraphim (sic) fathered four children (the Nephilim) with a mortal woman. The Nephilim were deformed humans with the souls of angels, and the seraphim was sent after his children to save their souls from the Devil. He then says, 'Dana, the Nephilim is a story (sic). The text in which it appears isn't even recognised by the Church.' Wrong! Well, partly. It's certainly wrong to imply that the Nephilim aren't in the Bible, as they're mentioned in Genesis 6. However, McCue is partly correct, as the story of their origin appears only in the Apocrypha, specifically the Book of Enoch. The Watcher Angels visit Earth, descending 'like stars' to land at Mount Hermon. In a very Promethean way they teach humanity many wicked things, including warfare. They also mate with human women, leading to the creation of the Nephilim, monstrous human/angel giants, who are only defeated when four good angels arrive and destroy them. The above story is a staple of 'ancient astronaut' theories, so it's interesting to see it here being used literally, albeit that we might assume the Nephilim genetic line has surfaced again, rather than that more Watcher Angels have been up to mischief. However, it does provide an interesting metaphor: Scully herself is part of a human/alien mating, and the child she bore is the spawn of those who land at mountains in ships that look like stars. This half human, half celestial, thing was a bit of a monstrous hybrid, and was finally 'taken back' by the forces that made it. That this is all purely metaphorical (that is, we're not witnessing a part of the Shapeshifter civil war here) is shown by the presence of Emily, who is not literally the girl involved. That allows those who wish to do so to write this one off as Scully's religious interpretation of some baffling events (or, if you wish, a divine lesson designed to help her grief process). Gregory's *Book of St Peter the Sinner* is a weirdly stapled-together mix of the Gnostic Gospels (the self-contained books of the Gnostics, a sect associated with and perhaps predating Christianity, who believe God to be ultimately unknowable, and separate the divine into male and female godheads), the Book of Enoch, the Apocrypha (presumably those books which appear in the Vulgate, and thus in Catholic but not Protestant Bibles, which doesn't include Enoch), and the Book of J. 'J' is a designation for one of the two original authors whose work comprises Genesis and Exodus, as revealed through textual analysis of styles (the author is so called because he prefers the term Jahweh for God, while 'E' prefers the more formal Elohim). Each puts forward a separate creation tale in Genesis, and it seems that Gregory believes only one of them. He'd have to have made some major analytical breakthroughs to neatly separate them out, mind you!

The Bottom Line: KT: 'It's as if God Himself struck her down.' Loathsome. I defended 'Miracle Man' on the grounds of balance. I defended 'Revelations' because it was a nice attempt to do something different. This is just all of the worst bits of those two stories thrown up into the air and randomly assembled. And worse, it's cynical and depressing and stinks of too many bad days in church. I hate *The X-Files* when it's doing dark cynicism ('Roland', 'Hell Money') and I hate the *X-Files* universe when the goodies don't win because it becomes a very cold, godless and empty place full of hopelessness. In this episode, God wins, easily, by two falls and a submission, but I still feel unclean after watching it. I feel betrayed by something that seeks such rank darkness where there should be light. I cried at the end, not out of emotion, but out of relief that this hollow mess was over. Please, God, forgive them, they know not what they do.

PC: While Keithy was going through his . . . emotional experience . . . I was laughing out loud at the funniest *X-Files* episode since 'Bad Blood'. Only this time it probably wasn't intentional. I mean: the shadow with horns?! I splurted my drink at that one. The social worker (tiresomely) is the devil! But they expect us to be tricked into thinking it's the priest because . . . they've both got faces that are the same shape! As has the angel! Only he has four of them! (But shouldn't he have them at once, rather than in turn?) There's no reason for Emily to be in this either, and it's almost a re-run of 'Revelations'. So it's a mess, of course, but in thirty years this will be a *camp classic*. The feeling of alienation we get from these later episodes is, I suspect, because we as an audience long for Mulder and Scully to be sympathetic towards one another again. But the horns *made* this one for me, they really did . . .

MD: Really rather good, and a damn sight more interesting than 'Revelations'. This only becomes depressing if, like Scully, you automatically think that death must equal failure. Angels in the Bible are frightening, supernatural creatures – rather than little dudes with wings and harps and white frocks – and it's a refreshing change to see one of their number portrayed like this on TV. Frankly, I'd sit through all of Mulder's wonderful atheistic rants to see that weird creature again. I also enjoyed the post-mortem scene, where Scully thinks she sees Emily: it's so well-acted and intimate that one almost feels like a voyeur watching it. The only bit I really didn't like was the very silly 'horned beast' shadow: it had me giggling, which, like Paul, I imagine was not the desired effect.

115: 'The Pine Bluff Variant'

US Transmission: 3 May 1998
UK Transmission: 24 May 1998 (Sky One)
Writer: John Shiban
Director: Rob Bowman
Cast: Daniel Von Bargen (Jacob Haley),
Michael MacRae (August Bremer), Sam Anderson (Leamus),

J.B. Bivens (Field Agent),
Douglas H. Arthurs (Skin-Head Man),
John B. Lowe (Dr Leavitt), Ralph Alderman (Manager),
Dean McKenzie (Army Tech), Kate Braidwood (Usherette),
Armin Moattar (Goatee Man)

Washington, DC: a joint FBI/CIA task force stake out a meeting between Jacob Haley, a member of the New Spartans terrorist militia, and an arms dealer. The meeting ends with the dealer being killed by flesh-eating bacteria, and Haley escaping. Scully suspects that Mulder may have aided the terrorist, and tails Mulder as he goes to a meeting with the militia group in Delaware. She is stopped by agents and informed by Skinner and US attorney Leamus that Mulder is deep undercover, having infiltrated the terrorists. There is a power struggle within the New Spartans between Haley and leader Bremer. Mulder is questioned by Haley, who accuses him of spying on them. Meanwhile, Scully investigates fourteen deaths at a movie theatre in Ohio, concluding that this is another example of the lethal biotoxin at work. Mulder and the New Spartans raid a bank in Pennsylvania, contaminating the money that they leave behind. Later, Bremer denounces Mulder as a traitor, playing a tape recording he made of Mulder and Scully talking. However, after allowing Haley and most of the others to leave, he lets Mulder go. Mulder returns to the bank, which has already been sealed off by Scully and Skinner. Leamus tells them that the money has not been contaminated, but Mulder suspects him of having orchestrated everything that happened.

Don't Be in the Teaser: The goatee-bearded arms dealer has his flesh eaten by a toxic genetically engineered biological agent.

How Did He Do That?: The usher must have handled a lot more of the biotoxin a lot more quickly than those customers she gives change to, but they all get to their seats before she collapses.

Scully Here is a Medical Doctor: She sets Mulder's broken finger.

Ooze: Flesh-eating bacteria.

Phwoar!: Scully is vicious when she thinks Mulder has sold out ('Are you the wife?' asks the motel manager. 'Not even close!' she snaps). But even then she won't betray Mulder to her superiors, and it took Skinner's advice to make Mulder not tell her everything. Cool royal blue dress too. Her concern over Mulder's finger is very maternal. 'Let's get the swelling down,' she says.

Dialogue Triumphs: Scully: 'Exactly what agency are you guys from?' (Silence.) 'Obviously not the office of information!'

The Conspiracy Starts at Closing Time: The actual Conspiracy doesn't seem to be involved here. Instead we get an insight into Skinner's world of CIA suits, where he must be continually working out who's working for who and who knows what. (He obviously hasn't written off the whole CIA as a Conspiracy-riddled organisation, or, if he has, still feels he has to work with them.) The activities of the US government itself are here seen to be equally as dodgy as those of the Conspiracy, and without the justification of an alien foe. Or does Mulder's question to Leamus concerning using the bioweapons on 'someone else' suggest that he's got the Colonists in mind, and he thinks these are Conspiracy stooges?

Continuity: Mulder came to the attention of the New Spartans after he spoke at the UFO conference in Boston we see in 'Patient X', making allegations about a government conspiracy. He professes anti-Nazi sentiments even to the terrorists (so we now know where he stands on the militia thing). Mulder's role-playing makes him keep on lying to Scully initially even when she tells him what she knows (which harks back to the depth of his identification with the criminal mind in 'Grotesque'), and his subsequent words reveal he can't believe anyone is listening. Scully is used to Skinner being trustworthy and the CIA not being. Mulder's finger is broken in this episode.

The Truth: The US Army developed early versions of the bioweapons that Scully identifies as a virulent strain of streptococcus during the 1960s at the Pine Bluff facility, but the biological experiments were supposedly stopped in 1969 according to Richard Nixon (real world true). They've actually continued, with (CIA mole?) Bremer using the New Spartans to test the weapon on the public. Haley innocently got Mulder involved in the group, which eventually blew the cover on the CIA's whole plan, despite their attempts to have him killed.

Trivia: Pine Bluff is a city in Arkansas where the USA's biological weapons were created. Tom Braidwood's daughter, Kate, appears in this episode. Scully follows Mulder to the Aaron Burr hotel. Burr, Thomas Jefferson's Vice President, was convicted of treason, much as Scully suspects Mulder of becoming a traitor. The alias Mulder uses at the motel is Mr Kaplan. George Kaplan is the name of the 'fake' agent that Cary Grant's character is constantly mistaken for in Hitchcock's *North by Northwest*. (It's also a Jewish surname, again a hint towards Mulder's possible ethnic origins.) The episode makes oblique references to *Pulp Fiction*, *Reservoir Dogs*, *Killing Zoe* and *Point Break*. The masks worn by the robbers are nods to various classic horror movie monsters (Frankenstein's monster, Dracula, the Wolfman, etc.). *Die Hard With a Vengeance* is (appropriately) playing at the cinema, but what small town US cinema would be showing it these days?

The Bottom Line: KT: 'I have my beliefs.' It could be just me, but I sense the theme of betrayal all over season five – both intentional and otherwise. Just as seasons one and two concerned 'the truth' and seasons three and four were all about 'belief', so (conceptually) these stories seem to have at their heart questions surrounding just who *can* be trusted and believed in the cynical post-'Redux' *X-Files* universe. Scully's paranoia that she's been lied to by Mulder (previously central to 'Wetwired') is again the focus of this episode which tries hard to be profound but doesn't deliver. The torture of Mulder is very unsettling, and, as with the previous episode, there was a sense of betrayal to *me*, that this series seems to be getting away from what I'd always imagined its *raison d'être* to be. Nothing and no one in life is ever quite as dependable as you'd like them to be. Which is sad.

PC: Like a lot of these pre-movie episodes, this is rather trivial, but shows a basic competence. It's nice that we're allowed to see Mulder's innocence early on. Once more the episode insists, just in case we've missed it, that this series (tiresomely) blames the *actual* government for America's woes, but the ending at least asks us to confront the bizarre nature of Mulder's allegiances. Is he against the government, and so for the right-wing nutters? And if not, how can he work for the establishment he claims to loathe? Personally, I'd avoid calling a character 'goatee man' in an episode where every third character has a goatee.

MD: Not an unusually high amount of betrayal on display here (this is *The X-Files*, after all), and still less imagination or clarity of thought. I have no real idea what all this was in aid of: why let Mulder go? What *did* they spray the money with? Either I missed something, or the answers will come later. Either way, it left me feeling very unsatisfied. And, worse, bored. Good bank robbery, though, and the sequences in the cinema were excellent.

116: 'Folie à Deux'

US Transmission: 10 May 1998
UK Transmission: 14 June 1998 (Sky One)
Writer: Vince Gilligan
Director: Kim Manners
Cast: Brian Markinson (Gary Lambert),
John Apicella (Greg Pinkus), Roger R. Cross (Field Agent),
Cynthia Preston (Nancy Aaronson),
Dmitry Chepovetsky (Supervisor),
Brenda McDonald (Mrs Loach),
Grant Gladish (SWAT Teamer),
Steve Bacic (SWAT Commander), Leslie Jones (Ms Starns),
Nancy Kerr (Nurse), Owen Walstrom (Mark Backus),
Norma Jean Wick (Newscaster)

Mulder investigates a threat against a Chicago telephone sales company. One of its employees, Gary Lambert, is secretly trying to warn the world that his boss, Pinkus, is an insectoid monster, turning the other employees into zombies. Mulder shows up at the company at the moment when Lambert snaps and takes everybody hostage, demanding to make a TV broadcast. Mulder saves Pinkus's life as a SWAT team break in, killing Lambert. But in the chaos, Mulder also sees Pinkus as a monster. He discovers that Pinkus has been near many previous situations like this. He tries to prove that Pinkus is a monster, but Pinkus complains to Skinner. When Mulder tries to shoot Pinkus in Skinner's office, Mulder is hospitalised. Scully visits him, and believes his story enough to examine the body of one of Pinkus's 'zombie victims'. She finds a bite at the back of the neck, and, returning to the hospital, manages to save Mulder from his zombie nurse and the insectoid monster that came in through the window. She supports Mulder's story. Meanwhile, at another telephone sales company, the whole thing starts again . . .

Don't Be in the Teaser: A telephone sales operative is scared by a monster. He deserves it.

Scully Here is a Medical Doctor: In an echo of 'Bad Blood', she finds that Mulder has already scheduled her to do an autopsy.

Scully's Rational Explanation of the Week: *Folie à deux*, a madness shared by two.

Phwoar!: 'You're my one in five billion,' Mulder tells Scully.

Dialogue Triumphs: Zombie Nurse: 'Don't let the bed bugs bite.'

The Conspiracy Starts at Closing Time: There's nothing to directly connect these invading monsters to the Conspiracy, but it seems strange that another race of aliens with associations with the back of the neck is also planning a covert takeover using human institutions. Given the insect metaphor occasionally applied to the Shapeshifters ('Herrenvolk') and the insectoid possessors we've already seen ('Travelers'), perhaps this monster is a vehicle for the Black Oil we haven't seen before, injecting it into its victims to make them into Colonist-helpful zombies. What the Colonists would want with telephone sales is pretty baffling, but we've seen them overrunning institutions like Social Security before (in 'Talitha Cumi').

Continuity: Mulder and Scully have been working together for five years at this point, and Mulder is getting tired of being seen as the FBI's monster consultant. He's still got his finger bound up from it being broken in 'The Pine Bluff Variant', so this probably takes place less than five weeks later.

The Truth: Greg Pinkus is an insect who can psychically persuade those who aren't looking for his real appearance into thinking he's human, and that his zombies are still living people. (That effect must work at a distance, unless the zombies are also capable of it. If a hybrid like Jeremiah Smith can use the power of suggestion to control humans, as in 'Talitha Cumi', then a full Black Oil bearer should be able to do the same.) He controls his telephone sales workforce by biting them in the back of the neck, killing them, but re-animating them in some other fashion, possibly infesting them with Black Oil.

The Bottom Line: PC: A really scary monster in a fab comic book horror, marred only by the fact that Duchovny's acting so misses the beat these days that his accusations sound crazy to us as well.

MD: 'Oh man, did you come to the wrong place.' There's a cool, if derivative, monster, and it's nice to see Scully saving Mulder for real this time (cf. 'Kill Switch'). The hostage situation does drag on a little, though, which leaves no time for a satisfactory conclusion.

KT: 'Monsters? I'm your boy!' After the recent run of disappointing, often nihilistic and cynical tales, at last, the *real X-Files* again. The episode (though beginning as a hostage drama) develops into the kind of monster story they used to do every couple of weeks back in seasons one and two. It displays a number of homages to previous stories

('Blood', 'Never Again' and 'Duane Barry' notably), and the ending is a bit inconsequential. And, again, in keeping with the rest of the season, there's the betrayal element: Scully unable to tell the truth to Skinner at the end for fear of appearing to share Mulder's psychosis. A madness of two, indeed.

117: 'The End'

US Transmission: 17 May 1998
UK Transmission: 5 July 1998 (Sky One)
Writer: Chris Carter
Director: R.W. Goodwin
Cast: Mimi Rogers (Agent Diana Fowley),
Jeff Gulka (Gibson Praise), Martin Ferrero (Shooter),
Patrick Philips (Clinician #1), Paul Moniz de Sa (Clinician #2),
John Trottier (Clinician #3), Orest Blajkevitch (Russian)

The opponent of Gibson Praise, a child chess genius, is shot during a match. Meanwhile, a team led by Krycek capture the Cigarette-Smoking Man. Agent Spender is put in charge of the inquiry into the shooting, committed by an ex-NSA man, and objects to Mulder's presence at his briefing, where Mulder suggests that the captured sniper was after the boy. Also at the briefing is Diana Fowley, who knows Mulder of old. The Conspiracy want the CSM to solve the problem of Gibson. He agrees, and thus rejoins their ranks. Mulder and Scully discover that Gibson can read people's minds. Scully visits the Lone Gunmen to ask for help concerning Gibson's brain patterns . . . and to quiz them about Mulder's obvious attraction to Diana Fowley. Afterwards, she sees Mulder and Fowley together and, instead of disturbing them, phones in her information. Mulder discovers Spender meeting with the CSM in a car park, and unjustly accuses the agent of plotting with the CSM. Tests reveal that Gibson is capable of reading anyone's mind. The assassin wants to reveal what he knows about the boy and the Conspiracy in return for immunity from prosecution. He gives Mulder snippets. The CSM has the assassin killed, and Fowley shot as he kidnaps the boy and hands him over to the Conspiracy. Mulder blames Spender for the situation, and Spender promises bureaucratic retaliation. The CSM takes the file on Samantha from Mulder's office, then confronts Spender, telling him that he's his father. He has set Mulder's office alight. Mulder and Scully, having been told the X-Files are to be closed down, comfort each other in the ruins.

Don't Be in the Teaser: Gibson Praise's chess opponent is shot dead. It's all the boy's fault.

How Did He Do That?: Mulder assumes Gibson is psychic almost instantly. Why, exactly, are Gibson's abilities the solution to *everything* contained in the X-Files? Why, when a Russian is shot in Canada, is it FBI business? In Britain, it'd be unwise to have a one-armed man like Krycek drive your car, but we're told that with automatics being so common in the USA it wouldn't be such a problem over there.

Scully Here is a Medical Doctor: She tests Gibson's abilities.

Scully's Rational Explanation of the Week: She thinks that all the psychics she and Mulder have met were fakirs or lucky guessers. (Which is a bit hard on Clyde Bruckman.)

Phwoar!: A bit of a breakthrough. Scully is definitely suffering in the car as she contemplates Mulder and the woman she's never heard about holding hands. Part of the problem seems to be that Fowley is also a believer, so it's possible, but not likely, that Scully's jealousy is professional rather than personal. Her call to Mulder straight after begins with their biggest indication of togetherness, the shared catchphrase 'Mulder, it's me.' Mulder doesn't seem very interested in Fowley any more, telling her positive things about his relationship with Scully, that she makes him work for his conclusions. Gibson's insights into the minds around him reveals that Mulder is thinking about either Scully or Fowley, and one of them is thinking about him. He says that Scully doesn't care what anybody thinks of her except Fowley, indicating that Scully's holding in some major aggression towards the other woman. At the end, though, our heroes are very much together, inhabiting the same apartment, Scully lying her head on Mulder's chest.

Dialogue Triumphs: Frohike, when Scully seems to be considering psychic phenomena: 'Ooh, walk on the wild side!'

The Conspiracy Starts at Closing Time: Interesting to see that the Conspiracy train their assassins to shoot for the back of the neck (which, unless Gibson's alien heritage is to the fore, is merely a matter of procedure). Krycek now seems to be working for the Conspiracy proper again, instead of just being the Well-Manicured Man's dogsbody, though he remains his chauffeur. The CSM also rejoins their ranks without too much fuss about their attempt to kill him, obviously not believing the Elder's attempts at innocent disbelief. They think the CSM's interests are the same as their own, but in this episode we discover that he may have gone along with their plans simply to have the power (and here he once more has free access to the FBI) to advance Spender through the FBI (and, perhaps, to save Samantha, too). His advice to Spender, not to become part of a cause, may reflect his feeling that Mulder is lost to him now. Why the Conspiracy want to get hold of Gibson is never fully revealed. Obviously, they're concerned with their secrets being kept to themselves, and don't want Mulder to put one of them and Gibson in the same room, but also they're perhaps thinking of having Gibson read the mind of one of their alien masters to discover their real plans for Earth. The assassin describes Gibson as a 'missing link', which Mulder assumes means that he's proof of alien meddling with human biology. He uses genes that other humans don't, resulting in his telepathic powers. (This may either be the assassin playing on Mulder's well-known predilections to get out of jail, but if he's correct, then upon visiting Earth on the first occasion, the Colonists set up human genetics to produce just such mutants. Gibson is presumably, in about fifteen years' time, destined to be the host body for a particularly important incubating Grey.)

Continuity: Scully's protection of Gibson and her admission that she finds medical tests scary hark back to her experiences with Emily and her own cancer. Diana Fowley was Mulder's girlfriend (and not, according to the Lone Gunmen, his wife) when he was straight out of the Academy (before they knew him, so he must have told them about his past). She was 'there' when he discovered the X-Files (which means they were working together in 1990 at the time of 'Travelers', a time when Mulder was still wearing his wedding ring: was Fowley the reason for Mulder's marriage breaking up?). Mulder and Fowley spent time in psychiatric hospitals testing the inmates for psi-powers. When he started researching into the X-Files, she went to Berlin on assignment and no longer followed the paranormal, though she remains a believer. Spender doesn't know the CSM by sight, and is surprised at the news that he's his father. The Lone Gunmen seem to all live together in their (incredibly secure) office. The CSM has a scar visible on his chest, probably as a result of being shot.

The Truth: Gibson Praise can hear whatever's going on in anybody's mind, over at least the height of a concert hall through making use of the strange activity in the 'god module' of his temporal lobes.

Trivia: 'The Truth Is Out There' is replaced in the title sequence with 'The End', the only instance of an episode title shown onscreen. Clips are seen in this episode from *King of the Hill*, *The Simpsons* and *The Silver Surfer*. Mulder calls Gibson 'Karnak', after the mute strongman from Marvel Comics' *The Inhumans*. When Mulder considers *Baywatch*, Gibson says, 'You've got a dirty mind.' Before the original US run of this episode, the end credits of the previous show, *King of the Hill*, featured 'Fox President Peter Roth' fielding questions at a press conference over the apparent death of animated hero Hank Hill. Was he killed, the reporters asked, because he refused to move to LA with the show? (Neatly reflecting the speculation around David Duchovny as *The X-Files* made the same move.) A countdown to 'The End' was shown throughout the evening's programming. The teaser for this episode was the series' first venture to (fictional) Vancouver, complete with Mountie! Mulder mentions Newton, Galileo, Einstein and Hawking as 'different thinkers'.

The Bottom Line: PC: Solid, unusually direct, but rather empty. Carter's habit of hoping that we'll regard something as important because everybody says it is resurfaces, as Gibson's abilities are talked up into something pivotal, rather than merely interesting. The CSM's assassination plan is clever, and Scully's jealousy is delightful, but apart from that, this is just the same old runaround, the old elements being mixed up in yet another way. The presence of nearly every recurring character, for no good reason, echoes the *Simpsons* episode where everybody pops up to state their catchphrase.

MD: A squib so damp you could wash your hands on it. Oh dear. And I can't believe we've never heard about Diana before. All very contrived. Liked the kid, though.

KT: 'Checkmate.' An exercise in iconography that doesn't deliver anywhere near the shocks it could have. There are some good moments – the first CSM/Krycek sequence is the pre-titles from every James Bond movie never made, while Mulder and Skinner's initial exchange is joyous. But there's nothing at the core of this episode, except a few nice images and a lot of silly bits (the Conspiracy all standing around in a dark car park in their trenchcoats waiting for the CSM is mind-bogglingly funny!). Scully's catlike jealousy over Mulder's former love again ties in with the theme of betrayal and the ending is so downbeat it almost dares the audience to give up on the series. Not so much a case of 'Who's for Los Angeles?', more 'How do we get there from here?'

The *X-Files* Movie

121-minute cinema release

Created by Chris Carter

Associate Producer: Mary Astadourian
Co-Producer: Frank Spotnitz
Producers: Chris Carter, Daniel Sackheim
Executive Producer: Lata Ryan

118: *The X-Files*

US Release: 19 June 1998
UK Release: 21 August 1998
Writers: Chris Carter, from a story by Chris Carter,
Frank Spotnitz
Director: Rob Bowman
Cast: Martin Landau (Dr Al Kurtzweil),
Armin Mueller-Stahl (Conrad Strughold),
Blythe Danner (Jana Cassidy), Lucas Black (Stevie),
Jeffrey DeMunn (Dr Ben Bronschweig),
Glenne Headly (Barmaid),
Terry O'Quinn (Special Agent Darius Michaud),
Hrothgar Mathews (Paramedic)

In 35,000 BC, two cavemen find the ice-bound body of their companion underground. They also find a dangerous Grey creature, which attacks them. They kill it, but its black blood oozes into the rock, and into one of the cavemen. In modern times, a child playing in what is now the Texas town of Blackwood stumbles into the cave and encounters the same black ooze. Firecrew summoned to help him are lost, and a fleet of tankers and men arrive to bring the situation under control. Mulder and Scully, no longer working on the X-Files, are helping to search a federal building in Dallas where a bomb is supposed to have been planted. Mulder discovers that the bomb is actually in a nearby building. He tells his

superior, Michaud, who evacuates the building, but then sits
by the bomb until it goes off. Mulder and Scully are blamed
by an FBI hearing for not following correct protocol, and
Scully considers resignation. Mulder, on a drinking binge,
meets Dr Kurtzweil, who claims to have worked with his
father. He tells Mulder that the federal building was destroyed
to hide what it contained: the bodies from the incident in
Blackwood. Mulder wakes Scully and they head for where
the remains of the bodies have been taken. Meanwhile,
Conspiracy agent Bronschweig, at the Blackwood site, shows
the CSM the body of one of the firemen, infested with the
Black Oil. It's gestating into something else. Mulder and
Scully examine the other bodies, and find one with liquified
skin. Mulder contacts Kurtzweil, and finds the doctor is being
hunted on child pornography charges. Kurtzweil tells him to
continue searching in Dallas. There, Mulder and Scully find
fossil fragments that send them to Blackwood. Meanwhile,
the Black Oil has gestated into a full-grown Grey, which
leaves its corpse host and kills Bronschweig. The Conspiracy
seal up the site and him with it. The Conspiracy meet in
London, appalled by the revealed nature of the Black Oil: it's
a colonising force rather than a slave-creating weapon. The
Well-Manicured Man speaks out for fighting against the alien
colonists, but his is a lone voice. He is ordered by Conspiracy
leader Strughold to kill Mulder or abduct Scully. Mulder and
Scully find a playground where the dig in Blackwood once
was, and chase the tankers that took the Conspiracy agents
out of town. They follow the Black Oil tankers to a dome in
the middle of a cornfield that houses deadly bees. They
manage to escape the bees, but one remains in Scully's collar.
The FBI hearing elects to separate Mulder and Scully, and
Scully tells Mulder she is thus preparing to resign. He tries to
talk her into staying. Just as they're about to kiss, the bee
stings Scully. Mulder calls for medical help, but the ambulan-
cemen who arrive are from the Conspiracy. They shoot
Mulder and take the comatose Scully away. Mulder wakes in
hospital, from which he escapes with the aid of Skinner
and the Lone Gunmen. He tries to find Kurtzweil, but discovers that the Well-Manicured Man has got there first.
The Well-Manicured Man states that he was ordered to kill

Mulder. Then he shoots his driver instead, and gives Mulder Scully's location and a sample of the vaccine against the Black Oil. As Mulder departs, the Well-Manicured Man's car explodes. Mulder travels to Antarctica, and finds Scully, one of thousands of infected bodies kept on ice in a vast underground base. He injects her with the vaccine, but it also enters the system of the base, and havoc ensues, with Greys breaking out of containment. As Mulder and Scully flee from the base, it lifts off: it's actually a spaceship. Back home, Scully tells Mulder she's going to stay with him. In response to the agents' strange report, the FBI reopens the X-Files. The Conspiracy, meanwhile, continue their plans on an international basis.

Don't Be in the Teaser: Three cavemen, one Grey, one little boy, three firemen . . . all dead in just 37,000 years.

How Did He Do That?: How come, out of several soda machines, Mulder goes straight to the one with the bomb in it? What's the truth behind the bomb in the Well-Manicured Man's car? Was somebody watching to see whether or not he killed Mulder, and if so, why didn't they set it off with Mulder inside? Or, if it was just set to go off when the car restarted, why? That's a guarantee of not catching Mulder, and killing him seems to be the Conspiracy's aim at this point. (Perhaps this is the Cigarette-Smoking Man getting revenge for all those digs about his callousness.) What, exactly, is going on at the end? Mulder injects Scully with the vaccine, which means the Oil flees her body, the contaminant in the system which the Conspiracy aide refers to. So, suddenly mobile despite the temperature, this Oil attacks several of the already-Oiled humans in the pods, turning them instantly into Greys? (Which is, the novelisation makes clear, what is happening.) OK . . . we'll accept that, with the proviso that Mulder obviously didn't know that was going to happen. However, when these Greys are hatched, do they contact their Conspiracy helpers? No, they take control of the ship and fly off! And the Conspiracy all instantly know they're going to do that! (Presumably, a newly hatched Grey is a beast without much thought, and they were just escaping their presence. Or perhaps this is a Rebel ship, and the Conspiracy are keeping not only its crew, but all the infected humans they don't want dead here on ice as a matter of convenience. Which means we probably won't be seeing Marita again.) Whatever, as the ending of a blockbuster movie it needs an accompanying slide show and explanatory booklet. Also, Kurtzweil's distrust of FEMA is just plain weird. He sees this 'secret government' as a threat to freedom, despite the fact that they're so close to the Conspiracy that the latter need to bomb their offices in order to get their corpses back. (Presumably that's why the Conspiracy have let him continue publishing his non-Conspiracy conspiracy books.) And why does the Conspiracy's plan to abduct Scully seem to rely on that bee in her collar? Are we really to believe that the bee is biding its time, following orders? The speed of the Conspiracy ambulance's arrival would seem to offer no other explanation. (And indeed, we've seen these bees behave intelligently before, in 'Zero Sum'. Presumably, a bee can be controlled by the Black Oil it carries as easily as a human.) How do Mulder and Scully get back to civilisation at the end? And where did Scully's woolly socks come from?

Scully Here is a Medical Doctor: She carries out a rough autopsy on the Oil victims and diagnoses herself as she succumbs to the viral bee sting.

Ooze: Is, as it turns out, what this series has been about all along.

That's a Mouthful: Mulder to the bartender: 'I'm a key figure in an ongoing government charade. An annoyance to my superiors. A joke among my peers. They call me "Spooky". Spooky Mulder. Whose sister was abducted by aliens when he was a kid. Who now chases little green men with a badge and a gun, shouting to the heavens and anyone else who'll listen that the fix is in, that our government's hip to the truth and a part of the Conspiracy. That the sky is falling, and when it hits it's gonna be the shit storm of all time.' To which she replies: 'I think that just about does it, Spooky.'

Phwoar!: Mulder and Scully, on edge because of the impending end to their mutual crusade, are definitely about to share a genuine kiss this time, until Scully says 'Ouch!' At the end, despite his attempts to emotionally push her away once more, she holds his hand. Their relationship is presumably on a different plane now, but only next season will tell. (Despite all the pre-publicity, David Duchovny's bottom is nowhere to be seen.)

Dialogue Triumphs: After the bomb has exploded, Mulder to Scully: 'Next time, you're buying.'

And about which way to go to follow the tankers: 'Five years together, how many times have I been wrong?' Awkward silence. 'At least not about driving.'

The Conspiracy Starts at Closing Time: For fifty years, the Conspiracy have been working on the basis that the Black Oil that they were ordered to spread across the globe would turn humanity into a slave race, with themselves as their free commandants. Here they discover that another function of the Oil is to allow a Grey to incubate inside a human body, and finally burst free fully formed. The Well-Manicured Man takes this to be the last straw, a sign that the alien force is simply going to replace the population, but the rest of the Conspiracy are dedicated to continuing to strike a deal with them. The Well-Manicured Man tells Mulder that the virus that constitutes the Oil was 'the original inhabitant of this planet', presumably simply meaning, as he continues to elaborate, that it arrived here, in the form of the alien Colonists, before humanity evolved. (Considering the hints of genetic tampering we heard in the previous episode, one wonders if humanity was destined to be a host race for the aliens all along.) The Black Oil remained on Earth, underground (and he is presumably talking about all the deposits of it, the Tunguska event being simply the explosion that released it rather than deposited it), waiting to rejoin the Colonists when they returned. Presumably they did so around 1947, and explained their aims to the neo-Conspiracy, who ever since have been selecting suitable humans to donate eggs to create human/alien hybrids (whose function after the Black Oil release is not explained) and creating the genetically altered crops to pass the virus on to the genetically altered bees that will carry it. Presumably, the smallpox release in 'Zero Sum' was a 'blank' test of the delivery system. In the novelisation, in lines cut from the movie, the Well-Manicured Man goes on to explain to Mulder that his father (and/or we might assume, the CSM) arranged for Samantha to be abducted so that his genetic line would live on, albeit in the form of human/Colonist hybrid clones, immune to the Black Oil. He also hoped, so the Well-Manicured Man says, that his son would undo his work and save everyone. It is revealed that the Conspiracy have a nominal leader, in the form of Strughold. Although described by preview audiences as 'lizard like', the aliens in the movie are grey, with big black eyes and three fingers, which sounds like a Grey to us. And now we know why this creature of myth has eyes like that: full of the Black Oil! They're a lot more mobile and hostile than their cousins, the hybrid Greys.

EFFECTS OF THE BLACK OIL

The Black Oil can strike a human being in many different ways, according, presumably, to its intent. It can possess them, using them as an unaltered mobile vessel, able to emit a beam of hard radiation. (It's lucky for the Colonists that the Conspiracy stalked just such a version in 'Apocrypha', confirming their preconceptions.) It can make them fall into a coma, either when the Oil has no mission to perform, or so as to convince humans that it makes a good biological weapon. (As seen in 'Terma'.) It can infest them in order to use their biological mass to create a new Grey alien (which the Oil in the movie, presumably unaware of where Colonisation politics have gone in the last 37,000 years, does). Or it can kill them instantly through liquidising them. (Which may also be the form in which the Oil is used as a biological weapon by human armies.) This last raises a further interesting possibility, that a Shapeshifter is a human/alien hybrid that has had its skin liquified by the Black Oil component of its blood system, allowing it to change appearance.

Continuity: We discover that Skinner is not *the*, but *an*, Assistant Director of the FBI, as we meet another, Jana Cassidy. Scully lives in Georgetown. The Well-Manicured Man has grandchildren whom he visits at a large house in Somerset. (There's no sign of a Mrs Well-Manicured, though, so presumably his liaison with Dr Charne-Sayre in 'Tunguska' wasn't illicit.) Kurtzweil was a friend, 'a fellow traveller', of Bill Mulder, but left the Project decades ago.

The Truth: The Conspiracy have prepared, and, at the end of the movie, are still preparing, to release the Black Oil as a bee-distributed virus that will turn all of humanity, apart from the human/alien hybrids, into Greys.

Trivia: Mulder refers to the Lone Gunmen as the Cowardly Lion, the Scarecrow and Toto, characters from *The Wizard of Oz*. The circular spacecraft under the ice recalls *The Thing From Another World*. Mulder at one point pisses all over a poster for *Independence Day*, which we think is, frankly, a boast too far. The design of the giant spacecraft echoes that of *Alien*. It's interesting to speculate whether Nicholas Lea's absence wasn't a matter of prior commitments, as stated, but because he got wind of what was going to happen to the Well-Manicured Man's chauffeur, the function that Krycek was performing in 'The End'. Mulder quotes from Three Dog Night's 'One' (see 'Detour'). The song playing in the Doors' 'The Crystal Ship'. There is a possible oblique reference to *The prisoner*.

The Bottom Line: PC: Merely a double-length episode with a bigger budget, this disappointingly unambitious feature refuses to let go of the series' beloved Conspiracy enough to either offer closure or the inflation of expectations that a blockbuster movie should bring with it. It wastes its guest stars in minor roles, and the ending is only coherent to those who not only have been following, but also taking copious notes. The closeness of Mulder and Scully is entertaining, however, and Carter does pull out a few neat and clever surprises concerning the nature of the alien threat.

MD: In the summer of 1998, TV critic Sean Day-Lewis wrote about the decline of the single television play in *Broadcast* magazine. In part, he pointed the finger at Channel 4's *Film on Four* strand for encouraging the creation of TV-film hybrids. 'They were not cinema,' he said, 'and, worse still, I suggest, they were not truly TV either.' He could have been talking about *The X-Files* movie. It strikes me as being almost arrogant to pass off a trumped-up TV story as a 'motion picture'. Its narrative makes not one concession to the fact that this is a film, and it will make precious little sense to anyone who is not already a fan: a quick scene in a bar with Mulder calling himself 'Spooky' does not, in my book, count as character background. For all that, the scope and scale is marvellous, even if much of what we see is a revamp of TV episodes, and there are enough thrills and shocks to paper over many of the cracks.

KT: 'These men are negotiating a planned Armageddon.' Visually stunning. One wonders if Rob Bowman's influences (in terms of cinematography) lean more towards John Ford's dustbowl westerns like *The Searchers* than the SF genre. (Although overt influences include *2001*, both versions of *Invasion of the Body Snatchers* . . . And *North by North-West* and *Lawrence of Arabia*.) There are many memorable scenes (particularly the cornfield/helicopter chase) though the film is slightly disappointing in that, in attempting to stand alone from the series, it is required to reformat several aspects of the back story. Hence, we are introduced to an Assistant Director that we've never seen before, and a blatant Deep Throat clone in Kurtzweil. Too complicated, ultimately, to be really satisfying, but far too good to be dismissed as a failure, the movie is a curate's egg, and benefits hugely from repeated viewing.

CHRIS CARTER GOES ON RECORD

A secret track at the end of the *X-Files* movie soundtrack features the voice of Chris Carter talking about some of the Conspiracy back story. Ironic that this should be his chosen method of distributing this information, rather than the plot of the movie itself, but we are grateful. Carter reveals that:

The Colonists had ordered the Conspiracy to breed Colonist/human hybrids to move amongst humanity stealthily. They were cloned from human ova and Colonist bio-material, and are immune to the Black Oil. The Colonists regard Colonisation as *returning* to Earth. The Conspiracy members were guaranteed their survival in return for their help. The cataloguing of humanity was mainly to aid in the hybrid cloning programme, and that aspect of the Project was connected to many different government branches. (Carter names Social Security and the Department of Defense.) This operation, under the name 'Purity Control', began in 1948 as a continuation of Nazi eugenics experiments. (It is not clear from Carter's words that 'Purity Control' was initially aware of, or part of, the Colonists' plans. We use this grey area to allege that 'Purity Control' continued using Colonist DNA on humans even after the Conspiracy set up their hybrid breeding programme, because it explains many inconsistencies in the first season.) The Conspiracy began as a group of intelligence agents whose task was to create a cover-up for 'Purity Control'. (We allege that these people made greater contact with the Colonists and struck the Colonisation deal with them behind Purity Control's back.) Over the next fifty years, the Conspiracy slowly came to be in charge of matters alien in the US government and the UN. By 1990, they were a truly international group led by Conrad Strughold, a German industrialist now living in North Africa. In order to prevent them being discovered, and the collapse of civilisation that would result if they were, the Conspiracy continued their policy of disinformation, using secret US government projects (like 'Purity Control' and releases of bio weapons against US citizens, we assume) as a smokescreen. They also used the UFO believers' culture to make any belief in aliens seem ridiculous. They could also call on an arm of the Colonists themselves, the Shapeshifters (Carter persists in calling them 'alien bounty hunters') to police the hybrid breeding operations. Carter makes it clear that the Shapeshifters also reported back to the Colonists on what the Conspiracy was up to. The Black Oil is the medium the life force of the Colonists inhabits. If the Colonists discovered that the Conspiracy had a vaccine to this, they would certainly have destroyed the Conspiracy and moved more quickly towards Colonisation. The Conspiracy have maintained great loyalty to each other over the last fifty years, but with Colonisation looming, a struggle for power is starting. (Since we don't see much evidence of that in the movie, that's possibly a sign of where the Conspiracy are now heading.)

'I Want to Believe':
The X-Files and Faith

by Martin Day

'Jesus said "Everything is possible for him who believes."
Immediately the boy's father exclaimed "I do believe; help
me to overcome my unbelief!" '

Mark 9:23b–24

The X-Files suggests that there may be more things in heaven
and earth than the Western world's rational philosophy per-
mits: that there are paranormal and supernatural powers and
forces beyond the material world – and, indeed, beyond our
planet. This is both a radical suggestion, and a timely one.
Organised religion has been a declining influence since the
Second World War, and, in part, this has given rise to
a humanistic, materialist and consumerist society. As the
Cigarette-Smoking Man says in 'Talitha Cumi', 'They've
grown tired of waiting for miracle and mystery. Science is
their religion.' Despite this turning away from old patterns of
thought, studies have shown that most people in the West
still believe in (some form of) God. Chris Carter, who has
described himself as a lapsed Baptist, shrewdly anticipated
the increased interest in spiritual and metaphysical matters
engendered by the imminence of the next millennium.

Mulder and Scully (at least until the third season) aren't
shown as religious people in the usual sense of the word. But
belief, faith and even dogma courses through them. The early
episodes present us with a man desperate to believe in the
existence of alien life and in the supernatural and a woman
enslaved to logic and science. With Mulder – and despite
his frequent denials – almost everything about his current
character has a basis in the abduction of his sister. This single
incident prompted such a vast paradigm-shift that some form
of childlike trust in God was shattered and replaced in an
instant with contempt or disbelief and a new 'faith' in the
reality of alien life and the paranormal.

His Christian or biblical 'heritage' is clear, albeit less directly addressed than Scully's. In 'Die Hand die Verletzt' he states that 'Even the Devil can quote scripture to fit his needs', referring to Jesus's temptation in Matthew 4 and Luke 4; in 'Anasazi' he shows a familiarity with the fourth commandment (calling alien life one of God's 'side projects'). He is scathing about fundamentalist preachers and their 'literal' interpretation of the Bible in '3', but in 'Quagmire' he says (tongue-in-cheek?) 'Seek and ye shall find, Scully', a reference to Matthew 7:7/Luke 11:9. In 'Revelations' he clearly recognises the phrase 'He that has ears, let him hear', much used by Jesus in the Synoptic gospels. It is probably fair to say that in 'The Field Where I Died' his biblical knowledge outshines Scully's, although he seems a bit vaguer by the time of 'All Souls'. His (adult) view of the Bible is clear: he states that it is 'a parable, it's a metaphor for the truth, not the truth itself'. (It wouldn't be at all surprising if we were to learn that he considers the angelic visitation in Ezekiel, chapter one, to be the earliest recorded encounter with a UFO.) He certainly seems unusually sour and angry in this episode, attacking Scully's beliefs much more strongly than she usually does his. As Scully asks him in 'Revelations', 'How is it that you're able to go out on a limb whenever you see a light in the sky, but you're unwilling to accept the possibility of a miracle – even when it's right in front of you?', to which Mulder replies, 'I wait for a miracle every day, but what I've seen here has only tested my patience, not my faith.' The miracle he hopes for is the return of his sister ('Conduit' mentions an old ritual of closing his eyes and hoping (praying?) for her return). One can almost imagine Mulder saying to God, 'According to the Bible, you rose from the dead, but you can't even bring my sister back!' And thus he either has no faith in God, or holds Him directly responsible for the abduction of his sister. (In 'Talitha Cumi', the Cigarette-Smoking Man puts this Western paradox well, although the emotion here is fear rather than contempt: 'They don't believe in Him, but they still fear Him.')

Conventional religion, in particular, strikes Mulder as being too small and limiting. Where others might look to God for a reminder of our smallness in the cosmos, Mulder looks to extraterrestrial life. And thus in 'Anasazi' he calls the cover-up of alien life the 'biggest lie of all': it's his personal Holy Grail. Although at the beginning of 'Little Green Men' Mulder is saying that he 'wanted to believe', by the end of 'End Game' his belief is restored: 'I found something I thought I'd lost: faith to keep looking.' In 'Born Again' (and referring to his own hypnosis, as seen in 'Conduit'), Mulder states that he has a fundamental 'belief' in the beneficial powers of deep hypnosis. However, certain paradoxes remain: in 'Paper Clip' Mulder seems to indicate that he believes in fate, and 'Conduit' ends with Mulder praying and in tears in church before a stained-glass window of Christ crucified (strange behaviour if Mulder is, as David Duchovny claims and 'Kaddish' hints, Jewish).

Mulder's belief in the existence of alien life is counter-balanced by Scully's unshakeable faith in science. Never is this made clearer than in 'End Game': 'Many of the things I have seen have challenged my faith in my belief in an ordered universe, but this uncertainty has only strengthened my need to know, to understand, to apply reason to those things which seem to defy it. It was science that isolated the retrovirus that Agent Mulder was exposed to, and science that allowed us to understand its behaviour, and, ultimately, it was science that saved Agent Mulder's life.' This linking of science and 'salvation' (she calls science 'sacred' in 'The Erlenmeyer Flask') seems the ultimate in humanism, but with Scully things are not as clear-cut as that (after all, most Christian scientists – from Newton onwards – have seen the world as logical and ordered precisely because they believed a rational God created it). Science, for her, is the ultimate arbiter against irrationality and chaos (she says in 'Jose Chung's *From Outer Space*' that she'd never even considered the paranormal until she met Mulder). In 'The Blessing Way' Melissa says of Dana, 'You are so shut off to the possibility there could be any other explanation except for your rigid scientific view of the world.' And Scully seems to be at one with Mulder with regard to the Bible, as this exchange from 'The Calusari' clearly shows:

Scully: 'Wait a second, nothing just materialises out of thin air.'

Chuck Burk: 'You've read the Bible? You remember the story about Jesus creating the loaves and the fishes?'

Scully: 'But that was a parable.'

Unlike the Cigarette-Smoking Man in 'Talitha Cumi', she seems to believe that you don't have to believe in miracles to believe in God.

There are early hints that Scully has some residual religious belief (most obviously in the gold cross necklace she so often wears). In 'Beyond the Sea' she is adamant that hell will not be a cold dark place for her father or for Mulder, and in 'Miracle Man' her familiarity with the Bible leads her to believe that 'God never lets the Devil steal the show'. In 'The List' Scully mentions catechism for the first time, hinting at her upbringing as a Catholic, which is confirmed in 'Revelations'.

'Revelations' is a key Scully story, not so much in that it reveals these hidden characteristics as the fact that it explodes her previous character and presents us with a new one. Almost from the outset, and before she's seen enough to have her faith in science questioned (remember, this is the woman who will bend over backwards to make even the most obviously supernatural event an obscure scientific phenomenon), we're treated to scenes like this:

Scully: 'I believe in the idea that God's hand can be witnessed. I believe He can create miracles, yes.'

Mulder: 'Even if science can't explain them?'

Scully: 'Maybe that's just what faith is.'

This stands in complete contradiction to everything we've learnt about Scully up to this point, and is one of many reasons why this episode is somewhat disappointing. The story does, however, throw up some interesting nuggets: Scully believes in Armageddon, was raised a Catholic, but it's been six years since her last confession. She says she's not sure why she drifted away from the Church, but she states that she doesn't question God's word (she must mean in the general sense, given her previous attitude to the Bible). Certainly, this story (no matter how contrived the character change) is something of a watershed: by 'Apocrypha' she comments on a despairing mention of a 'sign from God' by saying, 'I've seen stranger things.' Of course, she has, but the fascinating conclusion of 'Revelations' shows how much she has come to rely on her 'detached' nature as a contrast to Mulder's willingness to believe. She begins to doubt the 'miracles' she has seen simply because Mulder didn't see them (when the positions are reversed Mulder has no problem with believing what he has seen on his own). When she says, 'It makes me afraid that God is speaking, but that no one's listening', one can imagine that she's thinking particularly of Mulder, having seen the depth of his hurt and anger (and how this – as in 'Nisei'/'731' – can seemingly stand in the way of 'the truth'). However, by 'Talitha Cumi' she's very much back on form, thinking the miraculous healings will be explained away rationally.

A number of episodes directly grapple with ideas of faith and belief in a religious, metaphysical or theological context. Not surprisingly for a programme as doggedly pluralistic as *The X-Files*, a consistent world view is eschewed in favour of contradiction and contrast. For example, the suggestion in 'Lazarus' that the bright light at the end of the tunnel seen when dying is 'beautiful' and 'nothing to be afraid of' clashes with '3', a story that – if what the vampires say is true – puts paid to any idea of a positive afterlife. 'The Field Where I Died' suggests reincarnation; 'Shadows' seems to feature an unequivocal ghost. Individual stories, too, sometimes find it difficult to tackle matters of faith in a coherent or unified manner, 'GenderBender' being very much a case in point. The occasional insightful comparison between the world of belief and the unfettered but fallen physical world gives way to a conclusion that is a mess of contradictory signifiers, effectively sweeping any real-life impact under the carpet of a weird alien faction.

By comparison, 'Miracle Man' verges on the unambiguous. Despite dealing very directly with matters of Christian faith and the existence (or otherwise) of miracles in the modern age, its targets aren't so much the religious community in general as a brand of Christianity in particular. The parody of a tent ministry with regular healing services is, however, undercut by the subtle presentation of the policeman's wife, who by the story's conclusion seems to feel that she would have been healed by the preacher's adopted son, had her sceptical husband allowed her to attend. Although it's difficult to know what to make of the boy's resurrection – bar that the dramatic structure required a powerful conclusion – the central concept (that a man healed, supposedly by the power of God, can have such a miserable new life) causes us to question the validity (or, rather, the 'goodness') of all that we've witnessed. Perhaps it's a tale about gullibility (a man in agony and suffering massive disfigurement is seen by many as exhibiting the abundant and overflowing new life that Jesus spoke of); it certainly contains a clever message about pride. The moment that the crowds – and Samuel himself – believe that the healings come from him, rather than from God, the boy's powers become corrupted and negative. The fact that the deaths have an earthly cause doesn't change the symbolism inherent in what we witness.

In 'Red Museum' the focus switches from Christianity to a New Age church. We're invited to see it in sinister terms as the story begins, but ultimately the group are shown to be (at worst) harmless – indeed, the story ends with a possible reconciliation between the 'cult' and the suspicious locals. Although not the focus of the story, the church believes in soul transference. In an interesting exchange, Mulder states that Abraham Lincoln, Mikhail Gorbachev and Charles Colson (but not, of course, Nixon!) are believed to have been the recipients of 'enlightened spirits'. It's difficult to know what to make of this, unless the production team are attempting a slight dig at the conversion of Nixon's notorious assistant to Christianity while in prison (New Age 'walk-in' rather than the intervention of the God of Christianity).

'Die Hand die Verletzt' subverts all our expectations of small-town Americana. In the opening scene, a meeting to discuss possible drama productions (*Jesus Christ Superstar* would not be 'appropriate', *Grease* contains 'the f-word') sets up the prospect of a Christian school ('Deborah, why don't you lead us in prayer?'). They're impatient to conclude, but realise that they've been 'letting it slip' – encouraging us to see the teachers as normal human beings, wrestling with faith in the modern context. Only then are we presented with the candles and the intoned 'In the name of the Lords of Darkness . . .' It's a wonderful and clever device.

The story continues to show that even the 'dark people' find belief difficult to maintain in the twentieth century (it's been 'years' since their last sacrifice: 'We haven't kept our faith'). Mulder is at great pains to stress that 'witches' – followers of Wicca – are religious, that they respect life and do not cast harmful spells, and that they don't worship Satan. 'Even the Church of Satan,' he says, with a completely straight face, 'has renounced murder and torture.' But as the story progresses it becomes clear that we're dealing with more than just white witches, and the ensuing events gain much of their impact from a well-portrayed change of attitude or world-view. Jim Ausbury was raised to see Christians as evil hypocrites, and to believe that man's basic nature is selfish rather than altruistic. Mankind is no more than a race of animals. However, after Shannon's death, he begins to perceive hypocrisy in himself and others (who seek to pin the blame on her, treating her death as a worthy sacrifice): 'And at that moment I knew that I am better than an animal, that my previous beliefs were responsible for her no longer being with us . . .' He explains that he forced his daughter to take part in rituals, but did not abuse her sexually. Mulder is dismissive of their 'watered-down' ceremonies. 'Did you really think you can call up the Devil and ask him to behave?'

'Revelations' returns again to miracles within the rational Western world, the preacher in the pre-titles sequence explaining one possible approach to the science–faith debate (that they are at odds with each other) via a story of a girl's Christian faith being disrupted by being told that the parting of the Red Sea was a natural (rather than a supernatural) phenomenon. But the man is shown to be a cheap fake and con artist who clearly doesn't understand the complexities of the argument, but does know how to fool the gullible (that theme again).

Gates – seemingly out to do more than expose false stigmatics – refers to Joel's Old Testamental description of the sun turning to darkness and the moon to blood prior to the Lord's coming. The same passage is part of St Peter's Pentecostal sermon in Acts and is referred to in Revelation after the opening of the penultimate seal. Gates believes that he was 'called upon' to kill the boy 'for the New Age to come', and that his actions are part of (or run counter to) some revised world-ending apocalypse. But nothing here matches the biblical book of Revelation, nor is presented with sufficient supernatural power (bar a few parlour tricks) to lead us to believe that we are witnessing a struggle between two spiritual protagonists. Instead, we're watching one madman attempting to kill the son of a madman – and, tragically, by the story's conclusion, even the boy has come to believe his father's hype. Scully says, 'Maybe I'll see you again sometime', to which Kevin replies, 'You will.'

'All Souls', on the other hand, at least has a clarity of vision about it, for all its mixing of biblical and apocryphal texts. We're left in little doubt that we're seeing a taste of Armageddon, of the ultimate battle between good and evil. Quite how this fits in with *The X-Files*' 'mythology' arc, as Carter calls it, is open to debate, although 'Patient X' uses appropriately biblical imagery to describe the battle for the Earth. It is perhaps not surprising that *The X-Files*' treatment of faith and belief is both strong and contradictory, with both characters and theology altering as any story demands. In its confusion, it reflects the modern mind, desperate to be rational and 'grown up' but still drawn to the stories of childhood (be they about aliens in spaceships or about a carpenter nailed to a tree). *The X-Files* has done much to expand our horizons and question the assumptions of its audience. Whether we're in turn drawn to God, or to other supernatural forces, or to little green men, doubtless depends on the individual. To put it another way, Christians believe that there is a God-shaped hole at the core of our psyche that will leave us unfulfilled unless we encounter God: Mulder's slot, on the other hand, is in the shape of the flying saucer that took away his sister. The desire to believe, even in the rational twentieth century, remains undimmed. As Scully says at the end of 'Avatar', 'That's why these myths and stories have endured – people want to believe.'

Acknowledgements

We would like to thank the following for their help, time and contribution: Ian Atkins, David Bailey, Daniel Ben-Zvi, Kini Brooks-Smith, Anthony Brown, Alec Charles, Paul Condon, Peter Cooke, Neil Corry, Peter Darvill-Evans, Helen Day, Helen Fayle, Lisa Gaunt, Liz Halliday, Jeff Hart, Kathleen Heck, Ian Hill, Andy Lane, Rebecca Levene, Claire Longhurst, James Margitich, Jackie Marshall, Paul Matthews, Audra McHugh, Cressida McLaughlin, John McLaughlin, John Molyneux, Carrie O'Grady, Kate Orman, Felicia O'Sullivan, David Owen, Anita Patel, Matthew Percival, John J. Pierce, Helen Rayner, Jac Rayner, Jim Sangster, Felicity Shea, Paul Simpson, Tucker Smallwood, George Solana, Kathy Sullivan, Jim Swallow, Jennifer Swanston, Susannah Tiller, Kathleen Toth, Colin Topping, Graeme Topping, Lily Topping, Andrew Walker, Geoff Wessel, Katy White, Peter Wickham, Simon Winstone, Janet Wood, Nicole Yates, Lucy Zinkiewicz.

We would also like to thank and acknowledge the help of contributors to uk.media.tv.sf.x-Files (especially Moira McLaughlin and Lee Staniforth), David Nattriss and his UK Episode Guide to *The X-Files*: (http://www.i-way.co.uk/~natts/x-Files/); Laura Witte and all the contributors to the *X-Files* In-Jokes List: (http://www. nashville.com/~subterfuge/xfiljoke.html); the *X-Files* online discussion group: (http://msnnews.news.com/msn.forums.sciencefiction.xfiles); and the inhabitants of all the other *X-Files* newgroups.

http://www.pathcom.com/~nooger/flameboy/darin_guide.html is the address of the Darin Morgan web page, by the way.

Dedicated to

'The Gally Gang': Elsa Frohman, Lisa Gaunt, Judi Grant, Audra McHugh, Mark McHugh, Felicia O'Sullivan, Jac Rayner and Trina Short.

Never Again

This is still our last book. These days, many different episode guides use the sort of format that we devised, and it's quite pleasing that this has now become the accepted way such books are constructed. Our subject this time changed radically over the course of the book, and so did our lives, and the way we react to the former always has a lot to do with the latter. That's a definition of how we went about writing books like this, and also of popular television. We remember where we were when we first heard the *X-Files* theme tune, saw a Darin Morgan episode, watched the movie. And so do you.

'We made this.'